Praise for *Web Analytics 2.0*

When it comes to the digital marketing channels and understanding what and why people do things online, there is no one smarter than Avinash Kaushik. His first book, Web Analytics: An Hour a Day, *should be on every marketer's desk. Now, with* Web Analytics 2.0, *there's a worthy accompaniment. When people ask, 'Who is the smartest guy in the room when it comes to online marketing?' only one name comes to mind: Avinash. I'd tell you to buy this book, but I would prefer if you didn't. I'd love to keep these concepts and theories all to myself and my clients. Yes, it's that powerful, awesome, and actionable.*

  —MITCH JOEL, president of Twist Image and author of *Six Pixels of Separation*

Analytics is vitally important, and no one (no one) explains it more elegantly, more simply, or more powerfully than Avinash Kaushik. Consider buying up all the copies of this book before your competition gets a copy.

  —SETH GODIN, author, *Tribes*

Lots of companies have spent lots of time and money collecting data—and sadly do little with it. In Web Analytics 2.0, *Avinash Kaushik helps us grasp the importance of this underused resource and shows us how to make the most of online data and experimentation.*

  —DAN ARIELY, professor of Behavioral Economics, Duke University and author of
      Predictably Irrational

Kaushik takes the witchcraft out of analytics. If venture capitalists read this book, they would fire half of the CEOs that they've funded.

  —GUY KAWASAKI, co-founder of Alltop & Garage Technology Ventures

Web Analytics 2.0

Web Analytics 2.0

The Art of Online Accountability & Science of Customer Centricity

Avinash Kaushik

Wiley Publishing, Inc.

Senior Acquisitions Editor: WILLEM KNIBBE
Development Editor: STEPHANIE BARTON
Production Editor: ELIZABETH GINNS BRITTEN
Copy Editor: KIM WIMPSETT
Editorial Manager: PETE GAUGHAN
Production Manager: TIM TATE
Vice President and Executive Group Publisher: RICHARD SWADLEY
Vice President and Publisher: NEIL EDDE
Media Assistant Project Manager: JENNY SWISHER
Media Associate Producers: DOUG KUHN AND JOSH FRANK
Media Quality Assurance: MARILYN HUMMEL
Book Designer: FRANZ BAUMHACKL
Compositor: MAUREEN FORYS, HAPPENSTANCE TYPE-O-RAMA
Proofreader: WORD ONE, NEW YORK
Indexer: TED LAUX
Project Coordinator, Cover: LYNSEY STANFORD
Cover Designer: RYAN SNEED
Cover Image: ISTOCKPHOTO

Dear Reader,

Thank you for choosing *Web Analytics 2.0: The Art of Online Accountability & Science of Customer Centricity.* This book is part of a family of premium-quality Sybex books, all of which are written by outstanding authors who combine practical experience with a gift for teaching.

Sybex was founded in 1976. More than 30 years later, we're still committed to producing consistently exceptional books. With each of our titles we're working hard to set a new standard for the industry. From the paper we print on to the authors we work with, our goal is to bring you the best books available.

I hope you see all that reflected in these pages. I'd be very interested to hear your comments and get your feedback on how we're doing. Feel free to let me know what you think about this or any other Sybex book by sending me an email at nedde@wiley.com, or if you think you've found a technical error in this book, please visit http://sybex.custhelp.com. Customer feedback is critical to our efforts at Sybex.

Best regards,

Neil Edde
Vice President and Publisher
Sybex, an Imprint of Wiley

To the wind beneath my wings, my inimitable wife Jennie.

Acknowledgments

Were it not for the love, patience, and support of my family, it would be impossible to write this book and hold down a few full-time jobs, advise three companies, write a blog, and travel the world evangelizing the awesomeness of data. I'm lucky. My wife Jennie is my biggest cheerleader and counsel, and for that I shall remain in debt to her for several lifetimes. My daughter Damini's courage and kindness is a constant source of inspiration. My son Chirag's intellect and energy reminds me to always be curious and strive for more.

I would like to express my deep appreciation to the readers of my blog, Occam's Razor. In approximately three and a half years I have written 411,725 words in my 204 blog posts, and the readers of my blog have written 615,192 words in comments! Their engagement means the world to me and motivates me to make each blog post better than the last. It is impossible to thank each person, so on their behalf let me thank three: Ned Kumar, Rick Curtis, and Joe Teixeira.

As the song goes, *I get by with a little help from my friends…* in the last few years I have benefited from the help of two dear friends in particular. Bryan Eisenberg, the author of *Always Be Testing*, has consistently shared life lessons about this business and helped a ton with my own journey. Mitch Joel, the author of *Six Pixels of Separation*, has helped me become a better public speaker and, as if that were not enough, connected me with anyone worth connecting to! Thanks, guys.

A huge motivation behind this book was the incredible work done by The Smile Train, Doctors Without Borders, and Ekal Vidyalaya. They make the world a better place, and I feel blessed that the money raised by my books helps me be a small part of their mission.

Last, but not least, my fantastic team at Wiley. This book was written and published at a pace that would drive mere mortals crazy, but not them. They worked harder than I did, they pushed deadlines (and me!), and they made the impossible happen. Stephanie Barton, Kim Wimpsett, Liz Britten, and Willem Knibbe, you rock!

About the Author

Avinash Kaushik is author of the best-selling book *Web Analytics: An Hour a Day* (http://www.snipurl.com/wahour). He is also the analytics evangelist for Google and the cofounder of Market Motive, Inc.

As a thought leader, Avinash puts a commonsense framework around the often frenetic world of web analytics and combines that framework with the philosophy that investing in talented analysts is the key to long-term success. He is also a staunch advocate of listening to the consumer and is committed to helping organizations unlock the value of web data.

Avinash works with some of the largest companies in the world to help them evolve their online marketing and analytics strategies to become data-driven and customer-centric organizations. He recently received the 2009 Statistical Advocate of the Year award from the American Statistical Association.

He is also a frequent speaker at industry conferences in the United States and Europe, such as Ad-Tech, Monaco Media Forum, iCitizen, and JMP Innovators' Summit, as well as at major universities, such as Stanford University, University of Virginia, and University of Utah.

You'll find Avinash's web analytics blog, Occam's Razor, at www.kaushik.net/avinash.

Contents

xiv

CONTENTS

Chapter 11   Guiding Principles for Becoming an Analysis Ninja   313

Introduction

I have a simple, if lofty, goal with this book: to change how the world makes decisions when it comes to online.

For far too long our online efforts have accurately been classified as *faith-based initiatives*. And why not? That's exactly how we made decisions for our offline efforts, and when we moved online, we duplicated those practices. But online, in the glorious beautiful world of the Web, we do not have to rely on faith.

We live in the most data-rich environment on the planet—an environment where numbers, data, math, and analysis should be the foundation of our decisions. We can use data to determine how to market effectively, how to truly connect with our audiences, how to improve the customer experience on our sites, how to invest our meager resources, and how to improve our return on investment, be it getting donations, increasing revenue, or winning elections!

You have a God-given right to be data driven, and this book will show you how to exercise that right.

Web Analytics 2.0 is a framework that redefines what data means online. Web Analytics 2.0 is not simply about the clicks that you collect from your website using analytics tools like Google Analytics, Omniture, or XiTi. Web Analytics 2.0 is about pouring your heart into understanding the impact and economic value of your website by doing rigorous outcomes analysis. It is about expressing your love for the principles of customer centricity by embracing voice-of-customer initiatives and, my absolute favorite, learning to fail faster by leveraging the power of experimentation. It is also—and this is so cool—about breaking free from your data silos by using competitive intelligence data to truly understand the strengths and weaknesses of your competitors.

This book answers four existential questions: *what*, *how much*, *why*, and *what else*.

The Second Little Book That Could

Like my first book, 100 percent of my proceeds from this book will be donated to two charities.

The Smile Train does cleft lip and palate surgery in 63 of the world's poorest countries. They help do more than give the smile back to a child. Their efforts eliminate a condition that can have deep physical and long-term emotional implications for a child.

Ekal Vidyalaya initiates, supports, and runs nonformal one-teacher schools in the most rural parts of India. By locating their schools in remote areas neglected by the government and development agencies, they help eradicate illiteracy and open new paths for children.

By buying this book, you will elevate your knowledge and expertise about web analytics, but you are also helping me support two causes that are near and dear to my heart. When it comes to helping those in need, every little bit counts. Thank you.

The Awesome World of Data-Driven Decision Making

The offline world is not going anywhere. But the Web is becoming central to every aspect of our existence. It does not matter if you are a small-business owner, a politician, a mom, a student, an activist, a worker bee, or just one of 7 billion Homo sapiens on this planet. It does not matter if you live in Athens, Antananarivo, Abu Dhabi, or Albuquerque.

We have access to multiple data sources (quantitative, qualitative, and competitive). We have access to an abundance of free tools that we can use to ensure our web decisions, from the tactical to the strategic, are informed by data. Those decisions may range from what content should go on which page, to how to purchase the right set of keywords for our search marketing campaigns, to how to find the audience with the perfect demographic and psychographic profile for our business, to how to delight visitors when they get to our website.

I have compared web analytics to Angelina Jolie; that comparison should suggest how sexy it is, how powerful it is, and what a force for good I think it is. By the time you are halfway through this book I am positive you'll agree with me.

What's Inside the Book?

This book builds on the foundation laid by my first book, *Web Analytics: An Hour a Day.* I am not going to beat around the bush; Chapter 1 starts with a bang by introducing you to the Web Analytics 2.0 framework. That is followed immediately by a strong case for why the *multiplicity* mental model is mandatory for success with tools. We go from 0 to 60 in 13 pages!

Picking the right set of tools might be just as important as picking your friends: pick the wrong one, and it might take a long time to recover. With Chapter 2, I walk you through a process of self-reflection that will empower you to choose the right set of web analytics tools for your company. You'll also learn questions you can ask tool vendors (why not stress them a bit?), the approach for choosing your vendor, and finally how to optimally negotiate your contract (stress them again!).

Chapters 3 and 4 cover the awesome world of traditional web analytics, clickstream analysis. In Chapter 3, using eight specific metrics, you'll learn the intricate nuances that go into modern metrics: what you should look for, what you should avoid, and how to ensure that your company has chosen the right set of metrics. You'll also learn my favorite technique for diagnosing the root cause behind poor performance.

Chapter 4 picks up the story and gently walks you through a primer on web analytics that will empower you to move very quickly from data to action on your website. I'll then explore foundational analytical strategies followed by six specific analyses for your daily life. In every section you'll learn how to kick things up a notch or two above average expectations. This chapter closes with a reality check on five key web analytics challenges (you are not going to want to miss this!).

Chapter 5 will be your best friend because it covers the single biggest reason for the existence of your websites: outcomes. That is, conversions, revenue, customer satisfaction, visitor loyalty, and more. You'll learn the value of focusing on micro conversions (a must do!). At the end of the chapter, I offer two specific sets of recommendations on how to measure outcomes on non-ecommerce and B2B websites.

In Chapter 6, the Web Analytics 2.0 fun really starts because I cover the wonderful world of customer centricity: listening to customers and doing so at scale. You'll learn to leverage lab usability, surveys, and other user-centric design methodologies. Finally, I give an outline of exciting techniques on the horizon—techniques that will dramatically change how you think of leveraging voice of customer.

Chapter 7 covers experimentation and testing. If you have ever read my blog or heard me speak, you'll know how absolutely liberating it is that the Web allows us to fail faster, frequently, and get smarter every single day. You'll learn about A/B and multivariate testing, but I think you'll remember this book the most for teaching you about the power of controlled experiments (finally you can answer the hardest questions you'll ever face!).

Chapter 8 will help you come to grips with competitive intelligence analysis. Like the rest of this book, this chapter is not about teaching you how to use one tool or the other. No sirree, Bob! You'll learn how to dig under the covers and understand how data is captured and why with competitive intelligence more than anywhere else the principle of garbage in, garbage out applies. By the time you finish this chapter, you'll know how to analyze the website traffic of your competitors, use search data to measure brand and identify new opportunities, zero in on the audiences relevant for your campaign or business, and benchmark yourself against your competitors.

Chapter 9 will clarify how to measure the new and evolving fields of mobile analytics; you'll see why measuring blogs is not like measuring websites and how to measure the success of your efforts on social channels such as Twitter. You'll start by learning about the fundamental challenges that the *social Web* presents for measurement.

Chapter 10 starts the process of truly converting you to an analysis ninja. I cover the *hidden* rules of the game, issues to be careful about, tasks to do more, and why some approaches work and others don't. You'll want to read the end of this chapter to learn why revolutions in web data fail miserably and evolution works magnificently. Oh, and as you might expect, I offer a very specific recommended path to nirvana!

Chapter 11 is about analytical techniques—the key weapons that you'll need in your arsenal as you head off to conquer the data world. You'll get to know context, comparisons, "what's changed," latent conversions, the head and tail of search, and really, really advanced paid search analysis. Oh my.

Chapter 12 contains material that will be worth multiple times the price of this book. It tackles the hardest, baddest, meanest web data challenges on the planet today: multitouch campaign attribution analysis and multichannel analytics. There's no dancing around here, just practical actionable solutions you can implement right now, today. Don't do anything in web analytics until you have read this chapter.

Chapter 13 was one of the most fun chapters for me to write. Web Analytics 2.0 is about people (not surprising coming from the creator of the 10/90 rule for magnificent success). Regardless of your role in the *data world*, this chapter includes guidance on how to plan your career to ensure maximum success. I offer best practices for keeping your knowledge current, but I don't stop there; I suggest ways to move to the bleeding edge. The chapter closes with advice for managers and directors about how to identify the right talent, nurture them, and set them up for success.

Chapter 14 collects all my experience and research in this nascent field and shares recommendations for tackling the one task that will make or break your success: creating a data-driven culture. I recommend approaches on how to present data, how to excite people, how to use metric definitions to influence behavioral change in your organization, and how to create a truly data-driven boss (yea!) and finally strategies for getting budget and support for your analytical program and people.

Does that sound exciting? Oh, it's so much fun!

Valuable Multimedia Content on the CD

The podcasts, videos, and resources on the CD extend the content in the book by making concepts easier to understand and offering additional guidance and instruction not in the book. For more information, see the book's appendix—or better yet, fire up the disc and start exploring.

Request for Feedback

I love preaching about the value of customer data, and I love practicing that mantra as well. I want to hear your thoughts about this book. What was the one thing you found to be of most value in the book? What was the biggest surprise? What was the one big thing you implemented and won praise for? What is one thing I should have done differently? What was the biggest missing piece?

You can email me at feedback@webanalytics20.com.

I'll learn from every bit of feedback, and I promise to reply to each and every person who writes to me. Please share your experience, critiques, and kudos.

One more fun thing: for my first book I requested readers to send me a picture with the book (of people, places, babies, buildings, and so on). That led to the wonderful collection of pictures you'll see here: http://zqi.me/wapeople. It makes the world a bit closer and more real.

I would love to get a picture of you or your hometown or your pet with this book. Please email it to me at feedback@webanalytics20.com.

Thank you.

The Beginning

I am sure you can tell that I had a ton of fun writing this book. I really, really did. I am confident that you'll have just as much fun reading it, learning from it, and changing the world one insightful analysis at a time.

Let's go!

Web Analytics 2.0

The Bold New World of Web Analytics 2.0

1

For years it has been clear that web analytics holds the promise to truly revolutionize how business is done on the Web. And why not? You can track every click of every person on your site. How can that not be actionable? Unfortunately, the revolution has not quite panned out. The root cause is that analysts and marketers have taken a very limited view of data on the Web and have restricted it just to clickstream data. In this chapter, I make the case for why you need to drastically rethink what it means to use data on the Web. The Web Analytics 2.0 strategy adapts to the evolution of the Web and dramatically expands the types of data available to help you achieve your strategic business objectives.

Chapter Contents

State of the Analytics Union

Let's start with a tale about the paradox of data. Professionally speaking, I grew up in the world of data warehousing and business intelligence (BI). I worked with massive amounts of enterprise data; multiterabytes; and sophisticated extract, transform, and load (ETL) middle layers—all fronted by complex business intelligence tools from companies such as MicroStrategy, Business Objects, and SAS. Although the whole operation was quite sophisticated and cool, the data set wasn't really that complex. Sure, we stored customer names and addresses, products purchased, and calls made, along with company metadata and prices. But not much data was involved. As a result, we made lots of great decisions for the company as we valiantly went to battle for insights.

But the lack of breadth and depth of data meant that often, and I say this only partly in jest, we could blame incompetence on the lack of *sufficient types* of data. So, we always had a get-out-of-jail-free card, something like, "Gosh darn it. If I knew our customers' underwear sizes, I could correlate that to their magazine subscriptions, and then we would know how to better sell them lightweight laptops."

I know, it sounds preposterous. But it really isn't.

With that context, you'll appreciate why I was ecstatic about the world of web analytics. Data, glorious data all around! Depth and breadth and length. Consider this: Yahoo! Web Analytics is a 100 percent free tool. It has approximately 110 standard reports, each with anywhere from 3 to 6 metrics each. That number of 110 excludes the ability to create custom reports covering even more metrics than God really intended humanity to have.

But after a few weeks in this world, I was shocked that even with all this data I was no closer to identifying actionable insights about how to improve our website or connect with our customers.

That's the paradox of data: a lack of it means you cannot make complete decisions, but even with a lot of data, you still get an infinitesimally small number of insights.

For the Web, the paradox of data is a lesson in humility: yes, there is a lot of data, but there are fundamental barriers to making intelligent decisions. The realization felt like such a letdown, especially for someone who had spent the prior seven years on the quest for more data.

But that's what this book's about: shedding old mental models and thinking differently about making decisions on the Web, realizing data is not the problem and that people might be, and focusing less on accuracy and more on precision. We will internalize the idea that the Web is an exquisitely unique animal, like nothing else out there at the moment, and it requires its own exquisitely unique approach to decision making. That's Web Analytics 2.0.

Before we go any further, let's first reflect on where we are as an industry today.

State of the Industry

As I reflect upon where we are today, I see a lot that has *not* changed from the very early days of web analytics—all of about 15 years ago. The landscape is dominated by tools that primarily use data collected by web logs or JavaScript tags. Most companies use tools from Google Analytics, Omniture Site Catalyst, Webtrends, Clicktracks, or Xiti to understand what's happening on their websites.

However, one of the biggest changes in recent years was the introduction of a free robust web analytics tool, Google Analytics. Web analytics had been mostly the purview of the rich (translation: big companies that could afford to pay). Sure, a few free web log–based solutions existed, but they were hard to implement and needed a good deal of IT caring and feeding, presenting a high barrier to entry for most businesses.

Google Analytics' biggest impact was to create a massive data democracy. Anyone could quickly add a few lines of JavaScript code to the footer file on their website and possess an easy-to-use reporting tool. The number of people focusing on web analytics in the world went from a few thousand to hundreds of thousands very quickly, and it's still growing.

This process was only accelerated by Yahoo!'s acquisition of IndexTools in mid-2008. Yahoo! took a commercial enterprise web analytics tool, cleverly rebranded it as Yahoo! Web Analytics, and released it into the wild for free (at this time only to Yahoo! customers).

Other free tools also arrived, including small innovators such as Crazy Egg, free open source tools such as Piwik and Open Web Analytics, or niche tools such as MochiBot to track your Flash files. Some very affordable tools also entered the market, such as the very pretty and focused Mint, which costs just $30 and uses your web logs to report data.

A search on Google today for *free web analytics tools* results in 49 million results, a testament to the popularity of all these types of tools. All these free tools have put the squeeze on the commercial web analytics vendors, pushing them to become better and more differentiated. Some have struggled to keep up, a few have gone under, but those that remain today have become more sophisticated or offer a multitude of associative solutions.

Omniture is a good example of a competitive vendor. SiteCatalyst, its flagship web analytics tool, is now just one of its core offerings. Omniture now also provides Test&Target, which is a multivariate testing and behavior targeting solution, and the company entered the search bid management and optimization business with SearchCenter. It also offers website surveys, and it can now power ecommerce services through its acquisition of Mercado. Pretty soon Omniture will be able to wake you up with a gentle tap and help you into your work clothes! As a result of this competitive strategy, Omniture has done very well for itself and its shareholders thus far.

Beyond web analytics, I am personally gratified to see so many other tools that exploit the Trinity strategy of Experience, Behavior, and Outcomes, which I presented in my first book, *Web Analytics: An Hour a Day* (Sybex, 2007).

We can now move beyond the limits of measuring Outcomes from web analytics tools, or *conversions*, to measuring more robust Outcomes, say our social media efforts. Obvious examples of this are using FeedBurner to measure Outcomes from blogs and using the diverse ecosystem of tools for Twitter to measure the success of your happy tweeting existence. We are inching—OK, scraping—closer toward the Holy Grail of integrated online and offline Outcomes measurement.

The Behavior element of the strategy has not been neglected either. Inexpensive online tools allow you to do card sorts (an expensive option offline) to get rapid customer input into redesigns on your websites' information architecture (IA). A huge number of free survey tools are now available; allow me to selfishly highlight 4Q, which is a free on-exit survey from iPerceptions that was based on one of my blog posts ("The Three Greatest Survey Questions Ever"; http://zqi.me/ak3gsq).

Then there is the adorable world of competitive intelligence. It did not have an official place in the Trinity strategy (though it was covered in *Web Analytics: An Hour A Day*) because of the limited (and expensive) options in the market at that time. We have had a massive explosion in this area in the past two years with tools that can transform your business, such as Compete, Google's Ad Planner and Insights for Search, Quantcast...and I am just scratching the surface.

Reflecting on the early days of web analytics, I am very excited about the progress the industry has made since the publication of my last book a couple years ago.

I am confident massive glory awaits the marketer, analyst, site owner, or CEO who can harness the power of these free or commercial tools to understand customer experience and competitive opportunities.

Rethinking Web Analytics: Meet Web Analytics 2.0

Remember the paradox of data? Just a few pages ago? So much data, so few insights. That paradox led me to create the Trinity strategy for web analytics when I was working at Intuit, and it has now led me to introduce Web Analytics 2.0.

Most businesses that focus on web analytics (and sadly there are still not enough of them) think of analytics simply as the art of collecting and analyzing clickstream data, data from Yahoo! Web Analytics, Omniture, or Mint.

This is a good start. But very quickly a realization dawns, as illustrated in Figure 1.1.

The big circle is the amount of data you have. Lots! After a few months, though, you realize the zit at the bottom of the circle is the amount of *actionable* insight you get from that data. Why?

Figure 1.1 The old paradigm of Web Analytics 1.0

You have so little actionable insight because clickstream data is great at the *what*, but not at the *why*. That is one of the limits of clickstream data. We know every click that everyone ever makes and more. We have the *what*: What pages did people view on our website? What products did people purchase? What was the average time spent? What sources did they come from? What keywords or campaigns produced clicks? What this, and what that, and what not?

All this *what* data is missing the *why*. It's important to know what happened, but it is even more critical to know why people do the things they do on your site. This was the prime motivation behind my redefinition of web analytics. For thorough web analytics, we need to include not just the *why* but also key questions that can help us make intelligent decisions about our web presence.

Web Analytics 2.0 is:

the analysis of qualitative and quantitative data from your website and the competition,

to drive a continual improvement of the online experience that your customers, and potential customers have,

which translates into your desired outcomes (online and offline).

This definition is specific, it's modern, and it results in rethinking how to identify actionable insights. Figure 1.2 illustrates Web Analytics 2.0.

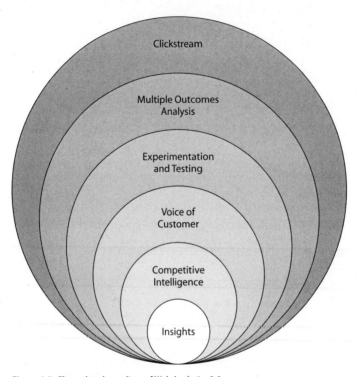

Figure 1.2 The updated paradigm of Web Analytics 2.0

With this definition, I wanted to expand the questions that could be answered by redefining what it meant to do web analytics, what sources an analyst or online marketer would access, and what tools would be put to use.

Clickstream answers the *what*. Multiple Outcomes Analysis answers the *how much*; Experimentation and Testing help explain the *why* (albeit analytically, Voice of Customer also contributes to the *why*), this time with direct customer input; and lastly Competitive Intelligence answers the *what else*, which is perhaps the most underappreciated data on the Web.

Figure 1.3 outlines how each of these four important questions map into each source of data/element of the Web Analytics 2.0 strategy.

Ain't that sweet? Now let's look at each element briefly; I will cover them in more detail in the upcoming chapters of the book.

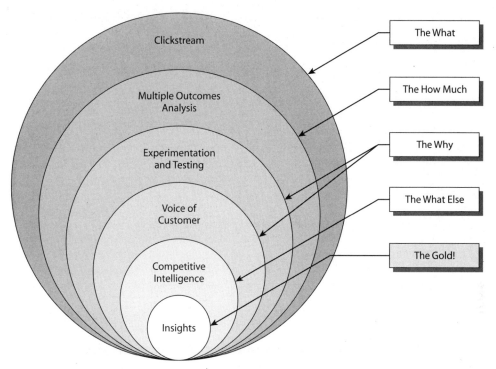

Figure 1.3 Key questions associated with Web Analytics 2.0

The What: Clickstream

The *what* of Clickstream is straightforward. If you have a web analytics solution hosted in-house, then the *what* is collecting, storing, processing, and analyzing your website's click-level data. If, like most people, you have a web analytics solution hosted externally or hosted by a vendor, then the *what* is simply collecting and analyzing the click-level data.

Click-level data is data you get from Webtrends, Google Analytics, and other Clickstream tools. You will have a lot of data—in the order of gigabytes in a few months and more if you store history.

Clickstream is also foundational data; it helps you measure pages and campaigns and helps you analyze all kinds of site behavior: Visits, Visitors, Time on Site, Page Views, Bounce Rate, Sources, and more.

The How Much: Multiple Outcomes Analysis

If you have heard me speak at a conference, you have heard this story. At my first web analytics job, the company was using Webtrends (a wonderful robust tool). I was new. I asked a lot of questions about the use of data and the 200 Webtrends reports that were being produced. At the end of two weeks, I turned off Webtrends.

For three weeks, not a single human being called about their missing 200 reports. 200! In a multibillion-dollar company!

After some reflection, I realized the root cause of this "unmissing" data was that none of these 200 reports focused on measuring Outcomes. A million visits to the site. So what? What were the Outcomes for the company? For the marketer?

Focusing deeply and specifically on measuring Outcomes means connecting customer behavior to the bottom line of the company. The most impactful thing you will do with web analytics is to tie Outcomes to profits and to the bonuses of your report recipients.

A website attempts to deliver just three types of Outcomes:

- Increase revenue.

- Reduce cost.

- Improve customer satisfaction/loyalty.

That's it. Three simple things.

Everything you do on your website needs to deliver against these three Outcomes, regardless of whether your website is for ecommerce, tech support, social media, or just general propaganda. You'll use your Clickstream tools, you'll use your enterprise resource planning (ERP) systems, you'll use surveys, you'll use Technorati, and more.

If you want the love of your senior management, you need to focus on Multiple Outcomes Analysis.

The Why: Experimentation and Testing

I believe that most websites suck because HiPPOs create them. HiPPO is an acronym for the "Highest Paid Person's Opinion."

You know how it goes. Someone presents a great idea, but the HiPPO decides what actually happens. If she or he wants the dancing monkey on the home page, well, then the dancing monkey goes on the home page.

The reality is that usually the HiPPO is 10 steps removed from the site, has never visited a Wal-Mart, and is too close to the business. The HiPPO is a poor stand-in for what customers want.

By leveraging the power of Experimentation and Testing tools such as the free Google Website Optimizer or commercial tools such as Omniture's Test&Target, Autonomy's Optimost, or SiteSpect, you can change your strategy. Rather than launching a site with one idea (the HiPPO's idea, of course), you can run experiments live on your site with various ideas and let your customers tell you what works best. So sweet. I call it the "revenge of the customers!"

There is a powerful hidden reason to be best friends forever (BFF) with your testing tool: you fail faster. It is very expensive to fail in all other channels, such as TV, radio, magazines, or big stores. But failing online is cheap and fast.

Consider launching a new product on Walmart.com vs. a Wal-Mart store. For example, why not launch a new product on Walmart.com first rather than at a Wal-Mart store and see how it does? Why not experiment with a few different promotional offers via email or search ads before you finalize your strategy and launch it using print, catalog, or TV ads? In each scenario you can take a bigger risk, launch faster, fail or succeed significantly faster online!

That is a massive strategic advantage. It is also the reason I am fond of saying "Experiment or die."

The Why: Voice of Customer

For me, a mechanical engineer with an MBA, the *why*—or the power and value of qualitative data—was a tough lesson. Consider this simple question: can you look at the Top Pages Viewed report from your web analytics tool and for your site—say, www.zappos.com—and understand the content visitors were most interested in?

How would you know which of the top pages visitors *actually wanted to see*? Maybe they could not find the pages because of a missing internal site search engine or the broken navigation on your site? You have no idea. Your web analytics tool can report only what it can record. What your customers wanted but did not see was not recorded.

That's why Voice of Customer (VOC) is so important. Through surveys, lab usability testing, remote usability testing, card sorts, and more, you can get direct feedback from customers on your website or from your target customer base.

I have had so many "aha" moments reading open-text VOC from website surveys. "Oh, this is why they abandoned" or "Darn, that's why no one is buying this product" or, usually, "Why was something so obvious hidden from us?"

If you marry the *what* with the *why*, you'll have a lifetime of happiness. I guarantee it.

The What Else: Competitive Intelligence

Of all the surprises on my web analytics journey, Competitive Intelligence was the biggest one. In the traditional world of enterprise resource planning, customer relationship management (CRM), and deep back-end enterprise systems, all you had was your data. You had very little information about your competitors. On the Web, though, you can gather tons of information about your direct or indirect competitors! And usually that info is free!

At www.compete.com, you can type in the URLs of your competitors and within seconds compare your performance with theirs. You can see how long people spend on your site vs. theirs. You can see repeat visits, page views per visitor, growth, and so on.

So, why should you really care about this?

Consider this simple analogy. If you are using your web analytics tool to measure your website, then it's like sitting in a car and watching the dashboard to see that you are going exactly 70 mph. But your windshield and windows are all blacked out. You can't see outside.

Using Competitive Intelligence data is like scraping off that black paint and being able to see outside. Now you can see you are in a race (unbeknownst to you), and you can see that while you are driving at 70 mph, everyone else is racing past at 160 mph. Unless you make drastic changes, you'll be irrelevant.

That's the power of Competitive Intelligence data. Knowing how you are performing is good. Knowing how you are performing against your competition is priceless—it helps you improve, it helps you identify new opportunities, and it helps you stay relevant.

In this book, I will cover how you can use free and commercial tools to get Competitive Intelligence related to audience (demographic and psychographic) attributes, keywords, traffic sources, website customer behavior, and more.

That's the magnificent world of Web Analytics 2.0. This world is broader than you imagined. It is sexier than you imagined. It is all about focusing on the customer.

Change: Yes We Can!

You will need to make two critical changes to succeed in the world of Web Analytics 2.0. The first is a strategic shift—a change to the mental model you apply. The second is a tactical shift—one that will challenge your current thinking about tools and how to use them.

The Strategic Imperative

The big challenge for crossing any modern chasm is rarely technology or tools. The challenge is entrenched mind-sets. For all of us, the biggest challenge to changing our web analytics strategy will be to evolve our mind-set to think 2.0.

Figure 1.4 illustrates the mind-set evolution that you absolutely need to move you or your organization to Web Analytics 2.0.

In the world of Web Analytics 2.0, clicks don't rule; rather, the combination of the "head and the heart" rules. When you are ruled by the head and the heart, you care equally about what happens on your website as you do about what happens on your competitor's. All the while you are automating as much decision making as you can to eliminate reporting and even some analysis. Your world is one of continuous actions (that is, surveys, testing, behavior targeting, keyword optimization) and continuous improvements, where customers, not HiPPOs, rule.

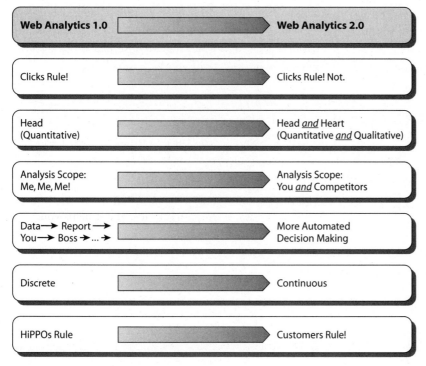

Figure 1.4 Mind-set evolution mandated by Web Analytics 2.0

The Tactical Shift

With the second change, you embrace a fantastic, now mandatory, concept of Multiplicity.

In the traditional business intelligence world, we were taught to seek the "single source of the truth." Bring all data into one place; build massive systems, usually over multiple years; and celebrate. Sadly, this strategy is toxic on the Web.

At the eMetrics summit in 2003, Guy Creese presented the concept of Multiplicity. The concept was brutal in its simplicity: multiple constituencies, tools, and types of data sources make it much easier to do effective analytics.

I have come to believe that Multiplicity is the core reason for the awesomeness of the Web. Consumption of data is vastly more democratic for your web business; everyone needs access to data now. You have a wealth of effective tools to do jobs that you never thought possible. You have not just a lot more data, as in clicks, but a lot more data types (qualitative and quantitative) that make life worth living!

Multiplicity is the only way for you to be successful at Web Analytics 2.0.

As Figure 1.2 illustrated, Web Analytics 2.0 gives you a holistic picture of your website performance. Under that strategy, every solid web decision-making program (call it *web analytics* or *web insights* or *digital customer insights*) in a company will need to solve for the Five Pillars: Clickstream, Multiple Outcomes Analysis, Experimentation and Testing, Voice of Customer, and Competitive Intelligence.

Figure 1.5 shows the approach your tools strategy must take to meet the need of Multiplicity.

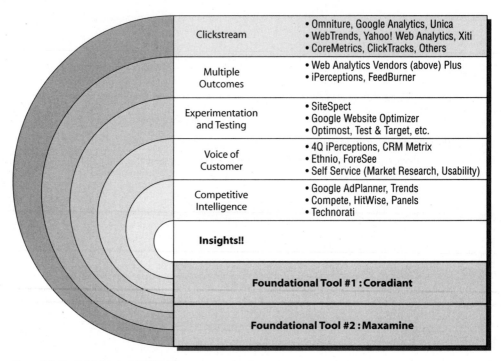

Clickstream	• Omniture, Google Analytics, Unica • WebTrends, Yahoo! Web Analytics, Xiti • CoreMetrics, ClickTracks, Others
Multiple Outcomes	• Web Analytics Vendors (above) Plus • iPerceptions, FeedBurner
Experimentation and Testing	• SiteSpect • Google Website Optimizer • Optimost, Test & Target, etc.
Voice of Customer	• 4Q iPerceptions, CRM Metrix • Ethnio, ForeSee • Self Service (Market Research, Usability)
Competitive Intelligence	• Google AdPlanner, Trends • Compete, HitWise, Panels • Technorati
Insights!!	
Foundational Tool #1 : Coradiant	
Foundational Tool #2 : Maxamine	

Figure 1.5 The Web Analytics 2.0 Multiplicity strategy and tools

As clearly illustrated in Figure 1.5, you'll need a specialized tool to solve for each element of Web Analytics 2.0.

Clickstream You'll use Omniture tools, Google Analytics, Unica's NetInsight, Webtrends, Yahoo! Web Analytics, Lyris HQ (formerly ClickTracks), Coremetrics, and so on.

Multiple Outcomes You'll use your web analytics tools mentioned for Clickstream but also the likes of iPerceptions (to measure Task Completion Rate!), FeedBurner (to track Subscribers), and various other tools to measure social media success (your traditional web analytics tools are not very good at this last one).

Experimentation and Testing You'll use Google Website Optimizer, Omniture's Test&Target, SiteSpect, Optimost, and so on.

Voice of Customer You'll use iPerceptions, CRM Metrix, Ethnio, ForeSee, and self-service options such as Lab Usability.

Competitive Intelligence You'll use Google Ad Planner, Insights for Search, Compete, Hitwise, Technorati, and so on.

For optimal success, you'll need only one tool from each of the previous categories to cover the base for each of the Five Pillars. That's Multiplicity.

Data from each tool is not meant to duplicate the other areas or relate to the other areas. Each tool provides insights that, taken together, give you the data you need to succeed.

Don't feel overwhelmed by the Multiplicity strategy.

Notice that in each row in Figure 1.5 you have an option for a free tool, so don't worry about cost right away. Mercifully you also don't have to do everything right away. Your company's size, needs, and sophistication will help you determine your personal strategy.

The following is my list of the must-have elements that different businesses should consider to join the Web Analytics 2.0 world; they are ranked by priority and show the minimal areas that should be addressed:

- **Small businesses**: 1. Clickstream, 2. Outcomes, 3. Voice of Customer.
- **Medium-sized businesses**: 1. Outcomes, 2. Clickstream, 3. Voice of Customer, 4. Testing.
- **Large, huge businesses**: 1. Voice of Customer, 2. Outcomes, 3. Clickstream, 4. Testing, 5. Competitive Intelligence, 6. Deep back-end analysis (Coradiant), 7. Site structure and gaps (Maxamine).

For each category, just choose a free or commercial tool listed in Figure 1.5.

Bonus Analytics

You probably noticed two tools at the very bottom of Figure 1.5. They are bonus items.

When we talk about web analytics, we typically don't think of Maxamine and Coradiant first. For large companies, Fortune 1,000 especially, both of these tools are almost mandatory. Neither measures what a traditional web analytics tool does, so there is no overlap, but each brings its unique strengths to the business of web data.

You should use Maxamine because it gives you critical data relating to search engine optimization gaps, missing JavaScript tags, duplicative content, broken website functionality (yes, broken links and "bad" forms), security and privacy compliance, black holes not crawled by your internal search engine, and more. Maxamine essentially provides everything you need to know, measure, and report about the existence of your website itself. Another competitive option is ObservePoint.

You should use Coradiant because it gives you critical data, down to an individual user level, about the "matrix" that powers your website—that is, the bits and bytes, the pages and packets. (Disclosure: I am currently on the Advisory Board of Coradiant.) Coradiant includes every single thing you can imagine going out from your web servers (anywhere in the world) to your customers. You can find problems on your website quickly and hold yourself and your IT teams accountable.

With Coradiant, you can also understand why, for example, your conversion rates are down. Is it because suddenly your cart and checkout pages were slow and not making it to your customers? Or is it because of 404 errors on your important pages? These are key questions that traditional tools have a hard time answering, if at all.

That's the Multiplicity strategy: Clickstream data, a better view of the landscape through Multiple Outcomes, and quicker paths to failure and success through Experimentation and Testing. These are the basic steps toward tackling a competitive industry. And don't forget to adopt the mental model of "heart and mind," where you are as vigilant of your competitor's web activity as you are of your own (outlined in Figure 1.4). Multiplicity provides you with the keys to go out and change the world. Rock on!

The Optimal Strategy for Choosing Your Web Analytics Soul Mate

2

In the new world order of Web Analytics 2.0, you must move beyond the mental model of a "single source of truth" to a true Multiplicity strategy to identify actionable insights faster. How do you do that? Tools! You must pick 'em right and make sure that one step forward is not three steps back.

In this chapter, you'll learn how to do deep introspection to understand your needs better, how to get the truth out of analytics vendors, how to compare analytics tools, and how to run a pilot and negotiate a contract.

Chapter Contents

Predetermining Your Future Success

We are blessed to have a number of robust free or commercial tools to solve for Web Analytics 2.0. Unfortunately, we significantly underappreciate how critical picking the right tool is. Or how much a wrong tool can regress the organization.

For example, my company chose a web analytics tool after sending a glorious request for proposal (RFP) that contained every question on Earth. The chosen tool took us 15 months to completely implement and then 6 months to get the first inkling that it was completely wrong for the company. Guess that RFP was not so robust after all! By then, we were too vested in the tool—via people, systems, and processes—to change anything quickly. In another 6 months, the senior leader who helped choose this expensive tool left the company. The new leader immediately saw the problem and started the process of choosing a new tool. The company had been stagnant now for more than two-and-a-half years. It took us another 9 months to pick and implement the right tool.

Total time to making strategic web decisions: terribly longer than it needed to be.

You might think this situation happens only at large companies or only at other companies. Trust me, it is probably happening at your company.

We tend to pick tools like we are picking a marriage partner. When we choose wrong, we don't want to accept it. The reality is that few things will impact your chances at success more than picking the right set of tools for the unique needs of your company—small or medium or large.

The 10/90 Rule

My entry into the world of web analytics was enlightening. The company had one of the best tools money could buy, yet decisions were gut-driven, and all that data was for naught.

The lesson I learned from that experience caused me to postulate the 10/90 rule (published on my blog on May 19, 2006):

- Our goal: highest value from web analytics implementation.

- Cost of analytics tool and vendor professional services: $10.

- Required investment in "intelligent resources/analysts": $90.

- Bottom line for magnificent success: it's the people.

The rationale was simple because of four basic problems:

- Websites are massively complex, and although tools can capture all that data, they don't actually tell you what to do.

- Most web analytics tools in the market, even today, simply spew out data. Lots of it.

The 10/90 Rule *(Continued)*

- We don't live in our simple Web Analytics 1.0 world. We now have to deal with quantitative data, qualitative data, results of our multivariate experiments, and competitive intelligence data that might not tie to anything else.

- One of the most powerful ways to convert data into insights is to keep up with the "tribal knowledge" in the company: unwritten rules, missing metadata, the actions of random people (OK, your CEO), and so on.

To solve these four problems, you need an analyst, that is, a person with a planet-sized brain. Invest multiple times more in her or him, or more of them, if you truly want to take action on your data. Otherwise, you are simply data rich and information poor.

With the proliferation of options online and the sophistication of the Web now, the 10/90 rule is even more relevant today.

Nitpicking: I currently work as the analytics evangelist for Google. Lots of people, mathematically superior people, tell me that with the existence of free tools the 10/90 rule is invalid: the tools ($10 part) are now free. My answer to them is that the tools are still not "free." If I want to use Google Analytics or Yahoo! Web Analytics, the cost of the tool is zero, but I may have to spend $5,000 working with an authorized consultant to implement it correctly. There's your $10. Now go spend $90 in getting people with planet-sized brains to make sense of all your data!

Step 1: Three Critical Questions to Ask Yourself Before You Seek an Analytics Soul Mate!

The biggest mistake we make in the process of selecting tools is that we never pause to reflect on our own awesomeness or, more likely, a lack thereof. We jump into bed with the closest tool that will sleep with us. We rarely consider the qualities that might determine whether that tool is right for us.

So, step *numero uno* is self-reflection and a brutally honest assessment of your own company, its people, and its position in the evolutionary cycle.

Use the following three questions to prompt the critical self-reflection that should help you pick the right Web Analytics 2.0 soul mate.

Q1: "Do I want reporting or analysis?"

This is a very difficult question to answer because most organizations have a hard time being honest about their needs. Every company says they want analysis, yet few organizations (especially those with greater than 100 people) actually do. They want reporting.

The following are some reasons for choosing reporting only:

Decentralized decision making The organization is structured so that lots of different leaders make decisions, and their buy-in is required for any action. These leaders need *data that they can process*, not *analysis that tells them what action to take.*

Company cultures How does your company reach consensus? Do you need to always "cover your back"? Does it have layers of management? Is it matrixed? Paperwork-driven? Often the culture dictates checks and balances, with multiple oversights and the need for proof. This kind of culture requires a supply of information (data).

Availability of tools/features A number of tools are geared toward reporting and not analysis, which sets the pattern for what gets used.

History Older companies historically have worked by people publishing reports and data. "Think smart and move fast" is not the mantra.

Propensity of risk Does your company empower risk taking? Or is taking risks a career limiting move? Doing true analysis means letting go of some control and trusting people who know how to do their jobs. If your company's culture does not encourage that then you need reporting.

Distribution of knowledge in people/teams (tribal knowledge) If you really want to analyze data, you need to know the context to make sense of the numbers. If information and execution are isolated in your company, no amount of empowering the analyst will help. If your analysts are not plugged in, the best they can do is provide data to people who might be plugged in (ideally the company leaders).

Availability of raw analytical brainpower Bringing it back to the 10/90 rule, if you have invested appropriately in analysts, then it makes sense to choose a tool that allows your company to do true analysis.

Despite these extenuating circumstances, the analytics team is told to go out and buy the tool that is "God's gift to humanity."

If you are choosing a web analytics tool, you should take a hard look at your company, its decision-making structure, and its needs. Then be honest and decide whether reporting or analysis provides the most benefit. If your company really needs robust reporting, choose a tool that does that. If your company thrives on analysis, then choose accordingly.

Consider the following three stories.

The Wrong Affordable Tool

For my company, I chose a tool that was really affordable, and it could slice and dice data like no tomorrow to give the Senior Leaders true analysis. Now this was a large company, with about $2 billion in overall revenue and with several hundred million online. What the company really needed was distributed data to lots of people. That is, reports. My chosen tool failed miserably because it stunk at reporting. Each person had to process the data, it took too long, and people were impatient and pressed for time, so the company remained gut-driven, and our web opportunity was squandered.

The Expensive Tool with the Wrong Staff

My friend at a much larger company, with a multibillion-dollar revenue, chose the most expensive web analytics tool. It was chic, it was black, it offered colorful bars and graphs, and it did real-time processing. It could answer any question, not just online but also offline questions, with phone integration and everything.

But after 15 months of implementation, this "God's gift to humanity" tool could process only 45 days of data at any given time. An even bigger problem was that only two people knew how to use the tool. For four years, senior management was ecstatic with all this data in a chic interface. But they had yet to make a single strategic decision (or even 10 tactical ones) from all that data. Meanwhile, the web analytics vendor collected approximately $2.5 million in fees each year.

My friend's company would have been better off with Google Analytics or Yahoo! Web Analytics. Both give powerful, free reporting tools that would have gotten people using data.

Over time, if the culture, organizational structure, and level of risk taking all lined up, the company would have gotten smarter.

The Switch to the Right Tool

The third story is about a start-up. They were nimble, agile, and deeply data-driven because their existence depended on it. Yet they had unwisely chosen a tool that did reporting well but did deep analysis poorly. I recommended that they change their tool and buy a "high-end" analysis-rich tool. It was a sacrifice to pay that much. But these guys could really take advantage of rich analysis. The decision to purchase a high-end tool changed their trajectory; they could do deep analysis, do it fast, and take advantage of customer behavior to make rapid changes to their software-as-a-service (SAAS) application. They are very rich now.

Admitting that you simply want reporting is sacrilege. But be honest about it, or you'll regress your company by years. Realizing you need analytical horsepower is also important, so go spend the money, and the ROI will be there.

Q2: "Do I have IT strength, business strength, or both?"

Some companies are good at information technology (IT), and others are good at business (marketing, analysis, and strategic decisions). A very rare few are good at both. You need to stress test the core strength of your company, especially in the context of web analytics, because it will play a key role in your success.

Pulling off a successful web analytics implementation is complicated, and it is easy to get it wrong. A company that provided web analytics consulting services recently shared with me that 7 out of 10 times when they start their client engagement they find that the tool implementation is wrong (which means the client has been using the wrong data thus far!).

If you have solid IT and business strength in your company, then you can go at it all by yourself, and you'll be fine. Someone in your company, in the worst case, will have the part-time job of assuring that technical issues happen as expected.

If you don't have solid IT strength (by that I mean IT folks who know and get web analytics), then you'll have to add an external partner. Many authorized consultants or one-person-army folks outside your company can do this for you. Make sure you plan for this.

One last reason to assess your IT strength is if you want to develop your web applications in-house and not with an application service provider (ASP). If you hope to host the data collection and analysis in-house (say with Urchin, Webtrends, or Unica's Affinium NetInsight), then you need some serious IT strength to pull it all off. Ensure that you are covering this critical area.

If you don't have solid business strength, honestly acknowledging that weakness already puts you ahead of your peers. You are going to budget for bringing external consultants or an organization to teach you and help you evolve your sophistication. Page 406 of my book *Web Analytics: An Hour a Day* has a four-step life-cycle model with recommendations about exactly the type of engagement you should have with an external consulting agency to dramatically enhance your level of business sophistication. You can also view the article online at `http://zqi.me/wabizplan`.

Q3: "Am I solving just for Clickstream or for Web Analytics 2.0?"

The Clickstream vs. Web Analytics 2.0 question is a mind-set. It is a question that tries to judge what you are solving for to help you understand the level at which you are approaching the solution set. This question is all about knowing whether you need a tool to help you "understand clicks" (which is OK) or whether you need a tool to do a lot more. The question helps you crystallize your short-term and long-term goals.

The Web Analytics 2.0 mind-set and strategy call for robust qualitative and quantitative analysis in your web analytics approach with specific goals: to understand the customer experience explicitly and to then influence customer behavior on your site.

Your consideration criteria will be vastly different depending on where you are today, your point of view, and your approach. In one case, a simple log parser is fine, in another case you need a tool that integrates with other data sources, and in yet another case you need a tool that will play ball with your data warehouse.

For example, if you just want to quickly jump into web analytics, you may not care that the tool integrates with a survey system or that it can accept metadata from your company ERP or CRM systems. In that case, you want a tool to help you understand clicks.

On the other hand, if you plan to start testing from day one, then you need to know that you can easily integrate your Clickstream data with your A/B or multivariate testing (MVT) vendor. In that case, you want a tool that can do a lot more for you.

Remember, it is a terrible strategy to buy the biggest, baddest tool, because in the distant future you'll want to integrate your analytics data with your refrigerator. No one can predict how the world will be in three years, so buy a tool today that will serve your needs along that two- to three-year horizon. On the Web, everything changes too fast, which makes any other strategy imprudent.

Step 2: Ten Questions to Ask Vendors Before You Marry Them

The most common process for selecting an analytics vendor involves going around your company and asking everyone remotely related to the website to list the data they would like, compiling their answers into one giant list, and tossing it to the vendor as an RFP. The vendors reply with "yes" to everything, and you pick the vendor you really like, the one with the best schwag, or the cute one.

If you are selecting a fee-based web analytics tool for your company, the following sections give you 10 questions to ask. These questions are short, but they will separate the wheat from the chaff pretty quickly.

Q1: "What is the difference between your tool/solution and free tools from Yahoo! and Google?"

You might as well acknowledge the purple elephant in the room. If good, free analytics tools are available, why should you pay for a good analytics tool? Why not focus on following the 10/90 rule for web analytics success?

When you ask this question, ask the vendor to share their top five—and only five—reports that are different and unique to their product.

The answer you are looking for is not that Google and Yahoo! are big and bad and your privacy is under threat. That's a cop-out. You also don't want to hear that you won't get support for a free tool or that free tools will die and wither away. All of those answers are false: your privacy is not threatened, support is available with free tools (often from the same company that supports your paid tool!), and free tools are not going away.

You want your fee-based vendor to provide specific and tangible examples of reports and metrics that the free vendors don't provide. Any analytics vendor worth their fee will have a crisp answer that focuses on their best features, reports, metrics, integration points, and so on, and not scare tactics.

No global rule says that Omniture or Google Analytics or Webtrends works for everyone. Each company needs a unique solution. You should carefully consider the fit of those tools for your company. Your decision should be based on facts, not vendor FUD (fear, uncertainty, and doubt).

This question applies for survey tools (compare commercial tools with free solutions like 4Q), for A/B or multivariate testing solutions (compare these solutions to the free Google Website Optimizer), and for competitive intelligence tools (compare these tools to Compete, Ad Planner, Insights for Search, and so on).

It goes without saying you'll do a cost-benefit analysis; that is, if you can get 95 percent from a free/inexpensive solution, is the last 5 percent worth x hundred thousand dollars a year? If the answer is yes, go for it!

Q2: "Are you 100 percent ASP, or do you offer a software version? Are you planning a software version?"

One challenge vendors face is the client who wants a software-based, in-house solution rather than an ASP. Currently most analytics vendors, whether free or fee-based, provide an ASP-based tool with no software-based offerings. Some vendors, such as Webtrends, Unica, and Google (with Urchin), offer solutions you can buy and implement in-house.

With this question, you are probing how the vendor is preparing for the future with differentiated offerings. You are also looking for the intangible—how they react to this question—as much as the content of their answer.

You can also ask the vendor about first-party and third-party cookies, including which type they use as a default as well as the pain and cost of using first-party cookies. You should almost always use first-party cookies, and most vendors enable this.

You are looking for a reaction when you ask about first-party cookies. Did the vendor proactively advise you to have first-party cookies? Did they insist on it? The response shows the mind-set of the vendor.

Q3: "What data capture mechanisms do you use?"

You can capture data from your website in a number of ways. JavaScript tags are currently the most common method. You can also use web logs, packet sniffers, or web beacons.

 Note: For more details and the pros and cons of using each method, please refer to Chapter 2 in *Web Analytics: An Hour A Day*.

The answer you are looking for from the vendor is...wait for it...Multiplicity! Although they can accommodate the current standard, which is JavaScript tags, they can also deal with different data capture formats. You want a vendor that can evolve beyond just tags (or logs or sniffers) as the Web evolves and becomes harder to track.

That is, you want a vendor that will evolve to work with rich media, Flash, Flex, RSS, mobile platforms, mash-ups, and so forth.

You are not looking for a vendor to brainwash you that JavaScript tags or other common mechanisms are the answer to all your prayers. If they try that tactic, give them a dirty look, and move on to the next vendor.

I also urge you to take special caution as you review answers to this question when you are choosing competitive intelligence tools. There are so many different ways of collecting data (panels, ISP data, company server logs, search log files, monitoring software, control groups, and more), and each brings a bias to the game. It is important you understand what you are buying. I'll cover competitive intelligence in delicious detail in Chapter 8.

Q4: "Can you calculate the total cost of ownership for your tool?"

Really, really pay attention here. You are in "I am going to get promoted for this" or "I might get fired and blacklisted for this" territory.

Most vendors will quote you a price (or publish it in an ad) that will be something like this: "Solve world hunger with our analytics tool for just $5,000 a month!"

You need to look beyond the first number (the cost) you get from the vendor and compute the total cost of ownership (TCO). The TCO can be massively different depending on a host of factors, including you as a company, the tools you have in place, your vendor, and their pricing strategies.

You need to consider the following elements of TCO:

- Cost per page view (most ASP-based vendors charge per page view).

- Incremental costs beyond the initial lump sum. You incur such costs if you go over your allotted page views, if there are any "advanced" features (say, RIA tracking or RSS as extra modules that would cost more), and if you need to buy other features later (for example, pay-per-click integration with Google/Yahoo! Search Marketing or a keyword bidding feature, a data warehouse, or segmentation available only in a different tool).

- Cost of professional services (initial install and then post-launch troubleshooting or customizations).

- Annual support costs after the first year.

- Additional hardware you need at your end (PCs, laptops, web servers, data storage drives, and so on). This cost can vary by vendor—be careful because investing $250,000 in a vendor solution could require investing $1 million in hardware!

- Cost of "administration"—that is, the staff to manage the vendor relationship. This cost could be a partial head count, representing someone to create all the reports and publish them and someone to coordinate between vendor, IT, and marketers. All these roles could be filled with one person, but it's better to know now.

- Cost of analysts needed to draw insights. You could lump this element with the previous one, but it is important to be aware of the 10/90 rule and realize that you can't just buy the tool; you also have to hire a relatively intelligent brain to interpret the data.

- Additional head count (partial or full) to maintain the tags, liaise with your IT, update pages on the site, and so on. If relevant, this also includes the head count required to coordinate with marketing and sales and internal BI teams to ensure the data is tagged, collected, and passed on accurately.

Total up these factors across vendors, and make an informed choice. It is not hard to imagine that the TCO could easily be multiple times the cost quoted by the vendor.

It is critical to realize that you have to compute TCO even if you use a free tool like Google Analytics or Yahoo! Web Analytics. Only the cost of the tool is free (the first two items in the previous list). You'll still have to bear the rest of the costs (professional services, analysts, and other folks).

I encourage you to poke and dig for data to get a clear understanding of what the TCO is for each vendor. And I'll say this throughout the book: remember the 10/90 rule. A great tool in the hands of your reporting squirrel is useless. A free/inexpensive/ underpowered tool in the hands of your analysis ninja will yield massive results that impact your bottom line.

Q5: "What kind of support do you offer? What do you include for free, and what costs more? Is it free 24/7?"

During vendor pitches you'll hear that everything is free. And some web analytics vendors do indeed offer a bunch of absolutely free support as long as you stay with them. But often some limits and caveats are not explicit; you'll have to ferret those out. You want to learn how far the vendor will go to answer "silly" questions from your business users.

Signing a contract and implementing a solution signifies the start of your tool problems, not the end of your data problems. It is critical that you understand exactly what services are included and exactly how much it costs to get the services you need. For example, if a vendor provides free support only during business hours, what is the cost for 24/7 support? Or if they will answer questions only about the tool, what will it cost to determine why the tool is not working at your site? These situations are just suggestions to get your juices flowing; you'll have to work out your own unique questions.

You will need support and professional services, so you need to fully understand what the vendor will provide or what the vendor's *authorized consultants* will provide.

Q6: "What features in your tool allow me to segment the data?"

This is another principle I'll repeat frequently in the book: segmentation is the key to finding insights. You segment, or you die. So, you can imagine why this one feature is so key. You need to understand how much segmentation power is in the tool and how simple it is to use.

Put these questions to your vendor: "do I have to precode everything in custom JavaScript tags on each page of my site to segment the data post-capture? Or can I capture data with a standard tag and do segmentation later?" I call the latter *postfacto segmentation*.

Most vendors are in the former camp—custom JavaScript tags on pages to enable any segmentation. That makes segmentation much harder. How can you think of all the questions you'll ask of the data up front before you install the tool?

Often you have to try the process yourself and see whether you can segment data in the tool. Ask for a three-month free trial and stress test the tool.

Again, understand whether the vendor offers the feature you need, and make an informed choice.

Q7: "What options do I have for exporting data from your system into our company's system?"

That seventh question really needs to be broken down into four subquestions:

- "Can I get all the raw data?"
- "Can I export processed data?"
- "How easily can I export 100,000 rows of processed (not raw) data out of your tool into my other company systems?"
- "What happens if I terminate my contract with you?"

OK, I admit that's a lot of questions, but they all form one really important question: *who owns the data*? If the vendor stores it and you want to export it, do you get the raw logs (huge data files with no intelligence in terms of computed metrics, which you must decipher), or do you get processed data (computed data that is much easier to integrate)?

Typically most vendors will say you can export everything. Ask them the specific questions listed, and understand exactly what you can export (remember that an Excel dump is not the answer, which is why I mentioned the 100,000 rows earlier). Then you can determine whether their answer is sufficient for your company.

Let me stress that I am not recommending that you insist on getting all your data or getting it in a particular way. I am recommending that you ask the hard questions so you won't be disappointed later about the data you get.

Ideally, the vendor has an application programming interface (API) that allows you to pull out the data you need. Super ideally, you can pull out that data without incurring heavy additional fees (many vendors will charge you heavy fees after you download just a minor amount of data).

Q8: "What features do you provide for me to integrate data from other sources into your tool?"

By now you know that as you execute the Web Analytics 2.0 strategy you'll have to integrate different sources of data to get a complete picture. (But you are wicked smart, so you won't integrate data willy-nilly; rather, you'll do it judiciously!)

Your Clickstream data, no matter what vendor you use, will feel limiting after a while. You will eventually want deeper insights, and you'll want to integrate it with other sources of data. Exporting data is not a pain-free process, and you'll have to bring data into your tools. You need to determine how easily your potential vendor can work with importing outside data.

You might want to bring some of the following types of data into your tool: metadata from other sources in your company, CRM data, data from your ad/search agency, data from surveys that contain the primary key (such as cookie values), and results from A/B or multivariate testing. You must be able to import data efficiently (without needing humans, if possible) and then use it for segmentation or reporting.

A good example of integration is Google AdWords and Google Analytics: you don't have to tag your paid search campaigns, and your campaigns show up in Google Analytics nice and pretty for your analysis.

A suboptimal example of integration is Google Website Optimizer and Google Analytics. You can measure the success of your experiments in Website Optimizer using one goal/outcome. But it would be more useful if the tools were integrated and you could measure more Outcomes.

Figure out the line in the sand with your potential vendor for the kinds of data you want to integrate.

Q9: "Can you name two new features/tools/acquisitions your company is cooking up to stay ahead of your competition for the next three years?"

This is a forward-looking question. You want to know whether your vendors are worried about tomorrow (a good thing) and what they are doing *today* to deal with future challenges.

Their answers will give you a sense of how much they know about their own position and that of their competitors. Hence, you are not asking what two things they are doing that are good; the question is framed in the context of competition. Some vendors are much better at taking a good reality check about themselves, and others are just parsing log files like there is no tomorrow.

You want to be impressed by at least one of the two answers you hear. Ideally, you want an answer that is a complete surprise. You also want to get the feeling that your vendor has a good sense of themselves and their competitors.

Ask this same question across a few vendors, and they will talk about each other: the differing perspectives are a source of valuable insights for you. It is always so much fun when they *kvetch* about each other! Evil? Yes. Useful for unearthing some truth? Yes!

Q10: "Why did the last two clients you lost cancel their contracts? Who are they using now? May we call one of these former clients?"

A vendor taught me this question, and it is truly fantastic. You want to be confident that you are making the right choice, and there is no better way than to learn why each vendor recently lost someone's business.

You will probably hear sales-speak rather than a practical answer. But even the sales-speak can be of value. In my experience of a whole bunch of vendors, only two have ever answered this question directly. We are doing business with both today, even though in both cases they were not the most awesome vendor technologically.

Remember, with any vendor, you are actually buying a relationship, not just the tool. In the long run, the value of good people will far outpace the value of the most advanced tool, and if you don't have a relationship with the people, you can't work well with the tool.

There you go: 10 simple questions and none of them asking for much technical detail. Yet each question will help you uncover the truth about a vendor and help you find your BFF.

Redefining Conventional Wisdom on "Enterprise-Class" Web Analytics

"Enterprise class has become a catchphrase that is so amorphous that it no longer supports precise communication. Mostly it's used by marketing flaks to create sound and fury, signifying nothing." —Charles Thasher

My friend Charles at Microsoft captures the essence of the term *enterprise class* and its use in ruling out tools, vendors, and options.

Analysts, gurus, and consultants, each with their own motivations, use the term *enterprise class* to push certain massive, usually expensive, solutions.

This mental model arose from the old world. In a Web Analytics 2.0 computing world, where anyone can create massively scalable and successful software, that mental model is not just quaint; it can be corrosive.

So, the first important lesson is to avoid ruling any solution out because it does not possess an arbitrary, ephemeral label called *enterprise class*.

Continues

Redefining Conventional Wisdom on "Enterprise-Class" Web Analytics
(Continued)

The second lesson is to internalize that the definition of *enterprise class* has morphed significantly.

Here's my definition of an enterprise-class vendor:

- The vendor has been around for more than 18 months. The longer the duration, the better.

- The vendor can scale its ASP infrastructure (or in-house software solution) to (a) capture the number of page views required by the client and (b) process that data and provide it on a timely basis (say every two to three hours—after that you hit diminishing returns on your ability to take action).

- The vendor has a support infrastructure to assist the client in need at a reasonable price. If you are willing to pay for support, you should pay a reasonable price and expect solid support from the vendor or its partners.

That's it. Nothing else matters. You need to know the vendor has been around and that the vendor will be there for the long term. No other golden rules.

There is no default rule that says you ("enterprise" or "little guy") need Omniture, Webtrends, or Yahoo! Web Analytics or that says Lyris HQ (formerly ClickTracks), Omniture, Affinium NetInsight, or Google Analytics is not right for you.

Each company is unique. You are unique and special and weird. Don't rule out a solution based on what others think or say.

Comparing Web Analytics Vendors: Diversify and Conquer

I am sure you have heard this kind of statement: "I was so frustrated with Omniture. Our company dumped it, and we got Webtrends." Or maybe it was Webtrends with Coremetrics.

Moving between similar tools is like jumping off the Titanic to another sinking ship called the Pitanic: there isn't much difference, and the outcome will be the same (though that might become apparent to you just before the Pitanic goes down).

Through painful experience I have realized that when we go through the process of comparing web analytics vendors, it is critical that we find true distinctions.

The Three-Bucket Strategy

From my experiences, I have formulated a simple "three-bucket" strategy for comparing web analytics tools. Before you compare tools, be sure to choose one from each of these three buckets, each of which contains a truly differentiated set of tools:

Bucket 1: Omniture, Coremetrics, Webtrends

Bucket 2: Unica's Affinium NetInsights, XiTi, Nedstat, ClickTracks

Bucket 3: Google Analytics, Yahoo! Web Analytics

Rather than choosing from tools that will give you kinda, sorta the same features or functionality, the bucketing recommended here helps you make an optimal decision from a diverse set of choices.

Let me hasten to add that any tool in any bucket gives you 85 percent of the features you'll need. The reason each tool ended up in its bucket is because that bucket offers something compelling and uniquely differentiated from the tools in the other buckets.

Here are quick sound bites about the unique properties of the tools in each bucket:

Bucket 1 sound bites Omniture will do anything you want it to do with an ever-expanding set of features and add-on tools. Webtrends is morphing from just doing web analytics to performing paid search optimization. Coremetrics has a few unique features for retailers.

These tools often come to mind when people first think of web analytics. Each does something a bit better than the other, but there is also a large overlap.

Bucket 2 sound bites If you want to do real postfacto analysis, then ClickTracks will shine. Under its new parent (Lyris), ClickTracks is a part of an integrated suite of web tools. Unica's Affinium NetInsight integrates efficiently with your online and offline campaigns, especially if you use Unica to manage your offline campaigns. XiTi and Nedstat are two excellent European-based companies that meet local and global needs.

Each of these tools provides a truly compelling alternative to buckets 1 and 3.

Bucket 3 sound bites Google Analytics and Yahoo! Web Analytics are free, robust analytics solutions with custom reporting and advanced segmentation built in, not to mention tight integration with their parent's core search and display business.

Both of these tools will prove that you have to pay for analytics only if your needs are complex enough to require a special tool.

By using the three-bucket strategy for comparing web analytics tools, you are choosing to compare truly diverse and differentiated tools. Hence my recommendation is that, for your vendor evaluation, choose at least one tool from each bucket. You'll end up making an intelligent and informed choice for your company.

The CD-ROM that accompanies this book includes a video titled *Web Analytics Vendors & Challenges*. If you are a multimedia type, please check out that video; it outlines the previous framework and goes deeper into each vendor's strengths and your challenges.

Step 3: Identifying Your Web Analytics Soul Mate (How to Run an Effective Tool Pilot)

You've done the introspection and asked yourself the three all-important questions. You have interrogated the analytics vendors with 10 questions. You have applied the three-bucket test to ensure you have diversity in your selection process.

Now comes the exciting part! You'll take the selection-process finalists and run a real, live pilot on your site, and then in a dramatic ceremony worthy of the TV show *The Bachelor*, you'll present a rose (actually, your money) to your chosen partner.

It is important to realize at the outset that the average time from implementing a vendor to recognizing your mistake to choosing to switch to and implement a new vendor is approximately two years. You are making a critical choice for your company, and you could lose a lot of time if you make the wrong decision.

A live pilot ensures you are making the right decision, not just one based on vendors duking it out in a PowerPoint pitch battle.

Vendor pilots are usually staged for success. Yes, staged. It is not that anyone has any Machiavellian schemes. Every salesperson wants to make a deal, they are most likely compensated on a quota, and each vendor wants to look good. It does not matter if you are selling the most expensive tool or a free one (yes, even free tools have to go through a pilot!).

The following evaluation list was originally created by a reader of my blog, Steve Medcraft. To give you some context, he created this awesome list as evaluation criteria for an extremely large content publisher.

These are the key areas you want to evaluate during the pilot:

Usability Determine the accessibility/intuitiveness of the tool. Establish whether your target audiences (for example, business, data analyst, and IT) can actually use and customize the tool set and reporting or whether you must get dedicated resources to create the necessary reporting and dashboards on their behalf. Get a feel for the extent of training needed.

Functionality Test the functionality in realistic business situations: does it really do what it said on the tin? Can you use out-of-the-box reports/features and page tagging, or do you need to customize and extend data collection to meet your needs? (You may need to run a handful of scenarios with vendors.) Ascertain what is of actual value to the business.

Technical Understand the effort to implement, configure, and customize—get a feel for the actual implementation plan. Determine any unexpected overhead on your environment. Test potential interoperability with your other systems/data sources. Attempt to identify any limitations with each solution. Understand where tags can be expanded, customized, or integrated.

Response Determine the level of response for both the ASP and software solutions (performance, ability to handle the volumes, availability of reports/data, benchmarking exercise) and the vendors themselves (first-line support, ability to step up to your specific needs, documentation, and customization).

Total cost of ownership Identify any additional costs that will be incurred for your business that are not obvious in the vendor's proposal (additional administration, licenses, and so on).

To complement Steve's recommendations, here are my lessons from a tough life in the frontlines; these are evaluation criteria that are not usually obvious when selecting the right tool:

Get enough time Tell your vendor that the six weeks (or other specified time) for the pilot starts *after* you confirm that the solution (JavaScript tag) is implemented on the site, not from the time the vendor sends you the code. You would need at least six weeks of the tool fully running to get a sense of whether it is right for you.

Be fair As much as possible, try to perform the same tasks in each vendor's tool. This seems obvious, but every tool is strong in its own unique way; hence, it is easy to end up doing different tasks in each. That would not be fair to any vendor.

Ask about data sampling You won't really get a feel for a tool's ability to deal with massive amounts of data, because you'll have only six weeks worth of data. But still ask each vendor what kind of data sampling it does to make queries go faster (there is a good kind and a bad kind of sampling—we dive deep into sampling in Chapter 4). Check whether all the vendors in the pilot sample data in the same way (if they say no sampling is required, don't believe it; you will need data sampling sooner rather than later).

Segment like crazy Segmenting is not as easy as one might imagine in any tool. You can segment by customer behavior (*x* pages, *y* amount of time, visited these pages but not those, and so on) and by source (referring URLs, direct marketing campaigns, affiliates, and so on). Segmentation will show you the true colors of any tool. Remember to ask what you must do up front to segment the data later (and what happens if you forget to do the up-front work).

Ask about search analytics Ask each vendor how it identifies organic traffic from search engines (this is a trick question). Ask each vendor what process would be required to track your pay-per-click/search engine marketing campaigns (this in and of itself can be a huge pain, with all the work required, so go with the least painful option). Also ask what is required to import your keyword bidding and search spend data.

Test site content grouping Test how easily you can group the content of your site in each tool and what happens when your predefined content groups change. Content groups for the *New York Times* could be Editorials, Features, International News, Sports, and so on. How much work will that take? Can you go back and redo history (say, if you forget or want to create different content grouping in your historical data to see how things might have been)?

Bring on the interns (or the VPs!) Make sure you have at least a few complete newbies in the user pool and a few smarty-pants analytics experts; you want to ensure different personas are hitting the tool. The newbies (interns or VPs) can expose whether you have a tool that will power data democracy or not.

Test support quality When you first run into a problem or can't solve anything, resist the temptation to call your account rep. Try to find help in the tool, on the vendor's website, via email tech support, or on user forums. During a pilot or trial, you will get far superior levels of support. After you make the purchase, though, support from some vendors goes down quite a bit. You might as well test the support reality, because you'll use help in the tool, forums, email tech support, or the 800 number.

Reconcile the numbers (they won't add up, but it's fun!) Compare the numbers across different tools with which you are doing the pilot, and then then ask the vendors to explain the discrepancy. They won't add up at all, and it drives people nuts (myself included). But the vendor's reactions and how it explains the deltas will tell you a lot. Make sure you give the vendors specific data for specific time frames (they will greatly appreciate this), and then ask for an explanation. In the end, remember that data quality on the Web is not perfect, and that is 100 percent OK.

Check the daily/normal stuff Check how easy it is to create customized dashboards and customized versions of the same reports for different business units or to add computed metrics. I don't think this will be an issue with most tools you select, but nonetheless the process of doing each of these tasks will be of value during the pilot.

Sweat the TCO I have discussed ad nausem why the total cost of ownership is important. Do it. Enough said.

In closing, here is one macro thought. You don't have to do *everything* on both of the previous lists. Pick the most relevant factors to your company, and give each a weighting so that you can go through your most important criteria during the pilot.

And remember to have fun; it is a blast to do pilots.

Step 4: Negotiating the Prenuptials: Check SLAs for Your Web Analytics Vendor Contract

Oh, so close!

You have one more step left: signing a contract.

Before you sign, you'll need to check the service-level agreements (SLAs), especially if you plan to sign a contract with a fee-based analytics vendor.

You may not be aware that the SLAs you require from your vendor will inflate the yearly contract by substantial amounts (and to some extent that is not the vendor's "fault"; they price certain standard components/SLAs into their base pricing, and anything you want beyond the standard obviously costs them more to provide). For that reason, it is critical that you thoroughly consider your needs and then ask for what you need—and price it out—during contract negotiations.

The following is another important list from Steve Medcraft that will help you check the SLA:

- Availability and response of software/functionality
  - Standard availability/guaranteed uptime

- Speed of service—e.g., screens to be returned in x seconds (probably tricky to enforce because it depends on bandwidth)
- Response of service in relation to unexpected increase to load/traffic volume, load distribution, and so on
- Permitted downtime (e.g., emergencies)
- Compensation for downtime—service credits, reduced contract period, and so on, for x minutes of downtime per month (outside of planned or emergency maintenance)

- Availability of reports/data
  - Collected data to be reflected in reports within x hours
  - Availability of results after initiating query

- Technical/best practice support
  - Vendor resources available/dedicated to you (number of account managers, technical, consultants assigned to project)
  - Response to customization/change requests (quotation, delivery of service, and so on)
  - Response to traffic volume increase
  - Issue escalation procedures (online, phone, email, priority levels, status reporting, and response times)
  - Supporting material (availability of online help, accuracy of documentation, live support)

- Security
  - Physical hosted environment, protection of data/servers
  - User access to the system, data
  - Backup, archiving, and recovery
  - Monitoring in place and availability of that data

- Communication
  - Agreed points of contact (on either side)
  - Timing of notifications (planned maintenance/outage, status reports, and so on)

As earlier, I've also included my lessons from a tough life in the frontlines; the following are additional issues to be aware of regarding the SLA:

- It is likely that you don't care about all the items in the previous list, so pick what you need.
- For each item you pick, identify your thresholds or limits (in terms of downtime, amount of best-practice sharing hours, how quickly you want data, amount of email support you need, and so on).

- Identify a range for the threshold and not an absolute number; give yourself some wiggle room. Share this with your contract negotiators.

- Be explicit with the vendors (it is the least you can do for them), and ask them to be explicit with you.

- Get stuff written down; it will make a nice addendum to the standard contract the web metrics vendor will send to you.

- When deciding which tool to pick, remember to judge based on features you want, size of the contract (total size of the contract), and the amount of value you can provide your company from each (lots of people do this last one wrong). Sometimes you might not pick the most feature-rich vendor because you can't imagine that it can provide $1.2 million dollars of value back to your company (with that being the total size of the contract, in other words, tool + support + SLAs). You might go with the one that is $.05 million dollars even if it does not have that one niche feature you need.

It is likely you'll go through the previous extensive list only if you are negotiating a very expensive or "enterprise" contract. But even as a small or medium-sized business, you can use the previous information to understand the deep nuances that go into buying an analytics tool and be prepared. After all, your company is going to be huge one of these days!

The Awesome World of Clickstream Analysis: Metrics

New Web Analytics 2.0 mind-set: got it. New shiny set of tools: yep. Ready to jump in? You betcha!

It's time to start exploring the awesome world of Clickstream analysis with the building blocks of metrics and key performance indicators (KPIs).

I'll destroy some myths, take down (with love) some highly recommended but unactionable methodologies, and help you get better at diagnosing the causes of poor performance.

That means, with this chapter, you'll start honing your skills to become an analysis ninja!

3

Chapter Contents

When people say "web analytics," they really mean web metrics. Your boss rarely asks for analysis; she asks for "data" (metrics) or "reports" (KPIs). You and I of course know better; we give her analysis only, and it's based on a tortuous examination of the metrics and KPIs. If you remember nothing else, remember this: life is about taking action, and if your work is not driving action, you need to stop and reboot.

We have made a ton of progress in the past few years. Through rose-colored glasses I recall how every webmaster was once ecstatic about simply reporting hits on their website. It took K.D. Paine (www.measuresofsuccess.com) to truly enlighten us about what *hits* represented: How Idiots Track Success. That is not meant to offend anyone. Rather, it's just meant to highlight that in 1992 perhaps hits meant something—that someone requested a page. Today, in a world where every home page sends 50 or 100 hits and rich experience dominates, hits mean nothing.

The next step in our evolution was *page views*. Since the early Web was dominated by ad-driven revenue models, we all started to obsess about page views. More page views meant more opportunities to annoy with a banner ad that featured a bouncing monkey. Page views are still a decent measure of success, but they are increasingly becoming useless—not just because of Ajax, Flash, and video-driven sites. Measured in aggregate, page views mean nothing.

We have been living in the era of *visits* for the past few years, or, as some tools call them, *visitors* (more on this later in the chapter). Visits have been the currency used to measure macro success. They do mean something: a person came to your site and consumed some content.

I believe we are now living through a transformative moment.

The Web is a serious business. Even really large content companies that have been living under rocks are realizing that they need to "go digital" in a big way. Because of all this pressure, we seem to be moving to using *outcome-based metrics* as a true measure of health and success.

Next time you see me, don't tell me how many visits your sites had; tell me the Conversion Rate metric if you do e-commerce, or tell me about the Revenue Trends metrics. If you are a content site, tell me how the Depth of Visit metrics look. If you are Facebook, don't tell me the number of profiles you have; rather, tell me about your Visitor Loyalty metric.

We've evolved from hits to page views to visits. Now, we have Outcomes.

Standard Metrics Revisited: Eight Critical Web Metrics

Now let's return to the basics, rethink our core beliefs, and move into the future. I'll discuss some of our bedrock web metrics, but in each case I will illustrate nuances and complexities behind the computation of these metrics and how they make our lives challenging. You'll certainly learn the definitions of these metrics, but my sincere hope is that you'll learn how to think in a more sophisticated manner.

Before we continue, here's a quick clarification: a *metric* is a quantitative measurement of statistics describing events or trends on a website. A *key performance indicator* (KPI) is a metric that helps you understand how you are doing against your objectives. That last word—objectives—is critical to something being called a KPI, which is also why KPIs tend to be unique to each company.

Visits and Visitors

Visits and Visitors form the bedrock of nearly every web metric calculation. You'll see them prominently displayed in your web analytics tool, but you'll also find them in your search reports, your exit pages, your bounce rate computation, your conversion rates, and so on. So, your Visits and Visitors are very important.

Figure 3.1 illustrates the problem: each tool seems to have its own sweet way of reporting these numbers. They also tend to compute those numbers differently. When StatCounter says Unique Visitors, it actually means Visits. When ClickTracks (a part of Lyrics HQ) says Visitors, it means Visits.

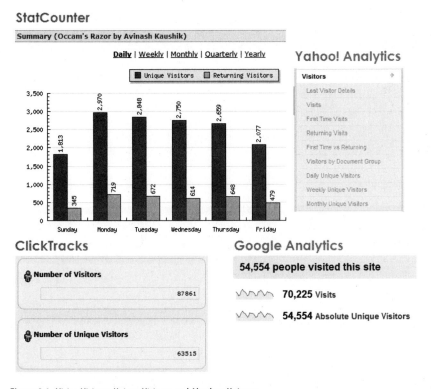

Figure 3.1 Visits, Visitors, Unique Visitors, and Absolute Uniques

So, here's lesson 1: as soon as you unwrap your shiny new analytics tool, spend five minutes identifying the details about these two important metrics the tool is reporting.

Although there is a lot of confusion about Visits and Visitors, at the end of the day each vendor is trying to measure the process of real people visiting your websites. And the vendors do that by measuring two important things: Visits and Unique Visitors.

Visits

Visits report the fact that someone came to your website and spent some time browsing before leaving. Technically this visitor experience is called a *session*.

Sessions are most commonly referred to as Visits (and perhaps only in ClickTracks now as Visitors). Sessions are usually a collection of *requests* from someone who is on your website. Here's how it works:

1. If you use a JavaScript tag solution, when someone requests the first page or item from your website, then your analytics tool starts a session for that person from that browser.

2. Each additional request from that person is attached to a unique session ID.

3. When the person leaves your site, that unique session ID is used to "stitch" together the pages viewed into one cohesive visit.

4. When you run a report for any given period in your web analytics tools, Total Visits is the *count of all the sessions during a given time period.*

In most modern web analytics tools, a session, or *visit*, is defined as lasting from the first request to the last request. If the person simply leaves the browser open and walks away, then the session is proactively terminated after 29 minutes of inactivity.

Please check with your web analytics vendor to learn what sessions are called in your tool. They could be masquerading as Visits, Visitors, Sessions, or some other label.

Unique Visitors

In computing Unique Visitors, the web analytics tool is trying to approximate the number of *people* who come to your website. Here's how it works:

1. If you use a JavaScript tag solution, when someone requests the first page or item from your website, your analytics tool will set a unique cookie on that person's browser.

2. This cookie remains on the browser even after the person leaves your website. It contains a unique anonymous string of numbers and characters. No personally identifiable (PII) information is included.

3. Each time someone visits your website from that browser, this persistent cookie ID is used to *recognize* that the same browser has returned.

4. When you run a report for any given time period in your web analytics tool, the Unique Visitors metric is the *count of all the persistent unique cookie IDs during a given time period.*

You should be aware of some important nuances and caveats when you look at the Unique Visitors metric. First, it is likely, but not always true, that each unique visitor is a unique person. Therefore, you must understand that although the Unique Visitors metric is a decent proxy for the number of unique individuals visiting your site, it is not a perfect measure.

Second, the Unique Visitors metric can be influenced by browsers that don't accept cookies or those that reject third-party cookies. Most modern analytics tools use first-party cookies that are rejected a lot less (the rejection rate is approximately 2 to 5 percent). Third-party cookies are rejected at a much higher rate (approximately 10 to 30 percent).

Even with the previous caveats, the Unique Visitors metric continues to be a superior approximation of the number of *people* visiting your website.

Compare it, for example, to the Visitors or People reported by panel-based systems, which use *monitoring software* to measure *people*. They usually use a small panel to mathematically approximate the *people* who visit your site (admittedly after applying complex algorithms). One commonly bandied-about company employs just 180,000 people who use the monitoring software to approximate the behavior of 200 million Americans who surf the Web. Quite suboptimal.

Perhaps in the future we will all have radio frequency ID chips in our bodies, and those chips will automatically alert a website that the same person is visiting (regardless of browser, PC, or mobile device). Until then let's not quibble; we'll use the Unique Visitors metric from our web analytics tool. It is useful, and it is actionable.

Next, let's really get *jiggy with it* and understand something complicated.

In many web analytics tools, you'll see Daily Unique Visitors, Weekly Unique Visitors, Monthly Unique Visitors, and, sometimes, Absolute Unique Visitors. Each metric gives you very different information, so let's examine this slightly yucky phenomenon using the data in Figure 3.2.

			Site Visits By. . .		
Month 1	Week 1	Day 1	Avinash	Dennis	Matt
Month 1	Week 1	Day 2	Dennis	Matt	Dennis
Month 1	Week 1	Day 3	Matt	Matt	
Month 1	Week 2	Day 1	Matt	Ian	
Month 1	Week 2	Day 2	Ian	Jim	
Month 1	Week 3	Day 1	Jim	Avinash	Bryan
Month 2	Week 1	Day 1	Jim	Avinash	Bryan
			Angie	Jennifer	Michelle

Figure 3.2 Website's Unique Visitors data

Now let's measure the complex set of metrics that stares back at you when you crack open Omniture (or another like-minded tool). But before you do, realize that what you see will depend on the time period you select. Arrrgh!

As you examine all the different types of Unique Visitors in your tool, keep an eye on the metric called Absolute Unique Visitors. I'll use that metric as a proxy for how unique visitors should be computed correctly, regardless of the selected time period.

Month 1 and Week 1 for End of Day 1

To make matters simple, I excerpted just one time period in Figure 3.3.

			Site Visits By. . .		
Month 1	Week 1	Day 1	Avinash	Dennis	Matt

Figure 3.3 Visits to the website on one day

In this example, if you run your reports at the end of day 1, your analytics tool will report the following details:

Daily Unique Visitors: 3

Weekly Unique Visitors: 3

Monthly Unique Visitors: 3

Absolute Unique Visitors: 3

That makes sense, right? Do a happy dance, high-five someone next to you—heck, give them a hug and a kiss (*only* if that is OK in your neck of the woods!).

Month 1 and Week 1 for End of Day 2

Now let's make our details a little more "complicated," as shown in Figure 3.4.

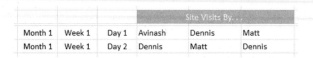

			Site Visits By. . .		
Month 1	Week 1	Day 1	Avinash	Dennis	Matt
Month 1	Week 1	Day 2	Dennis	Matt	Dennis

Figure 3.4 Visits to the website on two consecutive days

If you run your reports at the end of day 2, you will see these details:

Daily Unique Visitors: 5

Weekly Unique Visitors: 3

Monthly Unique Visitors: 3

Absolute Unique Visitors: 3

Slow down the happy dance a bit.

Note the silly effect on Daily Unique Visitors, even though the same folks from day 1, Dennis and Matt, visited on day 2. They get *counted twice*.

Life lesson: Daily Unique Visitors is a useless number if you are looking at a period of more than one day!

Month 1 for End of Week 1

Let's keep going. Figure 3.5 shows the data for one complete week.

			Site Visits By. . .		
Month 1	Week 1	Day 1	Avinash	Dennis	Matt
Month 1	Week 1	Day 2	Dennis	Matt	Dennis
Month 1	Week 1	Day 3	Matt	Matt	

Figure 3.5 Visits to a website during week 1

Crack open your analytics tool—it has been a long week—and look at the metrics; here's what you'll see:

Daily Unique Visitors: 6 (!)

Weekly Unique Visitors: 3

Monthly Unique Visitors: 3

Absolute Unique Visitors: 3

Note the continuing uselessness of the Daily Unique Visitors number.

Figure 3.6 shows the Daily Unique Visitors report from a web analytics tool and illustrates this point.

Day	Daily Unique Visitors	%
April 12, 2009 Sun	1,277	11.78%
April 13, 2009 Mon	1,812	16.72%
April 14, 2009 Tue	2,051	18.92%
April 15, 2009 Wed	1,710	15.78%
April 16, 2009 Thu	1,856	17.12%
April 17, 2009 Fri	1,436	13.25%
April 18, 2009 Sat	697	6.43%
Total	10,839	100.00%

Figure 3.6 Daily Unique Visitors report

By now you know why there is a frowning face in the Total row. Right? Repeat life lesson: Daily Unique Visitors is a useless number if you are looking at a period of more than one day!

Month 1 for End of Week 2

Let's solidify the lesson by stretching the time period a bit more, as in Figure 3.7.

			Site Visits By. . .		
Month 1	Week 1	Day 1	Avinash	Dennis	Matt
Month 1	Week 1	Day 2	Dennis	Matt	Dennis
Month 1	Week 1	Day 3	Matt	Matt	
Month 1	Week 2	Day 1	Matt	Ian	
Month 1	Week 2	Day 2	Ian	Jim	

Figure 3.7 Unique Visitors data for two weeks

Gather everyone in close proximity into the office, form a circle, hold hands, and now open your analytics tool:

Daily Unique Visitors: 10 (!!)

Weekly Unique Visitors: 6 (!)

Monthly Unique Visitors: 5

Absolute Unique Visitors: 5

The Weekly number is wrong because it counts Avinash, Dennis, Matt, Matt again, Ian, and Jim. It counts Matt again because he visited during both weekly time periods.

Life lesson: the Weekly Unique Visitors metric is useless if you look across multiple weeks. I covered earlier why Daily Unique Visitors is, to put it mildly, suboptimal.

OK, only two more scenarios left. Hang in there; it gets better.

End of Month 1, for the Whole Month

Figure 3.8 illustrates the data set that we'll consider now.

			Site Visits By…		
Month 1	Week 1	Day 1	Avinash	Dennis	Matt
Month 1	Week 1	Day 2	Dennis	Matt	Dennis
Month 1	Week 1	Day 3	Matt	Matt	
Month 1	Week 2	Day 1	Matt	Ian	
Month 1	Week 2	Day 2	Ian	Jim	
Month 1	Week 3	Day 1	Jim	Avinash	Bryan

Figure 3.8 One month's website visitors data

By now I am sure you are 100 percent up to speed on what you will see.

Daily Unique Visitors: 13 (!!!)

Weekly Unique Visitors: 9 (!!)

Monthly Unique Visitors: 6

Absolute Unique Visitors: 6

The tool has now triple- or double-counted both the Daily Unique Visitors and Weekly Unique Visitors.

Life lesson: both Daily Unique Visitors and Weekly Unique Visitors numbers are useless when you look at a period of a month.

Let's look at one last scenario, not to make your brain hurt but rather to ensure you reach the state of maximum analysis ninja enlightenment!

End of Month 2, for the Two Months

After all these dissections, Figure 3.9 takes us full circle back to the start of our journey.

			Site Visits By. . .		
Month 1	Week 1	Day 1	Avinash	Dennis	Matt
Month 1	Week 1	Day 2	Dennis	Matt	Dennis
Month 1	Week 1	Day 3	Matt	Matt	
Month 1	Week 2	Day 1	Matt	Ian	
Month 1	Week 2	Day 2	Ian	Jim	
Month 1	Week 3	Day 1	Jim	Avinash	Bryan
Month 2	Week 1	Day 1	Jim	Avinash	Bryan
			Angie	Jennifer	Michelle

Figure 3.9 Website's Unique Visitors data

You're probably tingling with excitement; here's what you'll see:

Daily Unique Visitors: 19 (gasping for air!)

Weekly Unique Visitors: 15 (oh my!)

Monthly Unique Visitors: 12 (!)

Absolute Unique Visitors: 9

The tool has now triple- or double-counted everywhere, with the Daily Unique Visitors, Weekly Unique Visitors, and Monthly Unique Visitors numbers.

The correct measure of *unique* is the Absolute Unique Visitors metric because it de-dupes the unique visitors across the entire time period.

Life lesson: both Daily Unique Visitors and Weekly Unique Visitors numbers are totally useless when you look across months. Use Monthly Unique Visitors with caution, knowing it merely de-dupes and then sums up the number for each month.

If your tool provides Absolute Unique Visitors, you are in luck because then you get true unique visitors across whatever arbitrary time period you choose. The bottom line is there are only two visitor metrics in web analytics: Visits and Absolute Unique Visitors (see Figure 3.10).

1,814,167 Visits

1,005,451 Absolute Unique Visitors

Figure 3.10 Visit metrics from Google Analytics

Do not get sucked into spurious versions of these two simple visit metrics. I am sure you are asking yourself, why do web analytics vendors put us through this torture? Simple: Computing power (or, really, the cost, for them).

The task of calculating your true real Unique Visitors number across an arbitrary time period or across multiple weeks or months is computationally intensive. That means more processing time and higher costs for the vendor. So, doing daily, weekly, and monthly counts (and then summing them up) is cheaper for them.

Google Analytics, XiTi, and Nedstat are amongst the rare vendors that provide the truly de-duped Absolute Unique Visitors metric by default, that is, at no additional cost to you.

Now, dear reader, you have truly achieved a higher level of analysis ninja proficiency! Above all else my fondest hope is that this section teaches you how to think critically about website metrics and that you should probe below the surface and ensure the metrics pass the basic sniff test. You should apply this critical thinking to all metrics you encounter.

Time on Page and Time on Site

After Visits and Visitors, perhaps the next foundational metric in web analytics is Time. It measures the time that visitors spend on an individual page and the time spent on the site during a visit (session).

Few people actually understand how time on a page or on the site is actually measured. As with most web analytics concepts, Time is more complex than you might realize. But the brave never fear silly things like complexity. We embrace complexity, and we conquer it!

To understand time, we will use a simple scenario, illustrated in Figure 3.11.

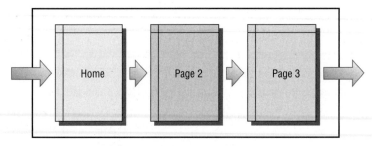

Figure 3.11 A representative visitor session on your website

Someone surfs over to your website and requests your home page, which starts a visit (session) on your website. The visitor then requests two more pages from your site before deciding to leave your website.

Figure 3.12 illustrates the metrics we want to compute for this visit:

Time on Page (T^p) represents the time spent on each page.

Time on Site (T^s) represents the time spent during that session on the website.

Let's walk through the process of computing each of these metrics. Figure 3.13 shows the time when the first request for the home page comes in.

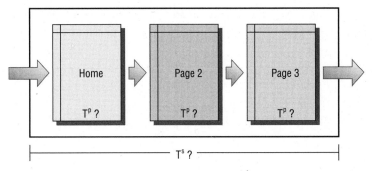

Figure 3.12 Time on Page and Time on Site

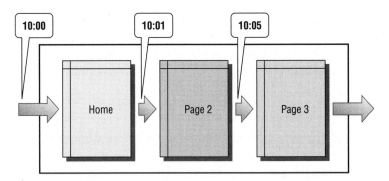

Figure 3.13 Home page requested at 10:00

There is an entry in your log file (weblog or JavaScript tag—it does not matter) that would read, "Someone has requested the website home page file at 10:00."

Technically, the message actually looks something like this:

```
111.111.111.111 - - [08/Oct/2009:10:00:00 -0400] "GET / index.html HTTP/1.1
200 10801 "http://www.google.com/search?q=avinash+kaushik&ie=utf-8&oe=utf-8
&aq=t&rls=org.mozilla:en-US:official&client=firefox-a" "Mozilla/5.0 (Windows; U;
Windows NT 5.2; en-US; rv:1.8.1.7) Gecko/20070914 Firefox/2.0.0.7
```

Notice the time stamp there? So far, all your analytics program knows is when a page was requested, which is why we have this:

T^p = N/A (not available)

T^s = N/A

Next, more fun happens on your site: someone clicks a link to page 2 from your home page, as shown in Figure 3.14.

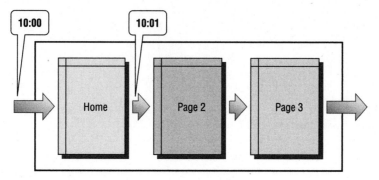

Figure 3.14 Computing Time on Page for the home page

Now there is a new entry in your log file that essentially reads, "The same visitor requested page 2 at 10:01." Now your web analytics program can compute some time metrics! The program knows how long the visitor spent on the home page. It subtracts 10:01 from 10:00 and gets one minute. Hence:

T^p (home page) = one minute

Notice that the only way the analytics tool knows how long someone spent on one page is by looking at the two time stamps: one from the request for the first page and one from the request for the second page.

Next, the blinking "get a $200 rebate on a $210 product" link on page 2 entices the person to click to page 3 to buy the product (see Figure 3.15). More sweet success!

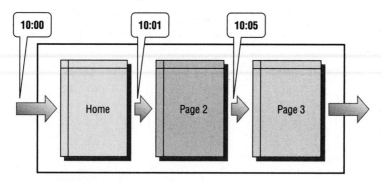

Figure 3.15 Time on Page for product page

The magical math outlined earlier happens (10:05 minus 10:01), and for page 2 here's the result:

T^p (page 2) = four minutes

The visitor reaches page 3 and notices that the rebate offer applies only to people who live in Antarctica! The visitor exits on page 3 (see Figure 3.16).

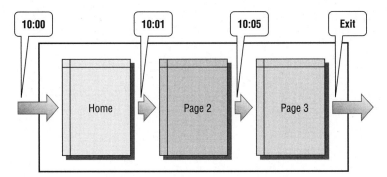

Figure 3.16 Complete visitor session

How long did it take to find and read the rebate fine print? You could reasonably guess if you knew how long the visitor spent on page 3. The problem is that your log file is missing one time stamp to do the magic math.

T^p (page 3) = The time of the page request (10:05) minus the time of next page request (N/A)

Hence:

T^p (page 3) = zero minutes

The analytics tool has no idea how long the visitor spent on the last page on your site. This flaw is true for nearly all web analytics programs in terms of default behavior.

Let's summarize the metrics using Figure 3.17.

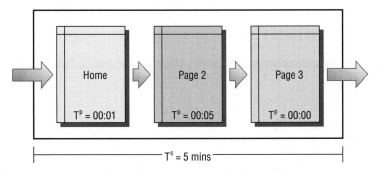

Figure 3.17 Computing Time on Page for each page and Total Time on Site

T^p (home page) = one minute

T^p (page 2) = four minutes

T^p (page 3) = zero minutes

T^s = five minutes (Time on Site, also known as Session Length)

Now that we have Time under our belts, let's consider two special cases so the lesson truly sinks in.

Lesson 1: The Single-Page View Session

Figure 3.18 illustrates a visit to your website that had only one page view, and then the person left your website.

Figure 3.18 Single-page view website session

The challenge in computing Time metrics for this session is that the required second time stamp is missing. The analytics tool records when the page was requested (10:00), but it does not know when the exit happens.

Figure 3.19 shows the information computed in this case by your analytics tool.

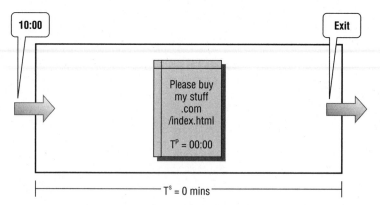

Figure 3.19 "Missing" Time on Site and Time on Page calculations

T^p = zero minutes

T^s = zero minutes

Be aware of this important fact as you report your analytics data.

Here's a slightly different scenario where the outcome is the same as earlier. The visitor came at 10:00 but leaves the browser open when they rush away as the visitor's spouse yells at them to do the dishes. Cleaning the dishes takes an hour. In the analytics tool, the session is terminated at the end of 29 minutes of inactivity (the default setting in most session-based web analytics tools). The metrics for that session will be as follows:

T^p = 0 minutes

T^s = 0 minutes

Options for Computing Time on Last Page

There is an exception to this "missing time on last page" rule: some hacks are available that allow you to compute the time on the last page (or the only page). One such hack involves adding extra code to your pages that would capture the fact that the page was "unloaded" (technically, the `onbeforeunload` event) in the browser. The `onbeforeunload` event provides the missing time stamp.

Even if you force a time for the page exit, your analytics tool will ignore this data unless you specifically ask your vendor to make an exception and redo their algorithms to take the data into account. If you parse your own web logs, then it may be a bit easier to accommodate this new piece of data into your calculations. Ditto if you use your own data warehouse.

Lesson 2: The Case of Tabbed Browsing

Nearly all browsers now allow you to open different tabs for links on a site. This creates an interesting scenario from a measurement perspective. Figure 3.20 illustrates the scenario.

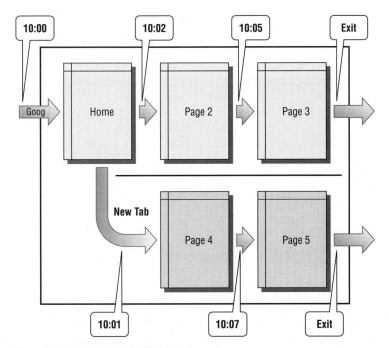

Figure 3.20 Website visit with tabbed browsing

A visitor comes to your home page. From there your visitor opens the first link in a new tab but continues to scan the home page. He clicks a link to page 2 from the home page, then on to page 3, and then closes the tab (or moves away and forgets about it).

The visitor goes to the tab opened from the home page to page 4 of your site, spends time there, and goes on to page 5 in that tab. Then the visitor exits. How is time on site computed?

Some, increasingly rare, analytics tools will simply create two sessions for this visitor and measure time separately for both sessions using the method that you have learned in this chapter so far.

Most web analytics tools will collect all the requests during this session and *normalize* the tabbed browsing behavior. Figure 3.21 shows how the *normalization* happens.

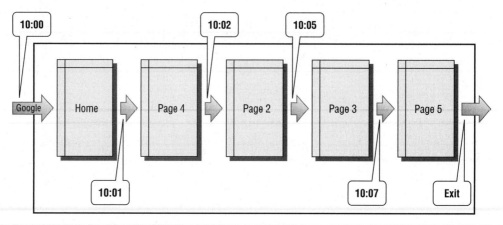

Figure 3.21 Normalizing the tabbed browsing experience

Now that everything is fine and dandy for the tool, it can easily compute the two metrics:

T^p (home page) = one minute

T^p (page 4) = one minute

T^p (page 2) = three minutes

T^p (page 3) = two minutes

T^p (page 5) = zero minutes

T^s (session duration) = seven minutes

That's it. Sure, it is a bit complex, but see how utterly logical it is?

None of the previous information should imply, overtly or covertly, that Time on Site is not a good metric. Far from it. For many businesses it can be a critical metric. Once you understand exactly how time is computed, you can make more informed decisions. In many cases, Time on Site can be a better metric than even Unique Visitors.

Bounce Rate

I have been known to call Bounce Rate the sexiest web metric ever! I am fond of measuring Bounce Rate for several reasons:

- It is a metric that is available as a standard metric in pretty much all tools. (In cases like Omniture, where it is not, you can still easily compute it.)

- It is really hard to misunderstand what Bounce Rate measures.

- It is actionable on multiple levels, especially at identifying the low-hanging "fix me now" fruit.

- It measures customer behavior, perhaps the most holy of the holy goals in measurement.

So, what does this mysterious, smoldering, sexy metric measure? From a website visitor perspective, it measures this phenomenon: "I came, I puked, I left." OK, the following is the technical definition: the percentage of sessions on your website with only one page view.

A few tools in the market allow you to use Time to measure Bounce Rate. That is, they measure the percentage of sessions where Time on Site was less than five seconds. It is increasingly rare to see this method of computation (which does make me a bit sad because I like this more aggressive definition).

Figure 3.22 shows how Bounce Rate might look in your analytics tool, in this case in the French tool XiTi.

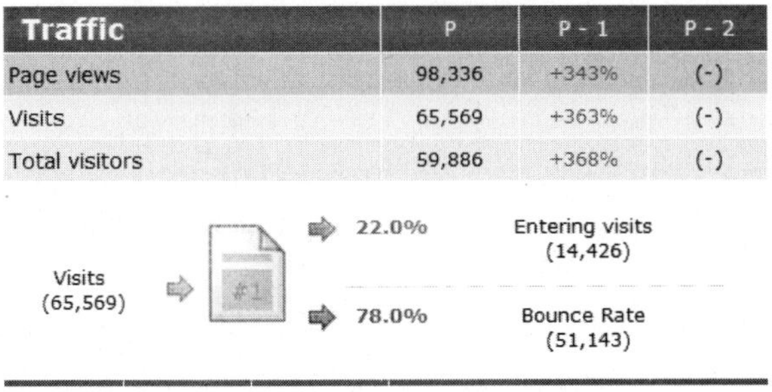

Traffic	P	P - 1	P - 2
Page views	98,336	+343%	(-)
Visits	65,569	+363%	(-)
Total visitors	59,886	+368%	(-)

Visits (65,569) → #1 →

22.0%   Entering visits (14,426)

78.0%   Bounce Rate (51,143)

Figure 3.22 Bounce Rate in XiTi

On the left are all the people who visited the website during this time period, 65,569. To the right of that, the number on the top represents those who chose to click any link on the landing page and see more than one page (22%). On the bottom is the big cry-inducing number: 78 percent of the people who came to this site refused to give the website one pathetic click.

Think about it. Not even one tiny click! It is the lowest bar of success: all you want from the visitor in terms of Engagement is one click, and you failed.

That is the beauty of Bounce Rate. At a macro level, it shows how much you stink. It doesn't matter who you are; you could be a B2B website, an e-commerce website, or a site with pictures of monkeys dressed as office workers.

So, you need to measure the Bounce Rate of your site on at least two levels. You need to measure in aggregate at an entire site level, as shown in Figure 3.22. And you need to measure the Bounce Rate of your top landing pages (also called the Top Entry Pages report), as shown in Figure 3.23.

Entry Page Title	Visits	%	Bounce rate
Web Analytics Blog	Occams Razor by Avinash Kaushik	69	21.84%	68.12%
Standard Metrics Revisited: Dail... Occams Razor by Avinash Kaushik	21	6.65%	66.67%
Googles Search-based Keyword Too... Occams Razor by Avinash Kaushik	14	4.43%	85.71%
Excellent Analytics Tip#2: Segme... Occams Razor by Avinash Kaushik	11	3.48%	81.82%
4Q - The Best Online Survey For ... Occams Razor by Avinash Kaushik	8	2.53%	87.50%
The Three Greatest Survey Questi... Occams Razor by Avinash Kaushik	8	2.53%	75.00%
Google Analytics Releases Advanc... Occams Razor by Avinash Kaushik	7	2.22%	85.71%
10 Insights From 11 Months Of Wo... Occams Razor by Avinash Kaushik	6	1.90%	100.00%
Blog Metrics: Six Recommendation... Occams Razor by Avinash Kaushik	5	1.58%	80.00%
Excellent Analytics Tip #8: Meas... Occams Razor by Avinash Kaushik	4	1.27%	100.00%
Subtotal	153	48.42%	75.16%
Total	316	100.00%	75.95%

« PREVIOUS 10   NEXT 10 »

Figure 3.23 Top Entry Pages report, Yahoo! Web Analytics

You want to take quick action based on your web analytics data? In 10 seconds this lovely report will help you identify the pages that are not doing their job by bouncing traffic like crazy.

The Bounce Rate metric also produces a lovely report because the world is dominated by search engines, and those search engines, not you, determine the home page of your website. In Figure 3.23, you see the top 10 home pages of your website. Fix 'em, and you'll have a colossal impact on your profitability.

Here are additional tips for actionability:

- Measure Bounce Rate for your website's top referrers. Your top referrers tell you who your true BFFs are. These are not the referring sites that just send you traffic but rather sites that send you traffic that does not bounce.

- Measure Bounce Rate for your search keywords (paid and organic). Perhaps you are optimized for the wrong keywords, or perhaps your landing pages stink; either way, you need to fix them.

See what I mean when I say that Bounce Rate is a hugely actionable metric?

Exceptions and Excuses for Bounce Rate

Exception

There is one obvious case where measuring the Bounce Rate metric in aggregate might be suboptimal: blogs.

Blogs are a unique beast amongst online experiences: people mostly come only to read your latest post. They'll read it, and then they'll leave. Your bounce rates will be high because of how that metric is computed, and in this scenario that is OK.

So, don't measure the Bounce Rate for a blog in aggregate. Segment your data, and measure Bounce Rate for your New Visitors. You don't want them to just come and leave after reading the post. You want them to subscribe to your RSS feed. (That's one click! No bounce!) You want them to read your About page (and be impressed with your magnificence and come to the site again). You want them to click ads (heavens!), and so on. All these actions are of business value to you.

Excuse

I have to admit, I get a bit miffed when I hear an excuse that goes something like this: "I don't have an ecommerce site. I don't have conversions. I don't have to worry about Bounce Rates." What?

I have a hard time imagining that any for-profit business exists where zero clicks from a visitor on its site is a success. Say I have, as an example, a dictionary website. I want people to see the definition and maybe also bookmark my page for future use (boom, no bounce) or check other definitions (and click ads and give me revenue). Another example is Yellow Pages websites. They exist to "bounce" you, or get you out to another site, namely, a site of their advertiser. Well, in that case, remember that Bounce Rate is one click, so you measure those people who come to your site and don't click an advertiser listing and leave your site (bad for you).

Bounce Rate equates to people taking absolutely no action on your site. If you make an "excuse," I'll push back because I don't fundamentally believe for any site—for-profit or nonprofit—that success is a one-page view. There are rare exceptions, as with blogs earlier, but think really hard before believing you are the exception. I'll cover more about measuring blogs and social media in Chapter 9.

Exit Rate

In discussing the Exit Rate metric, I want to accomplish two things: (a) question some conventional wisdom and (b) illustrate how a seemingly helpful metric can actually be completely unproductive.

Exit Rate metrics are all the rage. What Exit Rate measures is simple: how many people left your website from a certain page. Check out Figure 3.24.

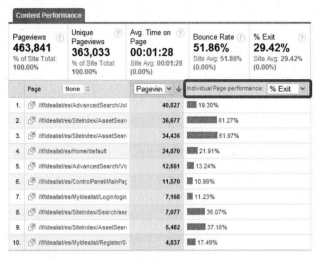

Figure 3.24 Exit Rate (% Exit) for website pages

On paper, this metric is supposed to show the *leakage* from your website. In other words, where do people exit after they start their session? It should illustrate pages that you should *fix* to prevent leakage and get customers to buy more or sign up more.

The problem is that everyone who comes to your website has to leave. They will browse around your website and leave from any arbitrary page. Their exit from a page is no indication of the greatness, or lack thereof, of that particular page!

Maybe they entered the site, completed a task (say, making a purchase or signing up for a credit card), clicked back to your home page, and left. That's not a failure, is it?

Here's another challenging case: Conversion Rates for most sites hover around 2 percent. Ninety-eight percent of visitors to your site will leave without delivering the outcome that you desire. How do you parse which exits were because you stunk and which exits were people who came, never wanted to transact, read what they wanted to, and then left—which is OK?

If you have to overlay your own opinions and interpret any metric to determine whether the data is "good" or "bad," then you have a bad metric on your hands. Exit Rate is one such metric.

So, should you not worry about exits? *Au contraire*! Can you separate good exits from bad exits without overlaying your own opinions on the data? *Mais, oui*! Use your new BFF, Bounce Rate.

Remember what Bounce Rate measures: of the people who enter your site on a given page, how many leave from that page without clicking anywhere on the site and without looking at any other pages? Those are "bad" exits.

To ensure there is no confusion, I'll reiterate: Exit Rate shows the percentage of people who entered anywhere on the site but exited from a particular page. Bounce Rate shows the percentage of people who entered on a particular page, did nothing, and exited from the site on the same page.

An Exit Rate Exception

There is one exception to the exit rates rule (I know, I know, life is nuanced and complicated!), and that's structured experiences.

Structured experiences are areas on your site where someone must go from page x to page $x1$ to page $x2$, and so on. When visitors move along through these pages, then that's success for you. Think of going from Add to Cart to Start Checkout to Complete Credit Card Info, and so on.

The Exit Rate, on any page, indicates a "bad" exit. But in this case it is called Abandonment Rate, to distinguish what is actually happening in terms of customer experience.

Use Abandonment Rate to measure submitting leads, signing up for an email newsletter, or completing any closed multipage process.

Conversion Rate

Is there any metric that we focus more of our love and attention on than Conversion Rate? Not yet. And perhaps that is how it should be. We are investing in our websites, so we should measure what comes of them.

Conversion Rate, expressed as a percentage, is defined as *Outcomes divided by Unique Visitors (or Visits)*. Outcomes are customarily the submission of an order on your ecommerce website.

That's fairly straightforward, right? It actually is—except one minor thing. Should you use Unique Visitors or Visits? You'll recall Unique Visitors measures unique browsers who visit your site, and Visits measures one particular time (a session) by that unique browser. Each unique visitor might visit your site multiple times (Visits).

The answer is, it depends on your business mind-set. If you choose Visits as the denominator, you assume that every visit to your website is a chance to get someone to place an order and get someone converted.

If you choose Unique Visitors as the denominator, you grant that it is OK for a person to visit your website multiple times before making a purchase. That behavior is a lot more common on the Web. Some might buy right away, but most will learn a bit, go home, and ask permission from their spouse to make a purchase, or they'll research a bit and come back.

So, in choosing the denominator, you are deciding which mental model is right for your company. That choice will influence which referrers, campaigns, keywords, and sources you'll value most.

A good place to use Visits is for sites where the same visitor will make multiple purchases during a short duration of time (say a week).

From my experience, working with different websites—ecommerce and non-ecommerce—I have concluded that most customer behavior is pan-session (across multiple visits). Hence, I strongly recommend using a mental model that reflects customer behavior, so use Unique Visitors in the denominator.

Using Unique Visitors will ensure that your conversion rate calculations more closely reflect the real-world purchasing and consideration process of your customers. It is not "BUY NOW! BUY NOW!" It is "Come visit our website. Thoughtfully consider whether we are a fit for you; it's OK to go back and check with your boss/wife and then conclude the purchase."

The metric you choose will have a broader mind-set, execution, and marketing impact on your organization. Check which denominator your web analytics tool uses. For example, Google Analytics and Omniture (and many others) use Visits by default.

Engagement

The Merriam-Webster dictionary defines *engaging* as "tending to draw favorable attention or interest." We should all try to create website experiences that draw favorable attention or interest. The challenge in the context of measurement is that "favorable attention or interest" is incredibly hard—if not impossible—to measure.

Much blood, sweat, and tears have been expended in the world of web analytics toward measuring Engagement. Some have gone so far as to create torturous, complex formulas that calculate the baby, the bath water, and the kitchen sink. Result: nada. OK, there is some output, but it's ugly and just about useless.

Metrics masquerading as Engagement in the analytics-o-sphere are not really metrics, they are an excuse to (a) not accept the limits of possible and (b) hide what is actually being measured.

Let's take the second excuse—hiding what is measured—first. Many people measure the time a Visitor spends on the website and call it Engagement. (With your permission to vent for a moment, might I just say that I fiercely dislike this trend of the "sexification" of metrics. If you are measuring Time on Site, call it Time on Site and not Engagement!) The challenge for an analyst, or a marketer, is to distinguish between someone who happily spent 10 minutes on www.nytimes.com soaking up all the news and someone who was frustrated for 9 minutes because they could not find the story they wanted. Both would be "engaging" experiences using this formula.

Ditto for folks who define Engagement as *the number of repeat visits by a visitor.* In this past week, I visited www.lenovo.com eight times because Lenovo decided to stop supporting System Update. I was stressed and frustrated because I had to locate drivers for my ThinkPad X301 by using its suboptimal internal site search engine! How do you distinguish those visits from someone who visits the Lenovo site regularly to learn about the latest products and updated features?

Now apply this type of emotional filter to any metric (or multiple metrics that you are mashing up) to measure Engagement. It's important to know that if you must overlay your own opinions and interpretations to understand the metric, then you might be on the wrong road.

We all want websites that engage customers. Why can't we measure them with web analytics tools? My friend Theo Papadakis shared this brilliant insight with me: quantitative data (web analytics) is limited in that it can measure the *degree* of Engagement but not the *kind* of Engagement.

Theo defines these terms as follows:

Degree The degree of positive or negative Engagement lies on a continuum that ranges from low involvement, namely, the psychological state of apathy, to high. An engaged person is someone with an above-average involvement with his or her object of relatedness.

Kind Customers can be positively or negatively engaged with a company or product. A more in-depth examination of kind would reveal its content, usually a mixture of emotional states and rational beliefs, such as in the case of positive engagement, sympathy, trust, pride, and so on.

The number of times someone visits your site, frequency of Visits, helps you understand the degree of Engagement. For example, "Visitors who come from search typically tend to visit our website 15 times in the subsequent 30-day period (degree)." There is no layering on top about whether those 15 visits were good or bad (kind).

Take another example: Depth of Visit, as shown in Figure 3.25.

Page Views per Visit	Visits	%
1 page(s)	192,518	78.12%
2 page(s)	28,948	11.75%
3 page(s)	10,899	4.42%
4 page(s)	5,225	2.12%
5 page(s)	2,830	1.15%
6 page(s)	1,832	0.74%
7 page(s)	1,120	0.45%
8 page(s)	794	0.32%
9 page(s)	554	0.22%
10 page(s)	418	0.17%
Subtotal	245,138	99.47%
Total	246,454	100.00%

Figure 3.25 Distribution of Depth of Visit, Yahoo! Web Analytics

The more pages a visitor sees, the deeper their journey and the higher the degree of Engagement. But this metric again does not distinguish the *kind* of Engagement.

Here are some other metrics and tasks that can capture degree of Engagement: Time on Site, registering on the site, subscribing to RSS feed or newsletter, submitting a comment, or downloading content. You can probably think of many others.

Two conclusions from this discussion are important to bear in mind throughout your web analytics journey:

- It is impossible to derive the *kind* of visitor Engagement (positive/negative) using web analytics alone, and, therefore...

- When we discuss customer Engagement in the context of web analytics, we are in fact discussing the *degree* of Engagement.

The next time you take quantitative data to your C-level executives, you should first state that your engagement index measures *degree of Engagement* only.

As you create your own metric to measure an engaging experience, consider these important challenges:

- Use web analytics data to measure degree of Engagement, and be open to using other sources to measuring the kind of Engagement.

- Each website and business tries to accomplish something unique. It is good to know what your competitor is doing or measuring, but you want to identify something that lines up uniquely against your website's goals. That something may be different even when compared to your direct competitor.

- In Chapter 1 we covered the importance of measuring Outcomes. A good engagement definition will measure some semblance of an outcome. So you had a high degree of Engagement, but what was the outcome for the business? This is a great stress test of whether you are on the right path.

- The term *engagement* means anything and everything to each person. Current definitions, even when used in the context of the Web, are overly broad (to cover every nuance) or sometimes too narrow (hence unique to just one business). Few people understand what the term means, and that poses a communication and actionability challenge. You don't want to measure a mouse and call it a lion.

Let me close this section with some ideas for measuring the *kind of Engagement* visitors had on your website:

- Use inline or on-exit surveys and ask your customers. You could ask them directly, "Hey, buddy, are you engaged with our site?" OK, maybe reword that a smidgen. The point is, get qualitative data.

- Go for an indirect approach with your surveys by measuring the *likelihood to recommend* as a metric. Likelihood to recommend is a strong proxy for Engagement because it measures the greatest gift you can get from your customers: that they will recommend your business to others.

- Use primary market research. A number of companies will go *door-to-door* (OK, phone call to phone call), ask brief qualitative questions, and report back to you the kind of Engagement your current or prospective customers have with your web business.

- Use the other awesome proxy: *customer retention over time*. Do long-term analysis of people who come back again and how often (non-ecommerce) or make repeat purchases (ecommerce). We're talking months of data, segmented for online and offline (then compare) and for various micro-segments of your online population. Super awesome.

We all want to engage with our customers. But as analytics practitioners our goal is to use the right metric. We must work hard to get to the root cause (rather than making an excuse) and share the cause and effect with our decision makers. Then and only then will the metric be actionable.

Engagement at its core is qualitative. It is difficult to measure via pure Clickstream (web analytics data). Think differently when you approach the Engagement metric. I'll talk more about surveys and other wonderful qualitative analysis in Chapter 6.

P.S. I picked Engagement as the last specific metric to introduce to you because I wanted you to see how incredibly difficult metrics and analysis can be. We have to understand the limits of data; there is no easy ride if you want glory. Good luck.

Web Metrics Demystified

I have stressed several times throughout this chapter that web metrics are unique to each business. By walking through eight different metrics in this chapter—Visits and Visitors, Time on Page and Time on Site, Bounce Rates, Exit Rates, Conversion Rates, and Engagement—you have also learned various life lessons about the nuances of picking web metrics.

In this section, I'll bring the whole thing together with a set of *rules* I have formulated from my own experience. These rules have come from painful lessons, but I now apply them with religious fervor in my web analytics execution, be it for my start-up, Market Motive, or for a large business I might be working with such as Dell or Sephora or Google.

You'll learn how to find diamonds in the rough, you'll learn how to know that a metric you have identified for your management dashboard is actually a good one, and you'll learn the process you can, and should, use to keep your web analytics metrics relevant. Excited? I am.

Four Attributes of Great Metrics

In a world where metrics and key performance indicators are a dime a dozen, how do you know which one is your *must-have darling*?

The following four attributes are all great—nay, magnificent—for metrics to possess.

Uncomplex

Great metrics are almost always uncomplex. Because we make little headway with the recommended metrics foisted on us, we create complex metrics. We'll have six things, each with its own unique multiplier, predicting the position of the sun when visitors click on our site!

Consider this: decisions in companies are not made by one person. If you want action, then the democracy needs to understand performance, and the democracy needs to make decisions. The democracy needs uncomplex metrics that they can easily comprehend.

If you are the only person who understands the metric or the key performance indicator, then you have just guaranteed that your company will not take action.

Don't sexify, uncomplexify.

Relevant

Is the metric you have chosen relevant to your business? Because we have so many metrics, we pick our favorites and then stick with them. The problem is that each business is unique, even businesses that seem similar.

In *Web Analytics: An Hour a Day*, I use the examples of Best Buy and Circuit City. You might think that they could measure their websites with similar web metrics. Nothing could be further from the truth.

The only thing they have in common is that they sell large-screen TVs on their website. Everything else is different: their business models, their priorities, and how each tends to use the Web in its multichannel portfolio. So, the metrics for each company to measure success are also different.

You can seek inspiration from your friends and competitors. But you must truly stress test that the metrics you identify are relevant to measuring the success objectives that are unique to you and your website. I'll discuss ways to measure success for different businesses in Chapter 5.

Timely

A few years back, I interviewed at one of the biggest companies on the Web. They had just closed their quarter, and it had been tremendously profitable. I asked them the reasons for that great success. The following anecdote is 100 percent true:

Them: "We just kicked off the query against our data warehouse; it typically returns the results in three months."

Me: Stunned silence.

I learned a very important lesson on that day: be on time or die.

That big company's stock price today is a fraction of its price then. Although not all of the decline is related to their ability to measure, you can imagine how hard it is to succeed in your business if it takes you three months to learn what worked three months ago.

Great metrics arrive in a timely fashion so that your business decision makers can…make timely decisions.

I am not a big fan of real time (see my blog post "Is Real-Time Really Relevant?" at http://zqi.me/akrealt). But between real time and three months, there is a sweet spot. Find out what your sweet spot is, and then ensure that you can collect and analyze your data—get your metrics with insights—in that sweet spot.

Even the greatest metric in the world is useless if it takes nine days while your world changes every three days. Be timely. Sacrifice complexity and perfection for timeliness.

Instantly Useful

Instantly useful is when you understand quickly what the metric is and you can find the first blush of insights as soon as you look at it. I absolutely love this one. Smooch, smooch, kiss, kiss.

I credit my early experience with ClickTracks for that love because Dr. Stephen Turner and John Marshall eliminated all the non-value-added stuff from the application. There were fewer metrics, which were presented in a way that made it easy to understand performance and get the first blush of insights.

Figure 3.26 shows a great example, the What's Changed report in ClickTracks.

Referrers

Rising ⇧		Was	Now	Falling ⇩		Was	Now
http://news.cnet.com		0	276	http://googleblog.blogspot.com		1639	508
http://multiply.multiply.com		0	177	Windows Live		2631	1988
Google		42027	47147	http://francoisderbaix.com		103	8
http://www.webdesignschoolsguide.com		0	119	http://www.stumbleupon.com		628	394
http://adage.com		41	214	http://analytics.blogspot.com		714	482
http://www.uberbin.net		0	71	http://www.seomoz.org		89	16
http://cuwebd.ning.com		0	51	http://www.kissmetrics.com		58	7
http://www.btobonline.com		0	49	http://conversionroom.blogspot.com		42	8
http://www.simulmedia.com		0	45	http://www.bloglines.com		141	75
http://www.networkworld.com		25	94	http://habrahabr.ru		32	4
More rows				More rows			

Figure 3.26 What's Changed referrers report from ClickTracks

Anyone can tell you what your top referrers were this month or last month. The ClickTracks report shows you *what you should care about*: referrers that rose in their importance this month and those that went down a cliff.

All the complexity is "hidden," and there is no junk. There's only the stuff you should care about. It will take some nice analysis and time to understand all the nuances and unlock the mysteries and deep stuff (just the way it works with your spouse and friends!), but the first blush is there.

In a data democracy, metrics have to meet the bar of being instantly useful. And not just that, think of your various levels of management at your company and how little they know. If you send them a metric and it is not instantly useful, then it will be instantly ignored.

You want instantly useful metrics, no explanations required, because that will give you an opening to show your deep stuff: to explain the nuances and highlight your analysis!

Smooch, smooch. Yes?

Example of a Great Web Metric

Let me give you a very simple example that I think will crystallize the previous methodology.

I think Bounce Rate is a great metric. Here is how it passes the required four attributes test:

Uncomplex It measures single-page-view visits. Or, "I came, I puked, I left." It's easy to understand, explain, and propagate. Enough said.

Relevant It identifies where you are wasting marketing/sales dollars and which pages stink when it comes to delivering on the "scent." Those two things apply to most web businesses. Bam!

Timely Bounce Rate is now standard in pretty much every web analytics tool and available in every report. Every day. Nice!

Instantly Useful You can just look at it and know what needs attention. You see a 25 to 30 percent Bounce Rate for your site, and instantly you know things are fine. You look at a page with a 50 percent Bounce Rate, and you know that page needs attention. You see a campaign or keyword with a 70 percent bounce rate, and you know there is a fire.

Set aside a half hour today or tomorrow to apply the four attributes test to your own important web metrics. What do you see?

Three Avinash Life Lessons for Massive Success

I've hinted at some painful battle scars that I've earned from waging my web analytics campaigns. The following are three lessons that come directly from the front lines.

Perfection Is…the Enemy of Good Enough

Data quality on the Web is not perfect; things change too fast, everyone wants a piece of data yesterday, and your competitors are strong. Don't spend time getting things perfect when it comes to your metrics.

If you have 90 percent confidence in the data, then make a decision. Don't wait for perfection. Too often we spend too much time distracted by missing tags or the hoopla of deleted cookies. Follow best practices, and then move on. Go for precision and not accuracy (more on this in Chapter 10).

As my friend Stuart Gold says, "An educated mistake is better than no action at all."

Critical Few, Baby, Critical Few!

I owe Steve Bennett, the former CEO of Intuit, all the credit for this important lesson. He constantly pushed everyone to identify their *critical few*, whether it's priorities, goals, or metrics.

My interpretation of critical few is this: when the entire proverbial platform is burning, what is most important? That statement has phenomenal clarifying power.

If your business is on the line, how do you know things are going well or badly? Cutting through all the clutter of data, which metrics are your *critical few*? You probably have at most three critical few metrics that define your existence.

I'll cover how to diagnose the critical few in the next section and get into more detail in Chapter 5.

The Web Metrics Lifecycle Process Is Your Friend!

Metrics, no matter how great, must stand the test of time and business changes. I recommend the simple Web Metrics Lifecycle Process outlined in Figure 3.27.

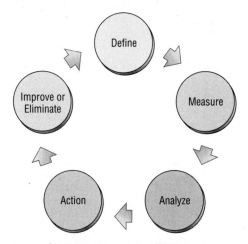

Figure 3.27 The Web Metrics Lifecycle Process

The idea is quite simple. Use the *four attributes of great metrics* test to identify your critical few metrics, go measure them, then analyze the data you collect, and take action.

Then there's the fork in the road. If you can't take action with anything, then perhaps you are using the wrong metric for your business. Eliminate it. If you can take action, figure out how you can improve it further.

Execute the Web Metrics Lifecycle Process in a timely manner; I recommend at least once a quarter. Some metrics will stay—those are your best friends. Others will outlast their value. Give them a warm hug and say, "Bye-bye."

Strategically Aligned Tactics for Impactful Web Metrics

In the next three sections, I will outline three strategic elements related to web metrics. The first element, *diagnosing root cause*, is a technique to help you unravel insights from your critical few metrics. The second element, leveraging custom reports, argues that creating custom reports can accelerate understanding of the site's performance. Finally I'll make the case for starting with a solid understanding of the macro view of your site's performance rather than wandering around in the weeds.

Taken together, these tactics should make you more than great at doing the kind of impactful analysis that transforms organizations.

Diagnosing the Root Cause of a Metric's Performance—Conversion

The simple process of identifying a metric as your key performance indicator and creating a graph of it rarely helps you find insights. There is more to it than that.

In one of his talks, my friend Neil Mason shared the slide in Figure 3.28. It was a very funny way of showing the variables he would use to predict how many people came to his talk.

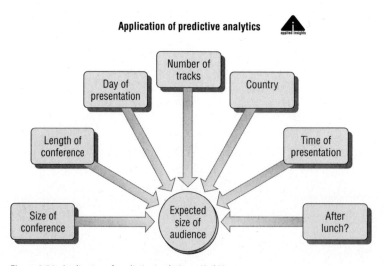

Figure 3.28 Application of predictive analytics—Neil Mason

Notice how incredibly well conceived it is! Neil thought of all the elements, and now he has a magic formula that spits out a useful number. But if estimating an audience is so complicated, imagine how difficult it might be to understand why your website is doing better this month or did worse last month.

I am going to adapt Neil's model to outline a methodology you can use to do real root cause diagnosis of your top key performance indicators. Let's use Conversion Rate as an example (though you can do this with any metric).

Your boss comes into your office and tells you to improve Conversion Rate by 10 percent. Not by 10 points, which would be huge! By 10 percent. What do you do?

Should you run out and spend a ton of money on affiliates, email campaigns, or paid search ads? Should you run to identify the demographic profiles of people who visit your website? (That was a trick question. The answer is no!)

Instead, I recommend going through an exercise, with your marketers and other smart people, that helps you identify all the variables that could cause Conversion Rate to go up or down.

Figure 3.29 shows the results of that exercise for my ecommerce website.

Root Cause Diagnosis Exercise: Conversion Rate

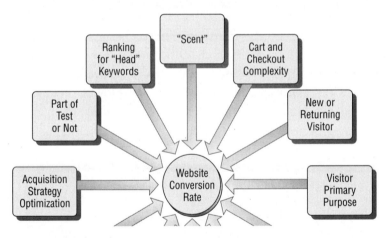

Figure 3.29 Root cause diagnosis exercise

Before you can figure out how to improve Conversion Rate, you need to identify all the influencing *levers*. That's what you see in Figure 3.29.

Conversion Rate depends on your acquisition strategy (where you spend money to acquire traffic), your organic search keyword ranks, the ease of your checkout process, the distribution of why people come to your site (primary purpose), the website "scent" (ability of your campaigns to deliver traffic to the most relevant pages), and so forth.

Next you need to collect data for each of the variables you have identified. Analyzing those variables will help you identify where the true opportunities for improvement are.

The output of this exercise will be something like this: "here are 3 areas out of 15 where we stink." Now do a cost-benefit analysis of where you can get the maximum bang for your buck. If you have done a good job of identifying all the variables, then after this exercise you'll be surprised at what you need to improve to win. It won't be the obvious areas.

You should take away three lessons about this humble process:

Lesson 1: This exercise is of tremendous value.

Lesson 2: This exercise is hard.

Lesson 3: You can't improve what you don't understand.

There is one important reason this methodology always works: it forces you to dig in a methodical manner and let the data, not opinions, drive action. It's work, but then there is no such thing as a free lunch.

Leveraging Custom Reporting

The most underappreciated problem with understanding the performance of your metrics is, wait for it…standard reports!

Our tools are full of wonderful standard reports that were created with the best of intentions by thoughtful people at our web analytics vendor. These people don't understand your business! It's not their fault, though—they're doing the best they can.

As an example, check out the standard report from Google Analytics shown in Figure 3.30.

	Visits 27,895 % of Site Total: 45.04%	Pages/Visit 1.54 Site Avg: 1.56 (-1.09%)	Avg. Time on Site 00:01:39 Site Avg: 00:01:52 (-11.62%)	% New Visits 76.52% Site Avg: 68.51% (11.68%)	Bounce Rate 78.92% Site Avg: 76.77% (2.81%)	
	Keyword / None		Visits ↓	Pages/Visit	Avg. Time on Site	% New Visits	Bounce Rate
1.	avinash kaushik		1,239	2.35	00:03:58	49.48%	52.95%
2.	avinash		707	2.94	00:04:19	37.77%	52.76%
3.	survey questions		671	1.10	00:00:13	99.11%	93.44%
4.	occam's razor		614	2.07	00:02:43	53.09%	57.98%
5.	4q		402	1.50	00:01:49	55.72%	77.86%
6.	working at google		215	1.18	00:01:00	93.95%	90.23%
7.	web analytics tools		188	1.74	00:02:11	75.00%	67.02%
8.	kaushik		167	1.96	00:02:17	55.09%	58.68%
9.	occams razor		160	2.05	00:03:40	40.62%	57.50%
10.	working for google		142	1.11	00:00:54	92.96%	90.85%

Figure 3.30 The standard Search Keywords report—Google Analytics

Nice. Lots of data and metrics. Hmm...I don't need Pages Per Visit. Time on Site is distracting. I just want the last two columns. Oh, and the best practice in judging the value of a referring site is to look at Outcomes or Conversions. Where is that? Oh, I have to go to another tab, which is shown in Figure 3.31.

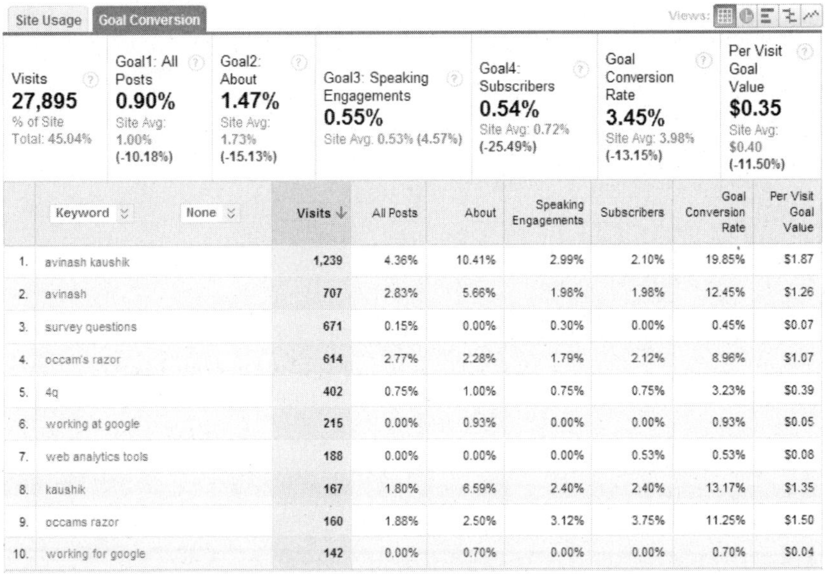

	Keyword	None	Visits	All Posts	About	Speaking Engagements	Subscribers	Goal Conversion Rate	Per Visit Goal Value
1.	avinash kaushik		1,239	4.36%	10.41%	2.99%	2.10%	19.85%	$1.87
2.	avinash		707	2.83%	5.66%	1.98%	1.98%	12.45%	$1.26
3.	survey questions		671	0.15%	0.00%	0.30%	0.00%	0.45%	$0.07
4.	occam's razor		614	2.77%	2.28%	1.79%	2.12%	8.96%	$1.07
5.	4q		402	0.75%	1.00%	0.75%	0.75%	3.23%	$0.39
6.	working at google		215	0.00%	0.93%	0.00%	0.00%	0.93%	$0.05
7.	web analytics tools		188	0.00%	0.00%	0.00%	0.53%	0.53%	$0.08
8.	kaushik		167	1.80%	6.59%	2.40%	2.40%	13.17%	$1.35
9.	occams razor		160	1.88%	2.50%	3.12%	3.75%	11.25%	$1.50
10.	working for google		142	0.00%	0.70%	0.00%	0.00%	0.70%	$0.04

Figure 3.31 The standard Goal Conversion report—Google Analytics

Lovely. I see my conversions, but I just lost the metrics I wanted. How do I judge quickly if things are going well?

This problem happens with pretty much every tool, and it is a below-the-surface issue that actually hinders progress. But you don't have to deal with this issue. You can fix it using the custom reporting feature available in most web analytics tools on the market. Hurrah!

Figure 3.32 shows the Google Analytics custom reporting interface.

The custom reporting interface is quite straightforward. On the left you type in the metric or dimension you want to report on. You drag and drop it on the right box (you see me dragging the Per Visit Value metric to the score card area), and you are done.

While I am at it, notice that I also added custom drill-downs into the data. I can go from Keyword to the Source of that Keyword and then to Search Term, which will help me see what searches people perform when they come from specific keywords. For example, the number-one search by people who come on the keyword *Avinash* is "compare analytics platforms." How interesting!

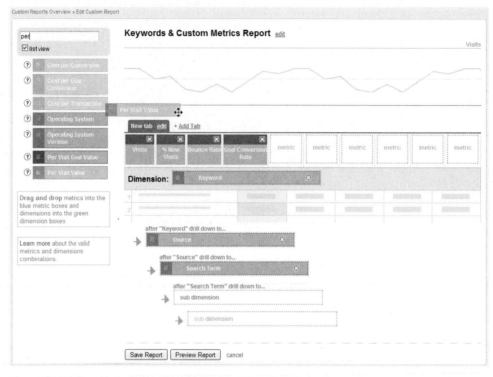

Figure 3.32 Creating custom reports with custom metrics—Google Analytics

Figure 3.33 shows my finished custom report with just the metrics that I am most interested in, which are metrics that in a single clean view will help me understand performance better and take action.

My Glorious Custom Metrics Report							
Visits 27,898 % of Site Total: 45.04%		**% New Visits** 76.52% Site Avg: 68.51% (11.68%)	**Bounce Rate** 78.92% Site Avg: 76.77% (2.80%)	**Goal Conversion Rate** 3.45% Site Avg: 3.98% (-13.16%)	**Per Visit Goal Value** $0.35 Site Avg: $0.40 (-11.51%)		
	Keyword	None	Visits ↓	% New Visits	Bounce Rate	Goal Conversion Rate	Per Visit Goal Value
1.	avinash kaushik		1,239	49.48%	52.95%	19.85%	$1.87
2.	avinash		707	37.77%	52.76%	12.45%	$1.26
3.	survey questions		671	99.11%	93.44%	0.45%	$0.07
4.	occam's razor		614	53.09%	57.96%	8.96%	$1.07
5.	4q		402	55.72%	77.86%	3.23%	$0.39
6.	working at google		215	93.95%	90.23%	0.93%	$0.05
7.	web analytics tools		188	75.00%	67.02%	0.53%	$0.08
8.	kaushik		167	55.09%	58.68%	13.17%	$1.35
9.	occams razor		160	40.62%	57.50%	11.25%	$1.50
10.	working for google		142	92.96%	90.85%	0.70%	$0.04

Figure 3.33 Finished custom report—Google Analytics

Let me give you one final example of how standard reports can fail you. The standard Landing Pages report in Yahoo! Web Analytics shows you Visits, % Visits, Page Views, and something called a Browse Rate. But you have already learned on this page that the most important metric for Landing Pages is…Bounce Rate!

Figure 3.34 shows how you can quickly fix this problem using the custom reporting interface of Yahoo! Web Analytics and make the report your very own.

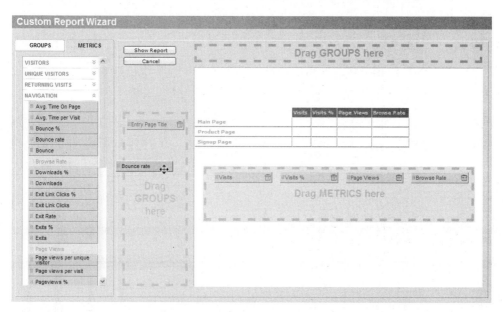

Figure 3.34 Customizing the Landing Pages report—Yahoo! Web Analytics

You drag the Bounce Rate metric to the Metrics box. As soon as you are done with that, go ahead and hit the trash box icon next to Page Views and Browse Rate, and you are done!

You'll understand performance better and take action faster simply by creating reports with metrics that are important to you.

Creating Micro-ecosystem Reports

Some tools such as Google Analytics allow you to add multiple tabs with data on your custom report. Currently you probably have a ton of reports running around the company for each person or group that wants their own nuanced report. Silly. You can eliminate this problem by creating just one report (hence one central place for people to go to) and customizing what each stakeholder sees with multiple tabs (see Figure 3.35).

The first tab shows the four metrics on which the acquisition team's performance will be judged. The second tab is for the Big Boss: he cares only about Visits, Conversion Rate, Revenue, and Shipping Revenue (money, money, money!). Finally, the third tab is for Amy, who wants to see Clicks and Visits only.

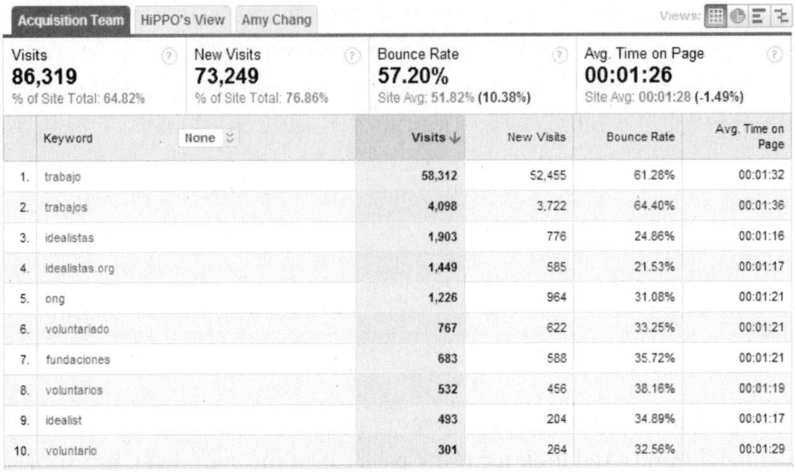

	Keyword	Visits	New Visits	Bounce Rate	Avg. Time on Page
1.	trabajo	58,312	52,455	61.28%	00:01:32
2.	trabajos	4,098	3,722	64.40%	00:01:36
3.	idealistas	1,903	776	24.86%	00:01:16
4.	idealistas.org	1,449	585	21.53%	00:01:17
5.	ong	1,226	964	31.08%	00:01:21
6.	voluntariado	767	622	33.25%	00:01:21
7.	fundaciones	683	588	35.72%	00:01:21
8.	voluntarios	532	456	38.16%	00:01:19
9.	idealist	493	204	34.89%	00:01:17
10.	voluntario	301	264	32.56%	00:01:29

Figure 3.35 The search "micro-ecosystem" report—Google Analytics

With one report, a *micro-ecosystem* report, you have provided everyone a central place to get all their data. And it's metrics customized to each stakeholder. That's the way to create a data-driven organization!

Starting with Macro Insights

This section will serve as a bridge between your newfound knowledge thus far about metrics and the next chapter, which specifically focuses on analysis and important analytical techniques.

You'll have access to lots of data, perhaps more than you ever wanted. Typically, you will open the tool and instantly start with "How is that page doing?" or "Can I report on all the campaigns that are driving traffic to these six pages and measure retention?" or "I have my key KPIs, and I want a detailed report across all top pages on the website."

Basically you jump gleefully into the weeds. Not that I blame you; it seems like so much fun. Sadly, though, this leads to a classic problem: you can't see the forest for the trees.

My recommendation is to *never* start in the weeds, but instead start with a profound understanding of the forest, of the big picture. I call it focusing on getting the *macro insights* first.

When you are in the weeds with your daily reports and your deep metrics, *everything* can seem important. It is tough to know what to explore and what to ignore. So you do everything. No surprise then that you fail to improve your company's bottom line in any significant manner.

Focusing on macro insights, however, is the simplest thing you can do. It is easier than analysis, and it's much easier than all the weed-level stuff. Yet few people spend time with the macro (perhaps it is hard to resist the allure of having every piece of data, for every page and every visitor, at your fingertips).

Before you put on the Tarzan suit and swing into the jungle, make sure that you ask four simple questions for macro analysis. Each question will help you figure out exactly where you need to dive deep into data. Your boss will love and adore you, because rather than shoveling reports, you'll identify specific, actionable items that have a strategic impact on the business.

Q1: "How many Visitors are coming to my website?"

Didn't I say this was going to be easy?

This is the simplest first question you can and should answer. Measure Visits to your website (sum of sessions) and measure Unique Visitors (sum of unique persistent cookie IDs).

For both of these metrics, focus on the long-term trends. Go as far back as you can to look for seasonal trends and look for other patterns in the data. Establish your comfort level, specifically, that you understand these metrics and that they are being measured correctly.

Tip: As you measure Visits and Unique Visitors, avoid diving into the number of repeat visitors, and this rate or that view, for now. Just for now. Hold your horses.

Q2: "Where are Visitors coming from?"

Ohhh...now it's getting interesting. This question is so full of promise and hope and goodness!

Look at two reports: Referring URLs and Search Keywords. You will almost always be surprised at how people find you.

Referring URLs help you understand which websites are sending you traffic and which are not. It is a great way to begin to understand both what you are doing that is causing traffic to come (relationships, direct marketing, other campaigns, affiliates, and so on) and what you have not done that might be causing traffic.

Look for surprises; you will find them.

With search dominating the landscape, at least for now, look for how much traffic you get for search engines (in your referring URL's report), and then dive deeper into what keywords and key phrases send traffic from each search engine. This is a gold mine of actionability, specifically for search engine optimization (SEO) and, if you are big enough, pay-per-click (PPC) marketing.

Look for nonbranded keywords. They will indicate that you are getting *prospects*—people early in the consideration cycle—and that you are getting traffic at the right level for your branded keywords.

At the end of this quick journey, you can go back to your boss and outline which acquisition strategies are more important and which are not working.

 Note: Notice we are not looking at countries, states, or ZIP codes. Unless you are in a deeply geo-specific business (say, in Europe), these can be a distraction at this early stage.

Q3: "What do I *want* Visitors to do on the website?"

The problem with web analytics data is that once you get access, it can be a huge time sink. Every place you turn there is a new piece of data—a new rabbit hole you can jump down. And it can be kind of fun.

Don't do that! Step away from your website, and take a long, hard look at yourself and your business.

Then answer these simple questions:

Why does your website exist?

What are your top three web strategies (paid campaigns, affiliates, trying to get Digg'ed)?

What do you think should be happening on your website?

Write down the answers, and publish them far and wide in your company and your local newspapers.

The output (your answers) could be metrics or KPIs that you think measure success. It could be simply a list of acquisition strategies for your website (SEO, PPC, DM, and so on), or it could be a mission statement that somehow ties to your company bottom line. You can calibrate the altitude later, but you must have some precision about what you want your customers to do on your website.

 Note: *Marketers, analysts, website owners*: Notice that "What do I want the Visitor to do?" is the third question and not the first one. That is because my experience suggests that you need some context from your web data to even think about visitor actions clearly. Often, sans the web data, you don't have enough understanding of basic web reality to help you answer these questions correctly.

Q4: "What are Visitors actually doing?"

It's the moment of truth, baby!

Now you take your first shallow dive into the data. Look at these four details in your reports:

Top entry pages Home pages are dead. Thanks to search and marketing campaigns, people come directly deep into your website. Identify the top 20 "home pages" of your website. Mark these as important, educate your boss, and start to wean her or him away from obsession with your website's home page.

Top viewed pages This is a great way to know what content is being consumed, and it will probably be different from what you think should be consumed. The top viewed pages can also help you, in conjunction with top entry pages, see why people end up looking at what they do.

Site overlay (click density) analysis For your top viewed pages, look at the site overlay report, and analyze the click patterns (only on the top 10 most viewed pages on your site, to keep it simple). It will help you understand navigational challenges on your website, it will help you understand visitor intent, and it will suggest optimization actions you can take.

Abandonment analysis You have surely created your first couple of funnels right now (for your order-taking process or for the steps it takes to submit a lead or take a donation). Check out the funnel steps where the highest abandonment is happening. Visitor behavior there will identify big opportunities that will improve outcomes for you, fast.

The goal is for you to simply get acclimated with content consumption and navigation behavior on your website. This will give you so much more context and a richer understanding of customer behavior. That in turn will be critical as you dive in to measure obvious famous metrics such as Conversion Rate.

> **Note:** The ordering of details is important. We tend to dive directly into measuring Conversion Rate, and it will turn out to be rather pathetic. Then we work our way backward (with our eyes closed), and inevitably we get frustrated. A better ordering is to understand customer experience to the extent you can with these simple reports and then work forward. Also notice we have not done path analysis. Thank goodness!

So, there you have four simple questions that help you look at the big picture. You can start calibrating what's most important for your website based on the data and begin to understand your priorities. The questions are simple and straightforward.

My goal in teaching you the life lessons of Web Analytics 2.0 is to encourage those who have just started with web analytics, or those who are currently frustrated to focus on macro analysis and not step into the quicksand of micro analysis. Far too often we all go micro, and sadly we are never able to go back.

Up next, the glorious world of deeper data analysis.

The Awesome World of Clickstream Analysis: Practical Solutions

It's time to get down to real work. Yeah!

In this chapter, you'll learn about some of the most important web analytics reports, and I'll cover how to apply cool and effective reporting for SEO, site search, widget analytics, and more.

Then you will move to the next level of analysis ninjafication. You'll learn how to deal with some of the most complex challenges that bedevil our lives as people of data on the Web.

If you have skipped directly to this chapter, I do recommend at least skimming Chapter 3, because it's foundational to this one.

Chapter Contents

A Web Analytics Primer
The Best Web Analytics Report
Foundational Analytical Strategies
Everyday Clickstream Analyses Made Actionable
Reality Check Perspectives on Key Web Analytics Challenges

When you crack open XiTi (or Omniture or your BFF analytics application), you'll face a bewildering array of reports. You'll start your lesson here by sharpening your skills in figuring out what's important and how to go about extracting value from your data.

A Web Analytics Primer

Web Analytics 2.0 is neither child's play nor impossible. Like everything in life, it is a complex journey. You can start simple and earn a white belt with easier tools, and then as you learn more, you can move on to more complex analysis and get a brown belt. Over time, as you get more experience and practice, you can work yourself to the all-powerful analysis ninja level!

With that in mind, we'll start with the understanding that you might be a *beginner ninja*, and with each recommendation, you take a path toward becoming more adept in your analytical strategy.

These recommendations are simple things that you can use on any website. My hope is that on a scale of ninjafication from a 0 to 100 (with 100 being the uber-master guru ninja), this section will move you from 0 to 35 in a matter of days.

I'll use an easy-to-understand structure for each recommendation:

- *What is it?* Understand what's in the report.
- *What is it telling you?* Know how to interpret the metrics and information.
- *What do you do next?* This is my little bonus gift for you; it's the next level of sophistication.
- *What is the bottom line?* Know what you should expect in the end.

Getting Primitive Indicators Out of the Way

Get ready to wade into some sweet numbers. Figure 4.1 shows you a snapshot of the key metrics you'll see when you log into a typical web analytics tool.

Site Usage			
49,111 Visits		57.78% Bounce Rate	
157,476 Pageviews		00:03:35 Avg. Time on Site	
3.21 Pages/Visit		65.01% % New Visits	

Figure 4.1 Base website key performance indicators

Because of their foundational nature, these six metrics—Visits, Bounce Rate, Page Views, Pages/Visit, Avg. Time on Site, and % New Visits—represent a great starting point for your web analytics journey.

Foundation metrics: what are they? Visits represent the number of sessions on your website, which is the number of times someone interacted with your site. Bounce Rate is the number of those people who left instantly! Chapter 3 has more detail on each of these metrics.

The Page Views number is how many pages were requested in those visits. Oh, and Pages/Visit represents how many pages were requested in each visit.

Avg. Time on Site represents how long people stayed on your site.

% New Visits shows the number of sessions from people who visited your website for the first time.

What are they telling you? First, bask in the glory of how good you are (or be sad at how low your traffic is!). See those spark lines next to each number? They are trends for individual metrics and show a trend over time of that metric's performance.

Here is how I analyze the numbers you see in Figure 4.1, and you'll do something similar for your website: Visits look like they are all heading in the right direction for the business. It looks like an event a few weeks ago caused a peak, so I make a note to investigate that.

Next, I get clues that we are doing something very right because Pages/Visit and Avg. Time on Site are seeing a nice upward trend. You'll actually be surprised that frequently those two numbers do not correlate: people see lots of pages, can't find what they want, and spend little time. Or vice versa.

The Bounce Rate at 57 percent is definitely a concern, but recent changes to the site and traffic acquisition strategy have had a positive effect and reduced the Bounce Rate (see that spark line next to the number 57.78 percent?).

Growth of every business (for-profits and nonprofits) relies on growing the franchise by attracting new prospects. Although 65.01 percent of New Visits might look positive, notice that the spark line is trending down, which means although the overall number is a healthy 65 percent, we are getting more repeat visits (which would explain fewer bounces and more time on the site).

At the end of this quick analysis, I do my happy dance.

What do you do next? Dive into detailed trends. Beyond the quick spark lines snapshot, see how the metrics look over the last few months, and compare metrics between this month and last month.

No matter what web analytics tool you use, these comparisons will require clicking two or three buttons at most.

The bottom-line demystification #1 With a tiny amount of effort (30 minutes or so), you have learned your core metrics, and you know how you are doing on the surface. That wasn't hard, right?

Working through the primitive metrics gave you 5 out of the 35 points of progress toward greater ninjafication. Feel good? Yes!

Understanding Visitor Acquisition Strengths

It is critical to understand, early in your journey, where Visitors come from (you'll learn a bit more about this in the section that immediately follows). Figure 4.2 illustrates a typical Visitor acquisition report at a high level, which is all you need for now.

All traffic sources sent a total of 357,912 visits

~~~ **21.12%** Direct Traffic

~~~ **15.07%** Referring Sites

~~~ **60.08%** Search Engines

■ Search Engines
215,037.00 (60.08%)
■ Direct Traffic
75,593.00 (21.12%)
■ Referring Sites
53,942.00 (15.07%)
■ Other
13,340 (3.73%)

Figure 4.2 Major Visitor acquisition methods

A whole lot of excitement is packed in this humble little pie.

Visitor acquisition methods: what are they? Direct Traffic represents all those people who show up at your website after typing in the URL of your website or using a bookmark.

 Note: It's important to code your campaigns with the right parameters to ensure that traffic does not show up in Direct Traffic.

Referring Sites represents other websites that link to you, including blogs, industry association sites, forums, competitors, your mom's site that proudly links to you, and so on.

Search Engines, well, that's you know who: Google, Yahoo!, Bing, Ask, and others. This bucket will include both your organic as well as your paid (PPC/SEM) traffic, so be aware of that.

Finally, there is Other. This bucket contains your display banner ads, email campaigns, social media campaigns, affiliates, and so on. Typically you are spending money with these places to acquire traffic (except for search).

What are they telling you? Look at the Direct Traffic first so you know how much traffic you're getting from people who already know your URL or have you bookmarked. Twenty-one percent is a healthy number for Direct Traffic. The best number will depend on the type of business you have, but a low Direct Traffic number could indicate issues with retention or truly connecting with customers.

Next, look at Referring Sites to identify sources that don't know you but are sending you traffic. You might visit the referring pages and see why. For some solid sites, you might want to establish a marketing relationship. Usually, referring sites link to you for free, and you want this number to be as high as possible, although it will never be 80 percent! Though, if this number is 2 percent, you may not be spreading your marketing message or value enough to get people to link to you. That is suboptimal.

The Search Engines bucket is very important. For many sites, search engines often account for at least a third and often half of the traffic. As more of the online population uses search engines to find information, this bucket is a key one to watch. In Figure 4.2, 60 percent is very healthy—though of course that depends on the business—but from my experience, I worry if I see, say, 10 percent. That's just too low.

Typically, Other will be a small part of your pie, which is a good thing because Other contains your acquisition strategies, in other words, things you are spending money on to get traffic. If, for example, your Other bucket is 45 percent, that is a sign you might not be working hard enough on getting *free traffic* (Organic Search, Referring Sites, Direct Traffic).

What do you do next? Look at longer-term trends for each bucket. Are you getting better or worse over time? Consider segmenting the data and diving deeper in higher-priority areas. For example, Figure 4.3 shows a simple and quick approach to segmenting Search Engine traffic.

Figure 4.3 Segmenting organic and paid search traffic

My initial interpretation of the segmented data in Figure 4.3 would be that there is perhaps *overreliance* on paid search. So, you dive deeper to understand why. See how it works?

I also recommend drilling down to specific websites that send you traffic and, of course, drilling down to keywords and key phrases that are sending you traffic. Both of those help you understand that critical customer *intent*.

Oh, and in both cases, look for surprises.

The bottom-line demystification #2 You probably spent 30 minutes looking at the previous figure and drilling down to the next level of report. You now know where your Visitors come from, and you have a first-blush understanding of whether your company is spending its marketing dollars effectively.

You are now 10 points into your 35 points of progress of ninjafication! Hurray!

Fixing Stuff and Saving Money

You've spent an impatient hour working on some reports; now it's time to fix stuff and save some money! First you must identify web pages that are a *key point of failure*. In

Chapter 3 I covered exactly how to do that: by examining your site's Top Entry Pages and the Bounce Rate for each.

Another immensely actionable way to find places to fix stuff (and save money) is to look at the top 25 keywords driving traffic to your website and their Bounce Rates (or as Figure 4.4 from Clicktracks calls it: Short Visits).

Search Keywords

	Total	Google	Windows Live	Yahoo!	MSN	Ask	AOL
Total	84.5%	83.2%	97.5%	88.3%	93.9%	91.2%	89.6%
avinash kaushik	49.2%	49.1%	64.7%	40.7%	100.0%	100.0%	66.7%
avinash	59.0%	48.2%	98.4%	34.1%	100.0%	-	100.0%
survey questions	94.4%	94.1%	100.0%	97.7%	94.1%	77.8%	100.0%
occam's razor	59.2%	58.8%	52.2%	73.3%	81.3%	-	100.0%
analytics	99.7%	89.2%	100.0%	-	-	100.0%	
working at google	86.2%	86.2%	-	88.9%	-	-	66.7%
4q	59.8%	60.1%	-	43.8%	-	-	50.0%
kaushik	66.0%	59.3%	96.7%	66.7%	100.0%	-	0.0%
working for google	87.9%	87.6%	100.0%	93.3%	100.0%	100.0%	100.0%
web analytics tools	72.3%	72.5%	0.0%	-	-	-	
occams razor	55.7%	55.7%	44.4%	50.0%	60.0%	-	100.0%
customer survey questions	93.5%	93.7%	100.0%	100.0%	92.8%	100.0%	0.0%
kpi	89.0%	89.0%	100.0%	100.0%	-	-	
web analytics blog	53.5%	53.7%	-	0.0%	-	-	
google trends	78.0%	78.1%	-	-	-	-	71.4%
google	96.6%	89.6%	100.0%	-	-	100.0%	100.0%
key performance indicators	89.8%	89.3%	-	100.0%	-	-	
occam's razor blog	49.6%	48.9%	100.0%	60.0%	100.0%	-	
tracking cookies	91.5%	92.7%	77.8%	62.5%	100.0%	-	100.0%
data driven decision making	91.7%	91.3%	-	-	-	100.0%	100.0%

Figure 4.4 Percent Short Visits (bounces)—Clicktracks

Top entry pages, keywords, and bounce: what are they? Here's a metaphor: you have many doors into your department store. With Top Entry Pages and Bounce Rate, you identify doors that are not letting people come into your store. Talk about a crime!

The Top Entry Pages report shows you the top home pages that let your Visitors, and precious little you, down. The keyword report helps you identify keywords where something is amiss. It's even better if you look at just your paid search keywords.

What are they telling you? Simple: Stinkiness. Your site's.

Remember, Bounce Rate measures stinkiness from a customer's perspective: "I came, I puked, I left." Pages with a high Bounce Rate are not delivering on the promise that drives customers to your site. The ones in the top ten entry pages report need your attention. You fix 'em, and you increase the likelihood that people will go deeper into your site and maybe convert.

The keywords report is even more interesting. Here you have *intent*. The customer is telling you why they might be visiting, and keywords with high Bounce Rates are where you are not meeting that intent. You may be ranked for the wrong keywords, or the pages these folks land on may not have the right calls to action. Fix it.

What do you do next? I'll discuss this in some detail in Chapter 7, but your real friend here is Experimentation and Testing. Start with simple A/B tests. Start with a free tool like Google Website Optimizer; it can do 95 percent of what any paid tool can do. If you already have a paid tool like Optimost, Offermatica, or SiteSpect, then go for it with one of those.

Pick pages you want to fix, create a couple versions of the pages, and put them into a test. Change copy, content, images, and calls to action—everything is fair game.

With testing, you improve the pages based on customer feedback.

The bottom-line demystification #3 It takes you about two minutes to get to each report and another minute to look at the numbers and click a few buttons. At the end of the half hour, you have created a specific list of focus areas. You know exactly where to start fixing pages on your site and potentially improving your paid campaigns.

You've spent an hour and a half, and you are up to 20 of your 35 points in the analysis ninjafication process. And now you know what you are doing! Priceless!

Click Density Analysis

I love the site overlay report. There, I said it. I love it.

You have improved the Top Entry Pages and key traffic-driving campaigns (key phrases). Now figure out why pages that you want to win on your site are not winning and why pages with key calls to action are not delivering. Look for the obvious things you are doing wrong. Figure 4.5 is the Google Analytics site overlay report for www.fotonatura.org.

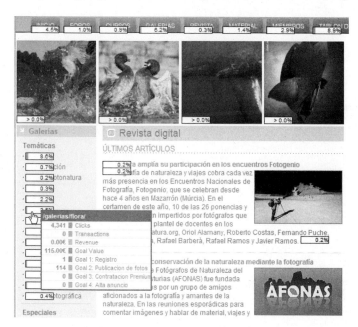

Figure 4.5 Site overlay report—Google Analytics

There are two reasons for my fondness for this report:

- For many people, numbers, metrics, and spreadsheets are still overwhelming. A site overlay report demystifies all that. You see the data visually represented.

- Even seasoned analysts are not as good at analysis as they should be because they rarely use the website they are analyzing. Using the site overlay report is a great way to walk in the shoes of the customers.

Site overlay: What is it? Click density analysis.

The site overlay report shows the number of clicks on each link on a page (as in Figure 4.5). It also shows you other helpful information such as Revenue from clicks on a link, Goal Conversions, and so on.

Each tool will show click density slightly differently. My favorite may be ClickTracks because it also shows context and key metrics about the page, right in the site overlay report, as you can see in Figure 4.6.

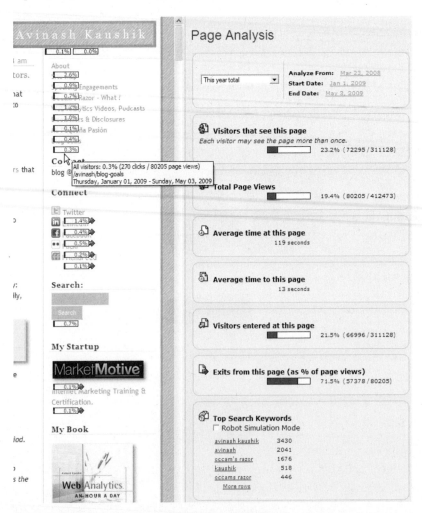

Figure 4.6 Navigation report with page-level metrics—ClickTracks

The site overlay report shows % Page Views, Time on Page, Time to the Page, % Exits, and Keywords that brought people to the page. In a nutshell, it's everything you would ever want to know to judge the performance of a page.

What is it telling you? When you look at the site overlay report, you are looking for clusters of heavy clicks. Look for the top two or three most clicked links, and try to reconcile that against links that you want Visitors to click. See what people are clicking "below the fold," and look for any surprises there.

Also, look at links that ultimately drive high conversions (you can have conversions on an ecommerce website or, as in Figure 4.6, a non-ecommerce website). Look for things that connect with people. For example, do more people convert on the site when they click Product Comparison on the home page or when they go directly to a product page?

Try to follow a few heavy clicks and see what people do next. Walk in their shoes, and experience your own website.

Check out referrers to each page; that could explain Bounce and Exit Rates.

Finally, look at Average Time to This Page. If it takes too long for people to find your key pages, then you have a problem with your core site navigational elements or merchandizing.

What do you do next? Identify improvements to your pages.

Consider merchandizing and cross-sell and up-sell opportunities now that you know what people like. For example, no one is clicking your blinking promotion in the middle of the page because it looks like an ad!

If your tool allows, segment the clicks. Where do people who convert click vs. everyone else or vs. everyone from a search engine or an email campaign?

Also, by segmenting the data, you not only understand things in aggregate, all Visitors, but now you can start to understand different types of people on your site. And now you can treat them differently!

The bottom-line demystification #4 Looking at the site overlay report is a very visual, easy-to-understand way to learn exactly how people browse your website, which methods are working on your site, and which are not. No tables, no numbers, no graphs—even your HiPPO will get this!

You can take up as much time as you have available on the site overlay report. Initially, you'll probably spend 30 to 60 minutes exploring your top pages. At the end of that, you'll be up to 25 out of 35 points of ninjafication!

Measuring Visits to Purchase

There is a unique phenomenon that many of us dismiss: people usually don't buy on the first visit. But most of us focus on getting people to buy right away, especially those of us who measure Conversion Rate as Outcomes or Visits.

The antidote to that suboptimal mental model is the Visits to Purchase report, as shown in Figure 4.7.

Visits to Purchase	Transactions	Percentage of all purchases
1 visits	237	42.70%
2 visits	106	19.10%
3 visits	72	12.97%
4 visits	49	8.83%
5 visits	26	4.68%

Figure 4.7 Visits to Purchase report

Visits to Purchase: what is it? Your web analytics tool starts anonymously tracking a visitor from their first visit. When they purchase something from your website, that event is noted. The Visits to Purchase report shows the distribution of the number of visits it took for someone to purchase from your website. A "purchase" can also be a submission or a lead or another such outcome. For example, if President Obama is collecting email and contact information of people interested in supporting his reelection in 2011, then his staff can track Visits to Lead submissions. Same method.

What is it telling you? You are looking for how evenly the numbers are distributed. In Figure 4.7, only 42 percent of the people purchased on the same visit. Then there is a nice drop-off that continues to *xx* visits.

You use this information to help you understand the intensity of the *pan-session* purchase behavior of your customers. You can learn what it takes to convince people to purchase the product you are selling. If you sell iPods and Ferraris on your website, it is incredibly valuable to understand that most people purchase Ferraris on the first visit, while they take 15 visits to buy an iPod. (What can you say? Midlife crises cause such odd behavior.)

What do you do next? The *sister* report of Visits to Purchase is Days to Purchase. The intersection of these two reports helps you understand how many days pass between visits.

For example, most people may make a purchase after three visits to your site. But those three visits could be more than fifteen days. Or it could be that those three visits were on the same day.

This analysis helps you understand customer behavior in a very actionable way. Now you can go back and optimize how you sell each item and how you advertise and market it, and you can even optimize your inventory system!

The bottom-line demystification #5 Reviewing the Visits to Purchase and Days to Purchase reports and understanding the data are not very time-consuming, and the reports are standard in most tools. The process may take, say, 20 minutes. It will take a bit more time, maybe the rest of that hour, to correlate the data and cross tab that with your selling strategy and find actionable insights.

Regardless, at the end of the hour, you will have earned all 35 points! You are now officially well on your way to uber-master guru ninja! High-five!

Consider this: in approximately three hours of work, you went from knowing a little bit about web analytics to a starter ninja, and along the way you were already taking actions based on the lessons you learned. Congratulations.

The Best Web Analytics Report

At pretty much every conference I present, I get asked this question: "If you could pick only one web analytics report to take with you on a deserted island, which report would it be?"

I can do a cop-out: well, it really depends on your business. What are the three strategies you are executing? Are you B2B or B2C? You catch my drift.

Those are tough questions, but you can't get paralyzed just because you don't know enough (an analysis ninja understands one can't ever have complete information).

There is one report that will work for any type of website, and it qualifies as my nominee for the best web analytics report: *Outcomes by All Traffic Sources.* Coincidentally, it also fits perfectly with the Web Analytics 2.0 core mental model and hence is immensely actionable. Figure 4.8 shows how an Outcomes by All Traffic Sources report looks, in this case in Google Analytics.

	Source	Visits ↓	Goal1 Conversion Rate	Goal2 Conversion Rate	Goal3 Conversion Rate	Goal4 Conversion Rate	Goal Conversion Rate	Per Visit Goal Value
1.	google	10,809	1.31%	2.07%	0.80%	0.70%	4.89%	$0.50
2.	(direct)	7,597	1.26%	2.36%	0.46%	1.09%	5.17%	$0.50
3.	google.com	1,575	1.08%	1.21%	0.95%	0.70%	3.94%	$0.46
4.	images.google.com	583	0.00%	0.00%	0.17%	0.00%	0.17%	$0.03
5.	twitter.com	560	0.18%	3.21%	1.25%	0.89%	5.54%	$0.56
6.	stumbleupon.com	469	0.00%	0.00%	0.00%	0.00%	0.00%	$0.00
7.	analytics.blogspot.com	453	1.32%	2.65%	0.66%	0.66%	5.30%	$0.50
8.	yahoo	389	0.26%	1.03%	0.77%	0.51%	2.57%	$0.31
9.	wilsonweb.com	223	0.90%	6.28%	0.45%	0.45%	8.07%	$0.56
10.	googleblog.blogspot.com	195	1.54%	1.03%	0.51%	1.03%	4.10%	$0.46

Figure 4.8 Outcomes/Conversions by All Traffic Sources

In a veritable ocean full of metrics in our web analytics tools, this report represents two things you should care about more than anything else: sources of traffic and Outcomes.

Sources of Traffic

I have come to believe that if you know the source of your traffic, then you can strongly infer what kinds of people are coming to your website and even a little bit of why they are coming (intent).

As an example, I am a huge fan of Direct Traffic, and I will talk about that more later in the chapter. If you tag your campaigns correctly, then Direct Traffic represents free traffic because it comes from people who arrive via using bookmarks, typing in your URL, or other such activities. Direct Traffic is also traffic that is familiar with you, so it typically represents returning Visitors and most likely your existing customers. In Figure 4.8 I was happy that Direct Traffic was so big—and notice that it converts higher, which is very typical.

But if during the last 30 days I had spent a boatload of money trying to attract new Visitors (*prospects*) to my website, a big number from Direct Traffic might not be such a good thing.

Notice the box drawn around twitter.com in Figure 4.8. In the prior 30 days, it was not even in the top 20, and now it's at 5. Immediately you can see how social media efforts might be paying off. You can also infer that these are much more tech-savvy people; in fact, they're the bleeding-edge kind. The source helps you better understand the persona of the audience.

Row 6, stumbleupon.com, represents new Visitors who might typically be interested in recent stories, or if this were an ecommerce website, it would represent recent promotions, product launches, and so on. Stumbleupon.com, digg.com, and others also represent a sense of validation that your content is good and it is being spread by others whom you don't know.

Row 9, wilsonweb.com, represents traffic that I would otherwise never reach, namely, very traditional direct response and traditional marketers. Dr. Ralph Wilson has written about the Web since 1995 and reaches a unique audience—and I am grateful to him for sending me free, valuable traffic.

Finally, the importance of Google to this website is very clear. The numbers validate that the work put into search engine optimization (SEO) is paying rich dividends. A specific example of this is row 4, which is traffic from images.google.com; that is a validation of the time and effort spent tagging each image on the website with relevant descriptions.

These examples should show you how much you can learn by understanding the sources that send you traffic. You can see what's working and what's not in terms of your core acquisition strategy and whether you are attracting the right audience to your site.

Now should these sites be on your *permanent BFFs* list? That depends on if they send you quality traffic, and here we go....

Outcomes

In Chapter 1, I stressed the importance of Outcomes; that's the reason they are a key part of the best Web Analytics 2.0 report. If you want to change the culture of any company, you start by focusing on Outcomes (not measuring Visits, Time on Site, or Top Exit Pages—yikes!).

Figure 4.8 shows Conversion Rate for a non-ecommerce website. At a glance, I can see the overall Conversion Rate (the one with the box around it), and I can also go down the list of the websites and very quickly identify which ones are sending me quality traffic, in other words, traffic that takes action that adds to my bottom line.

I can also quickly identify my BFFs (twitter.com in this case). I can quickly see sources that send me lots of traffic yet are not my real BFFs (stumbleupon.com in this case, or even images.google.com). Notice how in one view, Visits, you come to different conclusions than looking at another, perhaps more important, view.

You can dive into many more nuances in this report. Notice there are multiple goals for you to consider. Each part of your business might have different Outcomes, or *goals*, which are shown in the report as Goal2, Goal3. and Goal4.The report will tell each business unit or leader how they are performing against their unique goal.

The essence of the best web analytics report is that it highlights two questions to focus on first: *who?* and *how much?*

If you start with the Outcomes by All Traffic Sources report, you'll find that your senior executives suddenly care about your web analytics reports. They will ask you good questions, and they will seek you out rather than you knocking on doors that never open.

Ain't that sweet?

Foundational Analytical Strategies

The rest of this chapter will help you evolve your thinking about Clickstream analysis (frequently called *web analytics*). You'll learn a few to-die-for analytical strategies such as segmenting and focusing on Customer Behavior metrics. Then we'll leap into specific types of analyses you'll do in your daily life.

Through each lesson, my hope is that you'll focus not just on the metrics and reports being analyzed but rather on the reasons for choosing the metrics and the thought process around creating insightful analyses. That'll ensure that other types of analyses you do, not covered in this book, are actionable.

Segment or Go Home

Absolutely nothing is more important in analytics than segmentation. Why? Because monoliths don't come to our websites. I know that seems like such a shock. Yet most of our reporting and analysis happens at an aggregate level. That's like saying Figure 4.9 represents the traffic that comes to our site.

The reality is that your traffic actually looks like Figure 4.10.

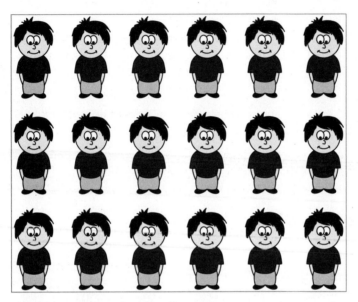

Figure 4.9 Representation of analysis traffic in aggregate

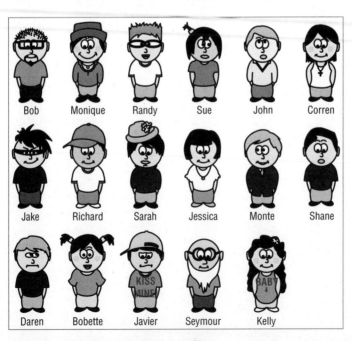

Figure 4.10 Actual reflection of your website traffic

Different types of Visitors come to your website. And they all come with different intentions, with different problems or solutions, and with different personas.

This unique phenomenon mandates that you have a very effective and persistent segmentation strategy as part of your web analytics process.

Benefits of Segmenting

The power of segmenting a metric is that you peek behind the curtain and find out more about the metric. These are the benefits that you will gain:

- It is impossible to create a segment of your data without putting in the effort to understand what is important to your business, what goals you want to accomplish. This means you'll have to spend time understanding the business, a good thing.

- By segmenting your data, you can quickly hone in on areas of deeper depth, which will reveal key insights that drive meaningful action.

- Our senior executives and decision makers don't understand all the complexity and magic of a web experience. Showing them segmented trends is an extremely effective communication tool. And the best part is you barely have to talk; the picture will tell the story!

Segmenting your data doesn't mean focusing on the *glob* but rather focusing on the *specific*. That focus helps make ideas actionable. To internalize the power of segmentation, let's look at an illustrative example.

Figure 4.11 shows revenue generated from a website over a period of 12 months. I am positive you have a graph like this running loose in your company.

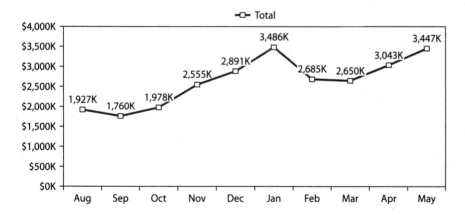

Figure 4.11 Monthly revenue trend over 12 months

Cute. You can see things going up and down. Your executives already know that December is always a seasonal high for the company, as is May. You have just shown them what they already know. The actual numbers are mildly interesting. But what decision can they make from this? Zilch. Nada. Zip.

Now try Figure 4.12, the same monthly trend, but this time illustrating important segments of the overall revenue.

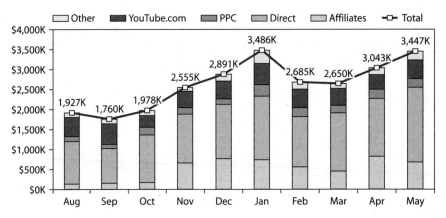

Figure 4.12 Segmented monthly revenue trend—sources of revenue

Sweetness! Your executives can now see a delightful monthly trend of the main contributors of revenue to the business. They can quickly conclude that for all the money going down the pipes, direct, *free traffic* dominates revenue contribution! The paid search, or PPC, program needs serious attention. Despite spending *muchos dineros*, it still does not deliver a proportional chunk of revenue. Oh, and look how a *rogue marketer* did a tiny experiment with YouTube. Now she deserves a bonus because her experiment has consistently produced revenue.

See what I mean? You can report the data, or you can effectively segment it and communicate more value to your decision makers.

Creating and Applying Segments

Although identifying the optimal behaviors, sources, metrics, and Outcomes to segment remains a skill you will develop over time (and ninjas *do* possess this skill), creating segments and applying them to your reports is pretty much a piece of cake.

Say I work at Intel and I am responsible for improving Intel's marketing in Eastern Europe. I could just segment www.intel.com's data using geographic segmentation. Or I could get way more specific and earn my salary by understanding customer behavior using segmentation.

Figure 4.13 illustrates my strategy. I open the folders on the left (under Group Selection) and drag and drop my metrics or dimensions onto the palette:

1. First I drag over Organic Search. I really want to know how I am doing with free search traffic.

2. Next, I am interested only in traffic that looks at content about microprocessers (sure, Intel does other things, but my bonus is tied to microprocessors!).

3. I am less interested in understanding what happens to traffic that bounces; I really want to know keywords that bring traffic that visits my site multiple times (Number of Visits greater than 3).

4. Finally, I'll restrict my analysis to just traffic from Eastern Europe.

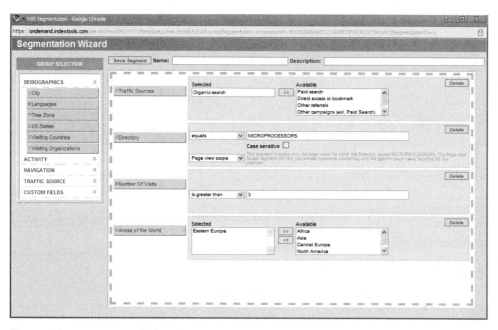

Figure 4.13 Deep segmentation of website data—Yahoo! Web Analytics

In the past, you had to know complicated SQL, and you had to know basic database design to segment this way. Now, you drag, you drop, and bam!

I can now go apply this segment to my content report, which helps me understand what kinds of microprocessors are most interesting to this precious traffic segment. I can apply it to the search reports and understand the search engine preferences of folks in Eastern Europe, as well as what valuable keywords send this kind of quality traffic. I can dive deeper to see whether they downloaded product specifications or submitted leads.

Here's a final example to illustrate how you can answer everyday questions that might seem to have complicated answers. My question was, how effectively does my home page engage Visitors so that they read lots of my content? Put another way, how good was my first impression?

That seems like a hard question, no? Figure 4.14 illustrates how I can get that answer very quickly. From the Dimensions and Metrics lists, I drag over the metrics I need: I take Page Depth first and then Visits where Visitors have seen more than three pages (a high *degree* of engagement—see Chapter 3). Next I choose Landing Page, because I want only those people who start browsing at my home page and not people who entered deep in my site and then surfed over to the home page.

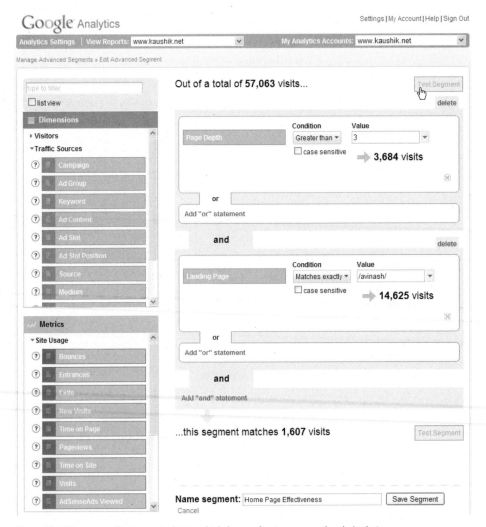

Figure 4.14 Home page effectiveness in driving a high degree of engagement—Google Analytics

In this time period, there were 57,063 Visits to my site. Of those, 14,625 entered the site on the home page (see what I mean when I say home pages are dead?). In total, 3,684 Visits had people reading more than three pages.

And my answer? 1,607. Only 1,607 out of a possible 14,625 thought my home page made a good impression! Me sad now. But do you see how simple it was for me to get the answer, once I knew my question?

That example illustrates a very cool feature in Google Analytics. In most web analytics tools, you must first tell your vendor what data you might want to segment, and then they suggest implementing JavaScript tag updates. You wait a few days to get data, and then you must create the segment, submit it, wait for processing, and finally get the data you want.

In Google Analytics (and in Yahoo! Web Analytics), you don't have to tell Google up front what you want to segment, you don't have to change tags, and you don't even have to submit the segment and wait for it to be processed. You simply drag and drop, and when you are done, you click Test Segment (the top-right button in Figure 4.14), and you have your answer right there in your Advanced Segments creation window. Pretty yummy.

Now, you go do the same process with Google or Yahoo! Web Analytics and see how good your home page is.

To sum it up: you no segment, you no find insights. You no segment, you no have job for long time.

Segmentation is a strategy that has been applied thus far in this book, without you probably realizing it, and will be applied liberally for the rest of this book. My hope is that you'll use it just as liberally as you tackle the problem of answering tough business questions.

Focus on Customer Behavior, Not Aggregates

Aggregates again!? I hear you yell. Yes. But in this section, *aggregates* means something slightly different. I want to shed light on a different way of analyzing data. We will not focus on aggregate metrics such as Unique Visitors and Average Time on Site and such; rather, we will identify truly actionable insights and focus on metrics that report the behavior of customers on your website.

Measuring the number of Visits to your site during a month is interesting. Maybe a rise or fall in that number, or meeting a preset goal, will be of some value. What's more valuable is focusing on a *behavioral* metric like Bounce Rate because it measures, as you already know, this customer behavior: "I came, I puked, I left."

Analyzing your site Bounce Rates at various levels helps you understand what's working, what's broken, and what you need to do more or less (check out Chapter 3 for more specifics).

Let's look at an example. I am responsible for running the website news.bbc. co.uk. Success will typically be measured using an *aggregate* metric such as Page Views or Pages/Visit, as shown in Figure 4.15.

Figure 4.15 Three aggregate metrics: Visits, Page Views, Pages/Visit

There aren't too many insights there, sadly. The customer behavior that is of value to the BBC is people seeing more than four pages on the website. Figure 4.16 shows the distribution of Visits by the number of pages read during each visit.

Depth of Visit

Most people visited: 1 pages

Depth of Visit	Visits	Percentage of all visitors
1 pages	67,671.00	52.95%
2 pages	17,545.00	13.73%
3 pages	12,156.00	9.51%
4 pages	6,860.00	5.37%
5 pages	5,053.00	3.95%
6 pages	3,413.00	2.67%
7 pages	2,657.00	2.08%
8 pages	1,994.00	1.56%
9 pages	1,570.00	1.23%
10 pages	1,261.00	0.99%

Figure 4.16 Distribution of pages read during each Visit

Ahhh...now this is fantastic—and actionable. You can see that 76 percent of the website Visitors did not exhibit the ideal behavior. Now you can easily segment the behavior that is accretive to your business, four pages or more, and analyze customers (the 24 percent) who exhibit that behavior. You can dive in and understand what their preferences are. Do they like sports? Podcasts? International stories? You catch my drift.

This will help you understand what your valuable customers consume, which in turn helps you focus better. (Maybe dump entertainment? Or make it a lot more interesting?) Of course, you can create the inverse segment—that is, fewer than four pages—and see what that group is reading, where they come from, and what repulsed them.

Behavioral metrics are all around you. Loyalty, Recency, and Returning Visitors are just a few that come to mind. I'll talk more about these metrics in Chapter 5. Focus on behavior, and glory awaits you.

Everyday Clickstream Analyses Made Actionable

We are going to focus on five very common types of Clickstream analyses that you'll do when you have a bit more gray hair or, to be more politically correct, when you're more experienced: internal site search, search engine optimization, paid search, direct traffic, and email campaigns.

Internal Site Search Analysis

Almost all web analytics clicks data is missing one key ingredient: customer intent.

The keywords that people type into search engines such as Google, Bing, and Yahoo! contain a modicum of intent. The real gold is the search engine that you surely have on your website. What? No, you don't? You are the last website on the planet not to have an internal site search engine? Shame! Shame!

If you directly understand the intent of Visitors on your site, you can better understand the causes for success or failure on your site.

Here's an example. You can look at the top 10 most viewed pages on your site and understand what people who came to your site wanted. Or do you? How would you know which pages your Visitors *wanted* to see? If Visitors can't find those pages, then your web analytics tool won't record that action.

One way to overcome the challenge of intent is to look at your internal site search data and see what customers typed into your site search engine. You should perform three clusters of actionable analysis with your internal site search data: site search usage, site search quality, and, wait for it…segmenting.

Site Search Usage

When you look at how your internal site search is used, you need to answer the basic questions first: how much is the search function used, and what keywords are used most?

Figure 4.17 shows how a report that illustrates the trend for site search usage might look.

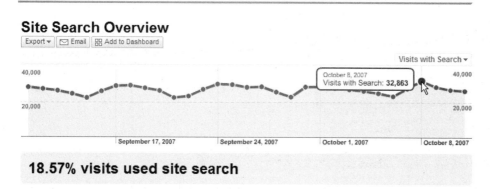

18.57% visits used site search

Figure 4.17 Trend for internal site search usage

At a glance, you can see how important site search is (18.57 percent) and how the trend tracks over time. Visitors will use no other navigational aid even a small percentage of the time; typically, site search will be the site navigational element they use most often.

Of course, this is not the kind of detail you want. You want the meat! Figure 4.18 shows how a report for the most frequent searches might look.

Internal Search Report 1 [Data dissection]

This report is currently showing values for the URL parameter 's'.

	Total	Jan	Feb	Mar	Apr
bounce rate	129	32	41	24	30
survey	82	18	15	20	29
dashboard	73	20	18	18	16
engagement	69	6	23	24	16
kpi	65	13	14	25	12
segmentation	65	10	17	17	19
seo	37	8	13	11	4
4q	35	5	8	14	8
trinity	35	11	13	7	4
reporting squirrel	33	4	1	1	27
None	305851	67895	81058	86477	67898

More rows

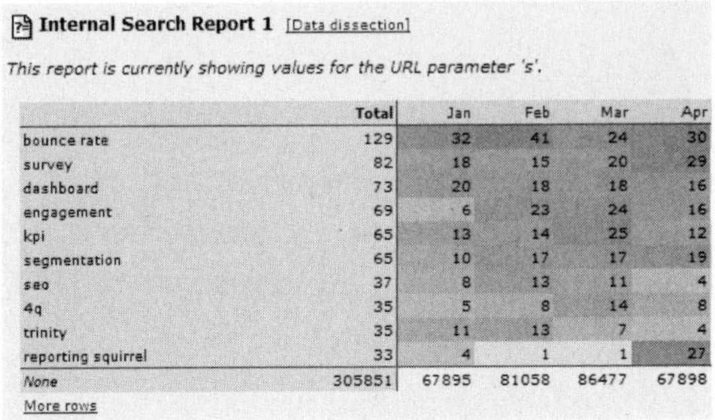

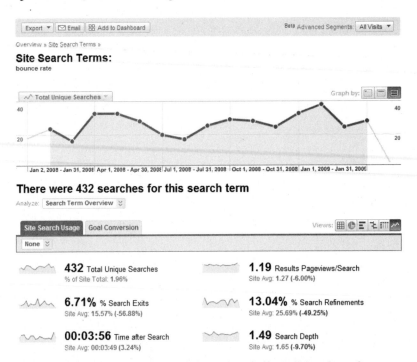

Figure 4.18 Report for internal site search keywords usage

This report gives an excellent peek into your visitor's mind and into what they are really looking for! You can take the report one step further by drilling down into a specific term, as shown in Figure 4.19.

Figure 4.19 Comprehensive site search data for keyword searched by site Visitors: Bounce Rate

You can see the trend or interest and the seasonal effects and start to understand the performance of this particular query, whether by looking at the detailed statistics or by clicking the Goal Conversion tab.

It's time to kick it up a notch.

Measuring Site Search Quality

Now that you have established the importance of site search, you need to find out whether your site search engine delivers quality results.

Remember Bounce Rate? Of course you do. Some web analytics tools provide a *Bounce Rate for site search*. It is called % Search Exits. It measures the same phenomenon as Bounce Rate: the number of people who leave your website immediately after seeing the results provided by your internal site search engine. Figure 4.20 shows the report.

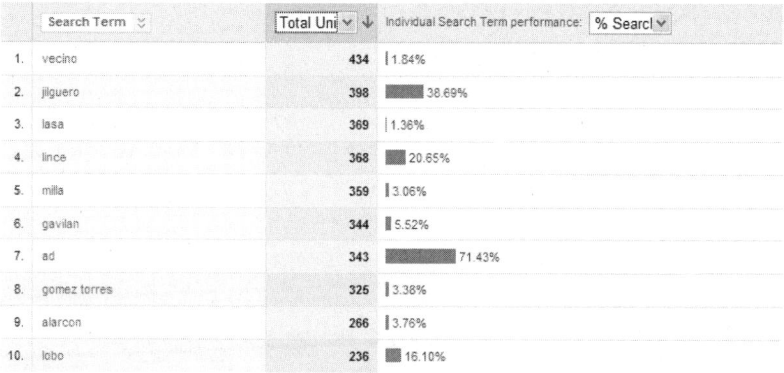

Search Term	Total Uni	Individual Search Term performance: % Searcl
1. vecino	434	1.84%
2. jilguero	398	38.69%
3. lasa	369	1.36%
4. lince	368	20.65%
5. milla	359	3.06%
6. gavilan	344	5.52%
7. ad	343	71.43%
8. gomez torres	325	3.38%
9. alarcon	266	3.76%
10. lobo	236	16.10%

Figure 4.20 Percentage of search exits. High = bad!

A quick glance at the bar graph on the right tells you which internal site search results are working and which ones are slacking off. In this case, queries 2, 4, and 7 (with a 71 percent exit rate!) need immediate attention. Perhaps your internal search engine algorithms are not right, or perhaps you don't have products, services, or pages relevant to them. Either way, it's cause for concern.

The other way to think about search quality is to measure the number of search results pages that are viewed by the visitor. We are all trained by major search engines to expect the most relevant result on top of the first page.

In measuring Results Page Views/Search, you can posit that if you provide the most relevant results on page 1, then Visitors will click one of the top listings and be on their merry way. Figure 4.21 illustrates how this metric looks in a report.

Search Term ⌄	Total Uni ⌄ ↓	Individual Search Term performance:	Results ⌄
1. brain	44	▇▇▇▇ 1.23
2. microscope	42	▇▇▇▇▇ 1.88
3. drinking bird	39	▇▇▇▇ 1.15
4. bella sara	37	▇▇▇▇▇ 1.68
5. globe	34	▇▇▇▇ 1.26
6. marble	34	▇▇▇▇ 1.41
7. quercetti	31	▇▇▇▇ 1.10
8. gears	26	▇▇▇▇▇ 1.92
9. robot	26	▇▇▇▇ 1.35
10. (not set)	24	▇▇▇▇ 1.71

Figure 4.21 Measuring search quality with Results Page Views/Search

The report shows the search queries where Visitors must dig deeper into your site search results to find what they are looking for. Consider the search query *gears*, with an average of 1.92 results views. It took two pages (on average 30 to 40 links to look through) to find what the visitor was looking for—that might be a bit much. It's time to look at what the results are on page 1 and fix 'em.

Note: Some analytics tools also automatically report on Time After Search (*time spent on your website after doing the search*) and Search Depth (*number of pages viewed after searching your site*). Both of these metrics might be interesting proxies for search quality, though it is hard to generalize them. For example, the visitor found what they wanted by using internal site search and bought the product right away (so, small Search Depth is better). Or the visitor found what they wanted on a content site and went on to read a lot more articles (so, large Search Depth is better). Use caution in how you end up using those metrics.

One final method of measuring search quality is, once again, to focus on customer behavior. Search Refinements help you understand how Visitors refine their queries to get optimal results.

Figure 4.22 shows the percent Search Refinements column in the Internal Site Search report.

Search Term ⌄	None ⌄	Total Unique ↓ Searches	Results Pageviews/Search	% Search Exits	% Search Refinements
1. bounce rate		39	1.33	2.56%	17.31%
2. cross domain		31	1.00	83.87%	3.23%
3. survey		25	1.36	0.00%	5.88%
4. segmentation		16	1.94	18.75%	22.58%
5. dashboard		15	1.73	6.67%	15.38%
6. engagement		15	1.40	13.33%	14.29%

Figure 4.22 % Search Query Refinements for site searches

You can quickly see that Visitors refine their query for the word *cross domain* only 3.23 percent of the time, a likely indication that they find what they are looking for right away. But for the word *segmentation*, Visitors refine the query 19 percent of the time. That's not great. If your internal site search engine is good, then Visitors should not have to refine their queries. That is, they should not have to try searching again.

There is a small blessing in disguise here. With the results of Search Refinement, you can get a peek into your customers' heads. Figure 4.23 shows the Search Refinement report for the keyword *segmentation*. It is very helpful to know that most Visitors wanted to learn more about data collection when they were looking for information about segmentation. This information will help the company improve its site search results.

Site Search Refinement

	Refined Keyword (None)	Search R	Search Refinements
1.	data collection	9	1.57%
2.	engagement	7	1.22%
3.	bounce rate	4	0.70%
4.	audit	4	0.70%
5.	Excellent Analytics Tip	3	0.52%

Figure 4.23 Search refinement report for *segmentation*

Segmenting and Measuring Impact

By now you are not surprised by my obsession with segmenting data. Segmenting is always a valuable exercise. Most web analytics tools will allow you to do *inline segmentation*, or segment directly from the report itself. Inline segmentation is a very cool way for you to dig deeper and find insights, as you can see in Figure 4.24.

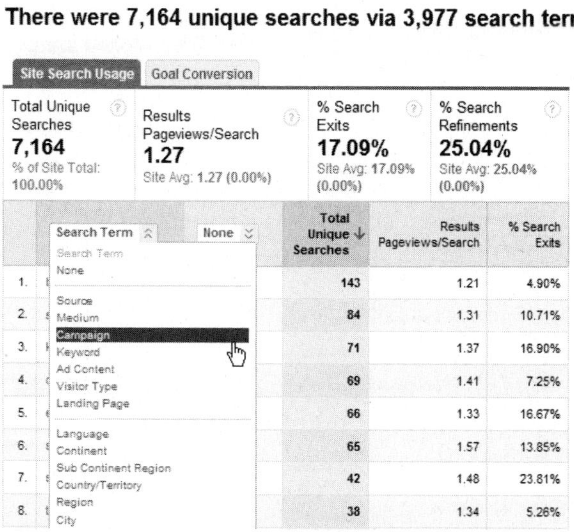

Figure 4.24 Segmentation options for site search data

When you do this kind of segmenting, you should be able to answer a few questions easily:

- Do New Visitors to your site search more than Returning Visitors? For example, for my real estate website, Visitors from which city search more, and for what?

- Is there a difference in internal site searches done by Visitors from yahoo.com vs. those from google.com? Visitors who enter the site from my campaigns on custom landing pages should not be doing internal site search because I have created the most glorious and relevant landing pages, so are they still searching?

Finally, with segmenting, you can show the impact that site search has for the company's bottom line. When you start the process of analyzing this data, you might find that your site search stinks. So, you work hard to improve it to the extent you can. You want management to pony up for a new site search tool. They refuse. Are you stuck?

No. Show them, as with Figure 4.25, how Visitors who use site search end up converting at a higher rate than those that don't.

Figure 4.25 Goal Conversion Rate for Visits with and without site search

Although the number of Visitors who search is low, the Conversion Rate is multiple times higher. It is now easier to quantify the impact on Goals or Conversion Rate or Average Order Size if you invest in making site search better. You can measure the Conversion Rates, revenue, and so on, before you purchase the new tool.

That wasn't so hard, was it? You can do three simple and effective types of analysis on one of the most valuable sources of data in your possession.

There are related metrics and analyses you can do in your web analytics tool. For example, you can customize the JavaScript tag from your web analytics vendor and track the searches done on your site that did not yield any results back to your Visitors. This information can be important, especially if your site search is really poor. Typically, though, these kinds of searches are done by a very small number of your website Visitors. Therefore, you should first do the three types of analysis I have covered in this section. Eat all the yummy low-hanging fruit first; you'll have a larger impact on most of your website Visitors. Then move on to things that are important but will have a smaller overall impact.

Search Engine Optimization (SEO) Analysis

Search engines are a key part of any company's acquisition portfolio. For good reason, citizens of the Internet use search to find everything they are looking for, including you. The business impact of this customer behavior is that we all pour a lot of resources into optimizing our websites to show up optimally in search engines for relevant queries.

Figure 4.26 shows the search engine results page on `www.google.com` for a typical query.

Figure 4.26 Search results page on Google

Sponsored links are the paid search results (I'll cover how to analyze these in the next section). The search results in the main body are the organic search results, or those that the search engines list for free based on their unique algorithm.

You can improve your organic results by taking a number of actions on your website. These include having a website that is easily indexable by the automated robots from the search engines, ensuring your URL structure is clean, using JavaScript in links judiciously (robots don't execute JavaScript and hence won't follow those links), ensuring that the content on your pages is relevant and uses the right keywords, and so on.

SEO analysis is unique because the data partly exists in your web analytics tool (such as Omniture, Webtrends, or Affinium NetInsight) and partly in external tools such as Webmaster Tools provided by Google and Microsoft.

In the next section, I'll cover analysis that will measure four facets of your SEO strategy: current performance (traffic), content coverage (indexing by search engines), keyword performance (search engine results), and Outcomes.

Performance: Traffic from Organic Search

You always want to know whether you should be engaged in this whole endeavor at all! Luckily, every web analytics tool provides quick access to understanding organic search traffic trends, as shown in Figure 4.27.

Figure 4.27 Organic search traffic reports

At a glance, you can see key statistics as well as understand the performance of the organic search traffic by looking at metrics such as Bounce Rate (looks fabulous here!).

You can also click the Goal Conversion tab and quickly assess the value of organic traffic. Are they converting at an optimal rate? Higher? Lower?

But the truly insightful bit is to segment the overall traffic trend and understand the performance of paid search and organic search as a piece of that bigger macro puzzle. Figure 4.28 shows the report you need to create immediately. It includes a 13-month trend of overall traffic (All Visits), Paid Traffic, and organic traffic (Non-paid Traffic).

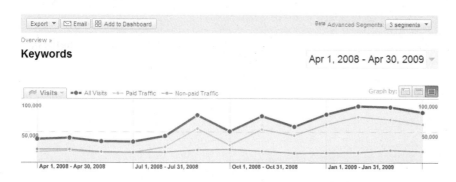

Figure 4.28 Segmented long-term paid and organic search report

From April 2008 through July 2008, organic and paid traffic contributed about the same amount to the overall traffic. Then something started to shift, and with almost every passing month (except October), the paid component kept growing and becoming increasingly more important to the business. Organic search, on the other hand, essentially remained flat.

Typically this type of trend should cause you to dig deeper. Why did the paid search strategy get increasingly successful while the organic search strategy went nowhere? What is unique about our website and content? Is our business (content, products, services) so dynamic that organic search won't work for us? Why the "over-reliance" on paid search?

An effective search strategy is a portfolio strategy. You must optimize for all major search engines, and you must effectively use paid and organic search. Doing only paid or only organic is suboptimal. Optimizing your organic search strategy starts with reports like those shown in Figure 4.27 and Figure 4.28.

Content Coverage: Indexing by Search Engines

With your organic search strategy, your explicit goal is to get your website indexed properly by the search engine. If this happens, then you increase the chances that your site will actually show up when people use search engines to look for *stuff* relevant to you.

You can measure the impact of your SEO efforts in terms of content coverage in two ways:

- You can measure the amount of content being indexed over time (this should go up if you publish new content).

- You can measure the number of pages on your site that get traffic from search engines.

All three major U.S. search engines provide a service affectionately called Webmaster Tools. This is your first stop in understanding whether your site is primed for search success.

Before you can use the tool, you or perhaps an IT person at your company will have to sign up with the search engine and authenticate yourself by placing a small XML or HTML file in your website's root folder (hence proving you own the site and can see the data).

In Google, you review the Crawl Stats report, as shown in Figure 4.29.

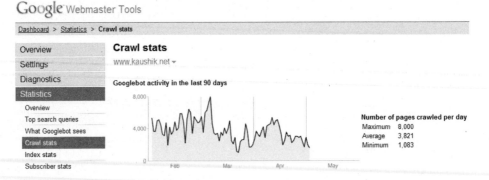

Figure 4.29 Google Webmaster Tools' Crawl Stats report

Contrary to expectations, as you publish more content on the website and you expend major SEO efforts, fewer pages were indexed in the last 45 days. You can't find this data in your web analytics tool. It is important to keep a close eye on it.

Figure 4.30 shows the statistics from Yahoo! Site Explorer.

Figure 4.30 Yahoo! Site Explorer's Statistics report

Same data, different numbers. It is confusing, but each search engine crawls and categorizes pages on your site in a different manner. Yahoo! shows 14,178, and Google shows around 3,821. Don't get stressed about the actual number; just compare the trends over time. The rule is simple: if you keep adding content to your site, the numbers should go up if the search engine is crawling your site optimally.

If your IT team is giving you a tough time, you can also try to use other tools to get at this information. Marketleap provides two useful reports at `http://zqi.me/ mktleap`. The Search Engine Saturation report shows you the number of pages a given search engine has in its index for your site, and the Link Popularity Check report shows the total number of links that a search engine has found for your site. The nice thing about the Marketleap reports is that you can trend the data over time.

Having checked the search engine perspective, you now need to check the view from your website's perspective. The content coverage report that you want to run is # of Landing Pages for Organic Traffic (meaning the entry pages on your site that get organic traffic from search engines, not the custom pages you created for paid or email campaigns).

Figure 4.31 shows how the report looks in Google Analytics; your web analytics tools should easily provide this precise view.

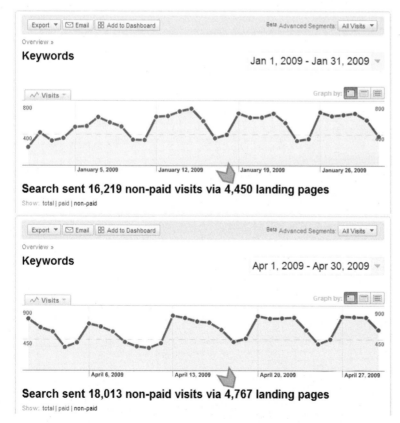

Figure 4.31 Content coverage report: organic search landing pages

The hypothesis is a very simple one. If your website is being indexed correctly and your SEO efforts are working, then over time the number of pages that get direct traffic from search engines will increase. In Figure 4.31 you can see how over a three-month period of exhaustive and often painful SEO work, both the number of Visits to the website as well as the # of Landing Pages for Organic Traffic has increased at a nice clip.

Keyword Performance: Search Engine Results

Search engines have increasingly moved beyond showing text results to including images, videos, and other relevant kinds of content. This concept is often called *universal search*. Additionally, search engines often customize results based on a whole host of factors such as your location, past search queries, language, and so on.

Therefore, you need to look beyond the keywords in your analytics reports and try to understand whether you are *showing up* for the optimal set of keywords in search engine results. And you want to know the surprises—unexpected keywords that show up in results.

An excellent way to measure these surprise keywords is to use the Webmaster Tools report. Figure 4.32 shows the Top Search Queries report from Google's Webmaster Tools (http://zqi.me/googwmt).

Top search queries ⓘ

www.kaushik.net/avinash ▾

▸ How do I use this data?

1 week ago All searches - All locations ▾

Top search queries
The top 20 queries in which your site appeared, and the percentage of the top 20 queries represented by each search.

Top clicked queries
The top 20 queries from which users reached your site, and the percentage of the top 20 queries represented by each click.

#	%	Query	Position	#	%	Query	Position
1	29%	google analytic	7	1	42%	hippo	8
2	11%	survey questions	6	2	9%	survey questions	6
3	8%	bounce rate	6	3	5%	water drop	17
4	6%	google analytics	40	4	4%	water drops	26
5	6%	analytics google	8	5	4%	trinity	12
6	5%	competitive intelligence	8	6	4%	enterprise	17
7	4%	embarrass	10	7	3%	choice	8
8	4%	king baby	7	8	3%	working at google	6
9	3%	working at google	6	9	3%	drop of water	9
10	3%	the bounce	5	10	3%	unique	6
11	3%	working for google	8	11	3%	evolution timeline	3
12	3%	statistically significant	7	12	3%	tear drops	7
13	2%	zaaz	3	13	2%	variables	7
14	2%	google anlytics	4	14	2%	to be or not to be	6
15	2%	coradiant	5	15	2%	google analytics	2
16	2%	4q	5	16	2%	liberty of the seas	17
17	2%	avinash kaushik	2	17	2%	problems	4
18	2%	avinash	2	18	2%	competitive intelligence	8
19	1%	work at google	9	19	1%	avinash kaushik	2
20	1%	"buy in"	5	20	1%	ripple	34

⬇ Download data   ⬇ Download all query stats for this site (including subfolders)

Figure 4.32 Top Search Queries report, Impressions vs. Traffic

On the left are Impressions, or user queries for which your website appeared in search results. On the right, Traffic shows queries where users actually clicked your website's link on the search results page and came to your website. As you might have guessed, the Traffic data will be in your web analytics tools, but your tools are completely blind to the Impression data because it exists only in the search engine. That is what makes the Impression data particularly valuable.

When you analyze the data, look for surprises. Your site shows up for a whole bunch of relevant results (1, 2, 3, 4) and less than relevant results (7, 8, 20). You can optimize your robots.txt file or your website content to ensure you are showing up for all the right keywords.

At the same time, not all keywords for which you have impressions (1, for example) result in traffic to you (or does not exist in Traffic on the left...sad). In this case, you should go back and look at the page that shows up—whether the page has the right snippet, whether the title of the page is right, and so on. Such changes will help make the page stand out again and yield more traffic to you.

The actionable insights from this data will feed into your SEO program. As your team implements these keyword-level strategies, you can measure their success by using the monthly data available from the search engine (see Figure 4.33).

December				April			
Top search queries The top 20 queries in which your site appeared, and the percentage of the top 20 queries represented by each search.				**Top search queries** The top 20 queries in which your site appeared, and the percentage of the top 20 queries represented by each search.			
#	%	Query	Position	#	%	Query	Position
1	24%	google analytic	9	1	18%	google analytic	9
2	19%	google analytics	39	2	13%	survey questions	10
3	9%	survey questions	8	3	8%	bounce rate	6
4	9%	analytics google	8	4	7%	google analytics	45
5	6%	bounce rate	3	5	7%	the bounce	5
6	4%	damini	7	6	7%	analytics google	9
7	3%	google	397	7	5%	competitive intelligence	10
8	3%	analytics	45	8	5%	working at google	7
9	3%	competitive intelligence	8	9	5%	king baby	6
10	2%	butt	54	10	4%	working for google	7
11	2%	avinash	3	11	3%	statistically significant	5
12	2%	zaaz	3	12	3%	avinash	2
13	2%	trinity tech talk	9	13	2%	next stop wonderland	9
14	2%	www "google be"	6	14	2%	survey examples	6
15	2%	metric	6	15	2%	zaaz	4
16	2%	occam's razor	15	16	2%	avinash kaushik	2
17	2%	google anlytics	4	17	2%	work at google	9
18	1%	razor	45	18	2%	work for google	7
19	1%	avinash kaushik	2	19	2%	coradiant	8
20	1%	what is bounce rate	8	20	2%	4q	7

Figure 4.33 Comparing improvement in Impressions over time

It is clear that the implemented SEO improvements have yielded positive results when you compare the Impressions data for December and April. For example, the phrase *statistically significant* was specifically targeted for optimization. It was non-existent on the left (December) but shows up at #11 in the report on the right (April). Hurray!

Outcomes: Goals, Revenue, and ROI

In the SEO business, we love our rankings, engines, and results, but we rarely give that same love to the Outcomes we are driving for our companies. We seem to be obsessed with playing with the search engines.

Consider this last point to be my plea to focus on measuring Outcomes, with the same vehemence you bring to your email, affiliate, or paid search campaigns. Doing so will ensure that you get the funding you need to execute your SEO efforts and show the value of this free traffic stream.

You can measure a whole host of ecommerce and non-ecommerce Outcomes. I'll recommend at least two.

First, measure the impact on your business of the traffic that comes from organic search (from all search engines), as shown in Figure 4.34.

Visitors completed 2,625 goal conversions in the "All Visits" segment

All Visits : **632 conversions, Goal 1**
Non-paid Traffic : **255**

All Visits : **1,178 conversions, Goal 2**
Non-paid Traffic : **423**

All Visits : **334 conversions, Goal 3**
Non-paid Traffic : **159**

All Visits : **481 conversions, Goal 4**
Non-paid Traffic : **144**

Figure 4.34 Segmented conversions: All Visits vs. organic search traffic (Non-paid Traffic)

Although organic traffic makes for a small percent of the website's traffic, it actually accounts for an outsized percentage of its multiple conversions. If you know a better way to get an immediate bonus as an SEO professional, then let me know.

If you have an ecommerce website, then you can dive even deeper into the data and analyze key performance indicators such as Revenue, Average Order Value, Products Sold, and so on, as shown in Figure 4.35.

Analyzing this data in context with your other campaign data will help you measure true ROI (remember to also add the costs of doing your email, affiliate, or paid search campaigns in computing ROI).

I'll give you one final example to illustrate the coolness of measuring Outcomes for organic search. Say you get a ton of traffic. You do your normal analysis and tell your boss that most of the traffic is irrelevant and you want to eliminate it. Your boss will faint. Get some cold water, and sprinkle it on her face. After she gets her wits together, tell her that the reduced traffic won't have any impact on Conversions; in fact, you can improve them.

Figure 4.35 Ecommerce metrics for organic traffic

The sweet delight is that you can easily measure the result of the shifts you are suggesting in your organic search strategy (see Figure 4.36).

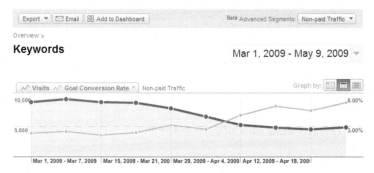

Figure 4.36 Correlating organic search traffic with Goal Conversion Rates

You can pinpoint when you started to implement your new and improved search strategy by focusing on the right keywords and web pages (March). Sure enough, traffic starts to go down, and mercifully Conversions pick up slightly. You have some sleepless nights, but your data-driven SEO strategy starts to clearly show results by the end of March (traffic is down almost 50 percent, yikes!). Of course, you are focusing on the line that's going up, and that's Conversion Rate).

As analysts, and as marketers, the strategies we follow and the recommendations we make might seem counterintuitive. But if you are wise and tie your recommendations to measurable Outcomes, you can get away with almost anything.

Pay Per Click/Paid Search Analysis

Paid and organic search are conjoined twins. You can't have one without the other. Any company that does both effectively (and holistically) stands to reap huge rewards.

Since there are entire books written about PPC analysis, in this section I hope to share with you the starting points of effective analysis of your PPC campaigns.

The very first thing you must do is *teach* your web analytics tool which click from the search engine is from an organic listing and which is from a pay-per-click (PPC) listing. Analytics tools (with the exception of Google Analytics/AdWords) don't come with native intelligence for separating organic and paid clicks. Each search engine is unique and sends a referral string that is distinct. Furthermore, each web analytics tool has its own way of storing search referral string data, which means if you put the wrong tracking parameter in the wrong place, you are hosed.

Let's look at an example. If you search the word *Omniture* on www.google. com today, you get two listings—one organic and one paid. The organic listing goes to the URL www.omniture.com. The paid listing goes to the URL www.omniture.com/ static/1923?s_scid=TC|5379|omniture||S|e|2831181395.

Everything you see after the question mark (?) in the previous URL is known as the *referral string*, and it contains a tracking parameter that tells Omniture which click came organically and which came via PPC. Without the tracking parameters, both clicks would be considered as coming from organic search.

If you had done a search on www.yahoo.com, you would also get an organic listing and a paid listing for Omniture. The paid listing goes to the URL www.omniture.com/ static/278?s_scid=680217600000000309&clicksource=standard&OVRAW=omniture&OVKEY= omniture&OVMTC=standard&OVADID=4822371011&OVKWID=130976483511.

You can see how the referral string is organized differently on Yahoo!

I cannot stress how important it is that you make sure that all your search campaigns are tagged properly and according to the rules imposed on you by your web analytics tool, or else your ability to do analysis will be kaput.

The only exception to this rule is if you use Google Analytics as your analytics tool and use Google AdWords to do your PPC campaigns. In this case, simply tying your AdWords account to your Google Analytics account will ensure that you don't have to tag your campaigns in AdWords to teach Google Analytics anything; Google does everything for you.

But when you analyze your Microsoft or Yahoo! paid search campaigns in your Google Analytics account, you must tag them properly (using the free URL Builder tool; http://zqi.me/urlbuild).

The following are the kinds of techniques that you'll use to optimally analyze your PPC campaigns.

Performance: Traffic from Paid Search

Some of the analysis you'll do for your PPC campaigns is similar to your organic search campaigns. For example, you will first impress your co-workers with the analysis shown in Figure 4.27 and Figure 4.28. The goal is to highlight the long-term trends for PPC campaigns. Are you getting better? Worse? Identify the major shifts in traffic, and identify the rationale.

The business impact analysis you'll perform for your PPC campaigns is also very similar to what I have already covered, as you saw in Figure 4.34, Figure 4.35, and Figure 4.36. The goal is to highlight how PPC campaigns add to the bottom line. Do you see the same kind of efficiency in your paid campaigns as you see for your organic campaigns in Figure 4.36? If not, why not?

Each of the following five analyses will help you understand how important your PPC campaigns are and help you understand priorities and initial focus areas.

Measuring the End-to-End View

The starting point of your PPC analysis will look like Figure 4.37.

AdWords sent 830 visits via 10 ad contents

	Site Usage	Goal Conversion	Ecommerce	Clicks			Views:
Visits		**Pages/Visit**		**Avg. Time on Site**	**% New Visits**	**Bounce Rate**	
830		**5.40**		**00:03:13**	**92.77%**	**18.80%**	
% of Site Total: 0.97%		Site Avg: 3.91 (37.96%)		Site Avg: 00:02:14 (43.96%)	Site Avg: 90.72% (2.26%)	Site Avg: 53.44% (-64.83%)	

	Ad Content ⋎	None ⋎	Visits ↓	Pages/Visit	Avg. Time on Site	% New Visits	Bounce Rate
1.	Icky Toys		209	6.41	00:03:41	96.17%	28.71%
2.	C3000 Chemistry Kit Sale		191	4.99	00:03:05	92.67%	14.14%
3.	Marshmallow Shooter Fun		134	4.66	00:02:25	90.30%	17.91%
4.	C1000 Chemistry Kit Sale		121	4.66	00:03:07	91.74%	11.57%
5.	C2000 Chemistry Kit Sale		50	4.20	00:02:51	86.00%	14.00%
6.	Perfume Science Kit Sale		50	4.46	00:02:20	94.00%	16.00%
7.	Give Smiles & Smarts		38	6.89	00:04:33	92.11%	23.68%
8.	Who gave you that toy?		37	8.30	00:04:57	94.59%	18.92%
9.	Smarter Smiling Toddlers		0	0.00	00:00:00	0.00%	0.00%
10.	Trainmech at BrainWaves		0	0.00	00:00:00	0.00%	0.00%
Find Ad Content: containing ⋎			Go	Go to: 1	Show rows: 10 ⋎	1 - 10 of 10 ◄ ►	

Figure 4.37 Clickstream analysis of paid search campaigns

You can quickly assess which keywords (or ad groups or user queries) bring clicks to your site and how each performs in terms of initial metrics (Time on Site, % New Visits, and so on). But look at the tabs in Figure 4.37, and you'll realize you can go deeper into the data. So in Figure 4.38, you can measure Goal Conversions, ecommerce, or, my favorite, the end-to-end view (Clicks).

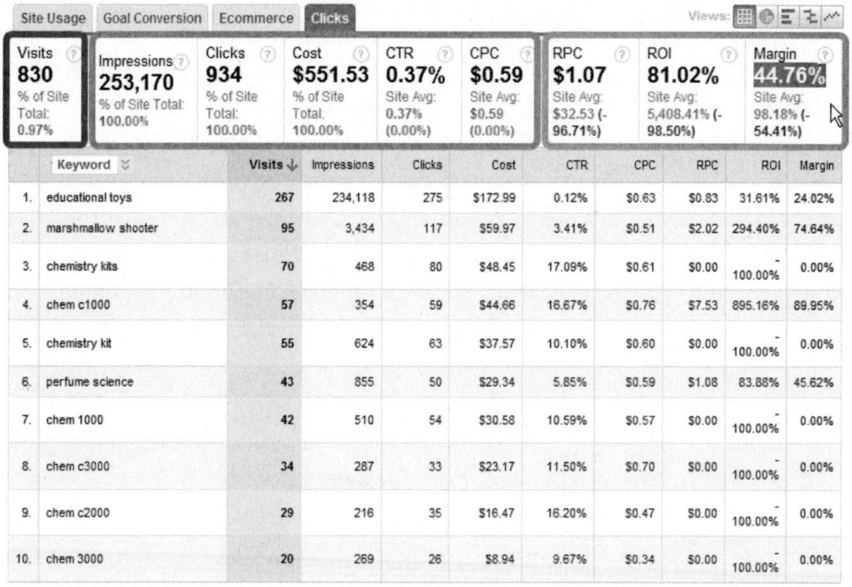

	Site Usage	Goal Conversion	Ecommerce	Clicks					
	Visits 830 % of Site Total: 0.97%	Impressions 253,170 % of Site Total: 100.00%	Clicks 934 % of Site Total: 100.00%	Cost $551.53 % of Site Total: 100.00%	CTR 0.37% Site Avg: 0.37% (0.00%)	CPC $0.59 Site Avg: $0.59 (0.00%)	RPC $1.07 Site Avg: $32.53 (-96.71%)	ROI 81.02% Site Avg: 5,408.41% (-98.50%)	Margin 44.76% Site Avg: 98.18% (-54.41%)

	Keyword	Visits	Impressions	Clicks	Cost	CTR	CPC	RPC	ROI	Margin
1.	educational toys	267	234,118	275	$172.99	0.12%	$0.63	$0.83	31.61%	24.02%
2.	marshmallow shooter	95	3,434	117	$59.97	3.41%	$0.51	$2.02	294.40%	74.64%
3.	chemistry kits	70	468	80	$48.45	17.09%	$0.61	$0.00	-100.00%	0.00%
4.	chem c1000	57	354	59	$44.66	16.67%	$0.76	$7.53	895.16%	89.95%
5.	chemistry kit	55	624	63	$37.57	10.10%	$0.60	$0.00	-100.00%	0.00%
6.	perfume science	43	855	50	$29.34	5.85%	$0.59	$1.08	83.88%	45.62%
7.	chem 1000	42	510	54	$30.58	10.59%	$0.57	$0.00	-100.00%	0.00%
8.	chem c3000	34	287	33	$23.17	11.50%	$0.70	$0.00	-100.00%	0.00%
9.	chem c2000	29	216	35	$16.47	16.20%	$0.47	$0.00	-100.00%	0.00%
10.	chem 3000	20	269	26	$8.94	9.67%	$0.34	$0.00	-100.00%	0.00%

Figure 4.38 Analyzing the end-to-end view of success

This lovely report manages to bring three different pieces of data together so you can judge effectiveness in one nice view. The first set of data, the middle box, is data from the search engine (in other words, AdWords). It shows the performance of your advertising via the number of Impressions, Clicks, Cost, CTR (which is the click-through rate), and CPC (which is the cost per click). You'll understand what it takes to get someone to your site by individual keywords. Check out the first row, "educational toys," with 234,118 impressions to get 275 clicks! Oh my.

The second set of data should be very familiar: Visits. Remember, a click is not the same as a Visit. During one session, a Visitor could have clicked three different ads from the search engine. That would show up in your reports as Clicks = 3, Visit = 1.

The last piece of data, on the right, illustrates the business impact metrics: RPC (the revenue per click), ROI (the return on investment), and Margin (typically revenue minus campaign cost). This is a great way to understand if you had a positive or negative impact on your business.

One caution, though. Notice I said "campaign cost" when computing Margin. By default, almost all web analytics tools will not include the cost of goods sold (COGS), that is, what it costs you to make the product or service you are selling, in the Margin calculation. Hence, you need to take that number with a grain of salt. If your web analytics tool allows you to import the COGS data, then do that and compute your true Margin. Omniture, Webtrends, Coremetrics, and many other tools allow you to do this.

Looking at your end-to-end view is important because you want more than clicks to your site. You want more than Visits. You want bottom-line magnifying impact. This simple report is very effective at showing you that impact.

Analyzing PPC Ad Position

So, here is how PPC campaigns work. You pay. Your bid goes into an auction. Others bid. They compete with you. A smart algorithm gets applied. Your ad gets listed on the search engine results page based on the algorithm + competition + bid. Now the cute part is that the position of your ad will also depend on those three factors (amongst others).

Hence, understanding the impact of different ad positions can be an insightful set of analysis you can perform. Figure 4.39 shows one such report, Keyword Positions, from Google Analytics. In other web analytics tools, you'll also easily find Average Position reports.

Figure 4.39 Keyword Positions report

The Keyword Positions report is always chockful of insights. Each box on the bottom right shows the number of clicks your ad received when it was listed in a certain position. You quickly realize that you pay a different amount of money to the search engine depending on the ad position—typically, the higher the position (Top 1, 2, 3), the more expensive.

Notice in Figure 4.39 that the keyword *trabajo* has an interesting distribution of clicks to your site. You get more clicks in position Side 1 than you do from Top 2 or Top 3. That seems counter to what you might believe ("Got to be in Top 1, 2, or 3 to get any clicks!").

So, your first insight is realizing which position to bid for your top keywords to ensure the optimal number of clicks. But, who cares about clicks? The Web Analytics 2.0 ninja cares about adding business value!

Besides displaying multiple dimensions of data in a way that an Excel table never can, the Keyword Positions report gives you that drop-down menu right above the search engine logo, Position Breakdown. Here you can choose the metric that is most applicable to your business, such as Pages/Visit, Time on Site, Bounce Rate, various Goal Conversion Rates, Per Visit Goal Value, and so on.

For our example, the company is a content-only website, with no ecommerce, and its goal is not simply to get a Visit but rather to get Visitors who spend a lot of time on the website. They'll choose Avg. Time on Site from the drop-down menu and see the report shown in Figure 4.40.

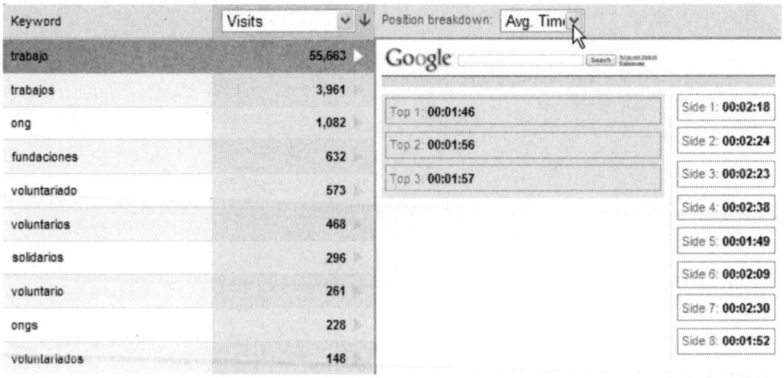

Figure 4.40 Keyword Positions report for Avg. Time on Site

You should notice two things. First, the report shows positions data from the search engine (AdWords in this case) with the metric for Time, which is from your web analytics tool. Without you realizing it, the report is making some pretty nifty connections. Second, you'll immediately notice that the *ego positions* (Top 1, 2, 3) are doing OK, but the top four positions on the side (cheaper bids!) actually deliver Visitors who spend more time on your website.

With these insights, you can balance between the number of clicks you can get from each position and your business success (time). You can tweak your bids to ensure you get the best position at the best cost.

Measuring PPC Customer Behavior

At the beginning of this chapter, I covered the importance of focusing on customer behavior rather than aggregate metrics. You can do some cool PPC analysis by applying that principle.

The setup is quite simple. Let's measure how long it takes for someone to convert from the first time they visit your website. The report is called Days to Purchase, which is shown in Figure 4.41. You'll notice, top right, that it is segmented to show only Paid Traffic.

Days to Purchase

Most purchases occured after: 0 days

Figure 4.41 Days to Purchase, PPC campaign traffic

This data is for a travel website. It might strike you as odd that only 46 percent of the people make a purchase on the same day, simply because airline tickets and hotels and cruises all tend to get more expensive with each passing day. That's odd behavior for Visitors.

OK, let's find out whether we see the same behavior with traffic from other sources. Figure 4.42 shows the report for Direct Traffic.

Days to Purchase	Transactions	Percentage of all purchases
0 days	163.00	70.87%
1 days	10.00	4.35%
2 days	7.00	3.04%
3 days	1.00	0.43%
4 days	4.00	1.74%
5 days	1.00	0.43%
6 days	2.00	0.87%
7 days	1.00	0.43%
8-14 days	5.00	2.17%
15-30 days	8.00	3.48%
31-60 days	11.00	4.78%
61-120 days	8.00	3.48%
121-365 days	9.00	3.91%

Figure 4.42 Days to Purchase, Direct Traffic

Whoa! With Direct Traffic, 71 percent purchase on the same day. That is normal behavior for Visitors for a travel site. So, what is up with the PPC traffic? Why don't they behave like *normal people*? If the behavior from PPC traffic is so odd, then how can we treat them better or differently?

These are all great questions, and they're the reason why I recommend this type of analysis. From my stress on segmentation, you already know that each traffic stream is unique.

In this case, the travel website took this data and reviewed the landing pages for its PPC campaigns. At the time of the previous report, it was geared toward converting Visitors quickly ("Buy now! Book now! Give us your money, now!").

The first action the marketers took was to soften the calls to action, because they realized a good chunk of the traffic does not want to buy right away. Then the marketers added a new feature, Save Your Itinerary. They realized Visitors would come back, so they might as well make it easy for them.

Finally, the marketers added another feature: "Email me if price goes up by x percent," where x was a number that the Visitors could input when saving an itinerary. This was a very clever move because the travel agency then had the contact information for the Visitors and could email them when the price went up by 10 percent or 20 percent or whatever number the customer input. This caused the customers to return and make a purchase sooner, and the customers were happier because they felt the site was watching out for them.

The net return for closely analyzing PPC customer behavior was that it brought forward Conversions to fewer days to purchase and tripled Conversion Rates. That's not too shabby for a simple segmented report, right?

There are lots of different kinds of analysis you'll do for your PPC campaigns. My hope is that these four *non-normal* examples—measuring traffic performance, measuring the end-to-end view, analyzing ad position, and measuring customer behavior—highlight the kinds of analysis that will help you maximize profitability. Advanced paid search analysis techniques are discussed in more detail in Chapter 11.

Direct Traffic Analysis

I am a huge fan of Direct Traffic because it is free. Who does not love free? Yet analysts and marketers constantly get enamored by campaigns and search and other perceived cool things and ignore this valuable source of traffic.

Direct Traffic is typically defined as *noncampaign, nonsearch, nonlinked* traffic, that is, Visitors who come to your website by typing in your website's URL or who come through a bookmark.

Direct Traffic is valuable because these Visitors know you already, they tend to be your existing customers, and you are not paying a campaign *bounty* to get them to come to your site. It pains me that some web analytics tools don't even have a clearly identified bucket for this traffic stream.

I highly recommend that you make a key part of your analytics strategy understanding free traffic and identifying strategies to nurture and grow this segment of your Visitors. You'll make your loyal customers happier, and you'll end up saving on acquisition costs. Do I hear a win-win?

The kinds of analysis you'll do for your Direct Traffic will be quite similar to what you do for your other traffic streams. Let me share a few reports that I use when I start with my analysis.

Reviewing Current Performance

First you want to educate yourself and your decision makers about the current state of affairs. That is, you want to know how you are doing today in terms of the performance of Direct Traffic and whether there are opportunities to grow. Figure 4.43 shows how the data appears in your web analytics tool, in this case Google Analytics and XiTi.

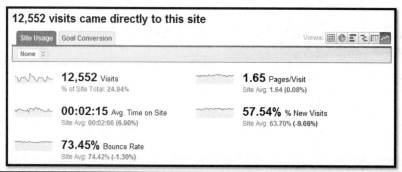

Figure 4.43 Direct Traffic reports for Google Analytics (top) and XiTi (bottom)

In this type of report, you need to understand what percentage of traffic is Direct Traffic. You can clearly see that percentage in the top part of Figure 4.43: 12,552 Visits form a total of 24.94 percent of website traffic. Not too bad, but it could be better. In the bottom, the Direct Traffic is 56 percent of the site traffic.

Next you need to dive into performance. Look at the base metrics such as Time on Site, Bounce Rate, Pages/Visit, and so on. It is very clear in the Google Analytics report (top) in Figure 4.43 that Direct Traffic performs very well when compared to Site Averages for those metrics.

An unsurprising close to this section is the recommendation to review the longer-term trends for Direct Traffic. Over the past 12 months, is the line graph up and to the right? If not, then you need to find out why not. How about when you compare it to other segments of traffic on your site?

Understanding the Opportunity and Educating Management

We will dive deeper into understanding Outcomes in the next chapter, but I want to stress here that you never convince decision makers to take you seriously without showing impact. Figure 4.44 shows a report that will be of incredible value in your effort.

3,674 visits came directly to this site

Figure 4.44 Ecommerce report for Direct Traffic

For your website, the impact might not look exactly like Figure 4.44, but it is not unusual at all for Direct Traffic to perform at a higher level than your other traffic sources. The reason is simple; these are people who found you without you having to incentivize them to come. They know you already, and usually they are going to deliver superior Outcomes.

Take both steps discussed earlier: identify the performance of the core metrics (as in 36 Transactions, $4,144 in Revenue, and so on), and clearly highlight that performance (as in the comparison to Site Total). The latter is cool because comparing the metric to the Site Total helps highlight value and gains you some love. For example, you'll notice that Average Value from Conversions of Direct Traffic is 58.79 percent higher when compared to the Site Average. That is rather sweet, and stuff like that helps you get support from your lovely management team.

Segmenting to Understand Uniqueness

Given the unique nature of the people who come directly to your site, it is extremely productive to understand them. It's like watching a pride of lions and taking notes. What is unique about them? What do they like to eat; that is, what content do they like to consume? Why do they return to the same place? You catch my drift.

The following are my favorite kinds of analysis:

Content analysis Note what pages/content directories these people visit most often. Look at their click pattern in the site overlay (click density) report—what does it indicate in terms of their preferences? Note whether the internal site search data indicates particular needs in terms of products, services, or other needs. For example, analyzing Visitor Loyalty and Depth of Visit could reveal that most Direct Traffic visits frequently and tends to read only about sports and entertainment, while all other traffic sources seem to gravitate toward politics and culture. Actionable insights!

Purchase behavior Visitors who come through Direct Traffic are often, but not always, existing customers, and understanding what they buy is an insightful exercise. Or in case of non-ecommerce websites, you want to understand the behavior around submitting leads or contributing donations and other such Outcomes. This data can be especially useful for future targeting possibilities; this is a delight if you have analyzed the behavior to understand seasonal impact.

For example, a business may recognize that in the first three weeks after releasing the latest version of a product, only existing customers made the purchase—with no need for any campaigns, coupons, or other enticements. Then came the new customers. You would execute your merchandizing and content strategy on the site completely differently if you understood this.

Direct Traffic is valuable. It offers an opportunity for you to maximize the potential of a relationship you already have for a source of traffic that does not typically cost you much, if anything, in terms of acquisition.

Email Campaign Analysis

It might seem incredible that, with spam the bane of our collective existence today, email marketing still seems worth pursuing. Not only is it worth it, but done right, email marketing can be one of the most productive acquisition channels for any company.

Analyzing email campaigns requires three important insights:

- You must use metrics that are unique to the medium.
- You can't track everything.
- You need to think end-to-end and not just in a silo.

As with paid search analysis, first you realize that you must deal with multiple sources of data. Your first source will be your campaign data, which in this case is your email provider. Your second source of data is your website.

Ensure that you have a tagging or tracking strategy for your email campaigns that allows you to merge the data after the fact. When I say your website data, I mean your broader data in Omniture, Webtrends, or Yahoo! Web Analytics. Tagging your site with the JavaScript tag from your email provider won't accomplish that. You'll have to ensure your campaign tracking parameters are set up so that the data will be captured by your web analytics tool.

You can break the analysis down into three important pieces: campaign response, website behavior, and business outcomes.

Campaign Response

The campaign response step involves the initial part of the customer experience: an email blast from you to get a customer response. The key metrics that you'll analyze will come typically from your email service provider (make sure you check that you can get these metrics before you sign up and fork over cash). Here are the metrics, beyond the standard emails sent, that will help you analyze performance:

Delivery rate = (# of emails sent – # of bounce backs) / # of emails sent This is your bread-and-butter Outcome metric when it comes to your campaign; it answers the following simple question: did we stand a chance at success? Note that the increasing use of junk and spam boxes means that bounce backs are not the cleanest way to measure deliverability. The emails might have just ended up in the junk email box where they never stood a chance of being opened.

Open rate = # of emails opened / # of emails sent Be aware that this metric is usually just directionally accurate. Most email programs now have preview panes that typically block images and scripts. Because of concerns about viruses and the like, the default settings on most email programs, including web-based ones, is to block images.

Click-to-open rate (CTOR) = # of clicks / # of emails opened

This is a key measure of the quality of your email list and of the effectiveness and relevance of your message. Segmenting this metric is really powerful. You can learn whether text messages or messages with images get a higher CTOR. You can compare customers in California, Idaho, and Florida; new and existing customers; or various demographics.

Subscriber retention rate = # subscribers – bounce backs – unsubscribes / # subscribers

This is the proof in the pudding, baby! This is perhaps as *strategic* an analysis as you could do for your email campaigns. Here you are measuring both the technical effectiveness of your email campaigns over time (reducing bounce backs) and the relevance of your messages and the targeting of the same (reducing unsubscribes). Measure retention rate over time in aggregate—or for optimal health, segment retention rate—and measure it for the various objectives you have set for your email marketing program.

Website Behavior

In my humble experience, email campaigns usually measure the emails sent and Outcomes (Conversions), but they rarely pause and measure what happens once the person comes to the website. In part, this is because marketers are incentivized based on Outcomes, which is not a bad thing. But everything that happens on the site will either deliver high conversions or kill the most valuable offer you have ever sent.

Here are two useful metrics to inspire the kinds of analysis you should do for website behavior:

Bounce Rate = # of email campaign visits with a single Page View / # of email campaign visits

"Never let your campaigns write checks that your website cannot cash." That's really what you are measuring. Are your landing pages delivering on the promise you made in the email campaign? It does not matter if you have a 100 percent response rate on your email campaign if the website Bounce Rate is 99 percent. This metric helps you find opportunities for immediate improvement—such as pages you should test and calls to action and content that fail to deliver.

Length of Visit = percent of email campaign visits that last longer than *xx* seconds

Here's the hypothesis: you are a content-only website, and you want people to come to your site and spend at least two minutes on it before they leave. You want to set a benchmark for the behavior of people who come from email campaigns. The *xx* in the definition forces you to think up front and plan for site behavior before you send an email blast and, of course, measure your performance against that goal. For a recent ecommerce client, I set a goal of three minutes and measured what percent of Visits from email campaigns exceeded three minutes. Why? For an average person, it would take six minutes from the time they landed on the site to learn about the product, compare options, start the purchase, and complete it. What the client wanted to know was how many Visits were *in the game*.

Depending on your type of website, other metrics will also be important to you. Do not ignore web behavior; it is an important part of measuring your email campaign success.

Business Outcomes

The next chapter is all about Outcomes and measuring success. That's super important. Of course, you need to consider specific outcomes that affect your business when you run an email campaign. Here are some key metrics that you'll analyze:

Conversion Rate = # of Orders / # of email campaign Visits

You need to measure Conversion Rate and segment it like crazy. Be ruthless at identifying causes for low performance. If you have a non-ecommerce website, no worries; you'll measure the # of *actions*, which could be lead submissions, # of Visits with more than nine Page Views, # of downloads, # of RSS sign-ups, and so on.

Average Revenue per Email Sent = total revenue / # of emails sent

I am very fond of this metric because it stresses productivity. Notice that you can play some really nice games by substituting the denominator with # of emails read or # of emails delivered. But I say, why settle for lower standards? Isn't the point of our email campaign to get maximum value? So, let's set a high bar; using # of emails sent will force quality in your email campaigns because it will mandate that the list be very clean and targeted. It is important in your journey as an analyst or marketer that you influence the positive behavior of your company by choosing your metric definitions wisely.

Email Campaign Profitability = (Revenue generated – campaign cost – cost of goods sold) / # of emails sent

Most email marketers will measure Revenue and Order Size and other such obvious metrics. But we rarely spend time measuring profitability. My analysis indicates that this is normally because it is hard to understand the true costs. In the case of email, that means the cost of the campaign: the cost of buying the list, sending the email, using resources, and so forth, as well as the cost of creating the products and services.

But that should not stop you from trying to measure Profitability along with Revenue. It is very easy to imagine that the most successful email campaign in the history of your company could very well cause bankruptcy (costs greater than revenue), and campaigns that look like potential losers could be most profitable. See why this is important?

Email marketing works. You just need to resist the temptation to abuse your customers. Don't preselect sign-up boxes and have an extra step to confirm opt-ins; always think of the customer benefit and not just what you will gain. You should have a big, clear, one-click unsubscribe link. Finally, you need to be relevant. That's really all it takes: treating your customers exactly as you would like to be treated.

Rich Experience Analysis: Flash, Video, and Widgets

Let's close this section with perhaps the toughest but coolest analysis you'll do: analyzing and understanding rich-media website experiences built with Ajax, Flash, Flex, or embedded pieces of rich content such as videos, widgets, and so on.

The challenge with analyzing these experiences is that they fundamentally *break* the core data collection mechanism in our web analytics tools, namely, the mighty Page View. Pretty much every analytics tool on the market today expects a Page View as a record of the interaction someone has with your website.

The problem? Most rich experiences don't generate Page Views. Consider something as simple as hitting Reply in Gmail: a box opens up at the bottom with no refresh of the page. Or consider hitting the Play button on a video on your website. Neither of these actions generate Page Views.

The strategy of past analytics tools was to get you to configure these rich experiences to generate *fake page views*. That approach allowed the tool to fit data into existing structures and enabled reporting (conveniently without the tool having to retrofit itself for the new world).

Event Tracking

Today, some tools provide next-generation data collection models such as Event Tracking to capture data from rich experience. This data is collected differently from your standard tag-based Page View data, it is stored differently (no square pegs in round holes as with fake page views), and finally it creates new metrics that capture the unique experience of rich media.

Although the approach differs from the kind of web analytics tool you use, Event Tracking works by giving you a few *empty containers* for storing data (key-value pairs) according to a hierarchal model. For example, Google Analytics provides you with four empty containers, called Category, Action, Label, and Value. Let's solidify how you track rich experiences using a fictitious example; see Figure 4.45.

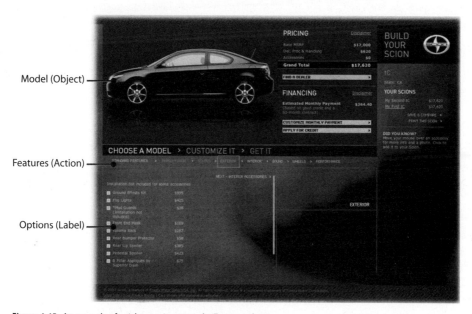

Figure 4.45 An example of a rich experience, on the Toyota website

The car configurator on the Toyota website is built using Adobe Flash; it is a beautiful *pageless* experience that allows Visitors to customize Toyota cars to their own preferences. The only way to do analytics on this experience is to step away from the traditional *page-driven* data collection mechanisms and use Event Tracking. The only challenge with Event Tracking (or tracking rich media experiences) is that you have to spend some time up front defining success. This is something new for analysts and marketers, who are accustomed to just getting data spewed at them.

Ideally, Toyota wants to know which cars customers choose to customize, what the most common features people add to their cars, and what optional elements are popular. Figure 4.46 shows how you might create an optimal data model for collecting this type of data.

Object	Action	Label
Car Model	Transmission	Manual, Automatic
	Color	White, Flint, Silver, Black, Crimson, ...
	Exterior	Ground Effects, Fog Lights, Yakama Rack, ...
	Interior	Security, Sport Steering Wheel, ...
	Sound	Navigation, Pioneer Premium Audio, ...
	Performance	Quick Shifter, Lowering Springs, ...

Figure 4.46 Car configurator Event Tracking data model

Creating this data model up front allows the developers of the application to ensure the proper encoding is in place up front.

As you can imagine, the data model would be different based on the kind of rich experience you build. For example, if I have a website with lots of movies, then I want to track which movie my Visitors watch, where they pause, where they stop, or whether they watch completely. Since the movie is in pieces, I want to know which parts people watch and which they skip. Finally, given that a lot of the world has a slow Internet connection, I want to track how long it takes each part of the video to load. Figure 4.47 shows my potential Event Tracking data model.

Object	Action	Label	Value
Movie Title	Play	Part 1, Part 2, Part 3, Part 4 . . . . . . Part xx	Video Load Time
	Pause	Part 1, Part 2, Part 3, Part 4 . . . . . . Part xx	
	Stop	Part 1, Part 2, Part 3, Part 4 . . . . . . Part xx	
	25%	Part 1, Part 2, Part 3, Part 4 . . . . . . Part xx	
	50%	Part 1, Part 2, Part 3, Part 4 . . . . . . Part xx	
	75%	Part 1, Part 2, Part 3, Part 4 . . . . . . Part xx	
	100%	Part 1, Part 2, Part 3, Part 4 . . . . . . Part xx	

Figure 4.47 Video website Event Tracking data model

The amazing thing is that the developer only has to encode the video player on the website once, and with that, all movies played become trackable. There is no need to encode all 2,500 movies on the site (well, not unless you like pain!).

You report and analyze this data through standard reports available in your web analytics tool or by extracting the data using the API and putting your own spin on it. For our car configurator example, a standard report for the actions taken by website Visitors would look like Figure 4.48 (not Toyota's data).

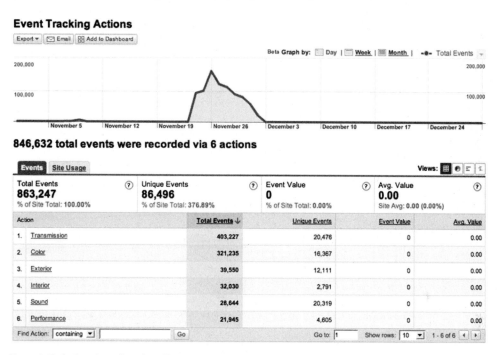

Figure 4.48 Options chosen by website Visitors

The configurator was live on the site for a few weeks. During that time, the most popular option customers chose was Transmission, followed by Color. The car company had expected Visitors to customize something as personal as the color of the car first. Hmmm…it's time to rethink the kinds of customers we have!

In our movies example, standard metrics would report the number of videos played on the site, the number of visits with video plays, the average number of videos played per visitor, the number of videos completed by Visitors, the funnel of how many people start and reach the end, and how far they watched if they did abandon the video (25 percent, 50 percent, 75 percent, and so on).

That's just part of the fun. Then you can dive deeper into your data and segment it! You can see preferences by geography (what color of cars Californians prefer compared to Texans) or for current customers vs. new customers—the sky is the limit.

These new mechanisms to collect data are quite malleable. For example, you can encode widgets (that run around the Web getting all viral and whatnot) and track behaviors or new metrics that might not otherwise be possible. A good example is tracking how many widgets are *grabbed* (the action of taking a widget and placing it on a new website), thus taking a step toward computing *viralness*. Since widgets are essentially small, built-in browsable experiences, you can compute new metrics such as Interaction Time, the amount of time in seconds a Visitor on any site integrated with the widget (using mouseovers, clicks, and so on).

In summary, Page Views are dead; the future of the Web will be substantially richer and immersive. To track these experiences, we must think of new ways of collecting data, understand up front what success means, and ensure all encoding is correctly done at the start. By keeping an open mind about metrics, you'll use them to measure success, and I guarantee glory will be yours!

Reality Check: Perspectives on Key Web Analytics Challenges

You'll realize very quickly that some issues in web analytics will become the bane of your existence. They will hound you in your dreams. Your bosses will throw hissy fits about them. You will come to question why you started with web analytics in the first place!

This section of the book is my attempt at truly *ninjafying* your mind. In other words, I want to get you a lot more focused, to appreciate value, and, perhaps most importantly, to selectively ignore distractions during your quest to find actionable insights.

Cookies, sampling, history, perfection, video playback, data reconciliation. Pay attention, grasshopper....

Visitor Tracking Cookies

Perhaps no other topic is more full of FUD (fear, uncertainty, and doubt) than cookies. Tracking cookies help fulfill a deep-seated desire in marketers and analysts on the Web: to track unique people who come to the website. But short of people embedding RFIDs in their bodies, which are scanned by every computer in the world, there is no way to track unique people.

So, as an ecosystem, we do the next best thing: we try to identify unique browsers (as in FireFox, Chrome, Internet Explorer, and so on) used to visit our websites. *Cookies* are small text files containing an anonymous unique identifier that stitches together Visits to the website by the same person (with the *assumption* that the same person uses the same browser).

We can do a lot of tracking without cookies; they are not the be-all and end-all of Visitor behavior tracking. But we currently track Unique Visitors using cookies. Some websites that make people log in to use key features, such as a bank, can use the login ID to count Unique Visitors, though that ID tracks only those people who log in—and many people won't because they are not there to check their accounts.

Let's attack the rest of this complex issue in a few bite-sized, understandable chunks.

Transient vs. Persistent

The web analytics software will set two types of cookies when you visit a website. They are commonly called *transient* and *persistent* cookies. Some folks refer to them as *session* and *user* cookies, respectively.

The job of the transient cookies is to help *sessionize* an experience on a website. Put simply, your Visitor will make a series of clicks and leave. That's a session. The transient cookie helps group those clicks efficiently.

The transient cookie is *set* when a Visitor visits the site, and it disappears when he or she leaves. The persistent cookie is set the first time the Visitor visits the website, and it remains there for a duration determined by the website (18 months is common, though some tools will set cookies for 50 years). Persistent cookies help identify a unique browser to your website, inasmuch as they are the closest thing to tracking a person or unique visitor. The persistent cookie is on your browser until you either delete it, reinstall your browser, or perform similar actions.

> **Note:** Persistent cookies don't contain any personally identifiable information (PII) data. They just have a random string of numbers or alphabets that only the company that set the cookie can read. For example, here is the identifier used to track me by a cookie that Webtrends just set on my browser as I visited www.webtrends.com: C8ctADY1LjU3LjI0NS4xMS00TU3MTQwMTc2LjI5OTQ0ONzE5AAAAAAAAAAACAAAAoM0AAINghUgWYIVI.

First Party vs. Third Party

Transient and persistent refer to the nature of cookies. *First party* and *third party* refer to the type of cookies.

A *third-party* cookie is set by, well, a third party when someone visits your site. For example, when you visit www.omniture.com today, the tracking cookies are not set using the .omniture.com domain; they are actually set from .2o7.net domain. That makes the tracking methodology used by Omniture *third-party cookie* tracking.

In the good old days, web analytics could more easily use third-party cookies, and such cookies were rampant. But other players then used these cookies in suboptimal ways. This led to default Internet browser settings that rejected third-party cookies and many antispyware and malware programs that autodeleted them. Suffice it to say, third-party cookies have fallen out of favor, and they are considered suboptimal for tracking Unique Visitors.

A *first-party* cookie, hence, is set by the web analytics tool using the domain of the website itself. For example, when I visit www.coremetrics.com, I see that it set cookies using the domain data.coremetrics.com—which makes these cookies first party.

First-party cookies are the preferred tool of choice for tracking Unique Visitors because they are deleted or rejected a lot less by any objective measure. Therefore, they are far superior at tracking Repeat Visits or the New and Returning Visitor segments.

First-party cookies are also rejected a lot less because much of the Internet does not work if you don't accept first-party cookies. Email providers such as hotmail.com or gmail.com, ecommerce websites such as amazon.com or crutchfield.com, banks, or even blogging platforms all require you to accept first-party cookies.

Almost every decent web analytics vendor now provides an easy way for you to use first-party cookies. Some, such as Google Analytics, offer only first-party cookies. Others, such as Omniture and Webtrends, give you a choice.

If you notice some initial pushback from your vendor to use the *easier-for-them* third-party option, push back yourself. Insist on first party. It's good for your health.

Exception for Third-Party Cookies

There are some relevant uses of third-party cookies. One of the most common uses is by ad-serving platforms, because third-party cookies are the only way they can track a *unique browser* across multiple websites. So, even if that third-party cookie gets blown away and rejected more often, they (you) really don't have much of a choice. That's just how the Internet protocols work.

Here's an example of how third-party cookies work on an ad-serving platform:

I notice that omniture.com is using .2o7.net third-party cookies. After going to omniture.com, I could go to ebay.com and then to nytimes.com. The .2o7.net cookie knows that I was at the Omniture site a little while back and knows I then went to eBay and then NYTimes.

Now, as I am reading the latest Maureen Dowd column, the .2o7.net cookie could serve me an ad for Omniture next to the Maureen Dowd column. Knowing I also went to eBay, it could even give me a deal on Omniture in that ad!

This is of course just one example to illustrate the use of a third-party cookie and why Atlas and DoubleClick and Yahoo! and all the others use them (and provide value to their customers).

First-party cookies can't be "read" and "carried over" as in the previous scenario. Their anonymous data is restricted just to that one site.

Cookie Choice and Data Storage

Whether you use first-party or third-party cookies, it does not influence where your data is stored. The type of web analytics software you use determines that.

If you use an ASP-based solution (say, NetInsight, Yahoo! Web Analytics, or XiTi), then both your first-party or third-party cookie data is stored in the data center of your application service provider (vendor).

If you use an in-house solution (such as ClickTracks, Urchin, or Webtrends), then your data is stored in your own data center, regardless of the kind of cookie.

Cookie Deletion Rates

Remember that cookie rejection is not the same as deletion. With rejection, the visitor browser didn't even accept the cookie, which worsens your ability to track. With deletion, you get to collect data for the session (Visit), but you worsen tracking for subsequent visits.

Everyone wants to know cookie deletion rates ("Help! My web analytics data is stinky!"). Bad news: there is no global standard. I have never seen an objective study, that is, a study that was not pushing the vested interests of the publisher. It is also extremely difficult for a third party—an external company or agency—to gain the kind of access required to actual data that would help them develop anything close to an objective standard.

The biggest determining factors for cookie deletion are your customers, their browser settings, and the software on their computer. And those factors can vary greatly from site to site.

My experience of measuring cookie deletion using the company's own analytics data across a number of ecommerce, support, and other corporate sites has helped me come up with a "benchmark" of cookie deletion rates of 3 percent to 5 percent for first-party cookies and 20 percent to 25 percent for third-party cookies. They all tend to fall in that range.

But it is critical to realize that your number will be unique to you. To find your number, you need to put in the sweat, blood, and tears to measure it on your actual site.

The most common methodology for measuring cookie deletion involves extracting your JavaScript-tagged data from the analytics tool and doing exhaustive analysis of visit patterns in that data vs. your website server log files. Each set of data tracks something unique, allowing you to identify Unique Visitors. For example, your server logs have the user_agent_id as well as IP addresses. If you also allow people to log into your site, you can use that piece of key data in this analysis.

If you want to know the exact number of cookie deletions, you can't just take someone's word for it. You need to evaluate your own web analytics data and get your own benchmark.

Without Cookies, Life Continues

If you use cookies, then your key metrics such as Unique Visitors and Visits will be more accurate. Not perfect, just more accurate. You will also get a better understanding of *pan-session* metrics such as Visits to Purchase or New and Returning Visitors or even Conversion Rates.

But if your company executives (the HiPPOs) or, more likely, website customers prefer that you not use cookies, then you don't have to use them. You won't be able to measure some of the previously discussed key performance indicators, but you can still get good value from the cookieless data that you do collect: Top Visited Pages, Revenue, Referring Websites (URLs), Search Engine Keywords, and so on.

Don't let the fact that you don't use cookies get in the way of using web analytics data in meaningful ways. Don't mope around! Use what you have, and you can still find actionable insights.

Data Sampling 411

Our minds usually refuse to accept that taking less data might sometimes be a better option. Hence, we tend to have an almost allergic reaction to hearing, "This is based on sampled data." We rarely accept that a slightly imperfect answer in 15 seconds is better than the perfect answer in 2 days. It is important to keep an open mind on this topic and realize that there are nuances to sampling—some very good and some you should use with care.

Pay special attention to the following two important challenges that drive data sampling:

- Almost all tag-based (and some log-based) paid web analytics tools bill you based on *pay per page view*. So, the more successful you are, the more you pay your analytics vendor (or often pay overages on top of your agreed Page View limits).

- You collect a ton of data and millions of Page Views, and now your simplest reports are slower than a snail on a hot day. Or you run massively complex, segmented queries against long time periods. Same snail outcome.

No web analytics vendor admits that either problem afflicts them. They will never tell you that data sampling might be important.

The standard operating procedure in dealing with these two challenges is to do data sampling, either selectively collecting data or selectively processing data. Although this practice is common, little is understood about its implications. Until now!

There are three primary ways of sampling your data:

- *Code Red*: Sampling web pages on your site

- *Code Orange*: Sampling data collected from each page

- *Code Green*: Sampling data processed when you run the query or report

Let's look at each approach in some detail.

Code Red: Sampling Web Pages on Your Site

Under the Code Red option, you add the JavaScript tag to only some pages on your website, either by choice or on advice from your vendor. Typically you might add the JavaScript tags to a bunch of your busiest pages and forget the rest (or as your CEO would say, "We should at least track our important pages even if we can't afford to track the site!").

This web page sampling is the least palatable of your three options. If you ever want to know anything interesting about your pages, you'll run into a dead end because you simply have no data!

You will not have a complete picture of your website. For example, if you forgot to tag page x and your marketing department sent off a million direct marketing emails pointing to that page, or if page y was indexed by Google and attracts a bunch of traffic, you have no idea.

Code Orange: Sampling Data Collected from Each Page

In the Code Orange scenario, rather than collecting every single Page View on your site, you can specify in the JavaScript tag code something like this: *just collect every 10th Page View.*

You do this to reduce the bill you get from your web analytics vendor. Data will be collected every 10th time the page loads, and that data will be sent to your vendor. This means less data is collected for the vendor to store and process, and when reports run, you get that sampled data.

Now, in the report you will have "lower" numbers than your real numbers, but usually some approximation is applied (say multiply every number by 10) to get the "correct" numbers for you.

This is a suboptimal approach for so many reasons, but it is still better than collecting no data at all. In this case, you have some representative data for all your pages. Even with the multiplier, you get an approximate view of your overall metrics.

For pages that don't get lots of Page Views, such as the pages beyond your top 20 or so pages, it also means that if you segment data, the quality of your reports will deteriorate very quickly. It is also suboptimal to sample Page Views; it is consistently better to sample sessions (Visits).

If you have a choice between Code Red and Code Orange, always choose Code Orange. Though you really want green!

Code Green: Sampling Data Processed When You Run the Query/Report

All data from your website is collected and stored by your vendor. The core challenge you face is getting fast results for your reports and queries, especially those that cover longer time periods or that perform complex queries.

There are two scenarios here. First, your web analytics vendor allows you to select the amount of sampling you want to apply to your data, which is a case of choosing your own *poison*, as shown in Figure 4.49.

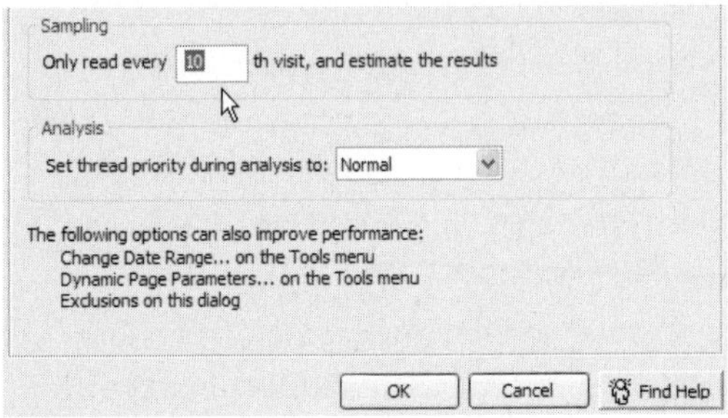

Sampling

Only read every [10] th visit, and estimate the results

Analysis

Set thread priority during analysis to: Normal

The following options can also improve performance:
Change Date Range... on the Tools menu
Dynamic Page Parameters... on the Tools menu
Exclusions on this dialog

OK   Cancel   Find Help

Figure 4.49 User-selectable sampling in ClickTracks

In this case, I tell ClickTracks to count behavior in every 10th Visit to my website (though I have all the data collected) to speed up the processing of the query. I get the answer I want much faster. If the count of Unique Visitors to my site last month was 18 million, then I might choose to sample every 999th session because, in the worst case, it will introduce an error of a few percent in my metric while providing me with the answer 500 times faster than if I crunched the whole thing.

In the second scenario, vendors such as Google Analytics don't have a user-defined sampling setting; rather, the tool will automatically trigger sampling when it detects that sampling will provide you with an answer quickly. Intelligent sampling is applied on the data, and your report might look like Figure 4.50.

At the very top of the report a message indicates that the report is based on sampled data. The table at the bottom shows the confidence intervals in the Visits column, which lets you know the *flex* in the data. For example, the number of Visits for New Visitors, 352,234, could be off by plus or minus 2 percent.

You collect all the data from your website, but rather than waiting hours to get your data back, both ClickTracks and Google Analytics allow you to get a fast answer within acceptable limits.

The ideal scenario is the one that ClickTracks uses, where I as a user can choose to apply the level of sampling on the data. For example, if I query hundreds of thousands of Visits over the past year, I might sample at, say, every 1,000th Visit. But if I query a very small segment of data, say everyone who came to my site on the keyword *avinash rocks*, I might set sampling at every ninth Visit. And if I really want to wait four days for my answer, I can run the raw unsampled query.

Most web analytics vendors are opaque about the kind of sampling they use (or impose on you) when they are trying to sell you their tool. Your job is to ask pointed questions and understand what type of sampling is applied, when, and how much control you have over it.

Figure 4.50 Statistically sampled report in Google Analytics

If your vendor gives you a choice, always choose Code Green over Code Orange and Code Orange over Code Red. But try to avoid Code Red; remember, in that case, you are guessing up front which data you don't need at all—and that's always unwise.

The Value of Historical Data

We have all been brought up to cherish data—to love it, marry it, and stick with it for better or for worse, to build increasingly vast and complex systems to keep it around, and to tap into cloud computing along with a small army of people in your company to keep that data happy.

This reverence sounds like a good mind-set, especially in the traditional world of ERP and CRM systems. But on the Web, this reverence can be a deeply suboptimal mind-set.

You need to divest yourself of the mind-set of keeping web analytics data around forever. If you, or your HiPPOs, have this mind-set, then a quickie divorce might be helpful.

Data Decay

Keep in mind that from the moment you collect your web analytics data, it starts to decay and lose value. Oh, it is useful on the first day and for the first month, but it's less so in six months. And click-level data is nearly worthless in a year.

Surely, you want an explanation! Sure. Let me give you six:

Your Visitors change too much Almost all the data you collect is anonymous, nonpersonal data from your Visitors. These darling Visitors swap browsers and machines and upgrades both from time to time. Thus, the data is less useful in identifying any usage trends and patterns tied to a unique person the further back in time you go.

Yet you make an implicit decision by hording data forever, hoping that you can use the data to make intelligent decisions about someone. Sadly, not gonna happen.

Your computations change too much You shift from logs to tags, and the core analytics data such as Visits, Visitors, or even Total Page Views now uses new and different logic. Even if you shift from Coremetrics to the capable and free Yahoo! Web Analytics, so from one tag-based solution to another tag-based solution, your data is not comparable because each tool uses its own logic to compute basic metrics or KPIs such as Conversion Rates.

Vendors and practitioners change their basic formulas for measuring core stats every so often. They rarely reprocess history (too hard!), making it difficult to provide continuity. As you evolve, comparisons become more like comparing apples and monkeys. There may be a relationship, but it's not one you're interested in knowing.

Your systems change too much At the end of the day, three pieces of information are captured by your analytics tool: the referrer, the page URL, and the cookie.

As you evolve your website CMS platform, say from Interwoven to ATG, or as you move it around or add or remove functionality, such as internal search or behavior targeting, you usually impact all three of those critical pieces of information that make up your data.

Resulting impact can make your data disjointed. And I am not even touching on changes such as moving from static HMTL to dynamic HTML or from personalized content to rich Internet applications (RIAs). All of these changes again impact the three pieces you collect.

Your website changes too much Google's home page has not changed very much in the last 10 years. That is the only exception I can find to the rule. However, your home page from three months ago is not your home page now (is it? I hope not!). You've killed half of your product-line pages last year, opting for product-detail pages for SEO reasons. There was no PayPal last week. Maybe 2009 was your first year with the support and ecommerce sites merged into one.

In the past six months, you have learned more about your business, about your data, about your Visitors, and about where you stand against your competition. Your web presence has changed accordingly. Every change changes the data you have, and it changes the value you can get from data three months from now.

Your people change too much   Sad as it may be, the hardest people to find now are web people—not just great web analysts, which we know are scarce, but web people in general. Front end, back end, thin, plump, newbies, experienced...all kinds are hard to find.

As people come and go, their actions have a subtle but important impact on all aspects of your data ecosystem. Given all these factors, would you still keep terabytes of data from two years ago? Should you invest 18 months building a data warehouse for your web analytics data?

I strongly encourage you to think of the pace of change. The chief reason for why historical data on the Web is not all it's cracked up to be is the decay.

The Goodness of Not Worrying About History

If you don't worry about history, then you are not tied to the past. You can think smart and move fast. If your current data will have less value in the future, then you will cherish the now more and try to get something valuable out of it.

Letting go of history also gives you the freedom to sever ties to legacy systems, legacy tools, or legacy data. You can move forward to better systems, tools, and data much faster than our sisters and brothers in the traditional world.

You can have a lot more fun because you get to learn, adapt, get value, and move on. It is damn exciting and damn liberating!

Saving What Matters

You do want to keep some history around, such as Weekly Trend (counts) of Visits and Unique Visitors, Top 10 Referrers to your website by month, and monthly Bounce Rate. You want to hold on to aggregated data for your critical few metrics, because that won't become less important with time. And keep some revenue stats just to prove that you're worth it!

Keep that data around as long as you have it. It will all fit on one tab in an Excel spreadsheet. That is all you'll need. Your historical data choices might be slightly different than the ones I mentioned, but I assure you it will fit in a spreadsheet.

To summarize, you should keep your click-level, detailed data around for a year (assuming seasonality!) and your session-level aggregated data for as long as you want or must, but it should fit in a spreadsheet.

It is extremely difficult to get anything out of your web analytics that you can take action on right now. I humbly recommend that in the drive to conquer history you don't forget the present. Don't ignore the price that you'll pay every day in the future for every day that has gone by.

History is important in other contexts, but in web analytics tools, for now, change on the Web reduces value from old data. This might cease to be the case at some point, but until that faraway day, you know what to do!

The Usefulness of Video Playback of Customer Experience

Video playback seems to make so much sense on paper: you can watch every Visit to your website like a sitcom. Sit back, and see what that person is doing! Finally, you can make more intelligent decisions.

The reality is that, except for one narrow and expensive case, video playback rarely produced the promised ROI. I especially wanted to cover this particular web analytics phenomenon because it illustrates the challenge of translating paper promises by vendors, or even our own marketers, into actionable insights.

The promise from companies like Tealeaf, ClickTale, RobotReplay, and others is simple: they will record all sessions on your website. You can then watch them at your leisure and figure out what's wrong with your website (or ideally what's great).

The following are a few challenges you face in finding insights.

Scale

If your website gets 100 Visits, then it is easy to do *random dips* into the data (videos), get a sense for things, and even get lucky and run into a problematic session. But, how do you do that if your website gets 100,000 Visits a month? How about 1,000,000?

It is incredibly hard to *get lucky*. Yes, you can still say this: "Let's find all sessions that end in an error and now narrow things down to those 1,800 sessions." But then, how do you watch all those sessions? How many hours are in the day? How many people do you need to watch the sessions to find something of value?

The promise of *individual* tracking is precisely what works against these solutions. It's a challenge of finding the signal in all the noise.

Interpretation

Video playback tools are sold as tools that perform usability. After all, you are watching someone doing something on your website. The problem, however, is not the watching; the problem is you: you and your interpretation of what you are watching.

When you study usability (remote or onsite), you have the context of what the person is trying to do in their own words. You are clear about their frustrations or about why they are failing because they tell you what they are trying to get done.

How do you do that in a *contextless* video? You guess. You impose your own interpretation on the data. Is it a surprise your insights are less than optimal?

If you notice that someone clicked Add to Cart and in the video you see a 404 error page, you don't need to interpret much: that's a problem. But you don't need to watch the videos of sessions to get that data. You could get the same data from Omniture or XiTi in two seconds by looking at the Next Page report from the cart.

"You Can Track Sara, Akio, and Roxana"

One of the most attractive on-paper values of session video playback is that if people call you or write to complain, then you can diagnose their experience. You can see what the problem on the site was.

But, here's the underappreciated problem: how do you find Sara's session on your website? How about Akio's?

Most people on your website will have anonymous sessions, even as they enter secure pages like shopping carts and checkouts because they haven't created an account. If Sara calls you on the phone, will you ask her to go into her browser, look for the cookies set, find the persistent cookie ID, and read off the 64- or 128-encrypted value that might possibly allow you to watch Sara's session and diagnose the issue?

This is not a problem on a bank's website. Visitors are forced to log in. When they call, a representative will ask for an account number or ID to find the problem session. Then the rep can watch the session and try to fix the problem.

Is your site a bank, or do you have a similar customer experience? Can you track "people" as they do? That answer is key.

If you are a small retailer, you can possibly "watch" all the sessions of people who added something to the cart and never purchased. Now you want to send those customers enticements to come back and buy. But then of course you'd need to find their contact information from the video of an anonymous session.

Cost vs. Benefit

A typical in-house hosted video playback service will require you to first buy the software from the company for a starting price of a couple hundred thousand dollars. Then you have to buy hardware in-house to host the software and service at a cost of another couple hundred thousand dollars.

You may go through months of implementation and integration processes with your company's websites and systems. You will have to hire a part-time or full-time person to baby-sit this software and hardware implementation. You'll hire more full-time analysts to make sure reporting works and to analyze some of the data (did you think I would forget that?).

That's what it costs to get going. Now, what must you get out of this to justify the return on investment? How long will it take? Please give very careful consideration to the portfolio of decisions you have to make across your entire web analytics ecosystem (see Multiplicity in Chapter 1) and then prioritize your choice of video playback.

Of course, if you use something like ClickTale, RobotReplay, or others, you can reduce both cost and *time to data* because it is an ASP-based solution, hosted in the cloud rather than in-house in your company. In that case, you worry only about the first three challenges in this section.

Hope for the Future

At the moment, Video Replay's key flaw, other than cost and *time to insights*, is its over-reliance on people to find the signal in the noise and to interpret the data. Likewise, the anonymity of most sessions makes it really hard to find any signal in the noise.

My hope is that this will change in the future, and I have a simple idea of how. Why do I need to watch 200 sessions out of 177,825 to find out that there was a problem? The technology should find logical patterns in the videos and data automatically so that I can watch one *aggregated* session to find interesting customer behavior. ClickTale provides you with one video for all Visits in which a page existed, and the video shows an aggregated view of how far all people scrolled down a page. One video = aggregated data and value. We need a ton more of that from video playback vendors.

Here's another idea. Today in these tools, if any modicum of segmentation or rules-based analysis exists, it then falls on my favorite analyst to use her intelligence and considerable expertise to go through the massive mound of data to find insights. These systems should be intelligent enough to algorithmically mine the data to highlight three things I need to look at or do for my site.

At some point, the video playback solutions will become smart enough to do more than just "puke out data." They will apply technology and match raw computing power to ensure that people have access to key processed starting points. Then we'll start to get somewhere. Until then understand the challenges outlined here and proceed with caution.

The Ultimate Data Reconciliation Checklist

I believe in having one Clickstream web analytics tool and sticking with it, because it is hard enough to understand just one tool well enough to start finding insights and creating a data-driven organization. You throw two or three into the mix, and it becomes akin to Sisyphus pushing a stone up a mountain.

But the sad reality is many people have more than one tool on their website. We often practice bigamy when we should be practicing monogamy. That leads to the bane of every analyst's existence: data reconciliation!

In this section, I'll share a helpful and effective checklist of how to reconcile the data, but more than that, I'll share the nuances and complexities of online measurement. My fondest wish is that you'll appreciate the challenge better and be even more ninjalike in your thinking as you tackle other problems.

Figure 4.51 illustrates the challenge very nicely; you see data for the same time period from three different web analytics tools.

Notice something delightful—the number of Visits reported for the same time period varies across tools: StatCounter: 53,123, ClickTracks: 56,184, and Google Analytics: 45,710. It is a difficult and thankless task to reconcile this data, and rarely is it worth the effort, but when you have to do it, use the following effective checklist.

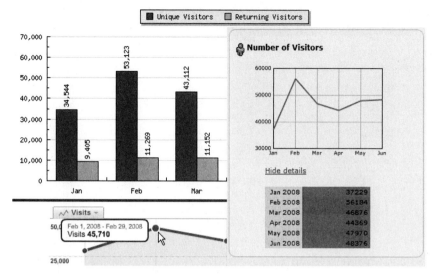

Figure 4.51 Visits measured by StatCounter, Google Analytics, and ClickTracks

#1: Don't Compare Data Collected from Web Logs vs. JavaScript Tags

Comparing web logs to JavaScript tags is like comparing apples and watermelons. It's just not right. These two methods of collecting data are very different, the processing and storage is different, and the things that impact are very different. Often, your numbers might not even come close.

Web logs primarily deal with effective and extensive filtering of robots (if you are not doing this, you are screwed regardless); the definition of a Unique Visitor (are you using cookies, just IP, or IP + user agent IDs?); and, this is increasingly minor, data caching at a browser or server level, which can also mean missing data from logs.

There is also the critical matter of rich-media content: Flash, video, Flex, apps, and so on. Without extensive custom coding, your web logs are clueless about all your rich-media experience. Most tag-based solutions now come with easy-to-implement solutions that will track rich media. So if you have a rich-media site, it will cause a big disparity between numbers you get from logs and numbers you get from tags.

The primary obstacles for JavaScript tags are browsers that have JavaScript turned off. Typically that will be 2–3 percent of browsers. In that case, the data will be missing from tag-based files but will exist in your log files. Be careful when comparing these two sources.

#2: The Gift That Keeps Giving: First- and Third-Party Cookies

I have covered cookie types a few times already, but the issue bears repeating. Using first-party or third-party cookies can have a huge impact on your key metrics such as Unique Visitors, Returning Visits, and so on.

Typically, if you use third party, then your numbers will be higher (and of course wrong), compared to numbers from your first-party cookie-based tool.

Cookie *flushing* (clearing cookies upon closing browser or by your friendly antispyware tool) affects both cookie types in the same way. Cookie rejection is more complex. Many new browsers don't even accept third-party cookies, which will impact your metrics.

Check your type of cookies; it will explain lots of your data differences.

#3: Imprecise Website Tagging

Other than cookies, imprecise tagging is the next most common source of data issues, and it shows up when you compare multiple JavaScript-based analytics tools.

The problem manifests itself in two ways:

- Incorrectly implemented tags
- Incompletely implemented tags

The standard JavaScript tags are pretty easy to implement. Just copy and paste, and happy birthday! But then you can add or adjust them to do more, which is why they can take eight months to implement. You can pass *sprops* and *evars* and *user_ defined_values* and *variables* and *bacteria* (OK, kidding on that one).

You should make sure your Webtrends, NetInsight, or other tool is implemented correctly. That is, make sure it is passing data back to the vendor as you expect.

To check that I have implemented tags right and that the *sprops* are not passing *evars* and that *user_defined_values* are not sleeping with the *vars*, I use tools such as IEWatch Professional, Firebug, Web Developer Toolkit, and Web Bug.

Now, incompletely implemented tags are a simpler matter. Your IT department (or brother) implemented Omniture tags on some pages and Google Analytics on most pages. See the problem? Unfortunately, this problem is astonishingly common. Make sure you implement all tools on all the same pages, if not all pages on the site. To check that my tags are completely implemented, I use tools such as REL Software's Web Link Validator and WASP.

If you want faster reconciliation between your tools, make sure you have implemented all your analytics tools correctly and completely.

#4: Torture Your Vendor: Check Definitions of Key Metrics

In Figure 4.51 the numbers are different, of course, but you'll notice that each vendor has given its own sweet name to the metric: Visits, Visitors, and Unique Visitors. How exasperating!

As an industry, web analytics has grown organically. Each vendor has either created its own metrics or taken standard metrics and, just to mess with us, decided to call them something else. This naming inconsistency makes reconciliation harder.

In the following list, honest to God, are three definitions of Conversion Rate I have gotten from web analytics vendors:

Conversion: Order/Unique Visitors

Conversion: Orders/Visits

Conversion: Items Ordered/Clicks

What? Items Ordered/Clicks? Kill me now!

So, before you tar and feather a particular web analytics tool, take some time to ask your vendors what the precise definition is of the metric you are comparing. Often that can help explain the difference.

With some vendors, getting a definition can be hard. Vendors are secretive, protective, or even embarrassed. You might have to badger them. Do it.

#5: A Tough Nut: Sessionization

Sessionization is the process of taking a series of hits or requests to your website and identifying a Visit by the same browser. The problem is that different vendors do this in different ways.

Here is an example: I go directly to www.recovery.gov and see some pages, then I go to Google and do a search, and finally I return to www.recovery.gov. This all happens in a period of a few minutes.

In some analytics tools, this whole process will be considered one visit because it happened in less than 29 minutes. But other tools will see it as two visits because I went to a search engine and came back to the site. Some vendors will time out sessions after 29 minutes of inactivity, and others will do that after 15 minutes. Arrrgh! See how session inconsistency makes reconciliation harder?

Another common issue arises when some tools set the "max session timeout" with a hard limit of 30 minutes while others set the limit at 12 hours or not at all. So, if you have long visits to your site, you may see one total visit or one visit broken up as ten.

Probe this important process because it affects the most foundational of all metrics, Visits.

#6: The Permanent Tripwire: URL Parameter Configuration

Life was so sweet when all sites were static. URLs were simple:

    www.bestbuy.com/video/hot_hot_hottie_hot.html

Any web analytics tool could easily understand visits to that page and hence count Page Views. But then the Web became dynamic, and URLs now look like this:

    www.bestbuy.com/site/olspage.jsp?id=abcat0800000&type=category

That's the page on Best Buy for the Phone category, and here's a page for a particular phone:

    www.bestbuy.com/site//olspage.jsp?id=1205537515180&skuId=8793861&type=product

See the additional parameters? See everything after the question mark? As a final example, the following is the URL when I am on the page of the same phone but I have clicked a tab to read more details about the phone:

www.bestbuy.com/site/olspage.jsp?skuId=8793861&productCategoryId=abcat080200
1&type=product&tab=7&id=12055375151

The problem is that while web analytics tools have gotten better and can probably understand that first page (phone category page), the next two pages are not as straightforward. These pages contain *tracking parameters* or *system parameters*. Junk. So, now you must sit down with your beloved IT folks and spend time documenting all the junk in the URL, in other words, the skuId, productCategoryId, type, tab, and id.

Some of these parameters make a web page unique, such as skuId, productCategoryId, and tab. That is, their presence and values contained mean it's a unique page. So, skuId=8793861 represents one phone, and skuId=8824739 is another.

But there will be some parameters that don't mean anything. For example, it does not matter if type=product is in the URL or not. Some of these different pieces of information are worth ignoring, and others you ignore at your own peril.

Your web analytics tool has a hard time taking all these pieces and counting the Page Views correctly. Each analytics tools has its own way of identifying and updating the settings for recognizing unique Page Views and ignoring the junk. If you want the data to reconcile, you'll have to make sure you do the same configuration in all tools.

If you are tracking rich media experiences using Event Tracking (as we covered earlier in this chapter) in one tool and generating "fake page views" in the other because it does not support Event Tracking, then your numbers will never match up.

#7: The Problem of the Big: Campaign Parameter Configuration

If you run lots of campaigns (email, affiliates, paid search, display, mobile, and so on), then you absolutely must tag your campaigns correctly and then configure your web analytics tools correctly. You do this to ensure your campaigns are reported correctly, your referrers are reported correctly, and your revenue and conversions are attributed correctly. This challenge typically afflicts larger companies.

Here is a simple example. If you search for Omniture in Yahoo!, you end up here:

www.omniture.com/static/278?s_scid=680217600000000309&clicksource=standard&
OVRAW=omniture&OVKEY=omniture&OVMTC=standard&OVADID=4822371011&OVKWID=
130976483511

If you search for Omniture on Google, you end up here:

www.omniture.com/static/278?s_kwcid=omniture|2109240905&s_scid=
omniture|2109240905

You'll note that Omniture has done a great job of tagging their campaigns. Let's say Omniture uses Webtrends and Google Analytics for web analytics. So, the analyst at Omniture must *configure* both tools with all the campaign parameters, the hierar-chies, and whatnot. That will ensure that when the analyst clicks the Paid Search tab in the tool, these campaigns will be reported correctly.

You'll have to repeat this for your affiliate, email, display ads, and all other campaigns you have. If you use two tools, you'll have to do it twice. And each tool might not accept this data in the same way. For Webtrends, you might have to place it in the URL stem; in Coremetrics, you might have to put it in the cookies; in Google Analytics, it might have to be a customized JavaScript tag.

Suffice it to say that setting up all these parameters is not a walk in the park.

#8: The Hidden Angel: Data Sampling

I covered data sampling earlier in this chapter. You can sample at the source (not col-lect data at all), or you can sample at *run time* (collect all data but sample sessions/ Visits). You want to ensure that you are applying the same kind of data sampling in all your web analytics tools.

The tragedy is that you rarely get a choice because the sampling is often hard-wired into analytics tools. In that case, you'll have to just accept that all, none, or some of your data will never reconcile.

But you should investigate and make sure the vendors are transparent with you. Once you have the information from the vendor, make sure you adjust your data recon-ciliation expectations accordingly.

#9: Order of Tags

The order of your tags, being the last item in the checklist, is not the hugest of deals. But on heavily trafficked websites, or ones that are just heavy, tag order can also affect the differences in the data.

As your web page loads, the tags are the last thing to load. This is actually a very good thing; you should always have your tags just before the [/body] tags. If you have more than one tag, then they are executed in the order they are implemented.

Sometimes on fat pages some tags might not get executed. This happens because the user has already clicked onward. Or it happens because you have custom-hacked the bejesus out of the tag, and it is now an obese tag and does not let the other, lean tags load in the time available.

If you want that least amount of extra checking, switch the order of your tags and see whether it helps. Tag order might explain the last percent of difference you are dying to get.

See what I mean when I say stick to monogamy?

Do data reconciliation when you have to, and now you know how. But my over-all recommendation is to accept that data will be off. If two tools are within 10 percent of each other, then just move on to doing the analysis.

The Key to Glory: Measuring Success

We analysts often don't get the love, respect, and funding we deserve because we do not adequately measure one golden concept: Outcomes. Because we have plenty of data, we jump into reporting Visits and Time and Returns. But only we care about those metrics. Our bosses, however, care about something far simpler: what has the Web done for me today?

This chapter will cover the art and science of measuring Outcomes from websites. It will cover the obvious (Conversions, yeah!), and it will cover life beyond ecommerce Conversion Rates. It'll stretch your thinking to consider other measures of success, such as how to compute the holistic economic value your website creates for your business.

5

Chapter Contents

Focus on the "Critical Few"
Five Examples of Actionable Outcome KPIs
Moving Beyond Conversion Rates
Measuring Macro and Micro Conversions
Quantifying Economic Value
Measuring Success for a Non-ecommerce Site
Measuring B2B Websites

Let me start with a personal story to illustrate the importance of focusing on Outcomes. I feel incredibly blessed that I have a full-time job as well as a start-up (Market Motive, Inc.) and many speaking engagements around the world. The impact of all those activities is that I have time to blog only well past midnight on any given day.

So, I go to my wife and say, "Honey, I'll be writing for the next couple hours." My loving wife, who is very concerned about my health, says, "Go to bed; you need the rest." I want my boss (wife) to commit the resources needed (me). So, I try to share how important this work is and say, "You do realize I am kind of a big deal?"

She says, "Go to bed."

How many times have you had a similar conversation with your boss or someone in senior management? Our first tactic when we want more of something, such as resources, analysts, or systems, is to stress how important a project is. It never works. Now back to the story.

I am not ready to give up yet. I go back to my wife with data. After all, data trumps everything, right? I say, "Did you know that in the past 30 days there were 79,631 Visitors who came to the blog from 176 countries? That includes Sudan, Mongolia, Panama, and Togo!"

Her reply: "That's great; go to bed."

I see you are smiling. You have tried this with your boss as well. To prove that you need support, you send them Omniture reports about Visitors and Page Views Per Visitors and Growth. No impact, right? The reason is simple. These numbers might mean something to you, but they mean little to an executive. Visitors is still a very *fuzzy* concept, and your boss cannot truly relate to it from a deep, heart-and-head perspective. So, much to our surprise, our gobs of reports and pretty PowerPoint presentations fail to impress.

I need to convince my boss but do it in ways that she can find impactful and valuable. So, I put on my thinking cap: why do I blog? What value does my *business* get from the blog? OK, so I have no advertising or consulting hours that people can buy and really no ecommerce of any sort. But I still have goals for my blog. I identify four goals: *faster customer task completion*, *expanding awareness* about me, getting *more speaking engagements*, and gaining *more RSS subscribers*. I implement those into my web analytics tool along with, and this is absolutely key, Goal Values (monetization impact). Figure 5.1 shows the result of that work.

I return to my boss and say, "You need to let me blog because in the past 30 days the blog created a total economic value of $26,210."

Pause. Then the response: "Work harder."

See the shift? By identifying the Outcomes generated by the website, I gave my boss something relatable, something that impacted the bottom line, something she could use to make her decision. That's the power of measuring Outcomes and communicating them to our decision makers. It changes the conversation from "Go away" to "How can I help you be more successful?"

Figure 5.1 Goals, Goal Values, and Economic Value

Computing economic value is a very powerful way of doing this; I'll cover the methodology in a bit more detail later in this chapter.

P.S. Now, to be completely fair (and ensure I don't get reprimanded), I must share that what my wife actually said is, "Go to bed now, but tomorrow you should figure out which of your five jobs you should stop doing so that you can keep your health and still create more economic value from the blog." She is the nicest wife in the world, and I am lucky to have her.

Focus on the "Critical Few"

Every successful web metrics story starts with a very simple question: "Why do you exist?"

OK, not *you*. This question is asking why your business (or nonprofit organization) exists. In a world where we are blessed with more data than God herself wanted us to have, it is often easy to skip past that question and just jump into reporting metrics. After all, metrics are so easy to find.

During my time at Intuit, I learned an important principle that is sourced from the world of Six Sigma/Process Excellence: *focus on the critical few, not the insignificant many.*

The principle of critical few encourages *focus* and, more importantly, a focus on the handful of things that matter. The process starts with asking yourself a series of questions so you can identify the most important factors for your business:

- From a strategic perspective, what is the most important thing that your website is solving for?

- If one metric could identify that your business is going up in flames or not, which one would it be?

- Which metrics will tell you that the three business priorities you are executing against are having an impact?

- Have you separated the *nice to know* from the *have to know*?

- If you had $100 to divide amongst all your web activities, how would the distribution of money look? Who gets the most investment?

- What is the biggest threat to your existence, and how do you know whether it is already harming you?

These existential questions will start the conversation with the senior decision makers in your company. At the end of this questioning process, you'll have identified two or three metrics that are head and shoulders above all others in their importance. These two or three metrics are your *critical few* metrics. Almost always, they will be dominated by Outcome metrics, as they should be. To know why you exist, you must understand what you are solving for, and hence you'll end up with Outcomes. If you don't end up with specific Outcomes, then you need to stress test whether you have answered the questions correctly.

Critical few metrics are so important because they give the entire organization a sense of focus and direction. They kill confusion. They help ensure that everyone knows where the company is going, with a clear line of sight from what they are measuring to what's important for the company.

You shouldn't have more than three or four critical few metrics. If you have more than four, then you have not done your job well enough. Go back and try again.

To inspire you, I'll share the example I got from Daniel Cotlar, the CMO of Blinds.com. Daniel and I were presenting at the same conference. In his talk he shared that what matters to Blinds.com the most was Gross Margin per Visitor (see Figure 5.2).

I had to admit that this shocked me. Until that point, I had not met any company that managed to distill the critical few down to one metric.

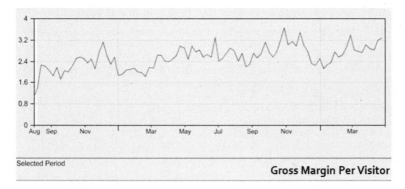

Figure 5.2 Critical few: Gross Margin per Visitor metric

The benefit to Blinds.com was quite simple: everyone in the company was crystal clear on what they were solving for. That is, when decisions were made about marketing, acquisition, people, systems, or products, each person answered one simple question: "How does this improve our Gross Margin per Visitor?"

That kind of focus is astonishingly powerful and productive. You'll notice in the graph that over the course of about two years the metric nicely moves up.

Of course, Blinds.com used other metrics, such as Repeat/Referral Rate, % of Sales Completed via Self Service, % Sales Private Label, Flee Rate, and Sample to Order Conversion Rate. Each of these metrics had a direct *line of sight* to the one metric they were solving for. If a metric did not have a direct line of sight, then it had to go.

For your business, you may not end up with one powerful metric. Try. But if you fail, know that you can't have 20. You can't even have seven. If you want focused business and execution, then you need to bring your metrics down to a handful—four or fewer is optimal.

Five Examples of Actionable Outcome KPIs

To solidify the concept of Outcomes, in this section you will look beyond the obvious things that come to mind when you think of Outcomes. I hope to inspire you to truly come up with key performance indicators (KPIs) of value for your business.

Task Completion Rate

Task Completion Rate is the percentage of Visitors to your website who rate if they were able to complete the primary purpose for their visit. We focus on ecommerce and Clickstream metrics far too often. As I covered in Chapter 1, most Visitors won't convert online, and even if you have an ecommerce website, they might not be there to buy. Instead of guessing, based on Clickstream data, whether visitors completed their intended tasks, you can use on-exit surveys. These surveys let your Visitors give you a qualitative perspective on whether they were able to complete their tasks.

Getting this qualitative perspective takes the focus away from why *you* built the website or what *you* want people do there. It shines a light on what people can get done and what they cannot.

The survey data helps you actively involve your customers in helping set priorities for where to focus your website improvement efforts.

Share of Search

Share of Search is the percentage of traffic you get from search engines compared to your key competitors.

You are doing search engine optimization, and you have invested in paid searches. You may be happy with your slow but steady improvements with traffic from search engines or from specific keywords. But what about your competitors? How are they doing, and how are you doing in comparison?

Tools such as Hitwise, Compete, and Google Insights for Search help you compute this fantastic Outcome metric. You'll note that although you have been improving at 5 percent per month, your competitors are improving at 25 percent per month. Or while you have made a dent for your brand keywords, you have lost a lot of ground in your generic or category keywords.

The Outcome here is not revenue at the other end. The Outcome is that your search acquisition strategy is yielding the kinds of benefits it should be. If not, then you can easily identify what you need to fix.

Visitor Loyalty and Recency

Visitor Loyalty measures the distribution of the number of Visits by each Visitor to your site; that is, it answers this question: "How many times did Avinash come to my website?" Recency measures the gap between two Visits by the same Visitor. In other words, it answers this question: "Avinash visited my site yesterday, but when was the last time he visited before that?"

I adore these twin metrics both because they measure Visitor behavior and because they measure the longer-term impact of your web strategy. They indicate whether your desired Outcome of building a long-term relationship with a person is working. Getting someone to visit your website once and read an article or buy something is fairly tough. But creating a value proposition on your website that makes someone come back again and again is where all the real work is.

Visitor Loyalty and Recency are fantastic Outcomes to study because they help you measure where the value of your website resides.

RSS/Feed Subscribers

RSS/Feed Subscribers measures the raw number of people who have signed up for your website or blog's RSS feed.

RSS (which stands for "really simple syndication") started getting popular with blogs, but it is now ubiquitous. I can *grab* the feed from CNN and get just the types of stories I want or *grab* the feed from my wireless router manufacturer's website and know when the latest software patch has been released so I can keep my gear current.

Measuring Feed Subscribers is key because the content from your site is being consumed *off-site*, in feed readers that might be web-based or software-based. This activity is usually invisible to your web analytics tool.

Feed Subscribers is a fantastic Outcome metric because you are measuring the behavior of your most committed valuable audience—the ones who pull your content from you rather than you figuring out how to find them and push it to them!

% of Valuable Exits

The % of Valuable Exits metric measures the percentage of people who leave your website by clicking something of value to you.

It might seem odd to have website exits as an Outcome metric. But consider a Yellow Pages website or a content website supported by display banner ads or even a blog that counts on revenue from AdSense for its income. In each case, the act of the Visitor leaving the website by clicking the business listing (with a referral code!) or the AdSense listing is the desirable outcome.

So, there are *bad exits*, which are people who simply bounce off your site, and there are *good exits*, which are people who leave your site by clicking options you provide them. Understand these two types, and track the good types as your actionable Outcome.

Most web analytics tools come with built-in features to do *outbound link tracking.* If your tool does not offer this feature, it is pretty easy to implement it on your own; it is simply a matter of adding an `onclick` event that will be captured by your web analytics tool. Once you have collected the visits that ended with a valuable outbound click, you can segment those visits. This will allow you to analyze where the traffic came from, what content interested them, and what they searched for on your site. All that behavior will help you understand your traffic better and optimize your site and campaigns.

In summary, keep an open mind about what kinds of Outcomes you can measure because your choices will guide the kinds of analysis your team does and the value of the insights they will provide. I hope these five examples inspire you to *think differently.*

Moving Beyond Conversion Rates

In Chapter 3, you learned not just the definition of Conversion Rate but also the nuances of choosing the right denominator: Visits or Visitors. My recommendation is Visitors.

Although you can have Conversions on a non-ecommerce website, in this section I'll focus on metrics that take you beyond the limited confines of Conversion Rate to identify opportunities to improve your bottom line.

Cart and Checkout Abandonment

Before someone converts on your site, you must get them through the checkout process. Even before checkout, though, you need to convince them to add your product to the shopping cart.

I stress measuring Abandonment Rate, because it is truly that: it shows the people who commit to buying a product on your site and then bail. Your job is to figure out where abandonment happens and why. The beauty of focusing on this metric is that you improve revenue not by spending more money on advertising or marketing but by fixing a few small elements on your site.

Many web analytics tools measure overall abandonment during the purchase process, that is, how many Visitors added something to their cart minus those who completed the checkout process. The calculation is mathematically accurate, but in my experience it complicates the analysis and focus of improvements.

You should instead measure two different rates:

Cart Abandonment (percentage) This is 1 minus (the total Visitors who start checkout divided by the total number of add to cart clicks).

Checkout Abandonment (percentage) This is 1 minus (the total Visitors who complete checkout divided by the total number of people who start checkout).

By measuring these rates separately, you can more efficiently isolate your focus.

Start with understanding Checkout Abandonment. The checkout process on most websites is just two to three pages, and sometimes fewer. Measuring Checkout Abandonment helps you understand how many people bail on those two or three pages, and with so few pages, you can very quickly figure out what needs to be fixed. Perhaps the pages are too long, maybe you have too many steps in the funnel, or perhaps the buttons are not clearly visible.

Cart Abandonment helps you understand the effectiveness of your merchandizing efforts on the site. Here people made an initial commitment to buy from you by adding something to the cart and then chose to bail. Although it is a matter of one click (Start Checkout), there could be any number of reasons why people don't actually start. You can focus on Visitor behavior immediately before the cart: what pages were seen, what campaigns drove the Visitors, what products they added to their cart, and so on. Cart Abandonment is a much bigger problem to understand and solve; each element is better done separately.

Any improvement in either of these two Abandonment Rate metrics is money directly into your pocket.

Days and Visits to Purchase

On the Web, many businesses believe that every Visit is an opportunity to convert. The reality is that just like few people will propose marriage on the first date, most people wait until they've had a few more dates. Visitors to your site might not buy on the very first visit, and that is perfectly OK.

Days to Purchase shows the distribution of the number of days it takes someone to make a purchase on your website. Visits to Purchase shows the number of Visits until purchase. Each metric helps you understand the stretch of time it takes someone to make a purchase on your site. Based on what the data reveals, you would change your marketing, messaging, and calls to action.

For example, if it takes multiple days to make a purchase, then you need to focus on giving more information to your Visitors, helping them research and make their purchase decision at their own pace. If you simply push them to purchase, nothing good will come of it. On the other hand, if the time period is short, then the purchase is more spontaneous, and you might play with pricing strategies or other such conveniences.

The intersection of these two reports can produce actionable insights. If a Visitor takes five Visits to Purchase over one day, you have a different understanding of your Visitor's consideration process than if they take five Visits over seven days.

Average Order Value

Can you improve your Conversion Rate yet reduce your revenue? Of course. When you get 200 Orders from 10,000 Unique Visitors, you get a 2 percent Conversion Rate. But if you reduce the amount of traffic to 100 Unique Visitors and get 20 Orders, you get a 20 percent conversion rate. That's a vast improvement, but the revenue from 20 orders is typically less than from 200 orders.

So, you need a perfect foil for Conversion Rate to ensure the right types of checks and balances are in place. Revenue is a very good foil, as I used in the earlier scenario. But I prefer using Average Order Value as a better starting point for deeper analysis to identify insights.

Average Order Value is a simple metric. It's the total amount of revenue divided by the total number of orders received. Figure 5.3 shows an example of the kinds of correlational analysis you can perform.

For the same time periods, I can see ups and downs in Conversion Rate, as well as in Average Order Value. An interesting quantity that jumps out of this comparison is the inverse relationship between Conversion Rate and Average Order Value. The biggest orders seem to be placed when Conversion Rate is actually lowest!

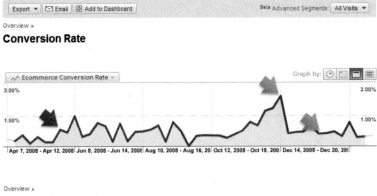

Conversion Rate

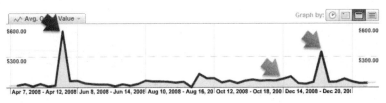

Average Order Value

$71.21 Avg. Order Value

Figure 5.3 Comparing trends in Conversion Rate and Average Order Value

Correlations don't imply causality. For that you need to collect more data and investigate. In this scenario, a deep dive into the acquisition sources (where converting people came from) and the campaign identified that this company did such poor marketing that each time they spent money to acquire traffic, they performed terribly. Hence, the traffic that did convert did not spend a lot of money. When the marketers got out of the way, the Average Order Value—and overall revenue—actually improved substantially.

As you can imagine, this kind of analysis helped the company do a major rethink of their marketing and sales.

Primary Purpose (Identify the Convertible)

One of the biggest hurdles in making optimal decisions for an ecommerce website is a poor understanding of what the opportunity is. Say 100 Visitors come to a site and 2 convert. That gives you a 2 percent Conversion Rate. You dutifully report that rate to your management team. They are initially sad but then seize upon the number of 98 nonconverting Visitors. You get your marching orders: "We have a massive opportunity. We converted only two Visitors. How hard is it to convert 10 more of the other 98? Go get it done!"

What your decision makers don't understand, and what you have not educated them on, is that the other 98 are not all there to buy, and some will never buy. The size of your opportunity is a lot less than 98. Your job is to capture and understand why the 100 people visited your website and then to calculate the size of your *opportunity pie* (the number of Visitors who are even remotely convertible).

You can do this by analyzing the content Visitors consume on your website. For example, 20 percent of the Visitors went only to Jobs, 20 percent downloaded your press releases, and the last 60 percent went to your product pages. There you go: a primitive realization that your opportunity pie is not 98; it's 60.

You can also gain this realization by using an on-exit survey for your website, where you ask people their primary purpose. You can ask the simplest of questions: "Why are you here?" The responses to the survey will allow you to create a graph like the one shown in Figure 5.4.

Primary Purpose of Website Visitors

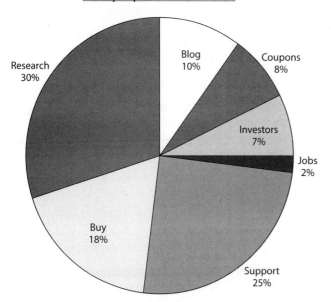

Figure 5.4 Reasons Visitors come to your website

With the survey, you get a much more robust understanding of the intent of your Visitors. You can see that people who come to learn about investing in your company (7%) did not come to buy. Ditto for those who come for tech support or to apply for jobs.

Clearly, the 18 percent who indicated their primary purpose was "Buy" are included in your opportunity pie. You can also throw in the 30 percent who were just there for research (they wanted to buy offline or just learn more, but maybe you can *convince* them to buy). So, your real solid opportunity is only with 48 percent of Visitors.

This information helps your management better understand the size of the opportunity and realize you are actually converting more than 2 percent!

Each company's opportunity pie will be different, based on different rules. It is very important that you identify your opportunities, educate your management, and then work with the marketers to adapt your execution strategy.

Measuring Macro and Micro Conversions

Macro Conversions and Micro Conversions are really simple, are really cool, and will change how you think about measuring success.

In the preceding section, you got a tiny hint of the importance I place on understanding all the reasons why people come to websites. There is no website on the planet that exists for just one reason. Therefore, we are not doing our best analysis by focusing on just the overall website Conversion Rate because that doesn't help us understand the complete picture.

Regardless of why your website exists, there are diverse reasons why people come to your website. Sure, you built a website to do ecommerce, but guess what? People come there to read specifications so they can buy the product on Amazon.com. Or they come to download the latest software patches. Or to apply for jobs. Or to research for products and services they will buy offline.

With all the passion in my heart, I make this recommendation: *focus on measuring your Macro (overall) Conversions, but for optimal awesomeness, identify and measure your Micro Conversions as well.*

Oh, by the way, when I say Conversion here, I don't just mean ecommerce conversion! Later in this section, we will look at Conversions for several non-ecommerce websites.

You want to know how to go about this? Sure. Figure 5.5 shows what we typically do and the question rarely asked.

Figure 5.5 Typical obsession of an analyst or marketer

You measure Conversion (orders, leads submitted, downloads, donations, widget grabs, and so on), but you ignore 98 percent of the site traffic that will never convert, because they visit for the other reasons we discussed earlier. So, should we ignore them? No!

Your website is still doing those other *jobs*. It helps people get support. It helps them research products. It helps people apply for jobs, print directions to your retail stores, get investor information, and do so much more! Why not measure the success of your website at doing those *jobs* to understand the complete impact of your site?

The one primary goal of your site is the Macro Conversion. But, all the other *jobs* your site does are Micro Conversions (see Figure 5.6.)

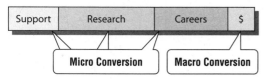

Figure 5.6 Macro and Micro Conversions on a typical ecommerce site

Hurray!

You have just provided your management team with a complete picture of your website's success. And you have shown that you are brilliant because you are measuring the success of all Visitors on your website. Priceless.

Awesome Benefits of Measuring Micro Conversions

As you learn more about measuring different conversions, consider the value you gain from measuring Micro Conversions:

- You'll focus on more than just the main reason the site was created.

- You'll measure multichannel impact well beyond your website. Most people don't get budgets for web analytics because all they focus on is measuring what happens during a small percentage of visits. Expand and conquer.

- You'll be forced to understand the multiple personas on your website. Trust me, that in and of itself is worth a million bucks. It will encourage you to segment Visitors, their behavior, and Outcomes. You'll realize the limits of a pure Clickstream strategy, and you'll be forced to expand beyond just Google Analytics, Omniture, or Coremetrics and execute a true Multiplicity strategy. That is good for your company, and it is good for your career.

- You'll be happy. Most people who do web analytics are sad and frustrated because they are hyperfocused on a small area with way more data than they could ever churn through. By expanding your measurement horizon and seeking insights from a broader area, you'll know what to do with all this data. That means you'll smile a lot more, because you'll feel a sense of accomplishment from your job. Happiness is good.

Examples of Macro and Micro Conversions

Some concrete examples of different websites and the Macro and Micro Conversions they might track should spark your creativity about your own site's measures.

Photo-Publishing and Sharing Website

My friend Fernando Ortega runs the Spanish photo website Fotonatura (www.foto-natura.org). For obvious reasons, his Macro Conversion is Visitors to his site uploading their own pictures to the website, which is Goal 2 in Figure 5.7.

Visitors completed 7,514 goal conversions
482 conversions, Goal 1: Registro
6,156 conversions, Goal 2: Publicacion de fotos
4 conversions, Goal 3: Contratacion Premium
872 conversions, Goal 4: Alta anuncio

Figure 5.7 Macro and Micro Conversions for a photo-sharing site

He now knows that there were 6,156 Conversions, and he can drill deeper to learn that he got a 1.58 percent Macro Conversion rate. But he has also identified three Micro Conversions:

- Goal 1: Visitor registration on the website
- Goal 3: People who sign up for premium content
- Goal 4: People who sign up for newsletters or announcements (great for future leads and driving brand value)

He measures these goals individually, as shown Figure 5.7. But this holistic measurement of success also helps him understand that his overall *Conversion* is much higher than he had anticipated. He also has a good idea of which *jobs* the website should be doing better than it currently is.

Technical Support Website

The main job of a tech support website is to solve someone's problem. So, its Macro Conversion is the Task Completion Rate. But a typical tech support site also does other jobs. Here are my suggestions for Micro Conversions:

- Call Avoidance: This is the amount of Visitors who see the phone number page (hypothesis: if the site is good, this amount goes down over time).
- Content Consumption: This is the number of Visits over time to each technical support core area (for example, different products or types of problems).
- Tickets Opened: This is the number of technical support tickets opened on the website (and over time compared to those opened over the phone).

- Sales: This is the Revenue from referrals from the tech support site to the ecommerce site (sometimes the best solution to fix a problem is to buy the latest version of the product or an upgrade).

- Net Promoters (or Likelihood to Recommend): This is the percentage of people (or an indexed representation) who will recommend the company products after an experience on the tech support site.

You'll note my stress is on understanding the overall purpose, which is getting people answers to their questions hyperfast, and also the other small but important things that the site might be impacting, such as improving your brand impression (and getting a higher Net Promoter score).

Multipurpose Ecommerce Website

By its nature, the Macro Conversion metric on an ecommerce website is to convert visitors to paying customers. But beyond taking the orders, the website is doing a number of other *jobs*, so it is important to identify Micro Conversions even when the focus is overwhelmingly on making money.

Figure 5.8 is absolutely self-explanatory; I wanted to share it because it does a beautiful job of identifying all the outcomes.

Visitors completed 8,626 goal conversions
98 conversions, Goal 1: Completed Order
3 conversions, Goal 2: Create Account
8,417 conversions, Goal 3: View Software Downloads
108 conversions, Goal 4: Contact Us

Figure 5.8 Macro and Micro Conversions for a multipurpose website

The primary focus for this site is Completed Orders. Then the site wants to get visitors to create accounts, wants them to download trial or full versions of the software, and wants to make it easy for Visitors to contact the company.

I hope these examples help you paint your very own unique picture. If you haven't focused on Outcomes until now, then measuring any Outcome is great progress. But you win the eternal love of your management team by measuring the complete success of your website. The other upside, of course, is that you can better value your website and deliver better customer experiences.

Quantifying Economic Value

I'll bring two different threads together now. At the start of the chapter, I shared my story of trying to convince my boss (my beautiful wife) to allow me to blog. I convinced her by sharing how the value of my blogging effort affected the bottom line.

You've just learned how to identify all the different jobs your website does and to model them into Macro and Micro Conversions. The real awesomeness is in not simply identifying the value of the Macro Conversions (which is usually quite easy) but in identifying the value of all the Conversions, Micro and Macro.

Say you are running an ecommerce website. It is a no-brainer to identify the value of the Macro Conversion metric. That's your revenue number. The value of individual Micro Conversions is not impossible to identify, just a little harder. You have to be creative and stretch the boundaries of your current thought process.

The term *economic value* has various definitions. In this context, it is the *imputed value* of an action taken by someone on your website. The question you must answer is, "As a result of this action by a Visitor, was any value created for my business?"

Here's an example. Two of the goals for my blog are to increase the number of Feed Subscribers and clicks on the Speaking Engagements page. Getting people signed up for my RSS feed is the purest form of permission marketing (as espoused by Seth Godin, author of *Permission Marketing: Turning Strangers into Friends and Friends into Customers*); my readers will pull content from me, and that becomes my marketing channel. My speaking engagements are all paid engagements, so sending the highly qualified Visitors of my blog to the conference site helps the conference get more attendees.

The way I compute economic value is to figure out the value of a highly qualified list of people. It turns out a recent qualified mailing list cost $4 per email address. I can take that as a proxy for each of the 23,000 Feed Subscribers I have. Last month I added 470 new subscribers. Value? 470 × 4 = $1,880. Now, I am not going to sell those email addresses or names of people who sign up for my RSS feed, of course, but that does not mean I can't compute the value of that asset.

Computing the value of the clicks on the Speaking Engagements page is easier. All the links on the page are tagged with a tracking code. After the conference ends, I'll ask the organizer how many people signed up for the conference from my blog's tracking code. Then I can compute the value of each click by computing the price of the conference divided by the number of clicks. A recent conference cost $1,900. I had sent 30 clicks to the site. Value? 1,900 / 30 = $63. I can follow that same process for the rest of the conferences, and to compute the value of each click on that page, I can, as an example, take the average of that value. Final economic value created? I received 338 clicks on that page, my average value was $25, so the total was 338 × 25 = $8,450. That money is not coming directly to me, but the conference organizer is paying me a fee to come speak, so it does come to me indirectly.

Now let's look at some other, perhaps tougher, examples of computing economic value.

If you are Burger King and accept applications for franchisees on your website, it's easy to compute that economic value. Simply ask your finance department what the

Conversion Rate is for offline franchisee applications and what the lifetime value is of a franchisee. Apply that information on your site.

Notice something very important: in the beginning, I am not asking you to figure out how to compute the value on your own; you can get help from your offline team. After that, you should ensure you are tracking offline conversions in your CRM system for the applications received online. That will help you compute real economic value from the online applications.

If you are Mazda and want to know the value of your site, why not track brochure downloads? Go to your finance department and ask for the metrics used to compute the ROI from sending the same brochures through physical mail. The finance people have that number, because they use it to send the mailers. Use that number for your online downloads. If you need to take a conservative approach, take the offline value number and divide it by 2, and then use the result for your online downloads (even though I might add that the physical mailers were sent to everyone, like spam, and online they were downloaded by people who wanted them!). Using the smaller number gets people to move beyond arguing about the number

If you are Intuit and you accept job applications online, then figure out the value of an application submitted by the candidate online vs. a referral from a recruiter. Many companies pay a bounty of about $2,500 for a referral. So, each application received online that ends up as a hired candidate is worth $2,500. Value? 200 applications × 2% Conversion Rate = $10,000 cost savings.

Economic value can increase revenue or reduce cost.

If you are Universal Studios and it costs you $9 million to show the ad for your latest movie to the 8 million people who watch a certain program over one week, then the cost to reach those people is $1.13. On your movie's website, the same movie trailer was watched completely 500,000 times. Economic value? 500,000 × 1.13 = $562,500. Again, you are actually computing the Web at a discounted rate because 75 percent of the 8 million people who were supposed to be watching the TV ad were in the bathroom and another 20 percent actually fast-forwarded the ad on TiVo. But why quibble?

If you are Target, you know the cost of sending someone a weekly mailer, as well as how many people see it online and print the coupons. Use the offline numbers to compute the value of the online weekly mailer views. And don't forget to compute the value of the people who sign up for the weekly exclusive email newsletters! You know how much it costs to get qualified mailing addresses; apply that value here. Calculate the reduced cost of getting people to sign up for wedding or baby registries or the value of Visitors who create wish lists because they are more likely to return to the site and buy. Just look at your historical data, and compute the value of past Conversions from the wish list!

It is criminal to simply focus on one job for your website and ignore the Micro Conversions. It is an offense of the highest order if you don't compute the complete economic value that your website adds. All it takes is two simple processes:

1. Seek out your offline peers to get the value of activities done offline. Your finance and sales departments are your best friends there.

2. Make sure the online data (such as leads, jobs, and catalog signups) that flows into your offline systems is clearly tagged as online so that you can compute offline conversions (leads converted, jobs accepted, catalogs mailed, and orders for those specific catalogs).

Your senior management will never look at you the same way if you accomplish this important task. As in the case of my wife, love for you will abound!

Measuring Success for a Non-ecommerce Website

In this chapter there has been a prevailing theme of looking past the obvious to measure the value delivered by a website. We have looked at measuring non-ecommerce activities, as well as ecommerce activities. As an example in the preceding section, we briefly touched on a number of websites that are primarily non-ecommerce in nature.

In the section about Micro and Macro Conversions, one of the examples I covered was a technical support website, which is as non-ecommerce as you can get. I identified six specific metrics for that site to measure success.

Now I'll cover a very special case: a content website that has absolutely no ecommerce of any kind. People come, they consume content, they bask in your greatness, and they leave. Maybe they come back again and again. For example, a news website or a blog or an academic journal website would fall into this category.

If you are one of these sites, how do you measure success? Don't say Visits or Average Page Views, or I will be very sad. You need to measure Visitor behavior, because in this case the behavior will indicate whether you are doing something of value. Four metrics are relevant for studying behavior: Visitor Loyalty, Visitor Recency, Length of Visit, and Depth of Visit. I'll suggest possible actions you should take based on the data you get from these metrics.

Visitor Loyalty

Visitor Loyalty tells you how often Visitors visit your website during the reporting period. Take a look at the graphs in Figure 5.9.

The number you see is *average Visits per visitor*. That number will usually be about 1.3. It's a metric that actively hides the truth.

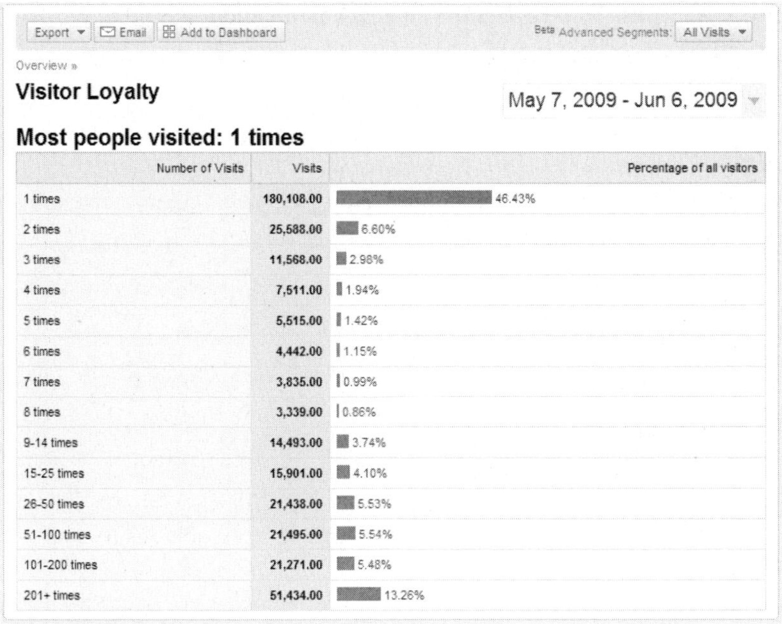
Export | Email | Add to Dashboard | Beta Advanced Segments: All Visits

Overview »

Visitor Loyalty

May 7, 2009 - Jun 6, 2009

Most people visited: 1 times

Number of Visits	Visits	Percentage of all visitors
1 times	180,108.00	46.43%
2 times	25,588.00	6.60%
3 times	11,568.00	2.98%
4 times	7,511.00	1.94%
5 times	5,515.00	1.42%
6 times	4,442.00	1.15%
7 times	3,835.00	0.99%
8 times	3,339.00	0.86%
9-14 times	14,493.00	3.74%
15-25 times	15,901.00	4.10%
26-50 times	21,438.00	5.53%
51-100 times	21,495.00	5.54%
101-200 times	21,271.00	5.48%
201+ times	51,434.00	13.26%

Figure 5.9 Visitor Loyalty report

By looking at the distribution of Visits over relevant buckets of Visits, you can understand the Visitor behavior. Figure 5.9 shows that 46 percent of the Visitors came to the site only once and never again (boo!), and yet there is that fine group at the bottom, 38 percent, who visited the site between 9 and 200+ times (yeah!).

You would make completely different decisions based on *average Visits per visitor*, knowing that 38 percent of the people are intensely loyal to your website.

Action (a) Identify a goal for your non-ecommerce website for the number of visits you expect from your website traffic in a given period (say one week or one month). (b) Measure reality using the Visitor Loyalty report. (c) Compare your performance over time to ensure you are making progress, as shown in Figure 5.10.

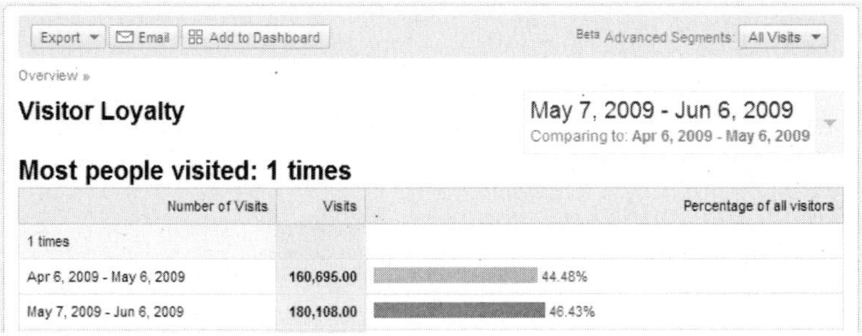
Export | Email | Add to Dashboard | Beta Advanced Segments: All Visits

Overview »

Visitor Loyalty

May 7, 2009 - Jun 6, 2009
Comparing to: Apr 6, 2009 - May 6, 2009

Most people visited: 1 times

Number of Visits	Visits	Percentage of all visitors
1 times		
Apr 6, 2009 - May 6, 2009	160,695.00	44.48%
May 7, 2009 - Jun 6, 2009	180,108.00	46.43%

Figure 5.10 Comparing Visitor Loyalty over two time periods

It is pretty clear in Figure 5.10 that in the current period (May 7 to June 6) the website actually performed a little worse because more people visited only one time.

Visitor Recency

Visitor Recency tells you how long it has been since a visitor last visited your website. Another way to think about this metric is that Visitor Recency measures the gap between two visits from the same person to your website, as shown in Figure 5.11.

	Last Visit	Visits		Percentage of all visitors
0 days ago		14,566.00		34.25%
1 days ago		4,689.00		11.02%
2 days ago		3,151.00		7.41%
3 days ago		2,330.00		5.48%
4 days ago		1,661.00		3.91%
5 days ago		1,449.00		3.41%
6 days ago		1,312.00		3.08%
7 days ago		1,051.00		2.47%
0-14 days ago		4,132.00		9.71%
15-30 days ago		3,457.00		8.13%
31-60 days ago		2,277.00		5.35%
61-120 days ago		1,526.00		3.59%
121-364 days ago		810.00		1.90%
365+ days ago		122.00		0.29%

Figure 5.11 Visitor Recency report

Often content websites are updated very frequently, from multiple times a week to perhaps multiple times a day. The Visitor Recency report shows whether people visit the site to get all that fresh content. In this case, 34 percent of the Visits were by people who were there less than 0 days ago (that is, people who were on your website less than 23 hours ago!). In fact, 69 percent of the Visits were by people who came to the site six days ago or less. This is superb because it reflects a commitment by Visitors to the site and a deeper relationship.

Measuring Recency works even if you are a jobs website, Craigslist, or any site whose business model relies on frequent visits by their audience.

Action Determine how frequently you add freshly updated content to your site. Set goals for how short the gap between Visits should be for Visitors to your site, and see whether you are meeting that goal. If not, figure out whether you need to improve the site content, the design, or the merchandizing. Should you "sell" harder the value of repeat Visits to your audience? Is that number going up or down? Deal with these issues, and you can create incentives on your site for people to visit more frequently than you can actually measure success!

Length of Visit

Length of Visit measures the quality of visit as represented by the length of a visitor session in seconds. Average Time on Site is perhaps the most common web analytics metric on Earth. But if two people visit your website, one for 1 minute and the other for 100 minutes, the average is useless. You want to look at the distribution, as shown in Figure 5.12.

Time spent on site	Visits	%
1 min(s)	264,068	83.77%
2 min(s)	8,797	2.79%
3 min(s)	5,557	1.76%
4 min(s)	4,144	1.31%
5 min(s)	3,173	1.01%
6 min(s)	2,655	0.84%
7 min(s)	2,175	0.69%
8 min(s)	1,911	0.61%
9 min(s)	1,736	0.55%
10 min(s)	1,596	0.51%
Subtotal	295,812	93.84%
Total	315,242	100.00%

Figure 5.12 Length of Visit report

So much information jumps out right away. Although the average time was 2 minutes and 53 seconds, the sad reality is 83 percent of the site traffic stayed for just 1 minute or less. There is a small but loyal group that stayed for more than three minutes. But it is clear what the issue is here.

Action Think of creative ways to engage traffic—what can you do to keep a Visitor for 60 seconds or more? Segment the Visitors who stay more than two minutes, and analyze the content they consume, where they come from, and so forth, so you can learn what you should be doing more. Create your own goals, and measure success for the percent of visits that are long and the percent that are short.

Depth of Visit

Depth of Visit measures the distribution of the number of pages in each Visit to the website, during a given reporting period. Depth of Visit is the sister metric to Length of Visit. I find it fascinating because time can sometimes be misleading. We might think,

"Oh, it's so sad people stayed on my site for only one minute." But in reality, the entire population on the Internet seems to be afflicted with Attention Deficit Disorder (ADD), and those people might have seen seven pages in one minute: *click, not this, click, interesting, click, wrong page, click*. See what I mean?

This standard report, especially when contrasted with Length of Visit, can help you understand the content consumption patterns of your Visitors. At the end of this process for your non-ecommerce website, you'll understand how many Visitors frequently visit your site, how many days elapse between their visits, how long they stay (contrasted to how long you want them to stay), and how many pages they visit.

Such powerful data can ultimately help you understand the kind of longer-term relationships you are building. These are the relationships that will help you grow your audience and business.

Here is a solid example. It is suboptimal to measure the success of Facebook by tracking the number of member profiles. Sure, Facebook wants more profiles, but the true value of Facebook is the number of active profiles and people who visit the site every hour of every day, people who *friend* others (deepening relationships), *superpoke* others, and send them annoying applications. This member behavior creates value for Facebook; hence, better measures of success are Visitor Loyalty, Recency, and Depth of Visit.

Action For your non-ecommerce website, determine what Visitor behavior will be of value to your business. Now measure it.

To ensure optimal success, you should bring on board your senior decision makers early in the process; educate them about the uselessness of averages, and work with them to create goals. Finally, to truly find insights, segment like crazy!

Measuring B2B Websites

Nothing, absolutely nothing, upsets me more than when I hear the owner of a business-to-business (B2B) website say this: "But I am in the B2B business; we don't really deal with customers like B2C sites."

Do robots visit B2B websites? As a B2B company, you are still trying to sell to other human beings; you are still selling products, services, or content just like Gap or Amazon; and you still want to influence other decision makers, just like every other site on the planet.

Real people visit your website, B2B or B2C. Yes, the sales cycles might be longer on some B2B sites, which is all the more reason to measure precious Conversions. It might take Visitors long consideration cycles to make a purchase, so you measure Loyalty, Recency, and Days to Purchase. You are trying to influence an organization rather than a single person; surely that means you still you need to create sites that are engaging, relevant, and easy to use because the people in those organizations will visit. Many conversions might happen offline, because all the site provides is information, but that only increases the value of web analytics in quantifying the impact of the information on your site.

I passionately believe that all sites exist to ensure that Visitors to the site can complete the tasks they came to the site for, whether B2B or B2C.

Let's take the example of the Texas Instruments (TI) website at www.ti.com. There are small aspects of the site that might be business-to-customer, though 99 percent of the website is as business-to-business as it can get. So, how would you measure the success of this B2B website? The following list shows some metrics I would use:

Percentage of Visits that viewed the Product Folder directories Lots of content on the TI website relates to details of its engineering products, and it is pretty comprehensive. Success for TI is when a majority of people who come to the site successfully read this valuable content. If the TI analysts want to dive deeper, they would segment those Visits by types of products they want to sell more (the latest, expensive ones) or understand what sources send this valuable traffic.

Percentage of selection and solution guide downloads Not only does the site have lots of downloads, these guides help the broader client employees make decisions about what to purchase. TI can track these downloads over time along with the products that are most popular in terms of guide downloads.

Number of free samples ordered This is the minor ecommerce component of the website. Visitors can come, customize the products (subsystem controllers, linear voltage regulators, integrated switches, and so on) and then purchase small samples to test and try. This increases the chances that the company will purchase 2 billion of those same integrated switches!

Number of new my.TI accounts opened Opening a my.TI account provides more benefits to the consumers; they can save their customizations to designs, sign up for training events, get special offers, and so forth. Translation: this creates a deeper engagement with ti.com and a much more positive brand impression. You have already learned that the raw number of accounts is not the core Outcome—TI wants to track the behavior of these account holders—but the number of new accounts is a start.

Number completed videos watched TI is very progressive because it has some fantastic video content. Except for the *Thank an Engineer* series, most of these videos speak a language that would send most folks into a tizzy, but not TI's target audience. These videos help TI provide information to its customers efficiently and help those customers make faster decisions.

Percentage of solutions posted by the same member ID This is pretty cool. TI has an engineer-to-engineer forum where the community is encouraged to participate and help each other. One key measure of success would be if people started to help each other. I would identify that by measuring the percentage of members who are heavily engaged in helping others (and thus of value to the community and TI).

Usage of decision support tools Littered all over the TI site are tons of tools that help you decide which product is right for you, from calculators to DLP projectors to micro-controllers. These tools help users figure out at their own pace what the right product is for their company. These decision support tools are extremely valuable to TI, and hence tracking their usage helps TI understand if the cost of the tools is worth it. By marrying sessions where tools usage resulted in Conversions (ordering samples, down-loading product specs, and so on), TI can measure the impact on the bottom line.

Now here's a secret. I have never spoken to anyone at TI, and I am not in its target audience of customers. Yet it took me a half hour of browsing their site to under-stand the goals (Outcomes) and value (Visitor behavior) of the site. After browsing and determining TI's potential Outcomes and Visitor behavior, I could put on my analyst hat and come up with a sampling of metrics that it can use to measure success. I can even attempt to guess the economic value of each of these Outcomes. If you work at TI, of course, you don't have to guess—you can actually calculate that.

Go through the same process for your website (focus on Micro and Macro Conversion and optimal Visitor behavior). Because it's your own site, you have one strong element in your favor: you actually know what the site's trying to accomplish! Leverage that knowledge. Oh, and don't forget to compute the total economic value!

Solving the "Why" Puzzle—Leveraging Qualitative Data

When I walk into a supermarket, I don't expect the employees to recognize me or rearrange the store for me. Yet when I visit an online supermarket, I am annoyed that on my third visit they still don't know I live in California and they are not presenting me with items on sale at my local store.

When people shop online, they have a different set of expectations. Therefore, your Web Analytics 2.0 strategy must include at least a few methods of actively listening to your customers. This way, you stay on top of their expectations, and you also gain the key context you need, the why, *for making sense of your* what, *which is your Clickstream data.*

Usability studies, remote testing, and surveys are among a handful of powerful techniques that help you plug your ear directly into the customer's brain and unlock the mystery of *why*. Why did they want this? Why did they react that way? Why did they not follow your simple instructions? Why…?

The Web has helped open up a whole host of new possibilities for listening to customers, from free, easy-to-implement surveys to affordable usability testing to cool things such as the *five-second test* (more on this later). So if you want to get started, the bar is low; you just need a minor time commitment and a major amount of love for your customers. That last part is key.

We all think we represent our customers. You're probably convinced that after years of doing online shopping or searches on Yahoo! you know exactly what an online shopper or searcher needs. The problem is you are completely and utterly wrong. True customer centricity—the thing that will power huge success for you on the Web—will come only from listening to your customers at scale and all the time.

Ready? Let's go.

Lab Usability Studies: What, Why, and How Much?

User research is the science of observing and monitoring how we interact with everyday things, such as websites, software, or hardware, and then drawing conclusions about how to improve those things. Sometimes we do the studies in a lab environment (complete with one-way mirrors and cameras pointed at the participants); other times we can perform the studies in people's native environments, such as their offices or homes. Lab usability studies are the granddaddy of all user-centric design (UCD) methodologies.

What Is Lab Usability?

Lab usability tests measure a user's ability to complete tasks. In a typical usability test, a user attempts to complete a task or set of tasks using a website (or software or a product). Each of these tasks has a specified goal for effectiveness, efficiency, and satisfaction in a specified context of use.

A typical study will have 8 to 12 participants. Early on—even during tests with as few as five users—patterns will begin to emerge that highlight which parts of the customer experience or process work well and which cause problems.

Lab tests are conducted by a user-centric design or human factors expert, who is typically supported by someone taking notes. Key stakeholders such as business owners, engineers, developers, analysts, and product managers participate as observers.

Tests can be conducted with a live version of the website, beta versions, on-screen HTML or PowerPoint prototypes, or even with paper printouts. These paper prototypes, sometimes called *wireframes*, approximate what a user might otherwise see on a computer screen but save the development team from having to produce an on-screen product.

In a lab environment, usability tests are typically held in a specially designed room called a *usability lab*. The lab is split into two rooms that are divided by a one-way mirrored window that allows observers to watch the test without being seen by the test subject. However, you can conduct a usability study without a lab. All you need is a room with a computer in it and a promise from all test observers that they will remain silent and out of the test subject's sight (that is, behind them) throughout the test.

As the test subjects work on their tasks, a test moderator observes, takes notes on user actions, and records outcomes. While the participant is working at their task, the moderator limits their own interactions to providing initial task instructions and occasionally prompting the participant to further explain their comments.

For example, if the participant says, "That was easy," the moderator might say, "Tell me more about that." This neutral prompt encourages the participant to explain what they thought happened and why it worked well for them. Because moderators make nonjudgmental comments and do not assist, the participant is forced to use their own devices—as they would at home or in their office—to complete their task.

Often lab usability tests are also recorded on video for later review and to present to a larger audience in a company.

Usability tests are best for optimizing user interface (UI) designs, optimizing workflows, understanding the Voice of Customer, and understanding what customers really do.

> **Note:** First things first. The CD included with this book includes a 25-Point Website Usability Checklist from User Effect. Use the checklist to grade your website on 25 basic usability best practices that every website should follow. You don't need a Usability test to fix these things. They fall in the *just do it* category.

How to Conduct a Test

There is as much art involved in conducting a lab usability test as there is science. It is very important to understand the end-to-end process to ensure that you can obtain valid observations and results from these studies.

Conducting a successful lab usability test involves four stages: preparing the test, conducting the test, analyzing the results, and following up.

Preparing

The preparation stage is perhaps the most important stage in determining success for your usability studies, because you'll help define scope, identify participants, and ensure all your ducks are lined up just right.

Here are the main steps in the preparation phase, using Amazon.com as an example:

1. Identify the critical tasks for which you are testing. (A critical task for Amazon.com might be this: how easily can customers return a product or request a replacement?)

2. Create scenarios for the test participant of each task. (A customer orders a Sony digital camera from Amazon.com, and when the box arrives, it is missing a lens cap. What does the customer do next to contact Amazon.com for help?)

3. Identify what success looks like for each scenario. (The customer finds the correct page on the support site, follows the link to the Contact Amazon.com web page, fills out a request form, and hits the Submit button.)

4. Identify who your test participants should be (new users, existing users, people who shop at competitors' sites, and so on).

5. Determine a compensation structure for the participants.

6. Contact a recruiter, in your company or outside, to recruit the right people for you.

7. Before actually conducting the test with live participants, do dry runs with someone internal to make sure your scripts and other elements work. You'll find issues in these pilots that you can clean up before you run the real test.

Conducting the Test

With all the preparation behind you, it is time for the proverbial rubber to hit the road. You finally get to see real people!

The main steps in the test phase are as follows:

1. Welcome your participants, and orient them to the environment. "Thank you for coming here to our company for this test. There is a mirror where people are watching you, and we are recording this. You can do no wrong, so don't worry, and just relax."

2. Start with a "think aloud" exercise. You want to "hear" what the participants are thinking, and this exercise you will train them to "talk their thoughts." The main goal is to really understand and uncover the problems they will surely have.

3. Have the participants read the tasks aloud; this will make sure they read all instructions and hence understand the task or scenario.

4. Now all company observers, pay attention, close attention. Carefully observe what the participants do, looking for verbal and nonverbal clues about where the participants fail in their tasks, misunderstand your web pages, or go down the wrong path.

5. The moderator can ask the participants follow-up questions to get more clarity. Be careful not to give out answers, and absolutely watch your own verbal and nonverbal clues; be as calm and reassuring as you can to the participants.

6. Thank the participants, and make sure to pay them right away (if you can).

Analyzing the Data

The fun is not over yet. At the end of the test stage, you have collected a ton of valuable observations, some expected and some not. It is key to strike while the iron is hot—to do your analysis now in a methodical manner.

The main steps in the analysis phase are as follows:

1. As soon as possible, hold a debrief session with all observers so that everyone can share their thoughts and observations.

2. Take time to note trends and patterns.

3. The moderator tallies up success and failures by each participant for each task.

4. Do a deep dive to identify the root causes for the failures based on actual observations. (For example, the FAQ answer on the website was too long. The Contact Us link was not apparent and hidden below the fold. It was not clear that they could not contact us via phone. Almost everyone complained that their expectations were not set about when to expect a reply.)

5. Make recommendations to fix the problems that were identified. Create a PowerPoint presentation that collects the scores, and then take the following steps for each critical task:

   a. Identify the points of failures.

   b. Make concrete recommendations that will improve the customer experience.

   c. Categorize the recommendations into Urgent, Important, and Nice to Have, to help business decision makers prioritize.

Following Up, Retesting, and Measuring Success

The traditional role of UCD experts and researchers might end at the previous step, but I think that their role continues after the test results are presented. Experts and researchers should collaborate with business owners to maintain the momentum from the test. The experts can help fix the problems identified by the test, offering their services and UCD expertise to partner with website developers and designers to improve the site experience.

Finally, don't forget to measure success post-implementation. You spent all the money on testing, so what was the outcome? Did you make more money? Are customers satisfied? Do you have lower Abandonment Rates? The only way to keep funding for testing efforts is to show a consistent track record of success that either impacts the bottom line or improves customer satisfaction.

Best Practices for Lab Usability Studies

Some salient best practices will help you magnify the results from usability tests. Collecting qualitative data is not simply a matter of following a regimented set of tasks; a ton of style and nuance is involved.

Here are some tips on conducting a successful test:

- Make sure you tell the participants that you are testing the website, product, or software and not testing them. People tend to blame themselves a lot; make sure to stress that any problems they have as they are testing are not their fault.

- Don't rely on what people say; focus on their behavior. People often report experiences very differently from how they experience them. It is amazing how many times I have observed a completely frustrating (or long) experience from a customer who in the end rates it as 4 out of 5. People are just nice; our job is to make up for that by observing.

- Try not to answer participant questions when they ask you how to do something. Instead, use statements like, "Tell me more," or "If this were the case at your home or office, what would you do next?"

- A tip from an earlier segment bears repeating: watch your body language to ensure that you are not giving participants any subtle clues.

Benefits of Lab Usability Studies

You would not perform lab usability studies if they didn't produce any benefits. Lab tests are great at getting close to a customer and observing them, and even interacting with them. I realize this description may sound like going to see an animal in a zoo, but the reality is that 99 percent of us will complete our employment with a company without ever seeing a real customer. Yet all the while we are supposed to be solving for them. Lab testing is an eye-opening experience for everyone involved. Be prepared to be surprised.

For complex experiences, lab tests can be a great way to get customer feedback early in the process to identify big problems. When you can get good information early, you save time, money, energy, and sanity.

For existing experiences, these tests really help identify what works and what does not. Testing is especially helpful if you are completely stumped by your Clickstream data, which can happen a lot.

Finally, usability tests are a great mechanism to generate ideas to solve customer problems. Not solutions, ideas.

Areas of Caution

In a world of finite options, you have to rely on lab usability tests for a full spectrum of answers. But in the world of the Web, you can leverage data in a much more nuanced way. As you consider leveraging usability tests, be careful about the following concerns:

- Twelve people do not a customer base make. Do your best to ensure that people in the test are a representative sample of your customers. But things like the *Hawthorne effect* can impact participant behavior. That is, people in artificial circumstances (like a lab with one-way mirrors and cameras) behave artificially because they know they're being watched. Don't jump to definitive opinions as a result of a lab test.

- Avoid doing complex, all-encompassing redesigns of websites or customer experience based purely on a lab test. You are asking too much of the lab test; it is impossible to control for all the factors that will occur on your real website.

- Remember that on the Web, *revolutions fail; evolution works*!

- Do not leave lab usability testing just to your UCD professionals and researchers. One of the best things you can do for your company is to pair up these experts with your web analysts. The latter will bring real work data from their tools and explain what that data means, and the former will take that data to construct real tasks and create good scenarios for each task. Both usability researchers and web analysts can benefit tremendously from a close, sustained partnership (the ultimate combination of qualitative and quantitative).

- Keep an open mind about the alternatives available. I'll cover a few in the next section. I find people just lock into lab usability as a panacea, and it is not. The results of lab tests should be one element of a portfolio of strategies available to you to collect Voice of Customer.

One of the most powerful uses of lab usability tests is to take 10 ideas and eliminate the complete losers. Take the remaining few ideas and put them live on your site as an online test. Now you have the best of both worlds.

> **Tip:** Some of the most important mental models for dealing with customers and customer data are contained in this section, such as the importance of letting participants complete tasks, getting many points of view, understanding the limitations of the sample, creating structured goals, or reading body language and other visual cues. As you execute other methodologies for listening to your customers, you want to remember and incorporate the key lessons you acquire from usability.

Usability Alternatives: Remote and Online Outsourced

The Web is an enabler if nothing else. I love it for that. In this section, I'll cover two delightful companies that solve important challenges related to user research and do so at scale. The first company provides a solution to the bias and challenges in our usability studies: recruiting! The second company provides a solution to democratizing access to user research to such a deep extent that even a small business with a few thousand dollars in revenue can access it.

Live Recruiting and Remote User Research

Two important challenges come with doing usability studies: finding optimal participants and getting them to come do the study. Often the way we solve these two key problems is by calling around and getting the best people we can in our location into our study. So, anyone who is close to our target participant is fair game, including Mom. We then tell the participants to think like someone who does business with us and give us feedback. We can also use a recruiting agency whose dedicated job is to find *people*. We schedule the studies around availability (ours and theirs). Unfortunately, with both of these methods, the results may not quite work out to be an optimal mix.

Live Recruiting and Remote Studies

A number of solutions, like Ethnio (www.ethnio.com), solve the previous problems in a clever way. You can recruit actual people who visit your site to complete a task, and you can conduct the study remotely (in other words, your participants can visit your site while sitting in bed if they like).

Here's how live recruiting and remote studies work:

1. You create a simple screener of a few questions, three to five, to ask visitors to your site. These questions help you qualify the candidates and hence get the right person.

2. You take a simple piece of code, typically one line, and insert it on your website (either on the entire website, on highly trafficked pages, or say only on the technical support pages if you want to test tech support).

3. Visitors to your site come and enjoy its glory. Based on your setting, some or all of them will get a sweet DHTML window that invites them to participate in a study (see Figure 6.1).

   You'll note the invite is not too intrusive, the Close button is clearly marked, there is a clear value proposition for the visitor (a possibility of an Amazon.com certificate), and it politely asks for 15–30 minutes of time.

4. The visitor can either close the invite or hit Continue. If they hit Continue, they will see a short questionnaire (see Figure 6.2).

   You can ask any questions you want, ideally ones that help you hone in on the right person. For example, in my first study, I wanted to know only why our tech support site had such low satisfaction ratings. My two questions were, "Are you an existing user of our software?" and "What is the reason for your visit to our site today?" The drop-down menus helped me find the right person.

Figure 6.1 Ethnio DHTML live recruiting window

Figure 6.2 Live recruiting survey

5. As soon as the visitors hit Submit, the data show up in a live database. You can identify Visitors who meet your criteria and, depending on your need, call them back right away or set up a convenient time to contact them. I cannot stress this enough: these are real people, who are really visiting your site to complete a task—not your Mom or the best person close to your location.

6. You can use your favorite screen-sharing application (GoToMeeting, WebEx, Yugma, Zoho Meeting, and so on) to contact your chosen participants, and off you go. You use nearly the same process as described in the prior section for lab usability studies: observe tasks, record video, do analysis, and then harass people in your company until they implement changes.

Solutions like Ethnio are most cost-effective if you have at least one user researcher in your company who can moderate and conduct the studies. But for a price, Ethnio and other companies can do the studies for you. Either way, you don't need to make a massive investment in usability labs and researchers, you don't need to use less-than-optimal participants, and you reduce the artificiality that comes with people being in a lab.

The downside is you lose the ability to physically observe people if you do a remote usability study. There is value in actually being able to see people.

Outsourced Online Usability

Outsourced online usability is great for people who don't have numerous resources: you don't have researchers in your company, and you just want to know what people think of your web experience.

A number of companies allow you to completely outsource usability. UserTesting.com (www.usertesting.com) is one such company. It has a large panel of people who have expressed an interest in participating in usability tests. You can commission usability studies, currently for an affordable price of $29 (or a bit less), where each participant goes through your test, and you get a video with the participant's experience as well as a short written summary of the participant's thoughts. That's not bad for the price.

Here's how outsourced online usability works:

1. You sign up for the study on www.usertesting.com. There you identify the following:
    - Your website
    - The tasks that you want test participants to perform ("find product x and complete the checkout process" or "find the solution to error code D78295 on our website")
    - The preferred number of test participants
    - The type of test participants you seek (specifying gender, age, income, computer savvy, and so on)

2. The company takes your data, converts it into a task list, and sends it to relevant participants in their database who meet (or come close to) the criteria you have identified.

3. You receive a video of the user, with audio, mouse movements identified, and other features, along with a short written summary. The summary contains answers to questions, such as what would have caused them to leave the site, how the site can be improved, and so forth.

4. You perform the same type of analysis as outlined for usability studies.

5. This step is always the same—you present your analysis and badger someone important in your company to implement changes.

So, you see this process is simple and cheap. You get real people telling you what problems they may have experienced with your site or what areas of your site delighted them.

The downside of using completely outsourced methodologies like this one are as follows:

- You don't have a lot of flexibility in getting the precise kind of test participants. Some companies like UserTesting.com allow you to use your own participants (perhaps ones you have recruited using Ethnio!), which would be optimal.

- As with lab usability studies, there is an artificiality about the situation, specifically because panel members may just want the $10 per study that UserTesting.com pays.

- You sacrifice the ability to test unstructured experiences, such as telling a user, "Just do what you would normally do on our site."

These downsides are trade-offs that you should carefully evaluate as you consider outsourcing. However, sometimes you want quick, direct feedback on your site: you want people, even random people, to poke holes and find problems that might not be visible to you. In those cases, outsourced usability provides a cost-effective way to get user feedback. You have no excuse, regardless of your size, not to use a method like this as a strategy to hear from real people out there using your site.

Surveys: Truly Scalable Listening

There is probably no other method of listening to your customers directly that is as efficient as surveys. For a wealth of reasons, surveys are an optimal tool for gaining more data about your visitors. Here are just a few of those reasons:

- Surveys are usually very affordable, and good free options are available.

- You can use surveys as a continuous listening methodology; that is, you can always have them on.

- They provide a mix of data that lends itself to quantitative and qualitative analysis.

- Surveys are timely; often you can detect problems and opportunities right away.

- You don't have to do a lot of surveys to get a lot of benefit; sample sizes can be small, so you don't need every visitor on your site to *talk* to get a statistically significant sample of data.

- Surveys have gotten very sophisticated; they have moved beyond the annoying, huge pop-up survey. Surveys can now use cookies, integrated with web analytics Clickstream data, and come in unique shapes and sizes for specific jobs.

Your quest for understanding the *why* question of user research should contain more than just surveys, but if you do not include surveys, you'll have a gaping hole in your ability to truly understand your customers.

Types of Surveys

Did you think all surveys were big, ugly pop-ups that show up during the middle of a website visit? You have other, better choices when you start using surveys. Specifically, there are two main types of surveys, each with distinct pros and cons and each with a distinct purpose.

Page-Level Surveys

Page-level surveys typically use a passive invitation model and collect micro-level data for a focused purpose or task. Figure 6.3 shows three examples of page-level survey invitations.

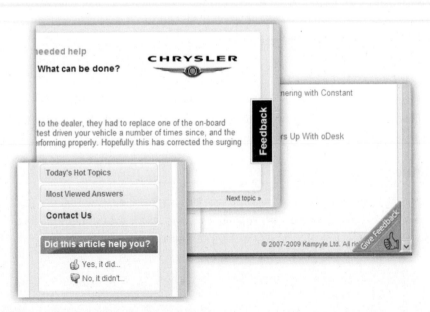

Figure 6.3 Page-level survey invitations

As you can see, the survey invitation can take different shapes; however, it typically sits close to the end of the browser. If the user is interested in giving feedback, then he or she will initiate the survey by clicking the invite.

Benefits of Page-Level Surveys

- Page-level surveys are always available on the web page.

- They focus on one task, such as getting user ratings on features, reporting bugs or questions about the site, or learning whether the page was helpful.

- Many free or affordable options are available, such as UserVoice and Kampyle. Also, it is fairly easy to create your own page-level survey; all you need is a modestly smart IT person, and as we all know, all IT people are more than modestly smart!

- You hear from your most upset or *engaged* customers. There is no better gift than hearing from those who love or hate you the most.

Challenges of Page-Level Surveys

- The invitation model for page-level surveys is passive; hence, only the people who really want to talk to you will talk to you. You can't get a complete picture (that is, if your user visits, is happy, and leaves, then it is less likely that he or she will stick around and give feedback—especially if the page-level survey is a tiny, pale plus sign on white background).

- Page-level surveys are at their best collecting *local feedback*, that is, feedback about the specific page where the user clicks the invite or feedback about a specific task.

- These surveys are not very good for collecting feedback about intent or complete site experience.

- It is difficult to control or get large enough sample sizes from page-level surveys—your invitation is specific to a page, you have lots of pages, and a small number of visitors will fill them out for each page. This makes is hard to stitch together survey results from across your website pages and identify important patterns in the data.

Page-level surveys are fantastic for measuring the effectiveness of individual pages or content on pages (think: technical support website). They are also great for collecting feedback on focused tasks (think: rate this list of features).

Many companies that provide page-level surveys will tell you that they can function as site-level surveys. They are not being completely truthful. The invitation model simply does not lend itself to collecting site experience data.

Site-Level Surveys

Site-level surveys have a much more proactive invitation model. They collect macro-level data about customer intent, behavior, and customer experience.

The world seems to have settled on two types of invitation modes for site-level surveys. The first method is to use pop-ups or pop-unders. In this case, as soon as the visitor enters your site, or at some point during their visit, a window pops open with the survey (see Figure 6.4). The window typically includes all the questions that you want the visitor to answer, usually between 25 to 38 questions.

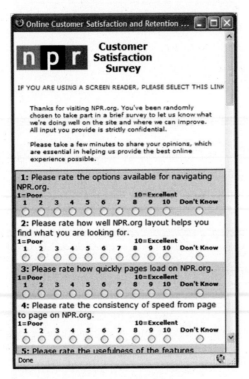

Figure 6.4 Pop-up/pop-under site-level survey

The survey that pop's up in the middle of a Visitor's session is increasingly falling by the wayside because of negative customer perceptions and better technologies, such as Ajax, to deliver the survey invite experience.

The second method is to use a permission-based model for the survey invitation. In this case, when the visitor enters your website, they are politely asked for permission to participate in a survey—and this is important—at the end of their visit. In Figure 6.5, you'll notice I get a DHTML layer asking for permission to participate in the survey on both the iPerceptions and Crowd Science websites (both of whom are site level survey providers). There is a clear Yes or No choice. If I click Yes, then at the end of my visit, I'll get a survey. Permission-based surveys are increasingly common on the Web.

Figure 6.5 Permission-based site-level survey

Benefits of Site-Level Surveys

- Site-level surveys are exceptionally good at capturing the macro experience, intent, and Outcome-level information about the visit (for example, "What brought you here?" or "Why do you love us so much?" or "How likely are you to visit our retail store?").

- These surveys provide a great deal of control over who sees the survey. You can set it up so only 5 percent of your site traffic gets the invitation. You can leverage cookies so the same person will see the survey only once every three months.

- If your site-level survey is not one long, precreated pop-up, you can use technologies such as Ajax to make the experience much easier and use conditional logic to focus your questions (for example, the user already said she was a student, so why in God's name are you asking her the size of her business?).

- The invitation model is proactive, which means you'll get a significantly more diverse sample of participants. You'll get people who are on your site for multiple purposes, and you'll get people who are happy or sad or just OK. The feedback is much more representative.

Challenges of Site-Level Surveys

- Typically, the sophisticated site-level surveys are not free (simple surveys like 4Q are free and can be very actionable; I'll talk more about this in the next section).

- You will need someone at your company—or a consultant from your survey provider—to help you sift through a good amount of rich data.

- Although you can easily identify big problems, such as the shopping cart is broken, it is harder to identify micro problems using site-level surveys (for example, "What did you think of page *xyz*?").

Site-level surveys are fantastic for measuring the effectiveness of your website, the macro experience of your customers, and the projected impact on your company, brand, and offline existence.

Many companies that provide site-level surveys will tell you that they can function as page-level surveys. They are not being completely truthful. The invitation model simply does not lend itself to collecting page-level experience data.

Each type of survey has a specific purpose in life. Stress test what you want to get done, whether it's getting feedback about a specific page or getting a sense of the full customer experience on your site, and choose the right weapon.

The Single Biggest Surveying Mistake

As humans, when we are presented with an opportunity to know something, we go crazy. I think we are simply hardwired to want to know as much as possible.

In the context of surveys, this thirst for knowledge translates into creating long, complex surveys with every question possible, or more likely every possible question anyone with any authority in our company would want answered. The result is Figure 6.6.

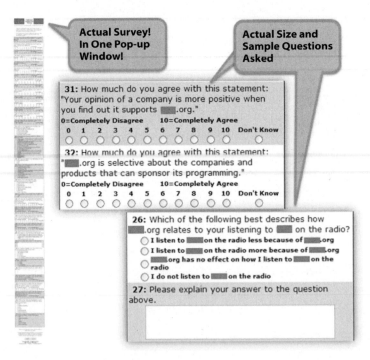

Figure 6.6 Balancing the *knowable* vs. *actionable*

Although we can *know* a lot, we have severe limits to what we can *do*. We constantly fail to balance what is knowable vs. what is actionable. We can ask our website visitors for their underwear size and the color of their eyes, but that information is completely useless because we can't take action with it. So, why ask?

When we ask too many questions, we are insulting the customer. Every touch point with our customers is our opportunity to reinforce our brand experience. By asking our customers so many questions, many of which are unnecessary and unactionable, we are implicitly telling our customers: "We don't value your time; we don't think enough of you to respect you by asking only what you need."

Figure 6.7 shows an actual survey, with the company's name hidden to protect the not-so innocent. Note the length of just one question and the progress dots at the top window; each dot represents one complex question.

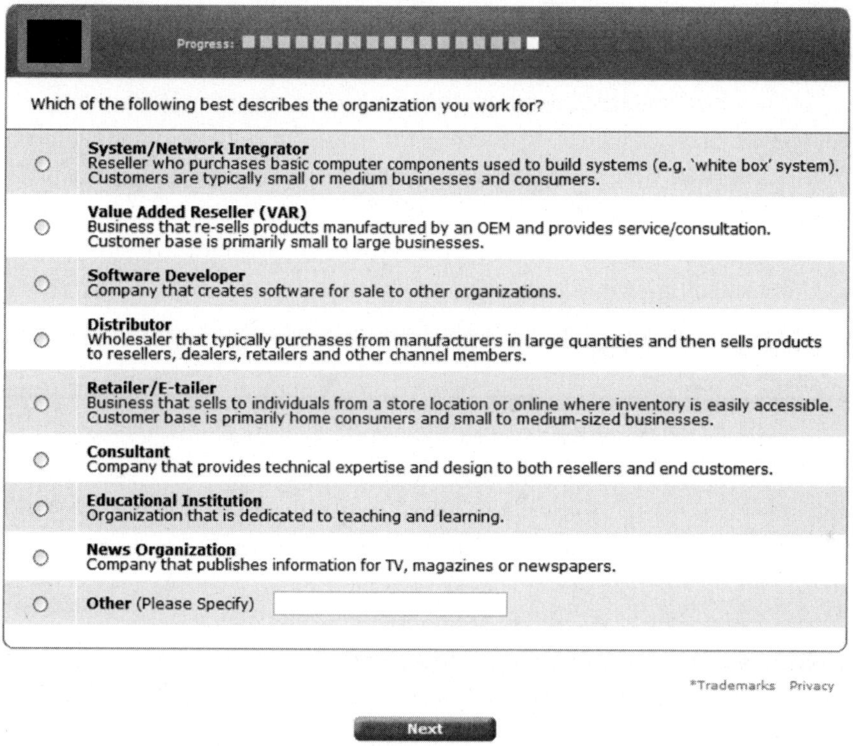

Figure 6.7 Example of a long, complex, time-consuming survey

Respect your customers and their time. Ask only what you can act on. It's good for your customers, and it's good for you—remember, after you collect all this data, you still need to spend time analyzing it!

Three Greatest Survey Questions Ever

We already know that our Clickstream data (*what*) needs qualitative data (*why*) to find truly actionable insights and give you the "A-ha, so that is what they wanted!" moments.

If you do nothing else in terms of user research, you *must* ask the following three questions of people who come to your website. Of course, do so using an on-exit survey.

These three simple questions will supply answers that fill major gaps in your knowledge about your customers and give you actionable data that will help you make a lot more sense of your Clickstream data. Not to mention, the answers you get will help give you specific ideas for improving your website and meeting your customer needs.

Q1: What is the purpose of your visit to our website today?

Most of us, whether analysts, marketers, or senior decision makers, will guess wrong when asked this simple question: "Why do you think people come to your website?" But now you don't have to guess.

Politely asking your website visitors why they visit your site is one of the best possible ways to find out that critical piece of information. The answers and distributions between different primary purposes will be eye-opening, and they will help explain so many things in your Clickstream data that previously did not seem to make any sense! For example, on an ecommerce website, you may learn that a minority of the site traffic is there to research a future purchase. Or on a nonprofit site, you may learn that most people don't make a donation because they could not easily find what percentage of their donation would be used for administrative purpose.

Q2: Were you able to complete your task?

I could ask you what's broken about your website, and you'll likely identify a few problems. I can ask Michele the analyst what she thinks, and she'll suggest other issues. I can ask the HiPPO, and he or she will suggest something else.

All those answers matter very little. What matters is what your customers think works well or what they think is completely broken. So, why not ask them instead of hypothesizing?

I am often asked what the single most important web analytics metric is. My answer is Task Completion Rate. It is more important than Conversion or Revenue or any other metric. With Task Completion Rate, I know why people came to my site (their primary purpose), and I know which tasks they could not complete (the Task Completion Rate), so I know exactly what to fix (see Figure 6.8).

2.2. Task Completion by Purpose of Visit

	Dec	Jan	Feb	Mar	Apr	May	Jun
Check my account	88%	69%	82%	86%	92%	90%	100%
Create an account	85%	83%	74%	89%	88%	84%	89%
Learn about products	78%	76%	79%	73%	79%	70%	58%
Learn about company / brand	79%	82%	77%	87%	72%	78%	80%
Seek support	63%	66%	71%	67%	65%	50%	50%
Other Please Specify	60%	54%	62%	56%	61%	70%	60%
Respondents	282	739	870	457	279	177	62

Figure 6.8 Task Completion Rate by primary purpose

Once I take this data and prioritize improvements on the site, there is no way that Conversion or Revenue won't go up (along with many other happy impacts!).

Q3: If you were not able to complete your task today, why not?

The third question in our Greatest Survey Ever provides a simple text box where the customers can type in anything they want; it's an open-ended Voice of Customer (VOC). It gives customers a chance to tell you, in their own words, the reasons they could not do what they wanted to do, and it allows them the opportunity, unconstrained, to share ideas and suggestions to fix things on your website.

You analyze this question by categorizing the responses into common themes and then rating the percentage of times each theme occurs in the open-ended VOC for those who could not complete their task. This becomes your to-do list of issues, directly from the horse's mouth, about what you should work on in order to improve the website experience for your customers.

Launching Your Customer-Centric Strategy

The previous three simple questions will provide a wealth of insights to help you deliver on your customer-centric strategy. You can create this three-question survey yourself and implement it on your website. Or you can use the free on-exit survey called 4Q from iPerceptions. (Disclosure: Currently I am on the board of advisors of iPerceptions.)

The 4Q survey (http://4q.iperceptions.com) is a permission-based survey that is available in 18 languages. You can control the percentage of website traffic that should see the survey, and 4Q also uses cookies to ensure that the same visitor sees a survey only once in 30 days (if they meet the sampling criteria).

When people exit your website, the survey will ask them the three questions outlined previously and one more question to compute Customer Satisfaction: "Based on today's visit, how would you rate your site experience overall?"

The CD that accompanies this book includes a video explaining the survey and how to set it up. So, you can get started for free today and tap into the wisdom that your website visitors want to share with you. How cool is that?

Eight Tips for Choosing an Online Survey Provider

At some point, you'll probably want to retain an external survey provider to help you with your surveying needs. There are whole rafts of companies today that provide very sophisticated surveying capabilities, in every possible niche you can imagine.

Remember that you want to decide not what company to work with but what your specific needs are. You also want to determine whether you need a page-level or site-level survey provider because they are not interchangeable.

From my humble and often painful experience, the following are eight factors you should consider before choosing a survey vendor.

Tip 1: Mathematical Rigor

No matter which company you choose, look for a partner that can apply mathematical rigor to your results. It is sadly common to find survey results that are misinterpreted, typically because of poor math applied in the analysis (or because someone decides to react to a *mouse with a megaphone*).

Measuring survey results is not simply taking the average of the answers, because averages lie; it is measuring distributions and doing regressions. When you use a survey, *you* shouldn't have to apply the statistics and statistical significance—stress test to ensure your *vendor* does that work. Then you can focus on analysis and not reporting.

Tip 2: On-the-Fly Segmentation Capabilities

Analysis is not static. Things change. You find intriguing patterns in your data, and you want to dive deeper. For example, if task completion dropped by 9 points in 24 hours for people coming from Microsoft Bing, you want to know why. Or you only want to read survey responses for people who visited your site three times to download a patch and whose task completion response is No.

You want to be able to segment your data quickly and efficiently.

Look for a vendor that can do on-the-fly segmentation of your data, because aggregates lie. With some vendors, you get no segmentation capabilities; send those vendors packing. With other vendors, you'll get segmentation *on demand*. That is, you must ask or beg for segmented data, and they'll send it to you later. If you have no other option, then work with these vendors. Your ideal vendors, however, will give you access to an online environment where you can slice and dice your data at will, from day one. This is your kind of online survey vendor!

Tip 3: Benchmarks and Indices

Context is king! Although it's fine to know your score went up from 53 to 57, you really want to know that the industry benchmark is 70. Few people in senior management will take action when you tell them your score, but they will get off their rear ends and give you money when you tell them: "Our score is a x, our main competitor is $x+10$, and the industry benchmark is xy."

Other subtle forces are also at play. By comparing your performance to the industry and competition, you depersonalize the data. It is no longer your opinion whether you are doing well or badly; the industry benchmark shows your standing. That kind of information works wonders with senior decision makers.

Look for a vendor that can provide a robust set of benchmarks and indices.

Tip 4: Open Text Categorization

Most valuable insights will come not from quantitative analysis but rather from qualitative analysis of open-text customer responses. This is the hardest kind of analysis for you to do, even if you are a medium-sized company.

No vendor is really awesome at categorizing and parsing open-text responses because it is a difficult problem to solve, but ask your vendor what kind of capabilities they offer. If they say they can do it all for free and instantly, take that response with a grain of salt, and ask them to demonstrate it on your website's data.

You want to pick the best among some less-than-optimal choices. The choices are poor not from any fault on the vendor's part—open-text categorization is an area where vendors are still working on improvements.

Tip 5: Type of Survey Invitation

Earlier you learned the various kinds of survey invites available: on-exit, pop-ups, pop-unders, active, and passive. Each type of invitation comes with its pros and cons.

Stress test your vendor to see what methodology it uses and whether it meets your needs. Ideally your vendor will allow you to experiment with different types of invites as well as the content, colors, and look and feel of the invite.

On-exit surveys work best for site-level surveys, but you want to validate that for your own case. Many page-level survey vendors now provide customization options as well. Use them.

Tip 6: Cookie Sophistication

In your search for a survey vendor, you want a company that can set cookies. The cookies ensure that once a visitor is served a survey, they won't see another one for, say, 90 days, regardless of whether they complete it. The last thing you want is to cause your customers survey fatigue.

You can also partner with companies that allow you to survey only certain types of customers, such as those who have seen x number of pages or those who came from www.zqinsights.com, and so forth. Ask whether your vendor provides you with such sophistication. Some do and others don't; depending on your needs, this option may or may not be important.

Nearly every vendor now allows you to set the sampling rate (the number of people on your site who see the survey). But just verify that you'll get that option as well.

Tip 7: Integration with Clickstream Data

Does your survey vendor allow you to integrate with your web analytics tool? Ask that question, and ask them exactly how they do it. Make sure you get one of your smart IT guys to look at the program with the FUD (fear, uncertainty, doubt) detector turned high.

Integration is important—not immediately, but after a few months of doing surveys—because you will want to know what your most satisfied visitors visited on the site, what campaigns or keywords drove the most unhappy traffic, and how people in your Clickstream data who saw the recommender tool felt about likelihood to recommend.

Integrating your survey tool with your web analytics data is complex, it takes some work, but it can yield solid rewards.

Tip 8: Pilot Friendly

When you ask the previous questions and make a choice, it is quite likely that you'll deal with the vendor's marketing and sales department. The best way to judge the real-world effectiveness of the survey is to do a pilot. If your vendor is any good, they'll be willing to do a pilot with you, say, for at least a month to six weeks. If the vendor refuses to do a pilot, then they may not have an effective tool for you.

Even if you have to pay a tiny amount up front to do a pilot, it is a very good idea to do one. You will learn whether the tool works for you, and perhaps more important, you will learn whether you can work with the vendor's people. Remember, you rarely buy tools; you almost always buy a relationship.

That's it: eight very simple traits to look for in a survey provider. These are traits that will help ensure you can establish a long, productive, and mutually beneficial relationship.

Web-Enabled Emerging User Research Options

One reason I am so crazy in love with the Internet is the massive amount of innovation and disruption that is enabled by the Web every single day. Even in our humble field of web user research, so many new options are available to us, and these options make possible what was once very difficult.

To close out this lovely chapter, I want to share four such options. Each is unique in its own sweet way. Each is an indicator of even cooler options around the corner—so keep your eyes open!

Competitive Benchmarking Studies

You have always wanted to know how bad (or good!) your checkout experience was compared to your competitors. Or how easily a visitor could answer a question or find a product between your websites.

In the past, it was difficult to find all the people you needed or to get the budget to do these kinds of studies. Not anymore. A number of companies on the Web now provide an easy and scalable way to make these comparisons. You tell them the task or process you want compared and who your competitor sites are. They get a number of users to execute the tasks; then they collect the data and provide an analysis. UserZoom is one such company, available at www.userzoom.com.

The cool thing is that the Web allows you to do these comparisons on a high scale and at a low cost, which you could never do in the past. I cannot tell you how powerful this type of data is for working with senior management and getting them to do the *right thing* (improve customer experience based on customer feedback).

Rapid Usability Tests

The concept implemented at www.fivesecondtest.com is brilliant in its simplicity.

You upload the image of the web page you want to test. Pick the type of test you want to do. You send out a url to a list of people (current or potential customers) or you can publish it on your Twitter account inviting feedback.

When a user lands on the site they are told that they will have five seconds to look at an image. Then the image (your image!) is shown. After five seconds elapse the image goes away and the participant is asked to list the things they remember from the image (/webpage) they saw.

It is fast, it is free (at least for now) and simple to execute.

The deliverables from the test are the open text summaries of what people recalled after a five second view of the web page (or an image). This is great for testing if your big calls to action are really all that clear on the page. What structural elements of your web pages stand out (and which ones don't). If people can read text in the image, what do they react to, etc.—you can even upload a screen of a competitor's site to see what people like about it.

Fivesecondtest is amongst a new breed of companies that are taking elements of traditional lab usability and massively democratizing access to them.

Online Card-Sorting Studies

One of the finest ways to improve the information architectures (IA) of a website is to do a card-sorting exercise. This exercise will help your users give you input on how your site should be organized. As usual, user input is always better than you creating an IA based on where *you* think things should go.

The traditional approach to card-sorting studies was to write the names of the main items on index cards, recruit a bunch of *representative* test participants, give them the shuffled set of index cards, and ask them to sort the cards into piles of related items. This reorganization helped you understand how to logically organize the website.

Of course, a study like this could get expensive, and it suffered from some of the same recruitment challenges faced when doing lab usability studies. Enter the Web, where two wonderful companies currently let you quickly and efficiently create card-sorting studies online: OptimalSort (www.optimalsort.com) and WebSort (www.websort.net).

Here's how it works: you log into the card-sorting vendor site, upload your items (create cards), identify representative users (use live recruiting methods like Ethnio or email people in your mailing list), and send an invitation email. Your users go through the sorting exercises quickly and efficiently online and then answer a few questions. You analyze the data. Everyone is happy.

You can do either open or closed card sorts. The primary difference is whether users are allowed to create their own categories or whether they must fit things into your predefined categories. When you start doing card sorts, I recommend using open sorts—it is always more intriguing to see where users would categorize items.

Artificially Intelligent Visual Heat Maps

Eye-tracking studies help you understand how visitors on your website consume content on your web pages: what captures their attention, how they *look around*, what influences their site navigation, and so on.

You have always wanted to do eye-tracking studies. Heck, you have even done them in the past and have a burning hole in your pocket to prove it (yes, they can be expensive). And, of course, there is the problem of the humans. It's always hard to find humans, get them into your labs, and make sure they are not too self-conscious as you ask them to *look around*.

Wouldn't it be great if you could still get the same kind of data without having to deal with *pesky* humans?

Enter Feng-GUI (www.feng-gui.com), a program that purports to "simulate human vision during the first five seconds of exposure to visuals and create *heat maps* based on an algorithm that predicts what a real human would be most likely to look at, as well as the *flow of attention*." Figure 6.9 shows the heat map created by Feng-GUI for my blog.

The intensity of the color represents more visitor interest, the hotspots are areas of interest, the number in the circle is the order in which the eyes looked at an area, and the lines represent movement.

Amazing, no? For free or at a very low cost—a fraction of what you would pay for eye-tracking studies—you can let a computer take care of the problem. We humans are so dispensable!

All kidding aside, the folks at Feng-GUI use some very sophisticated algorithms to power their solution. In my humble study, the program is not quite there yet when you contrast the results from the automatically created heat maps of Feng-GUI against actual eye-tracking studies. What is incredible is how good the results already are, and they will only get better with time.

Figure 6.9 Visual heat map of Occam's Razor created by Feng-GUI

I am unsure that computers and algorithms in the near term will replace the need for working with actual humans to understand emotions and answer your *why* questions. But computers are already good enough for quick and dirty analysis, and you should be prepared for computers and algorithms to offer even more valuable tools in the future.

Failing Faster: Unleashing the Power of Testing and Experimentation

Welcome to the awesome world of Experimentation and Testing!

If the Web holds one massive advantage over all other channels, it is in your ability to experiment and fail at a very low cost.

You can answer questions based on your gut about your site, the cost of products or shipping, or the layout of your landing page, or you can answer them through quick experiments, run live on your site, where customers help you pick winners. Experiments are fast, cheap, and scalable. So don't guess; learn to fail faster.

7

Chapter Contents

A Primer on Testing Options: A/B and MVT
Actionable Testing Ideas
Controlled Experiments: Step Up Your Analytics Game!
Creating and Nurturing a Testing Culture

People have been running experiments for a long time, not just in the chemistry lab or by cross-breeding plants in the name of biology. *Marketing experimentation* as a science has been around forever, from testing concept stores in different geographies before a worldwide launch to showing different television programs in different states, at different times, or to different audiences.

Despite that long testing tradition in the offline world, we tend to do very little of it online. It's a real crime, because we can learn so much from the offline experimentation techniques and have far fewer limitations.

Testing online is not optional. It is mandatory for every business of any size. Without leveraging some components of testing, your business will never scale the magnificent heights it deserves.

One of the most underappreciated aspects of testing is its comprehensive value proposition. Consider the following delicious benefits for your company:

- You can create an *ideas democracy*, that is, an environment where ideas come from anywhere and anyone, from the HiPPO to the janitor.

- You no longer have to guess what will work on your website.

- You can come up with bold and crazy ideas, but you manage risk by controlling how many people see the *crazy idea* and how many see the control.

- You can launch early and often and fail faster; your only limitation is the amount of traffic you get and the ideas you have.

- You control what success is—you identify the goal, and you decide what outcome you desire.

- You allow your customers to participate as they would normally experience your site and help you pick winners (all without knowing that they are in a test!).

- You can experiment for free if cost is a barrier, using tools such as the free Google Website Optimizer, and you can start tomorrow (no RFP, no complex product evaluation, no company bureaucracy).

- You don't have to buy a web analytics tool or worry about reporting or building your own multivariate or regression platforms for content or testing results. Every testing tool comes with all the analytics, reports, and complex math bundled in.

Convinced? I hope you are. Few things in web analytics are quite as cool, exciting, fun, and impactful as the subculture of Testing and Experimentation. It is a rare area where you can improve your bottom line while improving customer satisfaction.

Now you'll learn about the types of testing available to you, the kinds of tests you can run, why controlled experiments will change your life, and how to build a testing culture in your company.

A Primer on Testing Options: A/B and MVT

Although it might appear that you have a smorgasbord of testing types, essentially two types of testing techniques are widely used: A/B testing and multivariate testing (MVT). In the following sections, you'll get a glimpse at the pros and cons of each type so you can determine which is best for your situation.

A/B Testing

A/B testing is a technique for testing two or more versions of a page on your website. Each version of the web page is unique and can be visually differentiated from the control (the original page) without too much effort, as in Figure 7.1.

Figure 7.1 True A/B testing

The goal is to try a few versions of the page and identify which version delivers the desired outcome (for example, more click-throughs, more Conversions, lower Bounce Rates, or more donations). To accomplish the test, each version is randomly shown to a predetermined percentage of people who come to the page, usually 50 percent (or in the case of an A/B/C test: 33 percent, 33 percent, 34 percent).

A/B tests are best at testing big changes to the layout and templates of your web pages or for cases where you want to add or remove pages from a normal structured experience (for example, it takes four steps to apply for a credit card—you can test two steps or five steps).

Getting started with A/B tests is pretty straightforward. Start by looking at the Top Landing Pages report, and identify the pages with the highest Bounce Rates. Then have a brainstorming exercise for ideas to improve the page, coalesce the most promising, and get (beg) your designers and developers to create one or two versions with the new ideas. Launch the new ideas and measure. Simple.

Pros of A/B Testing

A/B testing is probably the *cheapest* way to start testing because you'll use existing resources in your company, the tools are free, or you can even use your website platform. A/B testing is not very difficult in terms of effort.

Without a doubt, A/B testing is the best technique to start your testing journey. Because of its inherent simplicity, you can get going quickly, and you can energize your organization while having some fun. In addition, the results are easy to communicate. You don't have to worry about multivariate tests, regressions, or other such (lovely) things.

Cons of A/B Testing

A/B testing is an all-or-nothing approach. In other words, you are testing pages, as in Figure 7.1, where you have changed many elements on the page all at once. You may know which page won quite easily, but it may be harder to tease out which elements contributed the most or not at all.

A/B testing will always be a key weapon in your arsenal, but too much reliance on A/B could mean you are making changes too slowly.

Multivariate Testing

Multivariate testing is a technique for testing changes to many different elements all at the same time on one web page. Let's use Figure 7.2 to illustrate this concept.

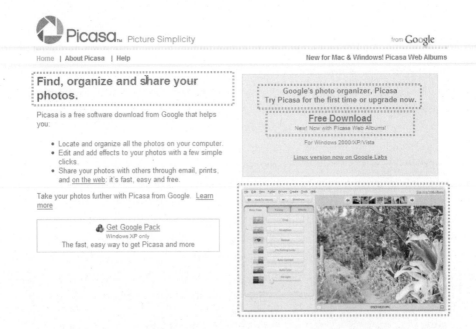

Figure 7.2 Control page in a multivariate test

You would like to optimize this page for Google. Four elements, identified in Figure 7.2 with double-dotted lines, are critical on the page and will be optimized in this test. For example, you would test four different versions of the main text on this page: "Find, organize and share your photos" and a few versions of the main image (bottom right). You would also test the page with no image at all and with three alternative calls to action instead of "Free Download."

To execute MVT, you would implement the JavaScript tags of the testing tool on the page. In the previous example, you would place tags around the four identified elements and upload the alternatives into the testing tool (for example, Google Website Optimizer, Optimost, SiteSpect). Then, let it rip.

Based on the settings you choose, visitors to the page are shown a dynamically created page with a variation of the elements in the test—in this case a different image, call to action, and main body text. Your MVT tool will start to produce the data almost immediately (see Figure 7.3), though typically you would not celebrate until you started seeing 95 percent or higher statistical significance in your results.

| Combinations | Page Sections | | | | | | |

Analysis

Sort By: ● Relevance Rating ○ Order Created   Download: T [img] [img] | 🖨 Print | 👁 Preview

Relevance Rating [?]	Variation	Estimated Conversion Rate Range [?]	Chance to Beat Orig. [?]	Chance to Beat All [?]	Observed Improvement [?]	Conversions / Impressions [?]
Section 3	Original	50.1% ± 0.4%	—	4.97%	—	12456 / 24859
3 / 5	Variation 3	50.8% ± 0.4%	94.4%	91.0%	1.42%	12693 / 24978
	Variation 1	50.1% ± 0.4%	46.9%	4.02%	-0.07%	12539 / 25042
	Variation 2	49.4% ± 0.4%	5.18%	0.03%	-1.46%	12404 / 25121
Section 2	Original	50.2% ± 0.3%	—	14.0%	—	16818 / 33532
2 / 5	Variation 1	50.6% ± 0.3%	86.0%	85.9%	0.82%	16936 / 33491
	Variation 2	49.5% ± 0.4%	5.65%	0.17%	-1.22%	16338 / 32977
Section 1	Original	50.3% ± 0.3%	—	94.6%	—	24944 / 49544
1 / 5	Variation 1	49.8% ± 0.3%	5.37%	5.37%	-1.00%	25148 / 50456
Section 4	Original	50.1% ± 0.5%	—	10.0%	—	10033 / 20035
0 / 5	Variation 3	50.5% ± 0.5%	79.8%	50.6%	0.83%	10109 / 20020
	Variation 2	50.3% ± 0.5%	66.1%	24.2%	0.41%	9964 / 19815
	Variation 1	50.2% ± 0.5%	57.3%	14.9%	0.18%	9994 / 19921
	Variation 4	49.4% ± 0.5%	10.0%	0.21%	-1.27%	9992 / 20209

Figure 7.3 Sample results from a multivariate test

In the case of Google Website Optimizer, you are keeping a close eye on the Chance to Beat Orig. column. Your bonus will be based, obviously, on the Observed Improvement column!

Notice the richness of the data in Figure 7.3 and how easily you can understand the Outcomes. This is one of the key strengths of MVT tools and the main reason they are a lot more accessible even to laypeople.

As in the case of A/B testing, be prepared for surprising results: the page shown in Figure 7.4 was the winner of the test.

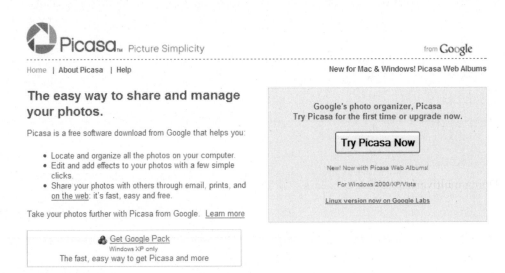

Figure 7.4 Google Picassa multivariate test winner

It is not a huge surprise that the text "The easy way to share and manage your photos" is better than "Find, organize and share your photos." It is surprising, however, that the image showing the program benefits did not help Conversions at all! Also, I was personally surprised because I have done tons of tests where simple text worked better than buttons, especially with the word Free, but in this case the "Free Download" text link did not work as well as the button "Try Picassa Now." See, we can all be wrong. Would you ever guess that "Try" works better than "Free"?

Common MVT Techniques

Two techniques are commonly used in executing multivariate tests: *full factorial* and *partial factorial* (also known as *fractional factorial*). With full factorial tests, you test all combinations of the pages that might occur as a result of your experiment. For example, in the previous test, you have four variations of all four elements—image, text, call to action, copy—so you have $4 \times 4 \times 4 \times 4 = 256$ combinations. With partial factorial tests, you test fewer combinations and *infer* results for what might happen with other combinations.

Rabid fans exist for each method, and they are not beyond completely trashing the other party. But nuances abound, and the technique you use depends on what you are trying to get done. A full factorial test is great at teasing out key data around interactions between each element, and it helps you make a more informed decision. But full factorial comes at a cost: the time required and the number of test participants (as you need enough data for each combination). A partial factorial test loses some richness of data, but you can get results faster. Another hybrid option is gaining acceptance; in this method you would use partial factorial to identify the worst combinations, prune them, and run a full factorial test for remaining promising combinations. The best of both worlds!

Each technique has value. Here's an example: if I am designing the perfect machine to reverse global warming, I'll use the full factorial technique, but if I am only designing a fix for the quickly disappearing ozone layer in the atmosphere, then I'll use partial factorial. Hyperbole? Yes. Encoded with a secret message to teach you how to make the right choice? I think so!

Pros of Multivariate Testing

Doing multivariate testing gets easier with each passing day. You can make things as complicated as you want, but you can also start very simply with just a few lines of JavaScript tags on a page.

Almost every aspect of MVT is outsourced; that is, MVT uses the powerful software-as-a-service (SaaS) model. Beyond adding tags to your page, you don't really need your IT team. You can start, run, and stop tests "remotely" using your MVT tool, and you can get all your analytics there as well. Bye-bye, IT! (OK, just teasing there, I love my peers in IT.)

The amount of data collected with MVT directly translates into an enhanced understanding of your visitor preferences and the value of your ideas. And all of that, in turn, directly translates into a more optimal website experience.

Cons of Multivariate Testing

MVT does require more effort and a higher level of commitment from your organization—from marketers, analysts, IT folks, and HiPPOs. Although the rewards are rich, you are also putting a lot of resources into the process.

With MVT, your experiments are only as good as the ideas you put into them. You'll need to invest in listening to customers (see Chapter 6), and you'll need to develop a solid understanding of what your website is trying to accomplish for your business. This is harder than you might imagine and why many MVT efforts fail.

Another problem, which is similar to A/B testing, is that you are optimizing a single page, but your website experience is not a single page. The number of pages it takes from entering your site to making a purchase could be 10 pages. Fixing just one page is a part of the victory, but if the other pages are suboptimal, you still lose.

Both A/B and multivariate testing are a critical part of improving your website experience and involving your customers. Choose the right weapon for the right purpose. Another technique, controlled experiments, is an extension of the testing philosophy. I'll discuss it a little bit later in this chapter.

Now go run your first test!

Actionable Testing Ideas

Conventional wisdom suggests that the first step is the hardest one. So, now that you realize the power A/B or MVT can unleash in your companies, I want to share specific ideas you can use as inspiration. These ideas come from my years in the trenches.

Before we continue, it is important to point out that every website is unique. What works for brand *x* might not work for brand *y*. That's because each business tends to execute a different online strategy. The other side of the coin, though, is the healthy cross-pollination of ideas. In a recent successful venture, I ran a series of experiments to optimize a nonprofit website, and most of my ideas came from the ecommerce space!

The bottom line: keep an open mind. The following sections contain a good collection of testing ideas to get you going, some obvious and most not.

Fix the Big Losers—Landing Pages

Most people start their testing with buttons or different hero images. But if you want a huge impact right away, start testing your Top Entry Pages, the ones with high Bounce Rates. These pages are heavily trafficked, they are not very hard to fix, and you can show a huge bang for the buck. You can start fixing them by looking at traffic sources, entry search keywords, and so forth.

If you want the heftiest impact, start with your campaign landing pages and your search, email, and affiliate pages. You are spending money acquiring this traffic, and if you fix the associated pages, you will reduce cost, and because you won't have to keep buying more traffic, you will increase revenue through higher Conversions, and you will save resources.

Focus on Checkout, Registration, and Lead Submission Pages

The checkout, registration, and lead submission pages are the classic funnels for your site. People enter a structured experience (page 1 → *click* → page 2 → *click* → page 3: done), and on the other side is money for you, through conversion, a lead, or an account registration. Focus on these pages because they are directly connected to Outcomes and your bottom line.

Most ecommerce sites have a four-page checkout process: cart/checkout → customer information → payment information → review order → confirmation. Some have a two-page checkout: cart/checkout → all information → confirmation. Which one is yours? Why not test it? Ditto if you are a bank that accepts credit card applications or a nonprofit that takes online donations. Test to find the process that works best for your customers.

Optimize the Number and Layout of Ads

Advertising is the primary source of monetization for numerous websites, and there seems to be little restraint in presenting ads. The prevailing strategy seems to be to slap as many ads on a page as possible. But the hypothesis that *more ads = more clicks = more revenue* never seems to get tested.

Just this morning I visited a major content website that had nine ad units above the browser fold! The ads were not just ineffective, but they made a terrible impression, making it likely that I'd never return. Double whammy.

So, test the number of ads you should have on a page. You can use a simple A/B test or a multivariate test. In one memorable test, a client actually reduced the number of ads on the page by 25 percent, and Outcomes improved by 40 percent. I kid you not, 40 percent! And guess which version made customers happier?

Let me give you a couple more ad-related ideas:

- If a banner takes up 30 percent of the real estate at the top of your web page, test a version without the banner, and see which one produces higher conversions.

- Try testing different ad layouts. Most ads in the header sit in a square box on the right or another obvious location. Visitors are blind to them. Test different locations on the page, and you may reduce banner blindness.

Test Different Prices and Selling Tactics

One way to reinvent your business model is to use testing. Here's a real story about how testing can change the business mind-set.

A company was selling just four products. But the environment got tough, and the competitors got competitive. How did the company fight back? Some "genius" in the company suggested they give the cheapest product, currently $15, away for free.

The CMO said, "Radical idea." The CEO said, "Are you insane?" The CFO said, "No way!"

The proposal did present a fundamental challenge: no one likes to give up revenue. And people worried about how successful the giveaway would be, how it would impact revenue, and why anyone would then *buy* a version.

Rather than create prediction models (with faulty assumptions!) or give up in the face of HiPPO pressure, the analytics team just launched an A/B test. They controlled for risk by doing a 95 percent control and a 5 percent version-A test (with the free product).

The free version of the product "sold" lots of copies. Surprisingly, the free version also helped shift the *SKU mix* in a statistically significant way; that is, the presence of the free product caused more people to buy the more expensive options. Hurray! Another benefit was that lots of new customers were introduced to the franchise as they "purchased" the free version. Nice.

Here are some bonus ideas for changing your selling tactics:

- Customers want to feel like they are getting a good deal, so if you give discounts, try 15 percent off rather than $10 off.
- Also try a $25 mail-in rebate rather than a $7 instant rebate. You get the idea.

Test Box Layouts, DVD Covers, and Offline Stuff

Let's say you are launching a new product or DVD. You want to figure out the most appealing layout for customers in stores. You could ask your mom to pick a version she likes. You could ask your agency to ask a few people. Or you could launch a test online and see which version your website visitors rate the highest.

If you are Wal-Mart, then it is expensive and time-consuming to put new products in your stores. That makes it risky to start stocking the "on paper hideous but perhaps weirdly appealing" zebra-print accent chairs in your store. What if they bomb? But you could add them to your site and see whether they sell. If the chairs get 15 positive customer reviews, then you know you have a winner on your hands.

By testing ideas for offline products online, you work with a faster launch process, you can reduce risk, and you don't have to rely on your employees to pick winners and losers.

Optimize Your Outbound Marketing Efforts

A/B and multivariate testing are not limited to your website. One of the most effective uses of testing is to improve the effectiveness of your email, affiliate, display, and search marketing efforts. You have unlimited possibilities for getting the maximum ROI from your testing efforts.

For your email campaigns, you can run tests for content, copy, calls to action, or the connected landing page experience. You can even do simple A/B tests by targeting different geographies or groups of your house email lists.

For your affiliates, you can try different offers across your network and reinforce successful offers in the site experience.

Many search engine marketing tools, such as ClickEquations (www.clickequations .com), let you do multivariate testing of your paid search ads. You don't have to guess which headline, copy, and links will work best. Run a live multivariate experiment on the search engines and let the click-through rates and conversions help you optimize your search campaigns.

My hope with this section on actionable testing ideas is that you will think beyond the obvious when you test. Yes, you can and should still test different calls to action, colors and sizes of buttons, and content on your web pages. But after your first few tests, try bigger and bolder ideas, because they tend to show the real value and power of Testing and Experimentation.

Controlled Experiments: Step Up Your Analytics Game!

According to the inimitable Wikipedia (http://en.wikipedia.org/wiki/Experiment), a controlled experiment "generally compares the results obtained from an experimental sample against a control sample, which is practically identical to the experimental sample except for the one aspect whose effect is being tested (the independent variable)."

Controlled experiments are effective for all kinds of scenarios in the real world, such as drug trials. In the online world, I have come to think of the methodology as a true friend. That's because we often come up with hypotheses that are tough to prove with the set of data available to us. We can't collect all the data cleanly. Or we can't control all the impacting variables.

Controlled experiments work very well in these cases. The goal is to create two or more similar conditions, change the desired variable, and then measure impact. You are trying to tease out cause and effect.

With controlled experiments, you can revolutionize the lessons you get from your online efforts. I'll now solidify this concept with a real-world example.

Measuring Paid Search Impact on Brand Keywords and Cannibalization

Here's the setup: you have the number-one organic search ranking for your brand term (for example, *avinash* or *Pantene*) on www.google.com. You have heard conflicting opinions about also buying a paid search ad. Some industry gurus say you should not buy search ads, but your friends say you should maximize the real estate on the search engine and use AdWords, AdCenter, or Yahoo! Search Marketing for your keywords.

What's the right answer? It is very difficult to tell. You can't quite rely on your web analytics data for a clean read because key data from the search engine is missing—you get x clicks, but x of how many? You can't rely on your friends or the "experts." You could go with your gut, but come on!

Why not run a controlled experiment?

Figure 7.5 shows some real data. In this case, the business received substantial traffic from organic search results for its brand terms, and the conversions were great as well.

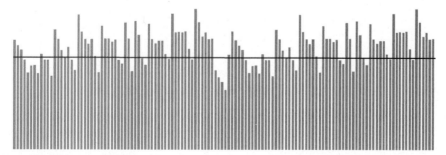

Figure 7.5 Organic search results

The x-axis represents time (days), and the y-axis represents Conversions. Normal variability appeared in the Conversions over certain weekdays and weekends. To understand the value of paid search, the company created a controlled experiment. It spent different amounts of money on its AdWords campaigns over a six-week period, as shown in Figure 7.6.

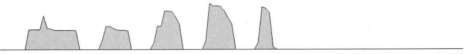

Figure 7.6 AdWords spending plan

Notice the hills and valleys in the spending levels: ramping spend at different levels, the days when spend levels went completely dark, and the difference in consecutive days of spending. The company strategy created an experiment where it could measure cause and effect more easily, while accounting for external factors that might cause variability in the data.

Figure 7.7 shows the impact of the campaigns on Conversions. The lower-level bars are the Conversions from organic search. The upper-level bars are the Conversions from paid search campaigns!

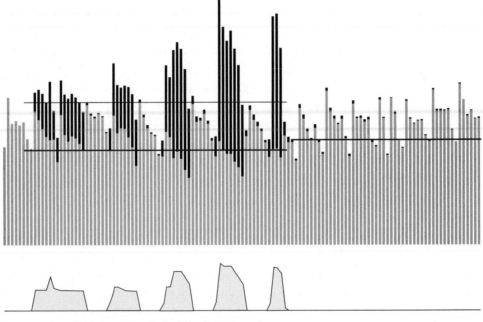

Figure 7.7 Controlled experiment results for paid and organic searches

You can work out the following key details from the data:

- The rise and fall of the paid search Conversions is duplicated as the paid search campaigns turn on and off. This shows the value paid search adds to this company's brand campaigns.

- After a certain spend level, starting with the third "bump" at the bottom of Figure 7.7, impact is multiplied. Outcomes go much higher, perhaps because of the ad position at that spend level.

- When you compare the impact on organic search, represented by the two disjointed lines of average conversions (or comparing Figure 7.5 and Figure 7.7), you can see some cannibalization. When paid search ads ran, there was a 12 percent cannibalization. That is, traffic that would have come via organic, free clicks clicked on paid search results and cost the company money.

- Overall conversions jumped up significantly, represented by the first line at the top in Figure 7.7. The effect was clear as spend levels varied by day or amount spent.

- In this case, the analyst was a true ninja who measured multiple goals. Goal 1 increased by 71 percent in the experiment, goal 2 increased by 7 percent, goal 3 increased by 31 percent, and goal 4 showed no change.

So, you see how the company answered the fundamental question of whether to buy paid searches, and it became much smarter about where paid search has an impact and where it doesn't!

Tip: Comparing average Conversions, as with the third item in the bulleted list, is a great strategy for understanding paid and organic search cannibalization.

At the end of the controlled experiment, the company decided to spend money buying brand terms in its AdWords campaigns. A difficult decision was made easy with a controlled experiment. This does not mean *you* should spend on branded search terms. You should use this technique to figure out the right answer for your case.

Examples of Controlled Experiments

One of the coolest stories I have heard about using controlled experiments to impact the bottom line comes from my friend Jim Novo, author of *Drilling Down: Turning Customer Data into Profits with a Spreadsheet.*

Jim ran an experiment where a company added a small thank-you gift and note along with the customer's online order. The hypothesis was that this small gesture would make a positive brand impression on the customer and increase future sales. Jim ran a small controlled experiment where some customers got the thank-you gift, and he measured results for that group vs. the control. Sure enough, more people from the test gift group placed repeat orders.

Zappos does something similar where they "delight" some of its customers by upgrading them to expedited shipping even though they paid only for normal shipping.

This controlled experiment proved it increased retention and repeat orders (not to mention the stories of joy these customers would spread).

In another example, an enterprising marketer at a big American retailer wanted to drive offline sales of bed mattresses by using online advertising. That seems like a huge stretch. Although some consumers do research online, mattresses are a deeply offline purchase, influenced by TV ads of comfortable people sleeping like babies. The marketer, however, ran online ads aggressively in four geographically different states (Texas, Oregon, North Carolina, and New York) and measured the sales lift in the physical stores in the weeks following the ad campaigns. Using this strategy, she isolated the impact on store sales between her test and control groups (states) and showed the company that online campaigns delivered a measurable percentage lift at one-tenth the cost of offline campaigns.

My final example of controlled experiments comes from my own experience. The question was quite simple: do radio campaigns effectively drive traffic online for a pharmaceutical company? The experiment involved running radio spots on stations of different genres (for example, pop, country, talk radio) in 100 cities across the United States. The resulting data, even by just studying Visits in the map overlay report, was sufficient for the client to recognize the effectiveness of the ads. The client could segment the data by market (city), radio stations, and genres to understand where the campaign was most effective and where it fell flat.

Imagine trying to make that kind of decision based simply on your web analytics data.

Challenges and Benefits

Running controlled experiments is not easy. It requires resources, a superior level of commitment from your company, clever experimentation creation, and complex coordination across online and offline teams, analysts, and marketers. But all things worth having come after some effort. With controlled experiments, you can realize the following benefits:

- You can answer fundamental business questions that yield powerful insights.
- You learn the impact of cross-channel online campaigns and multichannel campaigns.
- You adapt your marketing strategy to customer types, preferences, and locations.
- You can measure the impact of unmeasureable things such as branding campaigns.
- You make your analysts significantly smarter by exposing them to perhaps the most advanced way of doing analysis.

Bottom line: you can spend your precious marketing and advertising funds with increased confidence. Oh, and it's really fun!

Creating and Nurturing a Testing Culture

Creating a culture of testing can be much harder than it sounds. That's because you'll fail a lot, especially if your testing ideas are not bold enough or are not sourced in an actual customer pain. At various times, you'll need to involve your HiPPOs, marketers, designers, researchers, and analysts.

Here are nine tips that will help you create and then nurture a culture of experimentation and testing in your company.

Tip 1: Your First Test is "Do or Die"

No battle, or love, is won on day one, but I cannot stress enough how important your first test is. You'll read this book, you'll present nice slides to your management on the benefits of testing, you'll do a little rap song, and they'll be convinced. It's important that you make the best of this opportunity.

Make your first test an A/B test. It keeps things simple from an idea, execution, and measurement point of view, all of which are key to showing value and getting people to sign on.

When we test, we often mistakenly choose an irrelevant page or element to reduce risk. For example, we change the shade of blue in a button. With these weak choices, we kill any chance of showing impact: the page won't have enough page views, and the impact on Outcomes will be negligible. Pick a *big enough* page, though not necessarily the home page, and create bold alternatives to the control.

A and B versions of the page should be as different as you can make them (see Figure 7.1). Big differences in versions mean big differences in Conversions and Outcomes, and that means faster results and bigger success or failure.

Your first test will get your organization excited, even if you massively fail, and prove that testing is a valuable technique. Don't waste that opportunity on trying something minor. Remember, you can always control risk by deciding how many people see the test pages. If your product page currently has a bouquet of flowers and the test version has a naked man, then you send just 15 percent of the traffic to the test page and send 90 percent to the control. You reduce the risk, and yet you collect data that will prove the naked man can sell wireless routers just as well as a picture of flowers!

Tip 2: Don't Get Caught in the Tool/Consultant Hype

Companies tend to get caught up in the tool/consultant hype. "You can test 13 million page combinations," or "Our solution does automated optimization with artificial intelligence, and it'll cost you next to nothing." You catch my drift. Just get started. Don't waste months evaluating tools and sitting through the dog-and-pony shows of vendors and consultants.

In the world of Web Analytics 2.0, you can start right away with free tools like the Google Website Optimizer. If you have a deep relationship with Omniture, then you may be able to try Test & Target free for three months. So, why *evaluate*? Why not *just do it*? When you start for free, do a few simple A/B tests to prove value; you don't need to pick the perfect tool or the perfect consultant. Gain experience. Get smart. Then go evaluate options.

Tip 3: "Open the Kimono"—Get Over Yourself

If you need to convince everyone else that testing and validating opinions should be a way of life, you must first truly drink the Kool-Aid. You need to get over your own entrenched opinions.

When I talk about testing, I make my case by sharing the most recent times testing has proven me to be disastrously wrong. I share the worst stories—the big losers—to show that we don't really represent the customers and that validating opinions is great.

Remember, you'll get a receptive audience and change minds much faster if you are willing to "open the kimono."

Tip 4: Start with a Hypothesis

We tend to start by saying, "I want to test different colors of the home page" or "We should swap this image with text." Notice what's missing? Any semblance of intent. The golden rule is, always start with a hypothesis, not test details or test scenarios. Ask your client: "What is your hypothesis?"

This question forces people to take a step back and think. They might come back to you and say, "My hypothesis is that images of people make a more powerful connection than current box shots, and hence we will have a higher engagement score." Or they might say, "My hypothesis is that visitors to the site are more interested in user-generated content than our company propaganda." Super!

You have accomplished two important things: first, you can now contribute to the process of creating the test, and second, you have established a clear success measurement with a well-crafted hypothesis. Remember, if you don't see a success measurement in the hypothesis, then you don't have a well thought-out hypothesis.

Tip 5: Make Goals Evaluation Criteria and Up-Front Decisions

A mistake we make too often is knowing the success metric but not establishing the parameters to judge the *victory*. Choose the success metrics for the test before you launch, and don't forget to create a goal for those metrics. So, you are launching a test to improve Conversion Rate. Great. You need to establish by how much you want to improve the conversion rate.

Frequently we do not establish our measures up front, but these up-front decisions are critical for two reasons:

- You are forced to research the current trends of your success metrics and complete a goal-creation exercise for your test.
- You can judge whether you should do the test in the first place.

  If testing dancing monkeys on your home page will improve Conversion Rate by only 0.001 percent (your goal), then that test may not be worthwhile, and you should think of something more powerful.

Remember that you are trying to push the thought envelope and create tests that will yield more powerful improvements in customer experience.

Tip 6: Test For and Measure Multiple Outcomes

Testing for Multiple Outcomes is important once you have a bunch of tests under your belt.

Almost all testing focuses on a single goal. But life and customer experiences are significantly more complex; visitors come to your website for multiple purposes. If you use the current multivariate testing tools, then you need to integrate tools that let you measure the impact of your test on all those other purposes.

For example, visitors come to your home page to buy, to print product information, and so forth. If you solve only for Conversion Rate, then any changes you make may negatively impact your customers.

Integrating your testing tool with your web analytics tool can be a great start to measuring multiple goals. You can measure the goal you set in your testing tool, and you can segment the test participants in your analytics tool. Then you can measure other goals (Bounce Rates, loyalty, downloads, and so on). You can also integrate your survey tool with your testing tool and segment customer satisfaction or task completion rates.

Over the long term, by moving to a truly multigoal measurement model, you will convert the lessons you learned from your testing program into a sustainable competitive advantage.

Tip 7: Source Your Tests in Customer Pain

Do you remember the last question in our Greatest Survey Ever from Chapter 6? It was "If you were not able to complete your task, why not?"

That's your greatest source of testing ideas. Through surveys, usability tests, card sorts, or even site overlay heat maps, customers will tell you the problems they have with your website. Take that gold, and convert it into solutions that you can test.

Often our tests yield suboptimal results because we are trying to solve pain points that *we* think our visitors have. We take sources from our own experience and biases.

Flip the model. Source your testing ideas in customer pain, and you'll win because you are solving real customer challenges.

Seek out customer challenges on your site. Seek them out from your call center. Seek them out in market research. Seek them out from your regular customers. Solve an actual customer problem, and you kill two birds with one stone. Happy customers mean increased website ROI.

Tip 8: Analyze Data and Communicate Learnings

You have to celebrate failure and learn from it. You have to make sure that your peers and HiPPOs learn from it, too.

For every test you do, even the spectacular failures, analyze the data, and communicate what you learned. Companies improve from knowing what works, but they may learn more from what does not work.

Communicating your valuable lessons will ensure that your company and peers do not stigmatize failure; instead, they will try big, risky ideas. And they won't repeat tests that have already yielded results.

You are not just communicating data; you are trying to change a culture.

Tip 9: Two Must-Haves: Evangelism and Expertise

You need two key people in any successful program, a *testing evangelist* and a *testing expert*. This is important as you scale testing, especially if you are with a large company.

Most people don't yet get the testing religion, so to convert them, you need an evangelist—not just someone who "gets it" but someone who through their communication skills, pure love, business understanding, and position can preach the value proposition. If this person does not know what *r* squared is, that is OK. This is not a full-time position, but it does require full-time passion.

As you scale to run your program and actually execute many of these techniques, you need a testing expert. You need someone seeped in metrics and data who has enough business expertise to look at tests and provide good feedback—someone who can even help generate great value-added ideas.

My last tip is that you should have fun. Testing is incredible fun. You are dealing with complex challenges and helping your company come up with creative ideas to solve those challenges. It is fun to engage your peers. It is fun to *play* with your customers by putting them in tests and watching the results. It is fun to improve their happiness and yours by adding to your company's bottom line. Have fun.

Competitive Intelligence Analysis

In the real world, collecting competitive intelligence might mean hiring people to rummage through your competitors' garbage bins (actually happened!). In the virtual world, mountains of data are right at your fingertips—from referrers, destinations, and search keywords to demographic and psychographic profiles. Though it sounds too good to be true, much of this data is available for free.

Competitive intelligence data can radically enhance your decision-making process: you get additional context about your own performance, you can mine industry trends for actionable insights, and you can finally understand your competition in the near-frictionless environment of the Web.

8

Chapter Contents
CI Data Sources, Types, and Secrets
Website Traffic Analysis
Search and Keyword Analysis
Audience Identification and Segmentation Analysis

Quite simply, *competitive intelligence* (CI) is the analysis of data about your competitors, vertical markets, or the entire web ecosystem. For example, AMD, the microchip manufacturer, can use competitive intelligence data to understand how its direct competitor Intel performs. That means measuring growth rates of visitor trends or identifying good sources of traffic for Intel and using that information to inform AMD's strategy. Alternatively, AMD can access CI data for all businesses in the semiconductor industry and then index their competitor's performance against their own and identify new opportunities.

For a long time, the only options for getting competitive intelligence on the Web were solutions such as Alexa (a toolbar), comScore (a panel), and Hitwise (an ISP). Alexa data was free, but the latter options were expensive, and hence data was inaccessible to many. In the past two years, however, a host of paid and free tools have become available in the marketplace. These include Compete, Google's Insights for Search and Ad Planner, single-purpose solutions such as Wordtracker and Quantcast, alert-based solutions such as Trackur, and many more.

CI Data Sources, Types, and Secrets

You need to understand how any piece of data was collected so you can decide how best to use it. Browsers, search engines, vendors, and others collect CI data via many different avenues, and CI tools collect data very differently from your analytics tool.

So, I want to address a critical issue that trips up almost everyone. You crack open the yummy-looking CI tool, punch in your website's URL, and when the data comes back, the numbers don't match the data from your web analytics tool. You are confused; you lose your religion at that moment and give up. Big mistake.

CI tools have no access to your site (or that of your competitor), while web analytics tools do have access to your site. This fundamental difference in data collection means that the two sources will be close, the trends will look similar, but they will never tie. And that's OK!

Here's an analogy to help you think about CI data optimally. Consider the case of measuring how many people walk into your neighborhood supermarket. Using analytics tools such as Coremetrics or Yahoo! Web Analytics is like standing at the door of a supermarket and counting how many people walk in. They're pretty accurate. Using CI tools is like standing on the moon with a telescope pointed at the door of the supermarket and measuring how many people walk in. The data you collect by standing at the door of the supermarket will be better. But you can't get that data for your competitors—they'll kick you out in two seconds.

If you want to measure your performance against your competitors, the only choice you have is a CI tool. And although the data will never be perfect, it is good enough for you to understand important trends, identify opportunities, and ensure your strategy is informed by your performance *and* your competitor's performance.

Therefore, before you do CI analysis, you should spend some time understanding how your CI tool collects data. Ensure that there is as little bias as possible with the data sample and sampling bias (more on this later in the chapter).

Now, let's get familiar with data collection methods for CI to ensure you are prepared to make optimal use of your CI data. Later in the chapter, I'll talk about how to put the data to work.

Toolbar Data

Toolbars are add-ons that provide additional functionality to web browsers, such as easier access to news, search features, and security protections. They are available from all the major search engines such as Google, MSN, and Yahoo! as well as from thousands of other sources. These toolbars also collect limited information about the browsing behavior of the customers who use them, including the pages visited, the search terms used, perhaps even time spent on each page, and so forth. Typically, data is anonymous and not personally identifiable information (PII).

After the toolbars collect the data, your CI tool then scrubs and massages the data before presenting it to you for analysis. For example, with Alexa, you can report on traffic statistics (such as rank and page views), upstream (where your traffic comes from) and downstream (where people go after visiting your site) statistics, and keywords driving traffic to a site.

Millions of people use widely deployed toolbars, mostly from the search engines, which makes these toolbars one of the largest sources of CI data available. That very large sample size makes toolbar data a very effective source of CI data, especially for macro website traffic analysis such as number of visits, average duration, and referrers.

The massive use of search engine toolbars is also the reason data from Alexa, a toolbar deployed by fewer users, is not used very widely.

Tip: Toolbar data is typically not available by itself. It is usually a key component in tools that use a mix of sources to provide insights.

Note: Toolbars can make web surfing easier. As a user, you should familiarize yourself with the data being collected when you use a toolbar and how that data will be used. Before installing any toolbar, locate and read the privacy policy. Most toolbar privacy policies are hard to find and often harder to understand, but you should persist and hunt it down and familiarize yourself with it. You want to control what data is collected. You can find the privacy policy for the Google Toolbar at `http://zqi.me/gtpriv`.

Panel Data

Panel data is another well-established method of collecting data. To gather panel data, a company may recruit participants to be in a panel, and each panel member installs a piece of monitoring software. The software collects all the panel's browsing behavior and reports it to the company running the panel.

Varying degrees of data are collected from a panel. At one end of the spectrum, the data collected is simply the websites visited, and at the other end, the monitoring software records the credit cards, names, addresses, and any other personal information typed into the browser.

Panel data is also collected when people unknowingly opt into sending their data. Common examples are a small utility you install on your computer to get the weather or an add-on for your browser to help you autocomplete forms. In the unreadable terms of service you accept, you agree to allow your browsing behavior to be recorded and reported.

Panels can have a few thousand members or several hundred thousand. One of the largest panels in the United States is run by comScore; its U.S. panel has 1 million visitors (according to its website) http://zqi.me/cs1mil.

You need to be cautious about three areas when you use data or analysis based on panel data:

Sample bias Almost all businesses, universities, and other institutions ban monitoring software because of security and privacy concerns. Therefore, most monitored behavior tends to come from home users. Since usage during business hours forms a huge amount of web consumption, it is important to know that panel data is blind to this information.

Sampling bias People are enticed to install monitoring software in exchange for sweepstakes entries, downloadable screensavers and games, or a very small sum of money (such as $3 per month). This inclination causes a bias in the data because of the type of people who participate in the panel. This is not itself a deal breaker, but consider whose behavior you want to analyze vs. who might be in the sample.

Web 2.0 challenge Monitoring software (overt or covert) was built when the Web was static and page-based. The advent of rich experiences such as video, Ajax, and Flash means no page views, which makes it difficult for monitoring software to capture data accurately. Some monitoring software companies have tried to adapt by asking companies to embed special beacons in their website experiences, but as you can imagine, this is easier said than done.

The panel methodology is based on the traditional television data capture model. In a world that is massively fragmented, panels face a huge challenge in collecting accurate and complete (or even representative) data. A rule of thumb I have developed is if a site gets more than 5 million unique visitors a month, then there is a sufficient signal from panel-based data.

Tip: Panel data has been a primary source for CI analysis. But because of the methodology's inherent limitations, recently panel data is augmented by other sources of data before it is provided for analysis.

ISP (Network) Data

We all get our Internet access from ISPs, and as we surf the Web, our requests go through the servers of these ISPs to be stored in server log files. The data collected by the ISP consists of elements that get passed around in URLs, such as sites, page names, keywords, and so on. The ISP servers can also capture information such as browser types and operating systems.

The size of these ISPs translates into a huge sample size. For example, Hitwise (`http://zqi.me/hw10mil`) which chiefly relies on ISP data, has a sample size of 10 million people in the United States and 25 million worldwide. Such a large sample size reduces sample bias.

The other benefit of ISP data is that the sampling bias is also reduced; since you and I don't have to agree to be monitored, our ISP simply collects this anonymous data and then sells it to third-party sources for analysis.

ISPs typically don't publicize that they sell the data, and companies that purchase that data don't share this information either. So, there is a chance of some bias. Ask for the sample size when you choose your ISP-based CI tool, and go for the biggest you can find.

Tip: ISP data has been a primary source for CI analysis. In some cases, data from a small sample of toolbar data and some panel data are added to fill in some gaps.

Search Engine Data

Our queries to search engines, such as Bing, Google, Yahoo!, and Baidu, are logged by those search engines, along with basic connectivity information such as IP address and browser version. In the past, analysts had to rely on external companies to provide search behavior data, but more search engines are providing tools to directly mine their data.

You can use search engine data with a greater degree of confidence, because it comes directly from the search engine. Remember, though, that the data is specific to that search engine—and because each search engine has distinct roles, it is not wise to apply lessons from one to another.

Let's look at some examples. In Google AdWords, you can use Keyword Tool (`http://zqi.me/adwkwt`), the search-based Keyword Tool (`http://zqi.me/s-bkt`), and

Insights for Search (http://zqi.me/gi4s). Similar tools are available from Microsoft: Entity Association, Keyword Group Detection, Keyword Forecast, and Search Funnels (all at http://zqi.me/msacl).

 Tip: Search engine data tends to be the primary, and typically only, source for search data analysis.

Benchmarks from Web Analytics Vendors

Web analytics vendors have lots of customers, which means they have lots of data. Many vendors now aggregate this real customer data and present it in the form of benchmarks that you can use to index your own performance.

Benchmarking data is currently available from Fireclick (http://zqi.me/fcindex), Coremetrics (http://zqi.me/corebm), and Google Analytics (http://zqi.me/gabench). Often, as is the case with Google Analytics, customers have to explicitly opt in their data into this benchmarking service.

Both Fireclick and Coremetrics provide benchmarks related to Conversion Rates, Cart Abandonment, Time on Site, and so forth. Google Analytics provides benchmarks for Visits, Bounce Rates, Page Views, Time on Site, and Percent of New Visits. Figure 8.1 shows a sample of the data from each tool.

Figure 8.1 Performance benchmark reports

In all three cases, you can compare your performance to specific vertical markets (for example, retail, apparel, software, and so on), which is much more meaningful.

The cool benefit of this method is that websites directly report very accurate data, even if the web analytics vendor makes that data anonymous. The downside is that your competitors are unlikely to use the same tool as you; therefore, you are comparing your actual performance against the actual performance of a subset of your competitors.

With data from vendors, you must be careful about sample size, that is, how many customers the web analytics vendor has. If your vendor has just 1,000 customers and it is producing benchmarks in 15 industry categories, you may be able to compare numbers in some categories, while in other categories you may not have a significant data sample.

> **Tip:** Data from web analytics vendors comes from their clients, so it is real data. The client data is anonymous, so you can't do a direct comparison between you and your arch enemy; rather, you'll compare yourself to your industry segment.

Self-reported Data

You may be wondering how you can be using *competitive intelligence* if websites publicly report their own data. You are discounting the benefit of having your data public, especially if you are a website that runs on advertising.

It is common knowledge that some methods of data collection, such as panel-based, do not collect data with the necessary degree of accuracy. A site's own analytics tool may report 10 million visits, and the panel data may report 6 million. To overcome this issue, some vendors, such as Quantcast and Google's Ad Planner, allow websites to report their own data through their tools, as shown in Figure 8.2.

On the top right of the Quantcast report, the icon called Quantified indicates the report is showing data directly from the site. In Ad Planner, the small bar graph icon next to certain metrics—such as Unique Visitors (cookies)—indicates data from the site.

For sites that rely on advertising, the data used by advertisers must be as accurate as possible; hence, the sites have an incentive to share data directly. If your competitors publish their own data through vendors such as Google's Ad Planner or Quantcast, then that is probably the cleanest and best source of data for you.

You need to be cautious in two areas when you work with self-reported data. First, check the definitions of various metrics. For example, if you see a metric called Cookies, find out exactly what that metric means before you use the data. Second, incompletely implemented tags are the bane of our existence, and they can bias the sample. For example, if your competitor does not implement the Quantcast tag on all pages on their site, then that data will be incomplete and hence incorrect.

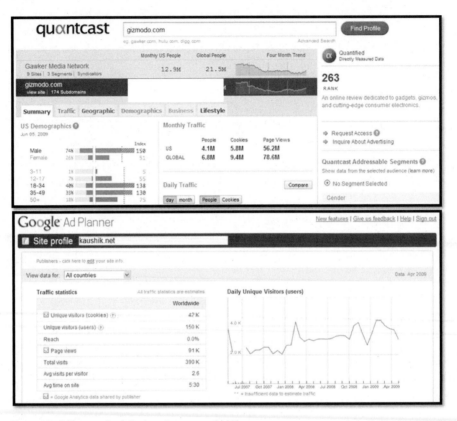

Figure 8.2 Self-reported website data, Quantcast and Ad Planner

 Tip: Because of its inherent nature, self-reported data tends to augment other sources of data provided by tools such as Ad Planner or Quantcast.

Hybrid Data

Rather than using just one source for data, some vendors now use multiple sources to augment their data set. There are two primary ways of doing this.

The first method is to *append* the data. In Figure 8.2, you saw that both Quantcast and Ad Planner still report data from their own sources, but they append data directly reported by the website.

The second method is to put many different sources into a blender, churn at high speed, throw in a pinch of math and a dash of correction algorithms, and—boom!—you have one number. A good example of this is Compete. Its analytics tool uses data from panels, ISPs, their own toolbar, and data purchased from other application providers.

Google's Trends for Websites is another example of a hybrid source. Here's the description directly from the horse's mouth:

> *Trends for Websites combines information from a variety of sources, such as aggregated Google search data, aggregated opt-in anonymous Google Analytics data, opt-in consumer panel data, and other third-party market research. The data is aggregated over millions of users, powered by computer algorithms, and doesn't contain personally identifiable information. Additionally, Google Trends for Websites only shows results for sites that receive a significant amount of traffic, and enforces minimum thresholds for inclusion in the tool.*

SOURCE: http://zqi.me/t4wdata

The benefit of using hybrid methodology is that the vendor can plug in any gaps that might exist between different sources. The challenge is that it is much harder to peel back the onion and understand some of the nuances and biases in the data.

Hence, the best-practice recommendation is to forget about the absolute numbers and focus on comparing trends; the longer the time period, the better.

> **Tip:** As the name implies, hybrid data contains data from many different sources and is increasingly the most commonly used methodology.

A lot of data is available about your industry or your competitors that you can use to your benefit. Here is the process I recommend for CI data analysis:

1. Ensure that you understand exactly how the data is collected.

2. Understand both the sample size and sampling bias of the data reported to you. Really spend time on this.

3. If steps 1 and 2 pass the sniff test, use the data. Don't skip the steps, and glory will surely be yours.

Excited? Let's dive deeper into a few different types of actual analysis and have some fun!

Website Traffic Analysis

When people think of competitive intelligence, the first question that crosses their mind is, "How many visits did my competitor get?" We can answer that question quite easily. Let's look at some of the wonderful analyses you can do.

Comparing Long-Term Traffic Trends

The simplest question to answer in the analytics world is, "How is my traffic doing compared to my competition?" Look at Figure 8.3 to find some easy answers for one market.

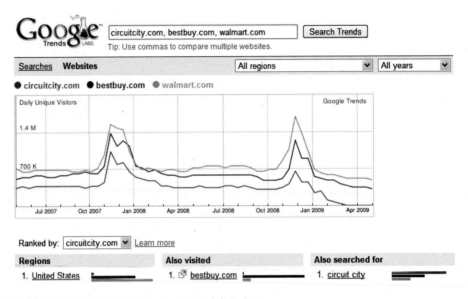

Figure 8.3 Website traffic comparison, Google Trends for Websites

Using Google Trends for Websites, I can easily compare Best Buy with its main competitors, Wal-Mart and Circuit City. I can easily see that through 2007 traffic was fairly competitive with Wal-Mart, but in Q2 2008, Wal-Mart started to pull away and has done well ever since.

Someone paid $20 million for the name and assets of Circuit City, which filed for bankruptcy in early 2009 (you see that in the graph, right?). Was that a good decision? From this chart, it looks like it was a great decision. Twenty million dollars is not a lot of money (in this context), and the chart shows that Circuit City held its own for the last few years against the others. In fact, even through Christmas 2008, when Circuit City was deeply in trouble, the site traffic held up really nicely.

Also note that Trends for Websites allows you to focus only on a certain region (countries) and further drill down into subregions (states). This focus provides great insights about the geographic strengths of your competition.

Compete is another excellent source of website analytics data. Figure 8.4 shows the report for the same query.

By now you know that the exact numbers at a given data point between Figure 8.3 and Figure 8.4 don't match because the two tools collect data far too differently. But note that the trends match pretty nicely.

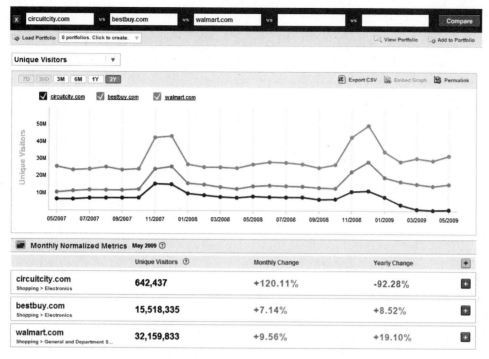

Figure 8.4 Website traffic comparison, Compete

Resist the temptation to compare precise numbers. Compare trends over time. Use the data to overlay your own actions, such as marketing campaigns, to see whether you made a real impact when you compare your numbers to the competition. For example, look at Figure 8.4; if Best Buy spent $100 million on marketing during Christmas 2008—five times its normal outlay—and could not even match the slope of the line for Wal-Mart, then the outlay was not worth it.

Analyzing Competitive Sites Overlap and Opportunities

The Also Visited data in Google Trends for Websites helps you recognize which sites are really your competition. (The metric shows which other sites Visitors to your site also visit, and trust me, this data is always full of surprises.) Figure 8.5 shows a comparison between homedepot.com and lowes.com.

An immediate scare for Lowes is that the number-one site its Visitors visited happens to be homedepot.com! Home Depot's biggest competitor comes in at 3. You can also see that some of their competition overlaps, though Home Depot might want to check why there is no overlap with certain sites that Lowes customers visit, such as tractorsupply.com, thisoldhouse.com, and askthebuilder.com. The latter two might be great advertising or sponsorship opportunities.

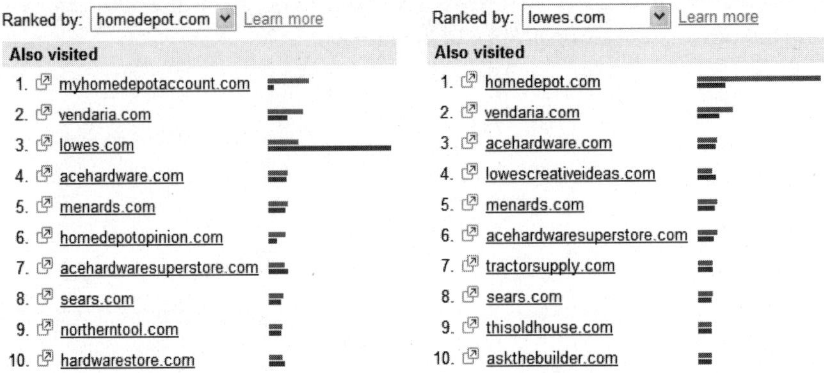

Figure 8.5 Also Visited report: websites visited overlap, Google Trends for Websites

The Also Searched For data in Trends for Websites shows which search terms Visitors of your competition are likely to visit. If none of those terms are yours, then you should be sad!

Analyzing Referrals and Destinations

When you open your web analytics tool, one of the first things to note is websites that refer traffic to you. But how do you know whether those are the best sites for getting traffic? You could look at your competitors and see who sends them traffic.

Here's another question that I am sure bothers you all the time: what websites do people visit after they leave your site? The answer, as you saw earlier, can be critical. For example, where do people go next after they bounce off your site? The answer may contain a clue about what they were looking for on your website and how you can improve it.

Figure 8.6 shows a composite report for referral and destination analysis for B&H Photo Video.

The report on the left shows all the sites referring traffic to B&H. It is easy to see that B&H sells through www.amazon.com as well as its own site, and that looks like a good decision: Amazon is listed as the number-three referrer. B&H is also strong in terms of search.

The report on the right shows the sites people visit after they leave B&H. It is a bit surprising that Google refers 32.5 percent of the traffic to B&H; if those people found what they were looking for at B&H, then 29.08 percent would not immediately go back to Google (presumably to search again). eBay also figures higher in the destination column, with an 8.5 percent increase of people going there this month. B&H could use content reports to check whether this traffic comes to do price comparisons or product research before they go back to eBay and buy there.

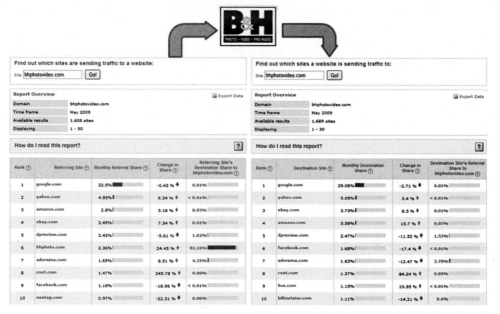

Figure 8.6 Referral and destination analysis, Compete

You can do this analysis for your own website, but it is a lot more interesting to pour over data for your main competitors and tease out their strategies.

Although simply comparing your traffic number with a competitor's is a good way to start, I hope the previous examples illustrate that more information is hidden beneath the surface. Figure 8.7 provides guidance on which data source to use for your analysis, based on the number of Unique Visitors you get on your site (or based on your best guess of that number on your competitors' sites).

		Toolbar	Panel	ISP	Search Engines	Hybrid
Website CI Analysis						
Size of Website	Very Large	X	X	X	X	X
	Large	X		X	X	X
	Medium			X	X	X
	Small					X
	* Size: Very Large: 5 mil or more Unique Visitors, Large: 1 mil or more, Mid: 100k more, Small: 10k or more.					

Figure 8.7 Decision matrix for choosing optimal data source for website CI analysis

Search and Keyword Analysis

Search engines are the starting points for most people who use the Web. Bing, Yahoo!, Google, Ask, and others are therefore a vital part of every company's acquisition portfolio. You want people to find you? You better have a solid organic and paid search strategy.

A key way to measure how you perform with search, and to find new opportunities, is to use CI tools to report on search behavior data. The following are some of the types of analysis that are possible today.

Top Keywords Performance Trend

Open Google Insights for Search (or Compete or Hitwise), enter your desired search terms, and—bam!—you see performance trends! Check out Figure 8.8.

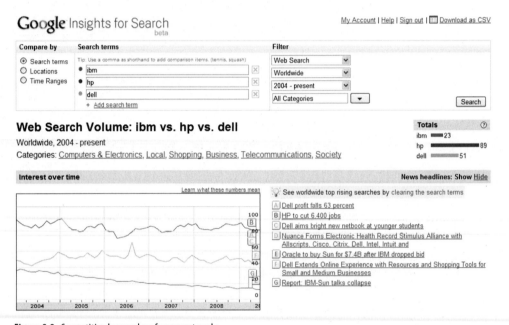

Figure 8.8 Competitive keyword performance trends

At a glance, you can see that both HP and Dell held steady with consumer interest, even if they declined slightly in recent months. But the number of searches for IBM dropped steadily over the past four years. This trend might be worrying for IBM, especially because IBM bought more magazine and TV advertising during that period; one would have expected a positive halo online from all that offline brand building.

Tip: When you use Insights for Search, a best practice is to do comparative analysis; that is, don't look at one line by itself, because the tool reports indexed performance. By making comparisons with other relevant terms, as in Figure 8.8, you get the context you need to judge whether a downward trend is necessarily bad.

Another excellent use of this data is to compare your performance to the category, as shown in Figure 8.9.

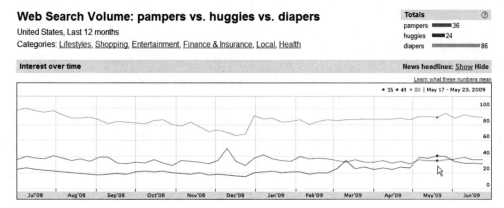

Figure 8.9 U.S. search interest for Pampers, Huggies, and Diapers

At a glance, you know the performance of the entire diapers category (interest dropped dramatically through the peak of the recession—July to December 2008—and has since shown a nice gradual recovery), the performance of the brand (Pampers has suffered somewhat less—possible promotions in early December yielded great results), and finally the performance of the competitor (Huggies has shown a very nice gain through end of Q1 2008 to the current period and in May 2008 overtook Pampers for the first time).

It is easy to look at your own performance in a silo in your web analytics tool. Analysis such as this, especially for your most important traffic terms, will help you understand the bigger ecosystem picture, and then you can take action.

Geographic Interest and Opportunity Analysis

One of the neatest features on all search engines is being able to target your advertising by geography. Each company or brand has its areas of strength, so why not take time to understand yours and figure out how to exploit opportunities?

I recommend this simple but effective analysis: use Google Insights for Search to look at your top brand terms and the industry category. We'll continue to use the Pampers/Huggies example to identify where opportunities exist for Pampers if it really wants to take down Huggies.

Figure 8.10 shows search interest by region for Pampers (this report is by state, though you can drill down to city level. I'll stay away from that for now).

There are some wonderful indicators in the map. States with big populations show up, such as Ohio and Pennsylvania, though it would be nice to have states such as California more interested in our brand. But how does our main competitor fare? Figure 8.11 shows the regional strength map for Huggies.

Quite different! There is some overlap, but the areas of strength for Pampers are not the same as those for Huggies. The disparity may be the result of different advertising or office locations.

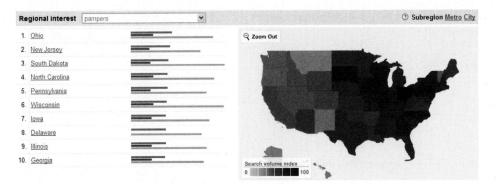

Figure 8.10 Geographic interest analysis for Pampers

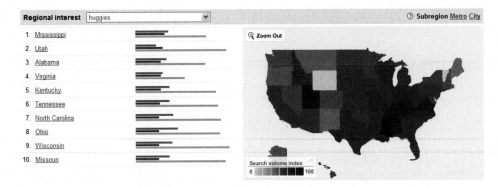

Figure 8.11 Geographic interest analysis for Huggies

As the brand manager for search, if I wanted to take Pampers head-to-head against Huggies, I might consider going after them in their strongest states like Mississippi, Utah, Alabama, Virginia, and Kentucky. Coincidentally, none of Huggies' strongest states show up in my own top 10. Or I could strengthen my brand in my own strongest states by doing more focused advertising.

The optimal move is to *grow the size of the pie*, that is, identify areas of opportunity by doing a complete category analysis. That way, I don't just *fight* the competitor I know; I also seek out overall market strengths and other competitors (more on this in the following section), as shown in Figure 8.12.

You get a different geographic interest map for the category than you do for the two brands that dominate the market, Pampers and Huggies. For example, look at the top-ranked state, Wyoming. It shows a huge interest in diapers (the intensity is searches for diapers relative to all searches), some interest in Pampers (the first line next to the name of the state above it), and nonexistent interest in the Huggies brand.

Now you get to decide as the *search person* for the company how best to take your meager advertising dollars and spend them better. Should you go after Alaska and Oregon more aggressively since there is so much interest in the category but not in you? Both are smaller states than New York and California, but they offer a nice way to grow sales. It's not much of a fight; you just increase awareness in those geographic locations. You can make other such key decisions based on this data.

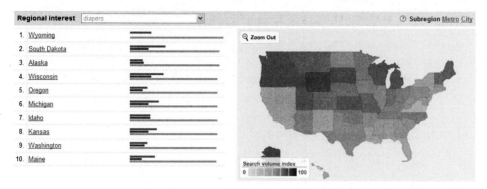

Figure 8.12 Geographic interest analysis for diapers industry segment

And if you are Bum Genius or a new player in the field, you can see how you can use this fantastic data intelligently to take on entrenched industry players.

You can also use geographic analysis for offline marketing and advertising. For example, in some states, you can only do so much to increase interest in your products through online advertising. Often the *inventory* simply does not exist online, but you can use the data to drive interest and increase brand awareness through TV, magazines, and billboards.

In a recent real-world case, marketers used geographic interest analysis to determine the optimal marketing strategy for a Brad Pitt movie, first for the offline ads by city and state and then how to geographically best target online users across the world. It was a simple matter of recognizing where interest was highest and promoting the new movie more heavily in those areas.

Google Insights for Search, the tool used in the previous example, will give you insights only into data from Google, obviously. Yahoo! and Microsoft (through adCenter Labs) currently do not offer access to their data. But you can use other tools to understand performance across all search engines. In Figure 8.13, I used Hitwise to understand year-over-year performance.

	State (51 returned)	Visits ▼ 05/23/2009		Visits 05/24/2008		Representation	
☐ 1	Texas	8.57%		7.77%		110	
☐ 2	California	7.35%		9.32%		79	
☐ 3	Florida	7.17%		6.55%		110	
☐ 4	New York	7.07%		7.28%		97	
☐ 5	Pennsylvania	6.20%		5.25%		118	
☐ 6	Ohio	3.95%		4.50%		88	
☐ 7	New Jersey	3.82%		3.41%		112	
☐ 8	Massachusetts	3.72%		2.96%		126	
☐ 9	Michigan	3.45%		3.89%		89	
☐ 10	Illinois	3.29%		3.13%		105	

Figure 8.13 Geographic delta analysis, using Hitwise

In this case, you can see states where brand interest improved and states where brand interest declined. The next step is understanding why.

Related and Fast-Rising Searches

A critical strategy in any effective search marketing program is to understand the complete ecosystem of the space and focus like a hawk on the customer's evolving interests. You can do both by focusing on two key tactics: constantly identifying *related search terms* and looking beyond the top 10 terms to find the *fastest-rising search terms*. The former helps you expand your view of the world, while the latter ensures you are plugged into your customers' fickle interests.

Figure 8.14 shows these two delightful pieces of information for our diaper category.

Search terms	related to diapers		United States, Last 12 months	
Top searches		⑦	**Rising searches**	⑦
1. cloth diapers	100		1. parents choice diapers	+60%
2. baby diapers	60		2. pampers diapers coupons	+60%
3. pampers	25		3. diapers.com	+60%
4. huggies diapers	25		4. parents choice	+50%
5. huggies	25		5. pampers coupons	+50%
6. pampers diapers	20		6. bumgenius	+50%
7. free diapers	20		7. white cloud diapers	+40%
8. disposable diapers	15		8. diapers coupons	+40%
9. diapers coupons	15		9. coupons for diapers	+40%
10. daily diapers	15		10. cheapest diapers	+40%

Figure 8.14 Top related and fastest-rising searches, using Google Insights for Search

It may worry me as the brand manager of Pampers that the top related search for my category is *cloth diapers*, a product that I do not sell. Combine that with the fact that five of the ten fastest-rising searches are all related to price (*cheapest, coupons*), and it is enough to give me an ulcer. But now I am more informed, and I can adjust my marketing strategies to emphasize affordability or offer strategic couponing without cannibalizing my bottom line. Consumer interest is clear; now I have to react.

If I want to identify influences on customers, then this search data can be very helpful as well. Notice that Parents Choice, a nonprofit guide for quality kids' products, is very influential, even above all other rating agencies.

Here is another practical example of using search data. My friend Shirley Tan runs American Bridal (www.americanbridal.com). She needs to keep up with the latest trends in her industry, and she needs to know what trends currently interest consumers. She can guess, or she can ask her friends. Or she can use consumers; declared interests by looking at terms they typed into search engines. Figure 8.15 shows the report Shirley would use from Hitwise.

Top Wedding Search Terms

The following report shows **search terms** for the industry 'Lifestyle - Weddings', ranked by **Clicks** for the **4 weeks** ending 06/20/2009.

Rank	Search Term	Clicks	
1.	davids bridal	1.78%	
2.	wedding dresses	1.51%	
3.	bridal shower games	1.25%	
4.	david's bridal	0.92%	
5.	wedding invitations	0.70%	
6.	wedding songs	0.61%	
7.	alfred angelo	0.54%	
8.	wedding cakes	0.52%	
9.	wedding favors	0.41%	
10.	wedding hairstyles	0.40%	

Fast Moving Search Terms

The following report shows **search terms** for the industry 'Lifestyle - Weddings', ranked by **largest increase** for the **week** ending 06/20/2009, compared with the **week** ending 06/13/2009. (Filters applied)

Rank	Search Term	Volume		Change
1.	questions to ask weddin...	1.07%		New
2.	paddle boat favors	0.49%		New
3.	maui-waterfalls-wedding	0.34%		New
4.	liquor wedding favors	0.33%		New
5.	burnt orange and chocol...	0.33%		New
6.	wedding cake toppers	0.33%		New
7.	davids bridal outlet	0.30%		New
8.	country wedding invitati...	0.28%		New
9.	womens evening or mot...	0.23%		New
10.	personalized wedding m...	0.23%		New

Figure 8.15 Top and rising searches for the wedding category, using Hitwise

Given the vagaries of consumer preferences, I'd tell Shirley to pay attention to the rising searches, where she'll find paddle boats, liquor wedding favors, and bridal themes that complement a Maui waterfalls wedding! She can get rid of her Seattle grunge–inspired favors and stock up on island-inspired decor.

In the offline world, we struggle to get real consumer interest data. Our only options are to call people on the phone or stop them randomly on the street. By using search engine data, you tap into the hearts and minds of actual consumers.

Share-of-Shelf Analysis

One of the most misleading reports you can get from your web analytics tool is the keyword report. I say that because you look at the numbers, you see them rising to the right, and you are thrilled. But is that rise to the right for 10 percent of the searchers, or is it for 90 percent? Or put another way, how much of the available inventory have I captured through my organic and paid search efforts? The ecosystem context is missing from your tool.

I use the term *share-of-shelf* because it is so well known in the offline retail world. P&G wants as many of its shampoos as possible on the shelves at Wal-Mart and Target. The same should be true for you when people search—you want as much share-of-shelf as you can of the available clicks for your category from the search engine.

Compete allows me to look at which websites received traffic for any keyword. Continuing the wedding theme, I want to know how much share-of-shelf Shirley gets for the keyword *wedding favors* (see Figure 8.16).

Americanbridal.com ranks 5 on the list, which is not too shabby; it also has 3.12 percent share-of-shelf. You can see how important the term is for Shirley; it accounts for 13.32 percent of her search traffic. Now she also knows who she is really competing against and can make informed decisions.

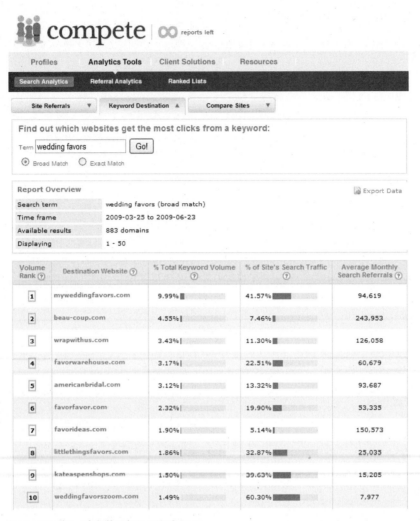

Figure 8.16 Share-of-shelf analysis, using Compete

You already know how easy it is to use this data to optimize your search campaigns, and now you have context for your web analytics numbers. You can see how much more headroom or growth a category has. You can figure out how to balance your paid or organic campaigns to increase your share of shelf.

There are always surprises in this data set. For example, for all the coolness and buzz around the Toyota Prius, honda.com is ranked 3 on the share-of-shelf report for the term *hybrid cars*, while irs.gov is ranked 2. That goes to show you what information consumers really want about hybrid cars. Ranked 12, toyota.com has less than half the share of Honda. The closest American car company on the list is GM, ranked 20 with a 0.92 percent share.

For your most important keywords, share-of-shelf analysis is a must.

Competitive Keyword Advantage Analysis

When you are duking it out with your main competitor, you want to know where they have an advantage (so you can crush 'em more intelligently!) and what your areas of strength are.

The test preparation market in the United States is very competitive. Like everywhere in the world, students must do well on standardized tests to get into top universities. A leading provider of these tests is Kaplan. To better understand its position in the market, Kaplan would analyze which keywords are strengths for Kaplan and which keywords are strengths for their competitors. Figure 8.17 shows the report Kaplan could run in Compete.

First, the good news: for all the brand terms, Kaplan (kaptest.com) is doing great. So if a student already knows Kaplan and uses its name in the search query, then Kaplan is fine.

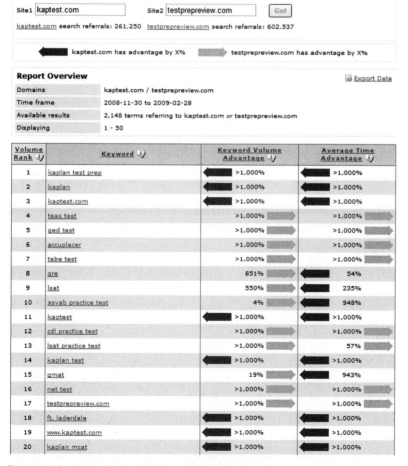

Figure 8.17 Competitive keyword advantage analysis, using Compete

Now the bad news: if students don't already know what they want, then they are more likely to find Kaplan's competitor first, `testprepreview.com`. This is terrible news for Kaplan because more people don't know them and are simply researching their options.

The great news is that now Kaplan knows the keywords that are stronger for their competitor, and they know those keywords are relevant to Kaplan. Hence, they can create a more competitive search engine marketing strategy—one that is hyperfocused!

Keyword Expansion Analysis

Keyword expansion is one of the most common types of competitive intelligence analysis in the search space. Your quest is simple: which keywords should you bid on?

The AdWords Keyword Tool (`http://zqi.me/adwkwt`) is one amongst many tools you can use to analyze keywords, average cost-per-click, search volume, trends, and so on.

Let's consider the problem. Say I am interested in taking advantage of President Obama's incentives for green energy, and I am building a massive wind farm in northern California. I have the fans running; now I need to get in front of customers who want to do some good and purchase wind energy. Figure 8.18 shows a report from the AdWords Keyword Tool that will help me.

I can see related keywords, which is information I can also get from other tools, and I can see the key data I need to make decisions, which is something I can't get easily from other tools. I can use this data to decide which keyword I want to buy based on cost, competition, search volume, and the trend. Ideally, my analysis will identify keywords with sufficient volume that trend in the right direction and yet are not too expensive, such as *wind power energy* in the report shown in Figure 8.18.

In the past, we had the famous Overture Keyword Tool from Yahoo! to provide this type of data for Yahoo! Unfortunately, that tool was discontinued. Microsoft adCenter Labs had some wonderful tools to analyze Microsoft Search's keyword data, but I've discovered that the data has not been updated since mid-2007. Search engines are the best source of search data, so it is my hope that, like Google, these other engines will start providing access to this incredibly useful information.

Alternative tools to look across multiple search engines to performance keyword expansion analysis include Trellian's Keyword Discovery (`http://zqi.me/keydisc`), Wordtracker (`http://zqi.me/wordtrk`), KeywordSpy (`http://zqi.me/spykey`) and many others—just do a Google or Bing search for *keyword research tool*.

Excited about getting your hands dirty? You should be. Over the past few years search has become critical as a channel for many businesses. The recommendations in this section should show you how easily you can use the data out there and ensure you get the highest possible ROI from your search campaigns.

How would you like to generate keyword ideas?	Enter one keyword or phrase per line:
⊙ Descriptive words or phrases (e.g. green tea)	wind energy
○ Website content (e.g. www.example.com/product?id=74893)	☑ Use synonyms ▶ Filter my results [Get keyword ideas]

Calculate estimates using a different maximum CPC bid: Choose columns to display: ⓘ

[US Dollars (USD $) ▾] [___] [Recalculate] ⓘ   [Show/hide columns ▾]

Keywords	Estimated Ad Position ⓘ	Estimated Avg. CPC ⓘ	Advertiser Competition ⓘ	Local Search Volume: May ⓘ	Global Monthly Search Volume ⓘ	Search Volume Trends (Jun 2008 - May 2009) ⓘ	Highest Volume Occurred In	Match Type: ⓘ [Exact ▾]
Keywords related to term(s) entered - sorted by relevance ⓘ								
[wind energy]	1 - 3	$1.34	▣	110,000	135,000	▂▃▅▆▇█	Apr	Add Exact ⌄
[wind energy technology]	1 - 3	$1.27	▢	720	880	▂▃▅▆▇█	Mar	Add Exact ⌄
[wind energy information]	1 - 3	$1.43	▣	Not enough data	1,000	No data	No data	Add Exact ⌄
[wind energy systems]	1 - 3	$0.73	▣	1,000	1,000	▂▃▅▆▇█	Mar	Add Exact ⌄
[wind energy association]	1 - 3	$1.93	▢	880	1,300	▂▃▅▆▇█	Apr	Add Exact ⌄
[wind energy cost]	1 - 3	$1.26	▣	Not enough data	880	No data	No data	Add Exact ⌄
[wind power energy]	1 - 3	$0.99	▣	4,400	3,600	▂▃▅▆▇█	Mar	Add Exact ⌄
[home wind energy]	1 - 3	$1.32	▣	2,900	1,900	▂▃▅▆▇█	May	Add Exact ⌄
[wind energy jobs]	1 - 3	$0.93	▣	8,100	9,900	▂▃▅▆▇█	Mar	Add Exact ⌄
[wind energy company]	1 - 3	$0.90	▣	1,300	1,000	▂▃▅▆▇█	May	Add Exact ⌄
[residential wind energy]	1 - 3	$1.46	▣	880	880	▂▃▅▆▇█	Mar	Add Exact ⌄
[wind energy project]	1 - 3	$0.74	▣	390	390	▂▃▅▆▇█	Mar	Add Exact ⌄

Figure 8.18 Keyword expansion analysis, using AdWords Keyword Tool

Audience Identification and Segmentation Analysis

In the previous section, I briefly touched on the value of relevancy for your ads. Most website users are not irritated by the ads themselves; they are irritated by irrelevant ads. As an example, I just read a story on news.yahoo.com about the Iranian crisis with an embedded ad about nursing jobs. I hit Reload, and the next ad was for online degrees.

I am a big Yahoo! user, and hence these ads use the massive behavior targeting information that Yahoo! and its partners have collected about me. Nothing in my profile indicates I want a degree or that I was remotely interested in nursing.

Yahoo!—or Adblade, its ad provider—is not unique in this fuzzy marketing. You'll run into ads with less-than-optimal relevance from DoubleClick (owned by Google) or Atlas Solutions (owned by Microsoft).

The solution? Do audience identification and segmentation analysis before you thrust money into the hands of your agency or marketer or best friend. A number of tools let you mine the demographic and psychographic data of your online audience in order to focus your media campaigns.

Demographic Segmentation Analysis

You use demographic segmentation to identify websites used by the audience whose profile you are interested in. Figure 8.19 illustrates the interface for demographic segmentation in Hitwise. In the scenario shown, my query was to identify websites with a likely audience of women between 25 and 44 whose household income is greater than $60,000 per year.

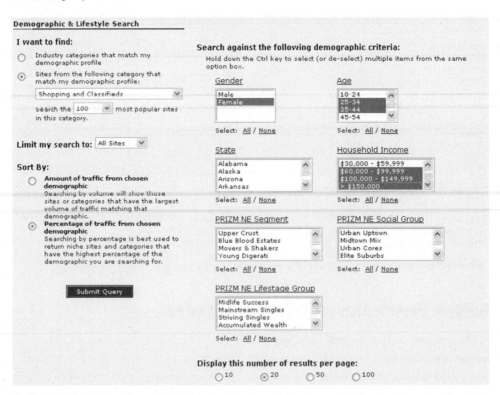

Figure 8.19 Demographic analysis, using Hitwise

You can also use the free Google Ad Planner to identify the optimal set of websites for advertising, as in Figure 8.20. I have sorted the data by Comp Index; and in that column, 340 indicates an audience that is three times more likely to be the one I want.

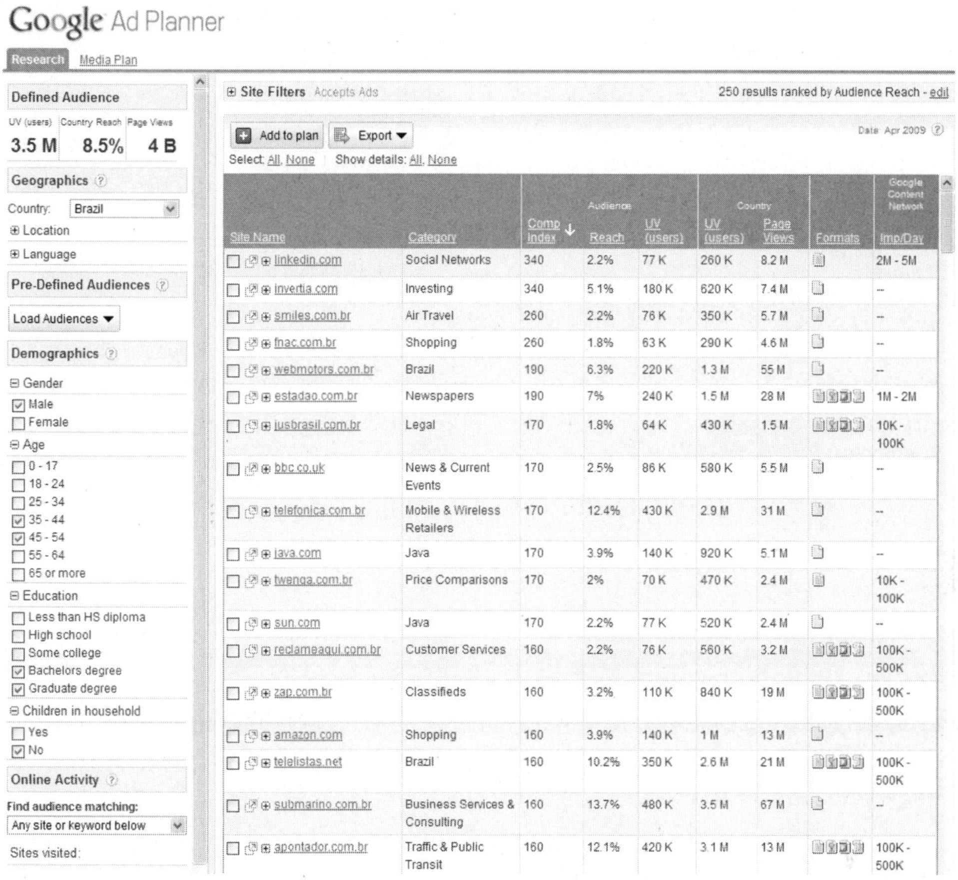

Site Name	Category	Audience: Comp Index	Audience: Reach	Audience: UV (users)	Country: UV (users)	Country: Page Views	Formats	Google Content Network: Imp/Day
linkedin.com	Social Networks	340	2.2%	77 K	260 K	8.2 M		2M - 5M
invertia.com	Investing	340	5.1%	180 K	620 K	7.4 M		--
smiles.com.br	Air Travel	260	2.2%	76 K	350 K	5.7 M		--
fnac.com.br	Shopping	260	1.8%	63 K	290 K	4.6 M		--
webmotors.com.br	Brazil	190	6.3%	220 K	1.3 M	55 M		--
estadao.com.br	Newspapers	190	7%	240 K	1.5 M	28 M		1M - 2M
jusbrasil.com.br	Legal	170	1.8%	64 K	430 K	1.5 M		10K - 100K
bbc.co.uk	News & Current Events	170	2.5%	86 K	580 K	5.5 M		--
telefonica.com.br	Mobile & Wireless Retailers	170	12.4%	430 K	2.9 M	31 M		--
java.com	Java	170	3.9%	140 K	920 K	5.1 M		--
twenga.com.br	Price Comparisons	170	2%	70 K	470 K	2.4 M		10K - 100K
sun.com	Java	170	2.2%	77 K	520 K	2.4 M		--
reclameaqui.com.br	Customer Services	160	2.2%	76 K	560 K	3.2 M		100K - 500K
zap.com.br	Classifieds	160	3.2%	110 K	840 K	19 M		100K - 500K
amazon.com	Shopping	160	3.9%	140 K	1 M	13 M		--
telelistas.net	Brazil	160	10.2%	350 K	2.6 M	21 M		100K - 500K
submarino.com.br	Business Services & Consulting	160	13.7%	480 K	3.5 M	67 M		--
apontador.com.br	Traffic & Public Transit	160	12.1%	420 K	3.1 M	13 M		100K - 500K

Figure 8.20 Demographic audience segmentation for Brazil, using Google Ad Planner

The specific query I ran, in the left column in Figure 8.20, is for males between the ages of 35 and 54 with a degree and no children in their household. This is the perfect audience to promote an expensive yellow sports car because these men may be dealing with a midlife crisis!

The results in Figure 8.20 show sites that I might not have considered. I might not have guessed that `linkedin.com` was a great place to reach my audience. Also, look at the diverse set of interests (Category) that this audience has. To the right of Audience, you'll see the information I need to make decisions: Unique Visitors, Page Views, Ad Formats, and approximate Impressions/Day.

With Ad Planner, you can also identify the demographic profile of any website of interest. Figure 8.21 shows the audience profile for my blog (`www.kaushik.net`).

Data about competitor websites is useful for your own website; it can help you understand the persona of the people who visit your website, and you can analyze the differences between your audience profile and that of your main competitors.

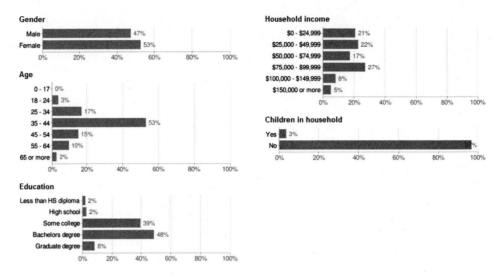

Figure 8.21 Audience profile for kaushik.net, using Google Ad Planner

Psychographic Segmentation Analysis

Often you want to analyze lifestyles and psychographic attributes to identify a relevant audience. Figure 8.19 showed the psychographic attributes available in Hitwise, referred to there as PRIZM segments and groups. Figure 8.22 shows the options available in Google's Ad Planner tool.

Figure 8.22 Lifestyle analysis for the United Kingdom, using Ad Planner

At the top right you can see the users in the defined audience (45 million) and the number of Page Views they consume (94 billion). In the Pre-Defined Audiences section, you can narrow down your desired audience to such categories as Brides-to-be, College Students, DIYers, Fantasy/Comic Book Enthusiasts, and a ton more audience segments. You simply select the segment you want to reach, and in a few seconds you get a list of optimal sites for reaching the desired audience.

Note that you can apply additional desired criteria. For example, you can use Language to identify Turkish speakers in the United Kingdom who are Celebrity Gossip Gurus. Or you can use Location and Language to identify an audience of German- and French-speaking Brides-to-be in England and Wales.

If you are a large website (greater than 5 million unique visitors), then you can also use various panel-based data sources to do psychographic analysis. Because of the sampling biases for medium and small sites, the panel data can get a very high ratio of noise and a very low signal very quickly.

Search Behavior and Audience Segmentation Analysis

The Holy Grail of marketing is targeting your display (banner) ads based on the search behavior of online users! For far too long, search and display have survived as two completely independent entities. As analysts, we do all our analysis for the display business, and then we repeat the process to identify search marketing opportunities.

Using tools such as the Google Ad Planner, you can identify relevant audiences based on their search behavior for free. Figure 8.23 shows an example of one such analysis to find relevant websites for running display ads for selling netbooks.

Netbooks are ultra-light, slightly underpowered, small laptops that are very cheap. In this case, I am an online retailer just getting into the netbook business, and I want to do display advertising to let people know I have launched this product. But rather than just segmenting by demographics, I can segment by search behavior.

At the bottom left of Figure 8.23 are the keywords I have identified (using the keyword expansion tool) as the most common among people looking for netbooks. I also know that many young people are interested in netbooks because they tend to be quite cheap (both the netbooks and the young people!). Hence, you'll notice in the age segmentation I chose 0–24 years old.

On the right are the websites visited by this audience. Hurray! No more guessing and wasting money: I can place ads where my desired audience is likely to see them most. Oh, and you know the data is good because of the interests listed in the Category column: Cheats & Hints, Lyrics, Music Streams, Online Games, and Photo Sharing!

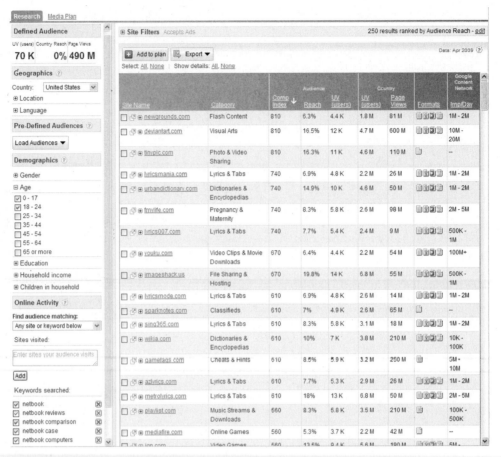

Figure 8.23 Identifying relevant websites for display ads based on user search behavior, using Ad Planner

Note: Although I used Google's free Ad Planner tool for the previous analysis, note that you do not have to then buy display advertising from Google. The folks at Google would certainly feel good if you did, but they have provided free access to the tool and you can use it, find insights, and purchase your display advertising wherever you want.

That's the beautiful world of competitive intelligence analysis. So much data is available, and much of it is free (and there's even more if you want to pay). You can use the data for better marketing and advertising, and you can use it to identify strategic opportunities for your business, to avoid being blindsided by competitors, and to ensure that you understand evolving customer behavior and preferences.

There is no other source of data on the planet quite like competitive intelligence data. Use it.

Emerging Analytics: Social, Mobile, and Video

The Web has seen an incredible evolution in the past few years: a shift from one-way conversation to two-way conversation; the richness of the web experience powered by video, Ajax, and Flash; and content distribution through multiple channels such as RSS and mobile.

These changes improve the web experience while putting users in charge. But that introduces a minor problem: how do you measure success?

In this exciting chapter, I will cover emerging analytics solutions to deal with how the Web is shifting from all content in one place and "you'll damn well consume it in static format" to its current model of content is rich, where you want it to be, and presented in a way that invites conversation.

9

Chapter Contents
Measuring the New *Social* Web: The Data Challenge
Analyzing *Offline* Customer Experiences (Applications)
Analyzing Mobile Customer Experiences
Measuring the Success of Blogs
Quantifying the Impact of Twitter
Analyzing Performance of Videos

Call it Web 2.0 or any other name bandied about, the Web is evolving in front of our eyes. Some evolution was expected—faster and better media, for example. Other bits were not, such as offline consumption or the rapid rise of *socialness* in every facet of the consumer web experience.

For some people, the social experience is Facebook or MySpace. For others, it is Twitter or YouTube. I tend to think of social as a shift from one-way monologues to two-way conversations. They might be happening on Twitter or Facebook, or they could be on your corporate website, on your ecommerce site, or on a nonprofit's project-listing website. Social is not a silo. Social is not a one-off. Social is the core integration of users and conversations into everything we do on the Web, personal and professional.

I personally cannot get enough of it. Beyond the obvious benefits to me as a devotee of the Web, this new world is really cool because it is a complex measurement challenge. All this evolution, with a dash of revolution thrown in, forces us to think differently and come up with new and innovative strategies.

In this chapter, I'll first outline how the fundamental model of content creation, content distribution, and content consumption is changing. In many ways, for web marketers and analysts, this change is at the core of the measurement challenge. Then I'll jump to the current bleeding edge of data collection for tracking offline web content consumption. I'll touch on mobile and what's possible with the current set of tools. Finally, I'll walk you through some specific measurement strategies for blogs, Twitter, and video, where the challenge is not so much data collection but thinking differently and inventing new metrics.

Excited? This is going to be fun.

Measuring the New *Social* Web: The Data Challenge

One of the least understood phenomena of the last few years is how the fundamental nature of content creation, distribution, and consumption has changed. Most marketers are unprepared to take advantage of this shift, most web analytics vendors have not evolved their core data collection mechanisms, and most analysts have not yet adapted their measurement techniques.

I have to admit it is a little depressing. But if you understand the problem, you can start formulating creative solutions. So, let's dive in and understand why measuring the new *social-powered* Web is both a challenge and a sweet opportunity. Figure 9.1 shows a simple sketch of how content was formerly created, distributed, and consumed on the Web.

The wonderful people at the BBC would create the content. They would then push the content out to their website. All of us grateful people would go to their website and consume the content. It was quite straightforward, really. And although I'm using a news website as the example, you could apply this old approach to any type of website: ecommerce, nonprofit, B2B, or B2C.

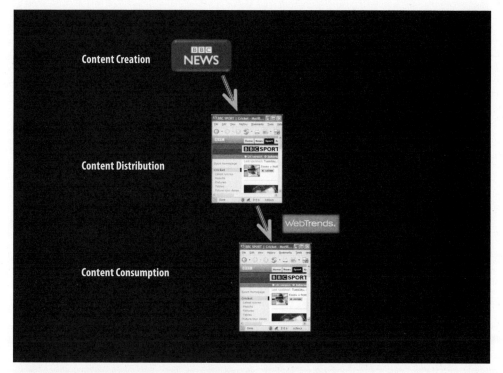

Figure 9.1 The traditional content creation, distribution, and consumption model

The Content Democracy Evolution

From a measurement perspective, we evolved into either a log- or tag-based approach for capturing data. In the case of the BBC news site, you could throw Webtrends, for example, onto the site, and in a few hours you had your web analytics data. The reports told you how many people visited the site, what content they consumed, what campaigns or acquisition strategies were working, yada, yada, yada. Life was simple.

The next relevant evolution was the rise of user-generated content (UGC) in two unique ways. First, websites opened up to users by allowing them to contribute comments, reviews, and even articles. This challenged the whole concept of when content was *done*. Was a page *complete* when you created it, or was it *complete* after five comments or customer reviews? How did you judge when the page became useful to your website visitors: when you published it or after users added their comments and perspectives?

Second, the rise of easy-to-use, and often free, self-publishing platforms changed the world of content. This phenomenon was most clearly illustrated with blogs, which allowed anyone to start their own publishing platform in a few seconds. For free. The challenge this platform posed was that visitors could talk about you on your own site and all over the Web. They could take excerpts of your content and expand the conversation in unimaginable ways. They could write reviews praising or bashing you all over the Web, and suddenly you were no longer in control of the conversation.

With the birth of blogs, the shift in content distribution was not far away. People consumed blog content on websites—either through your website or on a website where users had expanded your conversation—but this was still measurable for the most part. The advent of RSS and sites that scrape, syndicate, or mash up content, however, meant that content consumption fundamentally shifted. Users no longer had to come to your site to consume your content.

For example, I love reading about the Indian cricket team. I subscribe to the BBC Sports Indian Cricket Team feed, and all the news comes to me. I don't go to it. Sites like Alltop (`http://alltop.com`), JimmyR (`http://www.jimmyr.com`), or the Japanese site Qooqle (`http://news.qooqle.jp`) can push content out to users in mash-ups. Users might consume snippets or images from your stories there or come back to your site for more. Either way, your content is free and spreading in ways that you can't control or influence.

Figure 9.2 shows this evolution, and each number highlights an approximately incremental step.

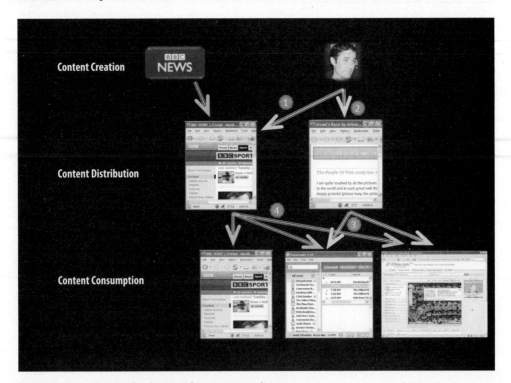

Figure 9.2 Content creation, distribution, and consumption evolves

There is an amazing democratic shift in who gets to publish content and how it gets distributed and consumed. Although brand, money, and influence are still important, they no longer determine access to distribution channels. Anyone can access the Web, and if they have something of value to say, they can reach a relevant audience.

So, the real picture is a bit more complicated than Figure 9.2; it looks more like Figure 9.3 where many, many others participate in the system and all of them create content, distribute it through different channels, and then some or all of that content is consumed at different places.

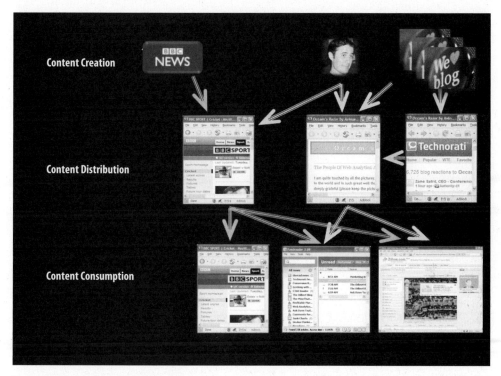

Figure 9.3 Everyone plays, the complex Web

Measurement now really becomes a challenge for these reasons:

- The JavaScript tag on your site measures only what was published on your site. And even then it measures only a *page URL*; it has a severely limited (or no) ability to measure a *living page* (one that constantly grows from user contributions, on a site or a blog).

- A lot of consumption happens *off-site*, that is, in feed readers, at aggregator sites, or at places you syndicate your content (or where nice people scrape it without your permission!) Your web analytics tools are blind to all this activity.

- Your existing metrics don't work in a world that looks like Figure 9.3. Visits and Unique Visitors are no longer enough; we need Feed Subscribers. Conversion Rate is OK, but *Conversation* Rate is crucial (more on this later in this chapter).

Figure 9.4 shows the extent of the challenge by identifying the number of tools you need to capture the data.

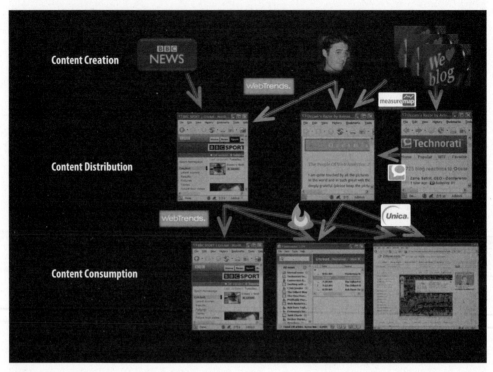

Figure 9.4 Capturing data in the new social web world

You need your traditional web analytics tool, in our example Webtrends, to capture your website data. You need something like the now-extinct tool MeasureMap to measure content contributed to your sites or blogs through comments or reviews. You need to dip into Technorati to measure Citations (other people talking about you and how much). You'll use a tool like Feedburner to get an understanding of your *offsite* content (RSS).

The last metric is the hardest. If your content is syndicated or scraped off your site, how do you track it (bottom right in Figure 9.4)? You could use the Event Tracking model (see Chapter 4) to capture that data using tools like Unica or Google Analytics. Or if you are using widgets for your syndication, then you can also use custom tracking from companies like Clearspring to collect data.

The challenge here is not simply using multiple tools, but using tools that collect and report new metrics each in its own way. Even if the same metric exists in two of these tools, it probably won't match.

Figure 9.4 does not even incorporate the latest *threat* to our way of thinking about measurement: Twitter, as shown in Figure 9.5.

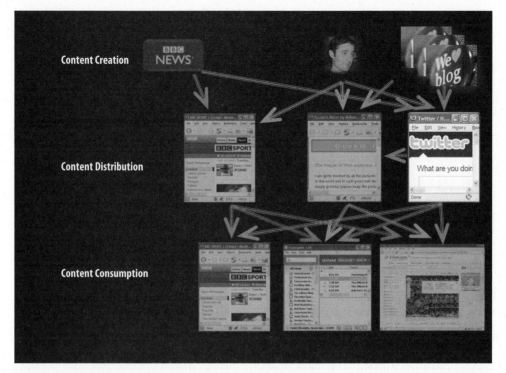

Content Creation

Content Distribution

Content Consumption

Figure 9.5 Twitter's impact on content creation, distribution, and consumption

The Twitter Revolution

Twitter empowers companies and individuals to create or publish content through Twitter to engage audiences. This content gets distributed through websites, RSS feed readers, aggregators, or desktop or mobile applications. Just imagine what this level of distribution does to our ability to measure. We can use some of the tools in Figure 9.4, if we try really hard, to measure some of Twitter's impact. But there are elements we simply can't measure, such as whether content we create and distribute through Twitter is consumed via applications like TweetDeck, Spaz, or Digsby. For the moment, we are completely blind to content consumed in apps, though we can append our URL with tracking parameters and measure clicks coming back to our site.

In a *social web world*, we don't have a single tool that can help us measure success. We have not even developed the new kinds of metrics that will define real measurement. We are still in the early stages of understanding the complete picture of the problem.

So, if your head hurts, that's OK. Now we can have an honest conversation and figure out how to address the problem. For the rest of this chapter, I'll cover two strategies to capture data in difficult situations, and then I'll dive deeper into three specific social channels: blogs, Twitter, and video. You will learn the new tools and metrics you should use to measure your success.

Although there are challenges in the social web world, every analysis ninja will have a ton of fun because you are exploring new worlds; you are creating innovative solutions.

Analyzing *Offline* Customer Experiences (Applications)

In the past year we have seen a massive increase in applications made from technologies such as Adobe AIR. These rich Internet applications are fully functional desktop-like programs, across multiple computing platforms, that you can use with or without an Internet connection.

I touched earlier on the difficulty of measuring applications. Although many of these applications provide content and functionality for a website, they themselves are not natively instrumented to collect data. This issue raises two challenges for traditional web analytics:

- If most user interaction is offline, how do you track offline behavior?
- If the standard *tag all pages with JavaScript* model does not work, how do you collect data?

I'll use the example of one of my absolute favorite Adobe AIR applications, the Times Reader from the *New York Times* (NYT), to illustrate how you can overcome these two problems with some clever ingenuity (see Figure 9.6).

Figure 9.6 Times Reader application powered by Adobe AIR

When NYT launched the Times Reader (`http://zqi.me/readnyt`) in early 2009, the NYT and Adobe teams set about identifying how to collect the necessary data to track user behavior. The following were some of the behaviors they wanted to track:

- Time spent in different sections (Front Page, Crossword, The Arts, and so on)
- Time spent reading individual stories (to get direct feedback on what users found interesting)
- Time spent consuming content online and offline
- Differences in behavior of Times Reader subscribers and nonsubscribers (notice the padlocks next to some sections in Figure 9.6; those were just for subscribers)

Rather than building a custom tool, the teams used the standard Event Tracking mechanism in Google Analytics to collect data. As discussed in Chapter 4, Event Tracking provides *empty containers* into which you can pass any type of *name-value* pair. Data is then processed and made available in standard reports, or you can extract it using an API for custom reporting. While building the application, the NYT and Adobe teams used the native integration of the open source version of the analytics tracking code and the ActionScript 3 programming language to enable the tracking of user behavior using events. That solved the problem of *how to collect data*. How about the first problem listed, "How do I track offline behavior?"

To track offline behavior, the teams did something very clever. The Times Reader comes with a very lightweight database. When I am offline (typically on a plane) and reading my beloved *New York Times*, data is collected, through events, and stored in the database. When the Reader detects that my Internet connection has been restored, it takes the events in the database and "phones home" (that is, sends the data to the reporting application). The logic built into the Reader sends the events only once a day to keep things supremely efficient. That solves the first problem.

In summary, a standard, flexible tracking methodology combined with an ingenious way of tracking offline behavior lets the NYT company track usage of its Adobe AIR application.

As you consider developing your own desktop or mobile application, you can use a similar approach to collecting the necessary data, thus making intelligent decisions based on actual customer usage of your apps. You should, however, be aware of two caveats:

- Put a lot of thought up front into what you want to track, and ensure your developers are aware of it so they'll do proper encoding.
- Use standard methodologies to collect and store your data so you can take advantage of the innovations your analytics vendor develops.

Note: To learn about the technical details, and see examples, of open source tracking methodology, visit `http://zqi.me/flashtrk`.

Analyzing Mobile Customer Experiences

Every year since 1999 has been dubbed the *year of the mobile*, yet I would say no year has delivered the expectations set by that lofty title. I make my sardonic observation because a ton of hype surrounds mobile and mobile analytics. The number of mobile handsets has certainly grown tremendously every year since 1999, and it is fair to say that iPhone's introduction in 2007 has turbocharged consumption of the mobile Web in the United States.

There is no doubt that we have to treat tracking and analysis of mobile consumption of our web content with a great degree of seriousness, perhaps just a tad bit under the level at which the hype meter is set.

Before the iPhone, web-enabled handsets could access the Internet, but the web experience itself was rudimentary. For example, you could access text-only, custom-created Wireless Application Protocol (WAP) sites with minimal information, although they were painful to access.

The iPhone and Android-based phones massively boosted consumption of web content by making it a far superior experience. Now with better browsers embedded in new phones from BlackBerry, Nokia, and others, this trend appears to be rising exponentially.

Such changes bode well for a higher ROI on any mobile efforts your company undertakes, which means you need to get serious about mobile analytics. The biggest challenge mobile poses is how to accurately collect data. Then comes the reporting and analysis, both of which are still nascent. Let's look at each of these challenges individually.

Mobile Data Collection: Options

We have not seen a massive adoption of mobile analytics yet because the industry has not settled on how to collect data from mobile platforms. At the moment three options are in play.

Logs-Based Solutions

A logs-based solution is a legacy option, though it may become a bigger player if the big telcos enter the analytics space or share their log files to ensure better accountability.

The web server log files for your website contain information in the headers and the URL string that might help identify mobile traffic. Some companies have written custom log parsers with filters and scripts to report on their site's mobile traffic. This method is cumbersome and only for the brave; hence, it is not common.

In Asia, some of the large telecom companies use their own server logs to experiment with creating and providing analytics to their advertisers. These solutions are not widely deployed, and it is unclear if they will ever be a viable source of information.

The benefit of a logs-based solution is that all you need is an enterprising IT person who has a way with simple code. That, and perhaps you'll have to buy them a lunch or two. The downside of a logs-based solution is that you must build and support your own software or hardware platform. Additionally, the reporting is only as good as the knowledge; your logs will be missing a lot of information that you can get with the other two solutions, described next.

Packet-Sniffing-Based Solutions

Packet-sniffing-based solutions try to solve two important problems: working with the telecom companies to get key data and tagging your site with JavaScript or image tags to enable reporting.

These solutions, like the one from Amethon (www.amethon.com), rely on a hardware-based methodology to collect data. You buy and install the platform inside your network (between the Web and your web servers), which enables the tool to collect all packets traveling between the Web and your servers. You can also get access to a whole raft of reports almost as soon as you deploy.

The benefit of using packet sniffers is that you don't have to touch your websites—mobile or otherwise—and you won't add code to your pages. The downside of packet sniffers is that if you host your sites in your own environment, then you must convince your IT team to implement and support a new piece of hardware. If your sites have a distributed architecture or are externally hosted, then deployment can be very complex because the hardware platform must be deployed in all those places.

Tag-Based Solutions—JavaScript or Image

Both tag-based solutions—whether JavaScript tag or image tag—work like most of your web analytics tools today, that is, in a hosted model.

Companies like Bango Analytics, Mobilytics, and Percent Mobile use an image tag to collect data. As an example, here is the Percent Mobile code that I use on my blog to track my mobile data:

```
<img src="http://tracking.percentmobile.com/pixel/70b263e0-6a49-11de-ab39-
12313900c5b8" alt="." width="2" height="2" />.
```

This tag will provide all the basic reports that I need, like percent of mobile traffic, devices, networks, countries, and mobile via WiFi. You can check out the live Percent Mobile analytics report for my blog by visiting this URL: http://zqi.me/akmobile.

Campaign tracking with tag-based solutions involves a bit more work, which differs slightly between JavaScript tags or image tags. Either way, you must create customer landing pages for all your mobile campaigns or create customer-tracking links. For the latter option, the visitor clicks your ad, goes to the landing page of your mobile analytics provider (say Bango), and is then redirected to your website. That second extra step allows the analytics tool to capture the campaign metadata it needs to enable tracking. It's a cumbersome process involving various teams at your company and manual configuration in your ad system and analytics tracking system.

Companies like Omniture, CoreMetrics, and Google Analytics use JavaScript-based solutions to collect data for web analytics. For a JavaScript-enabled phone from Apple, BlackBerry, Nokia, or HTC, that same tracking code will also capture the mobile browsing behavior of customers using those phones. You don't have to do any additional work as long as you follow the normal processes for tracking your web campaigns.

The benefit of using data capture solutions that are JavaScript-based is simple: you don't have to do any more work. For these modern phones, the data is already being collected and reported to you. But, there are several downsides of JavaScript-based solutions:

- Not all phones are JavaScript-enabled, which means you will be missing a chunk of your traffic. The vendors will tell you that non-JavaScript-based phones are not really used for ecommerce or for consuming web content; hence, they are not that important. That assumption is kind of true, but take it with a big grain of salt.

- These solutions primarily use cookies to identify a unique visitor, and many phones might not have cookies enabled. None of these solutions has yet enabled another way of tracking unique visitors. So, you'll have good Visits information, but a bit less than optimal Visitor information.

- Although you'll get all your page views, visitors, and campaign information, many traditional web analytics solutions have not incorporated key pieces of information such as handset, form factor, WiFi availability, and telecom carrier. This can limit your ability to segment the data.

Some of these problems don't exist with image tag-based data capture mechanisms. They will capture data for JavaScript- and non-JavaScript-enabled phones (see http://zqi.me/akmobile), and on some platforms vendors are developing non-cookie-based unique visitor data collection mechanisms.

Peering into the near future the winner of this three-way horse race will be determined by three factors:

- How quickly the world purchases iPhones or smart phones based on Android, SymbianOS, and such—phones that will accept JavaScript and cookies (and have both enabled by default).

- How quickly traditional analytics vendors enhanced their tags to include image tags to cover the small percent of data that will be missed by JavaScript-only solutions.

- How important web analytics vendors consider mobile tracking, which will drive them to incorporate databases like the one from WURFL (wireless universal resource file) to identify phone and manufacturer information and tele-com provider information.

With fast progress along these lines, we might see enhanced analytics tags that will collect data from all types of mobile phones as well as standard web access platforms. With slow progress, vertical-specific mobile solutions such as the ones from Bango, Percent Mobile, and Mobilytics might hold sway.

The sophistication of your company's mobile efforts will determine whether you choose to simply use the data from your web analytics tool and wait this battle out (knowing you are stuck with only 70 percent of potential data) or immediately switch to a specific vertical solution.

Tracking Mobile Applications

The technology to enable tracking for mobile applications on smart phones is similar to the Event Tracking model (discussed earlier and in Chapter 4). Web analytics vendors are starting to engage in this area, but the most robust solutions come from vertical-specific vendors such as Flurry, Localytics, and Pinch Media. Since the data collection by these vendors is embedded deep into the mobile application itself, the vendors can collect and provide detailed usage data and tie it to unique users. You get normal stuff like location, device name, and so forth, but more valuable data relates to actions users take in the application, how long they use it, the number of active users, and so on.

Mobile Reporting and Analysis

You've collected the data, so now for the exciting part—doing something with it! At its very core, the reporting you want for mobile users is pretty close to what you want for users who access your website from computers. You want to answer the following questions:

- How many visits did your website get?
- What were the sources of these visits?
- What are the screen resolutions of the mobile devices that access your site?
- What search engine keywords were used to arrive at your website?
- How long do users stay on your site?
- Did you get any conversions?

Figure 9.7 shows the Dashboard view from Google Analytics for the segment of users who visited the website using mobile phones.

Figure 9.7 Key metrics for mobile phone usage—Google Analytics

The Site Usage elements tell you the basic web metrics such as Visits, Page Views, Pages/Visit, Bounce Rate, and Time on Site. Below that you get traffic sources, 72.94 percent direct traffic. Throughout this book I have stressed the importance of Goals, and that's what you see next. As always, these Goals can be people making purchases, making a donation, or simply viewing important content. Then you have Screen

Resolutions and Map Overlay. Finally are the Pages Viewed by users and the Keywords they used to arrive at the site.

The metrics for your mobile analysis will be exactly the same as discussed, regardless of the web analytics tool you use. As we had noted earlier, this data, collected using a standard web analytics JavaScript tag, is only for JavaScript-enabled mobile phones.

Notice an important metric missing from Figure 9.7: Unique Visitors. Although an increasing number of devices and gateways do support cookies, there is still no accepted standard for cookies being turned on or off. This poses a challenge for traditional web analytics tools, which overwhelmingly rely on cookies to track unique visitors. So, you can get in-depth details about the sessions, locations, keywords, and conversions of your users but not the Unique Visitor number. Some vertical-specific mobile analytics solutions use proprietary *fingerprint* algorithms or store other PII information to track Unique Visitors. Currently there is no established standard for doing this, and when dealing with PII data, you must always be cautious with the evolving government regulatory landscape. Please stress-test what your mobile analytics vendor is using and that it complies with your privacy policies.

An important feature is also missing from your traditional web analytics tool: the deep device-specific information (except in a few tools like Nedstat).

Mobile-specific vendors, such as Bango and TigTags, collect multiple pieces of unique information about the mobile phones used to access your website. Figure 9.8 shows a report from TigTags that is a great example of a device-specific report. You can easily see the type of device accessing your website, the form factor of the device, and a summary of the brands at the bottom right.

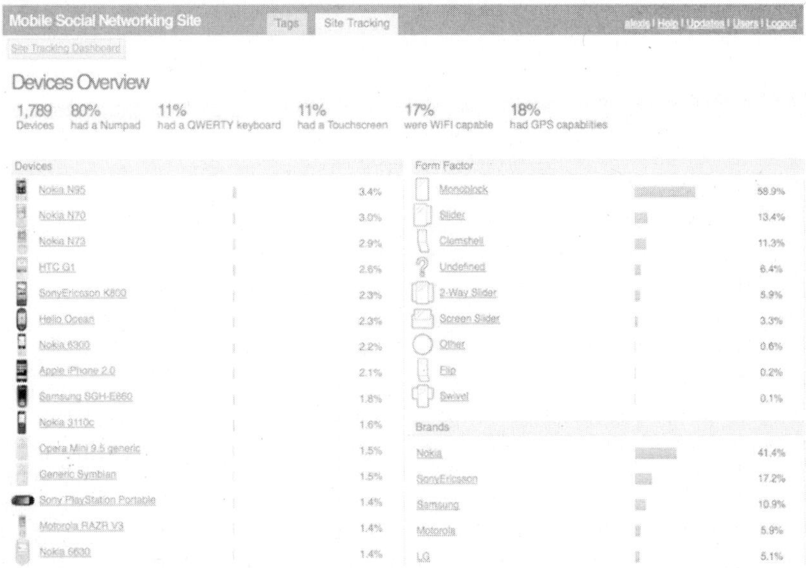

Figure 9.8 Devices Overview report—TigTags

When we analyze mobile data, we tend to get enamored by device information, because it looks cool. But remember that focusing on the customer experience and consumption is a lot more important than the *device* used to access the data. What is worth knowing is what is actionable.

In Figure 9.8, you can use the most interesting data, at the very top, to answer questions such as do people with QWERTY keyboards or touchscreens spend more time on your website or using our mobile applications? Do people with GPS capabilities use our maps and location features vs. those without GPS? When you do your analysis, consider focusing on those types of existential questions, connect them to the user experience and the outcomes you desire, and finally, segment your data!

Figure 9.9 shows a segmented report from TigTags (a tool from Percent Mobile) for a single device, in this case the Android-powered HTC G1 phone.

Figure 9.9 Detailed report for the HTC G1 phone—TigTags

You can see the popularity of the G1 amongst users who come to your website, and you can compare the trend with other mobile phones. You can see a visual map overlay and the countries of the users. With TagTags, and other vertically focused mobile analytics solutions, you get reports such as traffic sources, keywords, campaigns, pages viewed, and more.

If you choose a vertically focused mobile analytics tool, pick the one that gives you deeper segmentation of the data. Ask the following questions:

- Can you create two segments for visitors from iPhones and Android phones and compare their behavior?
- Can you compare the performance of phones without JavaScript functionality with phones that have that functionality?
- Can you look at two of the most popular screen resolutions and see the impact on Time on Site or Conversions?
- Can you do the valuable segmentation and analysis you are accustomed to with your web analytics tool?

These questions are important because of the oldest lesson an analysis ninja learns: actionable insights don't come from static reports; they come from segmented data.

Measuring the Success of Blogs

Blogs are the publishing platform for the democracy. That in a nutshell is what it's all about: giving a home to every voice and giving every voice the ability to find an audience. I love blogs—both because my blog, Occam's Razor, has given me a platform to be all that I want to be and because of how much I have learned from this global sharing of information.

We often think of blogs as websites: slap a web analytics tool on it, and go on our merry way. But blogs are a unique medium, and we need to think more expansively to develop a measurement strategy. Here are the questions you need answer to measure holistic success:

- Do I deserve to be successful?
- Is anyone *out there* reading my content?
- Am I just talking to myself, or am I having a conversation?
- Are other people talking about me or my company; am I causing a "ripple"?
- What is the cost of my blogging effort?
- What is the benefit (ROI) of my blogging effort?

You want to answer some of these questions for any medium, but others are unique to blogs. To answer each question, I have created a simple framework and a set of new metrics.

Raw Author Contribution

Raw author contribution is the foundation of all blog metrics, and it answers the first question, "Do I deserve to be successful?"

When we analyze our sites, most of us jump to the number of Visitors and Page Views Per Visitor. Stop. First measure yourself and your contribution to the world before you demand success!

Raw Author Contribution is measured using two metrics:

Posts per month = # of posts / # of months blogging

Content created = # of words in a post / # of posts

Neither of these metrics measures the quality of your contribution (we will measure that in a moment), but they indicate the frequency and consistency of your contribution. They help you understand if you even have a chance to be successful.

Figure 9.10 shows the data for my blog (www.kaushik.net).

Occam's Razor by Avinash Kaushik   Visit Site

Blog Metrics

Full Stats

Raw Author Contribution
5.4 posts per month
Avg: 2002 words per post
Std dev: 2272 words

Last 30 days

Raw Author Contribution
2 posts this month
Avg: 2941 words per post
Std dev: 3125 words

Full Stats		**Full Stats**	
Author(s):	1	Author(s):	1
Posts:	200	Words in posts:	5881
Words in posts:	400372	Comments:	40
Comments:	4021	Words in comments:	3827
Words in comments:	372065	Trackbacks:	12
Trackbacks:	1498		
Months blogging:	37		

Figure 9.10 The Raw Author Contribution metric

Posts per month = 5.4

Content created = 2,002 words per post

If you use WordPress, then these metrics are easy to calculate; you can install the Blog Metrics plug-in by my friend Joost de Valk. You can download the plug-in at http://zqi.me/yoastbm. If your blog has multiple authors, then Joost's plug-in will give you the Raw Author Contribution of each person—that is a great way to hold them accountable!

If you don't use WordPress, you can get the data from your blog's software—it will look like the bottom half of Figure 9.10—and you can compute the metric yourself.

Holistic Audience Growth

To answer the next question—"Is anyone reading my content?"—you must understand the unique nature of how people read blogs. Blogs exist as dynamic websites, and hence some content is consumed on your site. You can measure this consumption with your standard web analytics tool and compute Onsite Audience Growth (Visits and Unique Visitors).

But a cool thing about blogs is that readers can sign up for RSS feeds, which means those readers don't have to visit your site. They simply consume the content in RSS readers like Google Reader or FeedReader. You'll measure this audience with a tool like FeedBurner and compute OffsiteAudience Growth (RSS Subscribers).

Figure 9.11 shows the Visits and Unique Visitors trend for my blog.

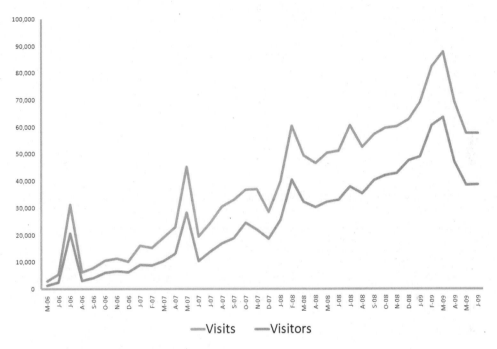

Figure 9.11 Offsite Audience Growth: Visits, Unique Visitors

As always, the trend should be the focus of your attention. By looking at the peaks and valleys, you can analyze what content gets you on the home page of Digg or StumbleUpon. On the flip side, you'll understand what content did not help you grow your audience. Notice the precipitous drop in traffic in May and June 2009 as I significantly slowed my posts to write this book!

Unless you are being *paid per page view* (as is the case for many blogs that make money on advertising), simply acquiring traffic is not the desired goal. You want relevant traffic; you want traffic that is engaged and committed to you.

That's where measuring RSS subscribers comes into play. Subscribers is my number-one metric because it is the ultimate form of permission marketing (a concept popularized by Seth Godin in his book *Permission Marketing*). By signing up for my feed, the subscribers are in effect saying: "You can publish whatever content you want, whenever you want, and I'll pull it from you automatically and read it."

Figure 9.12 shows two important metrics that you'll get from tools that track RSS feeds. Think of Subscribers as a number close to, but not equal to, the web analytics Unique Visitors number. It is an approximate measure of the number of individuals who are currently signed up to receive your feed. The daily Subscriber number approximates how often people requested the feed in a 24-hour period; hence, it tends to go up and down a bit each day.

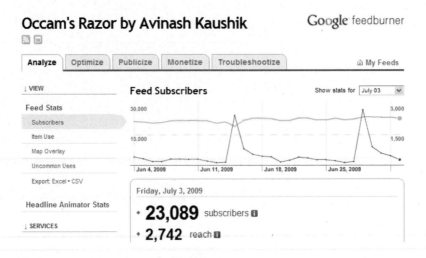

Figure 9.12 Subscribers, Reach metrics for RSS tracking

Reach is the number of people who viewed or clicked the content of your feed, in this case on one day. To use a magazine metaphor, of the number of people who subscribed to your magazine (blog), it's how many opened the magazine and read an article. This is a powerful number because it tells you whether all those Subscribers you pursued are actually reading what you send them.

The best practice with RSS Subscribers, and Reach, is to track the trend over time, as in Figure 9.13.

Notice that although the Visitors to the blog, shown in Figure 9.11, have dipped in recent months, the number of total RSS Subscribers continues to increase and at a higher rate during the same months. This is why I am not worried about short-term rises and falls in the Visitors number; my goal is to increase the number of relevant and loyal readers.

Conversation Rate

Blogs are the most social of social mediums. As mentioned in the opening, they offer a dialogue rather than a monologue. Conversation Rate answers the next question, "Are we having a conversation?" It also helps you identify whether you are actually publishing content that engages your audience.

Conversation Rate = # of Visitor comments / # of posts

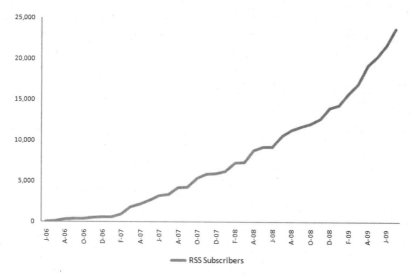

Figure 9.13 Three-year trend of RSS Subscribers for Occam's Razor

Figure 9.14 shows the Conversation Rate per post for my blog, as measured using Joost's Blog Metrics plug-in (available at `http://zqi.me/yoastbm`).

Occam's Razor by Avinash Kaushik Visit Site

Blog Metrics

Full Stats	**Last 30 days**
Raw Author Contribution 5.4 posts per month Avg: 2002 words per post Std dev: 2272 words	**Raw Author Contribution** 2 posts this month Avg: 2941 words per post Std dev: 3125 words
Conversation Rate Per Post Avg: 20.1 comments Std dev: 16.1 comments	**Conversation Rate Per Post** Avg: 20 comments Std dev: 2 comments
Avg: 1860 words in comments Avg: 7.5 trackbacks Std dev: 15.5 trackbacks	Avg: 1913 words in comments Avg: 6 trackbacks Std dev: 14.3 trackbacks

Figure 9.14 Conversation Rate for Occam's Razor

There are 20 comments and 7.5 trackbacks per post for the history of the blog. This does not include the comments I posted as replies to user comments. That's because you want to measure the fact that others are talking to you. Note also that the plug-in computes the number of words in comments submitted by visitors to the blog. Consider this: on average I write 2,002 words in each blog post, and the visitors write 1,860 words! They write almost as much as I do in each post.

That's what you want. You want the readers of your blog to have a conversation with you, contribute content, and truly create a social experience. That's success.

Citations and Ripple Index

So, you are talking, and people are responding to you on your blog. Great. But in a world of networks and connections, you need to measure your impact beyond your immediate blog. The next question is, "Are people talking about me or my company? Am I causing a "ripple"?

Validation for any blog is other people talking about what you are writing about. They reference back to you (with nice words or scathing critiques!). They link to you. I call these *citations*. People talk about you, discuss your point, throw up on you, or praise you. To measure citations, I use two different metrics:

- Technorati *Authority*, the number of unique blogs that linked to you in the last six months.

- Tweet Citations, a measure of how many people tweet about your post (think of it as measure of how *viral* your posts become).

In both cases, you measure the ripple caused by your blogging efforts. With the first metric, Authority, you measure the ripple caused by your blog as a whole. With the second, Tweet Citations, you measure the ripple caused by individual posts. Figure 9.15 shows the two metrics, measured at `www.technorati.com` and `www.tweetmeme.com`.

Figure 9.15 Technorati Authority and Tweet Citations

Authority simply measures the number of unique blogs that have discussed something related to your blog and linked back to you. If you don't publish quality content, then your *ripple index* will go down. It's the public voting with their links to you. My Technorati ripple index is 470 on this date.

Tweetmeme helps you compute the ripple caused by tweets of people who have linked to an individual individual post, talked about it, and passed it on to others. My Tweet Citations for a recent post on Paid Search Analytics is 114—pretty cool.

You don't have to use Technorati or Tweetmeme to compute your ripple index. What's important is that you measure the ripples caused by your blogging.

Cost of Blogging

Nothing in the world is free, so your blogging efforts, even if done in your spare time, cost something. That's the next question: "What is the cost of my blogging effort?"

A number of costs go into your blogging efforts. To keep things simple, I recommend measuring three components of cost:

- Technology (hardware/software)
- Time
- Opportunity cost

For me, technology costs are only the costs for hosting and for domain renewal. All software I use (for example, WordPress and BlogDesk) is free. So:

Technology: $25 per month = $300 per year + $15 domain renewal for a total = $315

According to my ever-vigilant wife, I spend at least 25 hours on blog-related activities (writing posts, editing them, and replying to emails specifically about blog posts). My time is conservatively worth $125 per hour. So:

Time: 25 hrs × 4 weeks × 12 months × 125 = $150,000 per year

Note I gave myself four weeks of vacation, though that is rarely true in a social world!

Businesses especially should measure opportunity cost. If you did not blog, the resources you put into blogging would go elsewhere, into a project that could earn you money. That is opportunity cost. You may have a great patentable idea or a solution to the Middle East crisis—these ideas are worth a lot. You need to price out your ideas.

If I apply this concept to myself, I know that if I were not blogging, I could be paid for other work. I could perhaps work a part-time job analyzing reports for a company and get paid $100,000 a year.

Opportunity cost = $100,000

So, either way, measure the value of the time you are putting into your blogging effort (cost of blogging) or the earning power or revenue from that time used to do alternative things (opportunity cost).

Benefit (ROI) from Blogging

Every honest effort, no matter how small, provides a benefit—a return on your investment, if you will. It is important to compute your ROI for your blogging efforts. In this segment, I suggest four values to consider, which add to your personal or business bottom line.

Comparative Value

If you create a decent blog, then you may create an asset that is worth something. So, compute that; determine the comparative value of your creation.

A number of tools can help you establish this value. Simply Google *blog worth* or *blog value*, and you can find tools that use either your inbound links or the current number of visitors, blog growth, feed subscribers, and so on, to compute the comparative value of your blog.

When I did this, one tool valued my blog at $740,000, and another one that used more robust metrics valued it at $950,000. Although no one is rushing to hand me that cash, it helps me compute a value for an asset I have created.

Direct Value

You can make money off your blog. People use AdSense or other services to display ads alongside their blogs. Or they maintain a job board, place ads in their feeds, find consulting engagements, or gain referrals to their business website.

All of these activities bring direct value to you in dollars. Calculate the money you earn from these actions, which are a direct result of your blogging, and you compute a direct value for your blog.

Nontraditional Value

A number of thought leaders, such as Seth Godin, have spoken of an evolution in marketing, sales, and influencing. A fundamental shift has occurred: companies with megaphones and TV ads are losing their grip. Today, marketing is about being where the customers and the conversation are. Marketing is now about engaging with customers in ways that are beneficial to them, without asking for anything in return. By engaging in the conversation and by listening to customers, we deliver something of value. This engagement creates customer evangelists, who will eagerly spread the word about a company and its products.

Your blog facilitates customer evangelism more than anything else you could do. Any business, big or small, that is not leveraging this medium in an honest attempt to have a new kind of conversation is committing a massive crime.

But if you have customer evangelists, then compute their value. You can fire your PR agencies (who might still be so lame that they send annoying email blasts to bloggers!). You can save on Super Bowl ads. You can move from expensive white papers written by you about your own glory, to leveraging meaningful user generated content.

See the big number? That's your nontraditional value!

Unquantifiable Value

With everything said and done, one more factor remains; it's a factor that is perhaps more important than all of the previous: your personal ROI from blogging. Let me explain.

My email address is listed on my blog, and many people write to me with questions, suggestions, and feedback. Just the other day I got this email:

Hi, You don't know me but I've loved your blog entries and your book. I just wanted to write and thank you. Today I was offered a job that I've been aspiring to for some time. Your writings and passion for analytics helped me gain an insight and understanding and in turn helped me secure this job. I just want to say thank you.

I wish I could tell you the happiness that email brought me. A stranger got actionable value from my blog. It touched my heart.

I blog because it makes me happy. I blog because I cherish the conversation with my readers. I can't value it enough. But in a world where so many things are based on data, this is my *faith-based initiative*. The blog still provides ROI, even if the value is unquantifiable. Your blogging efforts will be no different; they will create such unquantifiable value for you.

Here is a more quantifiable example of unquantifiable value.

My first book, *Web Analytics: An Hour a Day*, got its start from my blog. Hence, my wife and I decided to donate 100 percent of the proceeds from the book to the Smile Train and Doctors Without Borders. The book has been out for almost two years, and my part of the sales have amounted to $70,000. That translates into $35,000 donated to each charity. No direct ROI to me. But unquantifiable value to me and to people of the world.

In summary, in these six simple ways you can analyze the performance of your blog and its impact on your personal or professional efforts. Figure 9.16 shows a *decision matrix* to help you choose the optimal set of metrics for your type of your blog.

	Blog Success Metrics	Diary	Pesonal Blog	Business Blog
# 1	Raw Author Contribution		√	√
# 2	Audience Growth	√	√	√
# 3	Conversation Rate		√	√
# 4	Citations / Ripple Index			√
# 5	Cost	√	√	√
# 6	Benefit			√
	Remember To Set Some Goals, They Motivate!!!			

Figure 9.16 Blog metrics selection decision matrix

Quantifying the Impact of Twitter

Nothing has caught fire quite like the *micro-blogging* site Twitter. Its impact on the Web and information can't be understated. Sure, Oprah and CNN are on Twitter. But did you know about Kogi BBQ? It's a Korean barbeque taco truck in Los Angeles. And it tweets its locations so fans can rush to buy the twisted Korean quesadilla with jang-jorim chiles! Then, of course, there are you and me, using Twitter to share something of value, to stay in touch with friends, or to support the people's revolution in Iran.

This section of the book will talk about measuring the impact of your effort on Twitter. But before I go on, I have to share a bit of personal philosophy. I believe you should be on Twitter because that's where your customers are. We will identify metrics to help you measure success, but you must get into social media (Twitter or other media) because you want to be part of the conversation.

As with the other social media in this chapter, we are early in the evolution of Twitter in defining success and determining measurement strategies. In the initial excitement, you may want to measure anything measurable or try to measure fancy, dicey things like Influence or Engagement. That usually yields disappointing results.

My approach for measuring Twitter is not to focus on *activity* but rather to focus on *desired outcomes*. I want to share the four main measures of success that I recommend, and I'll close by sharing some emerging metrics.

Growth in Number of Followers

Think of Followers (people who sign up to receive your Twitter updates, or *tweets*) as a metric close to Visits. You want a high number of *relevant* people to visit your website, and similarly you want a high number of *relevant* people to follow your tweets.

There are many suboptimal ways to increase your Twitter follower counts, but ignore them! You want a relevant audience because of the emphasis on customers and conversation. You can use a variety of tools to track the growth of your followers; I use Twittercounter (http://zqi.me/twcount), as shown in Figure 9.17.

Notice that I not only track the growth for my Twitter account (@avinashkaushik), but I *index* my performance with that of my friend Mitch Joel (@mitchjoel). This is a great way of getting context about my performance.

You can also get this data directly from the Twitter API or from any number of other tools. Over time you want to grow the number of relevant followers, but there is no *right* number because Twitter helps you be part of a wider conversation. On Twitter people can start and stop following you as they please. At the moment there is no easy way to calculate this change, but a valuable metric would be Churn Rate: the number of followers you lose in a given time period. It could be expressed as a percentage of total followers.

Figure 9.17 Twitter Follower growth trend—Twittercounter

Message Amplification

If you tweet something of value (as perceived by the recipient and not by you!), then others will *retweet* it; that is, they will tweet it to their followers and thus spread your message much further than you ever could by yourself. This is *message amplification*, and you can use it as a metric to gauge the perceived value of your tweets.

I love this metric for two reasons: it helps instill discipline, and that discipline—tweeting something of value—helps extend your brand. Figure 9.18 shows the message amplification performance for my tweets for a 30-day period.

The graph in the middle of Figure 9.18 illustrates my retweet trend. I can match that up against my tweets and figure out which tweets were interesting to my followers, information I can use to focus my tweets.

But the really interesting metric is above the graph, *# of retweets per thousand followers in the last week*. It's 7.2 for me during that week. This metric is a great example of new metrics analysts invented to track success in new media. It helps you understand your degree of message amplification, and now you can easily compare your performance to others on Twitter. Others may have one million followers or ten thousand; you can now compare how effectively they tweet something valuable to their followers.

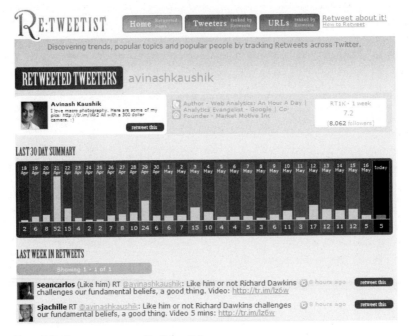

Figure 9.18 Retweets as measured by Retweetist

Another tool you can use to measure your relative quality is Retweetrank, at `http://zqi.me/retwrnk`.

Click-Through Rates and Conversions

Perhaps the most common use of Twitter is to share links to other websites or to your own website/blog. Measuring the activity that happens around these links can be super valuable—first as a method of gauging the interests of your Twitter followers and second as way to measure the impact, if any, from links that point back to your websites.

Average Shared Links CTR

Average Shared Links Click-Through Rate (CTR) is a tedious name, but stick with me, the metric is pretty cool. A common use for Twitter is to share links with your followers. These can be links to your own unique content, links to interesting articles on the Web, or, OK, links to hilarious YouTube videos.

Some Twitter measurement tools measure the number of links you share. That is akin to measuring the number of spam emails sent, or hits to your site. You want to measure *response rate*, that is, the click-through rate on the links you send.

Twitter has a hard limit of 140 characters, which means we all use services that can shorten our URLs. I use Tr.im (`http://tr.im`) to shorten my links on Twitter because it provides excellent reporting for the links I create, as shown in Figure 9.19.

Original URL	tr.im URL	Clicks	Stats	Options	tr.immed
http://thereifixedit.com/	qcVq	516		EDIT DELETE	04/07/2009
http://www.fancyfastfood.com/	qSKP	366		EDIT DELETE	04/07/2009
http://www.stuntdubl.com/2009/06/21/seo-history/	pi5H	398		EDIT DELETE	02/07/2009
http://thisisindexed.com/wp-content/uploads/2009/06/card2165.jpg	pGuf	852		EDIT DELETE	02/07/2009
http://politicalhumor.about.com/od/iran/ig/Iran-Cartoons/Stop-Or-I-[...]	pWKL	780		EDIT DELETE	02/07/2009
http://en.wikipedia.org/wiki/Dunbar%27s_number	qcmf	444		EDIT DELETE	02/07/2009
http://www.history.navy.mil/library/online/costs_of_major_us_wars.h[...]	pOYv	435		EDIT DELETE	02/07/2009
http://www.baekdal.com/articles/management/what-the-heck-is-twitter/	qyDc	1,018		EDIT DELETE	01/07/2009
http://www.ifc.com/news/2009/06/50-greatest-trailers.php	qxR2	427		EDIT DELETE	01/07/2009
http://www.twistimage.com/blog/archives/six-pixels-of-separation-li[...]	pp4h	408		EDIT DELETE	01/07/2009
http://designm.ag/resources/website-analytics-toolbox/	ppGl	913		EDIT DELETE	01/07/2009
http://blog.vkistudios.com/index.cfm/2009/6/5/The-Google-Analytics-[...]	pCXe	1,094		EDIT DELETE	01/07/2009
http://www.youtube.com/watch?v=bGJOmGL6mYM	qqfg	336		EDIT DELETE	30/06/2009
http://www.youtube.com/watch?v=QjUzzxAKs20&feature=PlayList&p=EA6F3[...]	qq9F	436		EDIT DELETE	30/06/2009
http://thisisindexed.com/wp-content/uploads/2009/06/card2178.jpg	qo2I	450		EDIT DELETE	30/06/2009

« Previous **1** 2 3 4 5 6 7 8 9 … 16 17 Next »

Figure 9.19 Click-Through Rate for shared links—tr.im

During the time period shown in the figure, I had about 8,500 followers on Twitter. That is a great context to better decipher my data: how many of my Twitter followers click the links I post, and not all of my followers pay attention to my Twitter stream all the time.

My Average Shared Links CTR was 604. This gives me a better sense of how many people I can expect to reach with my shared links.

As in the case of Message Amplification, the data in Figure 9.19 makes me more aware of my followers' preferences. I can see which links have huge click-through rates, such as links about analytics, Twitter, and Iran humor, and which links my followers are less interested in, such as philosophical items, SEO, and food. That data helps me focus my Twitter efforts.

Conversion Rate (Outcomes)

If you share links to your ecommerce (or monetizable) websites, then you can use Average Shared Links to measure referrals from Twitter to your site. To enable tracking, you simply encode the links you share on Twitter with unique tracking parameters. Figure 9.20 shows an example of a report you can create in your web analytics tool to measure success.

In this case I measure Visits, Bounce Rate, Time on Site, Goal Conversions, and Average Value. I can look at my Twitter *campaigns* (3) along with other traffic sources. In fact, I can even compare my performance (3) with others who share links to my site (7).

All Traffic Sources						
Visits ? **18,701** % of Site Total: 100.00%	**Bounce Rate** ? **51.76%** Site Avg: 51.76% (0.00%)	**Avg. Time on Site** **00:04:33** Site Avg: 00:04:33 (0.00%)	**% New Visits** ? **59.43%** Site Avg: 59.35% (0.14%)	**Goal1: Registered via Any Form** ? **0.67%** Site Avg: 0.67% (0.00%)	**Average Value** ? **$372.40** Site Avg: $372.40 (0.00%)	

	Source/Medium [None ⌄]	Visits ↓	Bounce Rate	Avg. Time on Site	% New Visits	Registered via Any Form	Average Value
1.	(direct) / (none)	7,640	53.74%	00:04:49	58.84%	0.76%	$379.00
2.	google / organic	4,466	52.78%	00:04:00	60.75%	0.31%	$469.82
3.	twitter.com / occamarazor ✦	1,411	27.92%	00:05:48	61.23%	0.78%	$136.50
4.	google / cpc	818	70.29%	00:02:22	83.01%	0.12%	$299.00
5.	grokdotcom.com / referral	379	51.72%	00:02:31	59.63%	0.79%	$39.00
6.	searchenginestrategies.com / referral	377	74.01%	00:01:16	78.51%	5.31%	$229.00
7.	twitter.com / referral ✦	304	57.24%	00:04:03	52.63%	0.33%	$39.00
8.	mail.google.com / referral	275	65.45%	00:03:11	37.82%	0.36%	$299.00
9.	kaushik.net / referral	245	44.90%	00:03:28	62.86%	0.41%	$299.00
10.	stuntdubl.com / referral	183	52.46%	00:02:04	68.85%	0.00%	$39.00

Figure 9.20 Ecommerce/Outcomes for shared links—Google Analytics

I can see that my conversion rate is higher (0.78 percent) with a higher average value ($136.50), compared to others 0.33 percent conversion and $39 value. That data suggests that my efforts are working.

We have measured Conversion Rate in Figure 9.20, but you can easily see how you can measure the impact of any outcome on your website. For example the number of completed movie trailers watched, downloads of your new chip design white paper, or simply the number of Facebook friends or fans that come from Twitter!

Conversation Rate

In social media, it is important to participate in conversation and to measure it. As with blogs, you should measure whether you are just talking at people or having a conversation.

TwitterFriends is one of many tools for measuring your conversation rate; you'll find it at http://zqi.me/twfriend. Figure 9.21 shows the set of metrics that you'll get from TwitterFriends.

Replies Sent Per Day, 6.4, is the average number of replies I sent during the last 30 days. That is higher than the benchmark (the Average column) of 2.4. Replies Received Per Day, 25, is the average number of replies I received during the last 30 days. The benchmark is 3.2. This analysis would suggest that I actively participate in the Twitter universe and have a high Conversation Rate.

A number of other metrics in Figure 9.21 might be interesting, but try not to get distracted by numbers that exist just because they can.

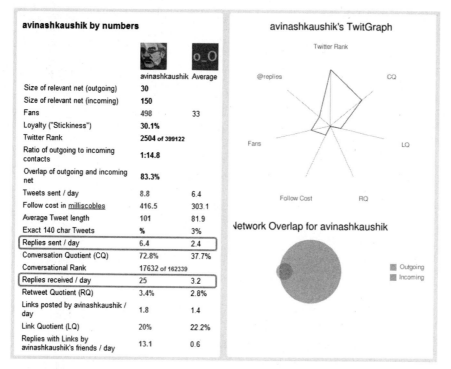

avinashkaushik by numbers		
	avinashkaushik	Average
Size of relevant net (outgoing)	30	
Size of relevant net (incoming)	150	
Fans	498	33
Loyalty ("Stickiness")	30.1%	
Twitter Rank	2504 of 399122	
Ratio of outgoing to incoming contacts	1:14.8	
Overlap of outgoing and incoming net	83.3%	
Tweets sent / day	8.8	6.4
Follow cost in milliscobles	416.5	303.1
Average Tweet length	101	81.9
Exact 140 char Tweets	%	3%
Replies sent / day	6.4	2.4
Conversation Quotient (CQ)	72.8%	37.7%
Conversational Rank	17632 of 162339	
Replies received / day	25	3.2
Retweet Quotient (RQ)	3.4%	2.8%
Links posted by avinashkaushik / day	1.8	1.4
Link Quotient (LQ)	20%	22.2%
Replies with Links by avinashkaushik's friends / day	13.1	0.6

Figure 9.21 Twitter Conversation Rate—TwitterFriends

Emerging Twitter Metrics

During this early stage of the Twitter evolutionary cycle, one tool, still in beta, is an indicator of the metrics that may soon become the norm. That tool is Klout (http://zqi.me/aklout). Figure 9.22 shows the Klout dashboard for my Twitter activity; it provides eight metrics in the scorecard and six additional dimensional metrics.

The scorecard metrics, Updates, Followers, @Messages, and so on, are pretty straightforward. Most of them provide an interesting snapshot of your activity. But they also include possibly meaningless metrics like Followers/Following—you don't have to follow everyone who follows you, and vice versa.

The definitions of the dimensional metrics are as follows (from http://sn.im/kscore):

Engagement How diverse is the group that @ messages you? Are you broadcasting or participating in a conversation?

Reach Are your tweets interesting and informative enough to build an audience? How far has your content been spread across Twitter?

Velocity How likely are you to be retweeted? Do a lot of people retweet you, or is it always the same few followers?

Username:	avinashkaushik						
Location:	Lat: 37.4 Long: -122.1						
Web:	http://kaushik.net/avinash						
Bio:	Author - Web Analytics: An Hour A Day | Analytics Evangelist - Google | Co-Founder - Market Motive Inc						
	View Twitter Profile						

K score

74

Tweet My Score

What does this score mean?

Summary

Stats

Content

Network

Twitter Analysis

Updates	Following	Followers	Followers/Following	Friends	@Messages	Messages Retweeted	Total RT's
1776	64	9873	154.266	40	311	251	1152

Engagement	Reach	Velocity	Demand	Network Strength	Activity
Slightly below average % of audience replies	Above average follower count	Retweeted by more unique people than almost anyone	Extremely high follower/follow ratio	Very high @ network score	Above average update count
Above average inbound/outband message ratio	Below average friend count	Very top percent in unique messages retweeted	Average number of reciprical follows	Very high retweet network score	Average updates for audience size
High unique @ sender count	Very top percent of total times retweeted	Average % of followers retweet	Very high @ reference count		Average tweet effectiveness
↑ 34.53%	↑ 35.19%	↑ 28.28%	↑ 36.32%	↑ 16.43%	↑ 24.39%

Trending Range: From Jun 20, 2009 to Jul 02, 2009

Figure 9.22 New Twitter impact metrics from Klout

Demand How many people did you have to follow to build your count of followers? Are your follows often reciprocated?

Network strength How influential are the people who @ message you? How influential are the people that retweet you?

Activity Are you tweeting too little or too much for your audience? Are your tweets effective in generating new followers, retweets, and @ replies?

As you know, I am not a huge fan of *sexifying* metrics names, and some of these labels fall into that camp. However, the definition of each is clean and valuable. For example, you might define Engagement differently (see Chapter 3), but Klout measures Engagement based on the diversity of people who reply to you and the diversity of conversation, which are both valuable data.

Klout's dimensional metrics are not based on fluff. An example of fluff would be calling a tweet high value (signal) because it contains a hash tag (#). Or fluff would be measuring how often you retweet; that's not a measure of value because originality is valuable, not forwarding other people's work.

One of Twitter's great gifts to humanity is its open API, which has fostered hundreds of applications that provide metrics. I hope now you feel better prepared to identify metrics of value to measure the success of your personal or professional Twitter account.

Analyzing Performance of Videos

What would life be without videos? In short order, videos have moved from clips of a Mentos commercial we send our friends to a key part of our strategies to deliver richer experiences to our users.

Amazon uses videos to sell books. The analytics world is full of videos that teach you how to use various tools. The Smile Train site uses videos to get you to donate money. Every news site in the world provides either a live video feed or clips and excerpts of the latest shows. Video is serious business.

Yet video remains a *faith-based initiative*. We create videos because we think we must. However, a wonderful outgrowth from the recent evolution in measurement techniques is some pretty cool video tracking and analysis, from features in your web analytics tools to metrics on video-sharing sites to tools like Visible Measures and TubeMogul that measure your video activity regardless of where the video is embedded. Now we can analyze how our visitors use our videos and create videos that meet their needs.

In this section, I want to touch briefly on data collection for videos, and then we'll dive into the metrics and reports you can use to measure success.

Data Collection for Videos

Most modern data collection methods involve instrumenting the video player you use on your website. That is, you implement the code your analytics vendor provides to track every interaction that can happen in your video. You can also leverage the Event Tracking model from your analytics vendor to customize the type of data you collect. Let's solidify this with an example.

Figure 9.23 shows the website of the wonderful PBS series *Frontline*. On the site you can watch complete programs that have aired on TV.

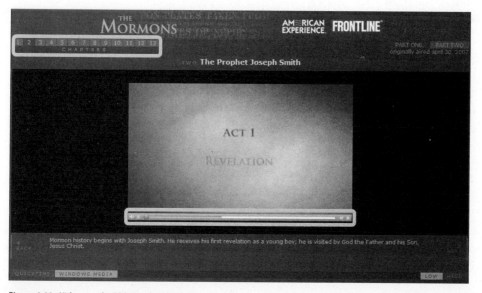

Figure 9.23 Videos on the PBS *Frontline* series

There are a lot of videos on this website. As the hypothetical owner of this website, I would love to track the following:

- Which videos are being watched
- How much of the video people watch
- Whether people watch all chapters in the video or just some chapters
- How long it takes for the complete video to load once people hit Play

I can pass any type of data into the Event Tracking model; Figure 9.24 shows the technical model for the values I want captured.

Object	Action	Label	Value
Video Tracker	Play	Ch 1, Ch 2, Ch 3, Ch4 . . . . . . Ch xx	Video Load Time
	Pause	Ch 1, Ch 2, Ch 3, Ch4 . . . . . . Ch xx	
	Stop	Ch 1, Ch 2, Ch 3, Ch4 . . . . . . Ch xx	
	25%	Ch 1, Ch 2, Ch 3, Ch4 . . . . . . Ch xx	
	50%	Ch 1, Ch 2, Ch 3, Ch4 . . . . . . Ch xx	
	75%	Ch 1, Ch 2, Ch 3, Ch4 . . . . . . Ch xx	
	100%	Ch 1, Ch 2, Ch 3, Ch4 . . . . . . Ch xx	

Figure 9.24 Hypothetical analytics video Event Tracking model for *Frontline*

To keep things simple, in the Action column I am tracking chunks of the video watched. That is one of the customizations you can do. You can track every second of the video watched, but you must balance your decision between the amount of data you'll get vs. the incremental value.

After you create your model, you'll work with your IT developers and your vendor-specific code to implement the collection of these events. With most vendors, you don't have to encode every video on your website. You simply encode the player once, and all your videos will be tracked.

All that's left is to open a bottle of champagne and wait for data to show up!

Key Video Metrics and Analysis

While the process of collecting data about video will be similar between many vendors, the reports and their metrics will not. The data model in Figure 9.24 hints at the metrics you will report. Hence, for this section, I'll use the reports from YouTube's reporting engine, YouTube Insights, which contains some of the nicest reporting for videos that you can get.

If you have ever uploaded a video into YouTube, you can access the reports in YouTube Insights. That will allow you to learn about important metrics and the analysis you should do, regardless of your web analytics tool. Let's look at five common types of analysis.

Baseline Performance Metrics

When you measure video, the first items you want to measure are overall and individual video consumption and location. Figure 9.25 shows this report.

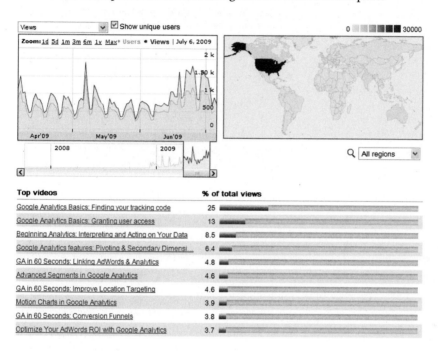

Figure 9.25 Views, Unique Visitors, and Locations

The three-month trend of overall video views shows you the peaks and valleys of consumption. These may coincide with new video releases or campaign launches.

The second line in the graph, top left, shows you the trend of Unique Visitors watching the videos. Notice how the two lines tend to stay close, but through the month of June they separate. The separation indicates that videos during that time were watched more than once by the same person. That raises a question for you: *why?*

The world map shows the locations of users who watch your videos, and in most tools you can drill down to region and cities, allowing you to hone in on where interest originates.

Finally, what would first-blush analysis be without understanding which videos are popular with your users. Note the drop-off between video 1 (which forms 25 percent of the views) and 10 (just 4 percent); this drop-off is normal.

With baseline performance metrics, you get an immediate grasp of your user's preferences.

Tracking Attention or Audience Engagement

You have the base metrics under your belt. Now it's time to dive deeper and see how your videos perform. Do they keep your audience's attention? When do people drop off? When do they perk up and really focus? The Attention Tracking report in Figure 9.26 illustrates just this data.

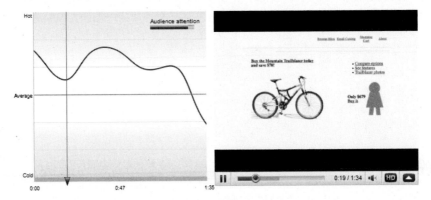

Figure 9.26 Audience Attention report with video timeline

The graph on the left shows the audience's attention, which is measured by the drop-off rate as compared to videos of similar length. When the graph dips below the Average line, the video is losing viewers at a higher rate than other videos.

This video starts with high attention and within seconds loses it as the video talks about the company's glory. Then, as the video shifts to features, attention perks up and stays high until the sales pitch starts and people bail!

A wonderful feature with this view is that the video sits on the right; you can review the content and learn what engages your visitors and what does not. After you observe these results, you need to chop off the uninteresting bits to optimize your videos.

Most web analytics tools with video tracking have a report similar to Figure 9.26, though the data they report may vary slightly.

Reporting on Social Engagement

Most websites now incorporate social elements into their videos, such as ratings (usually on a scale of 1 to 5), comments, and favorites. These three elements are the Voice of Customer (VOC) data that will form the qualitative part of your analysis (see Chapter 6 for more detail). Fortunately, you can focus your qualitative analysis by looking at quantitative data, as shown in Figure 9.27. The Social Engagement report shows you individual social elements, using the drop-down, or you can look at the total data for all three.

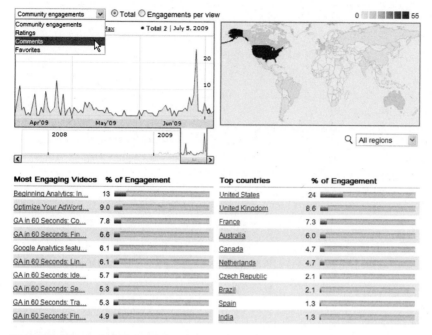

Figure 9.27 Summary Social Engagement report

You can easily identify time periods worth investigating or, by looking at the bottom left, which individual videos are achieving social glory. In a world of blogs, Facebook, and Twitter, there is perhaps no better validation of your video strategy than to understand engagement data.

Tracking *Viralness*

On some sites, videos stay on your website. But on other sites, videos are built to be shared and spread around the Web. Consider the example of a movie website that allows its visitors to take the video and embed it on their blogs or other websites—and thus provide free marketing! Figure 9.28 shows the report, Viral Distribution and Detail, for checking the routes your video has taken to spread around the Web.

The top list shows the methods used to spread your video. You can also drill down to get more detail. For example, by clicking the embedded player, you can track the websites where your video has been embedded and how many views of the video each site has contributed.

With universal search (search engines showing mixed text, video, and images in search results) becoming more important with each passing day, it is also important to track whether your video is being indexed and listed for the right keywords (bottom right in Figure 9.28).

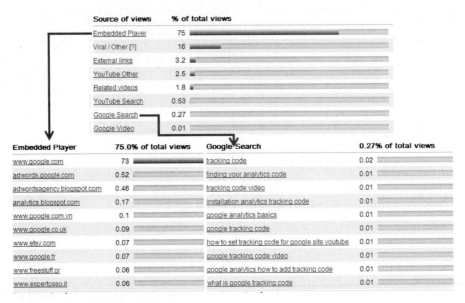

Figure 9.28 Viral Distribution and Detail report

Segment, Segment, Segment

Throughout this book, we have focused on Outcomes. You achieve true bottom-line impact with your videos when you focus on segmenting users who consume your videos and measuring impact.

Let's look at two examples. In the first example, you are a movie website, and you show trailers. Success for your site occurs when visitors completely view a video. Therefore, in your report, you need to segment people who watched the complete video. Then apply that segment to your campaign reports (affiliate, search, email) to see which campaigns bring traffic with a higher propensity to completely watch the videos (or embed those videos or forward to a friend).

In the second example, you are a news website. Videos are a key part of engaging your audience, and you define success as repeat visits to your website. In your report, you want to segment the sessions with video views and then wait 30 days (or a relevant time period). For that original segment, look for a statistically significant increase in repeat visits, as compared to a segment where people only read the news and did not watch the videos.

Analysis such as these examples helps your business leaders understand the bottom-line impact of effectively using video.

Advanced Video Analysis

You've looked at the video-viewing information, and you understand how many people are engaging with your videos. But is it worth the money in terms of bottom-line impact? You can measure the Conversion Rates for the segment that watches the video and the segment that does not and see whether conversions are higher with the video-watching segment. But there may be a self-selection bias; that is, likely purchasers will watch videos. How do you know?

The following are three advanced analyses that can answer these and other such complex questions.

Computing Contextual Influence

When you analyze video, two challenges stand in the way of using clickstream data and the "typical" measure of conversion rate to determine success:

- You might be looking at a *biased* segment, that is, only highly motivated people.

- By comparing all people who converted and viewed the video with those who converted and did not see the video, you are not comparing fair segments. You are also lumping all other marketing tools such as comparison charts, product screenshots, product information, and customer reviews into one large bucket. Your other tools might be converting people at a much higher rate.

By dumping videos and marketing tools together, you are not being fair, and you get a false read on the conversion impact of the videos. So, even if you use your web analytics tools to analyze video, try to compute *contextual influence*, or the value of each feature in context with others.

Computing contextual influence is difficult. It is difficult to calculate in most tools, including some very expensive ones. But one tool that does it with aplomb is ClickTracks, through its terribly named but easy-to-use Funnel report. You follow these basic steps:

1. Create a hierarchy of your website.

2. Add individual pages or groups of pages into each stage (notice I did not say *step* because your customers can jump between steps on your site).

3. Add an outcome (for example, the "Thanks for placing your order" page).

4. After you click Calculate, your final report will look like Figure 9.29.

When you read the report left to right, you can see how many people enter at each stage, which pages or tools they view and interact with, and how many people exit that stage compared to those who progress downward.

Then, each box represents a page or tool with videos, comparisons, and reviews, and each box is a different shade of blue. The darker the shade, the more influence the tool has in driving outcome. Influence is defined by that page or tool appearing in the visitor session, regardless of the path the visitor took, regardless of when the visitor saw the page or tool.

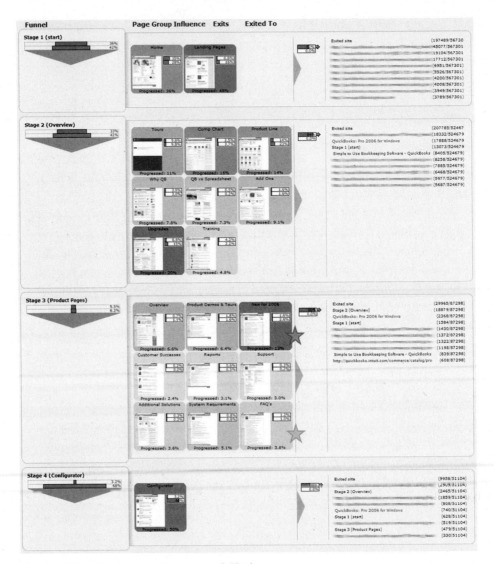

Figure 9.29 Content contextual influence report—ClickTracks

In Figure 9.29, the data from this website showed that Product Videos—the last box in the last row marked with a star—was the least influential tool on the site. The most influential tool—the last box in the first row marked by a star—was a tool that cost $10 to produce, a page that compared different versions of the product!

The report used actual customer behavior and it truly analyzed contextual segments, which helped focus precious company resources in the in the right area, rather than producing more videos.

Actively Collecting Voice of Customer (VOC)

When in doubt, ask your customers. There is perhaps no better advice when it comes to complex expensive efforts like videos.

Consider sending a simple post-purchase email survey to customers, and ask them for the key influencers of their purchase. You could list the tools on your site (product information, comparison tools, videos, customer reviews, and so on) and simply ask customers to *rank* those tools in order of importance.

Avoid asking customers to tell you how much they like certain tools or to choose tools they like, because they tend to pick all. Just ask them to rank the tools. The data customers provide tells you what works for those who buy.

For the 98 percent who will never convert on your website, consider an on-exit survey such as 4Q (http://4q.iperceptions.com) that asks for feedback when people leave your site. The survey will go to a small, random sample of visitors. You'll ask them three or four questions about why they visited (primary purpose) and then ask them what tools and features of your website they liked (and if your survey company can set it up, allow the customers to rank the tools).

Because conversion can also be thought of as a page-level issue, you can also use a page-level survey or poll, such as Kampyle, on your product pages and ask people to quickly rate various features. There is a Site Content feedback topic in Kampyle that you can customize.

Now you have the most important piece of data you need: your customer's opinion.

Testing to Measure Actual Customer Behavior

After reading Chapter 7, you will not be surprised by my next recommendation: run an A/B or multivariate test, and let your customers tell you the value of videos. For 30 or 40 percent of your test subjects, don't show the videos and check the impact on your data. You'll have your answer, without any bias.

A key benefit of using testing is that you define conversion for your videos. So if you run a content site, to measure success, you can use clicks on your AdSense or banner ads, subscriptions for your RSS feed, or visitors printing directions to your physical store after viewing the video.

Anything can determine value from videos on your website. And I can't say this enough—you are using your customer's actual behavior and not your faith to measure success. While the techniques shared in this section were for measuring the value of videos, you can use them to measure the value of any new features you launch on your website to connect with your customers.

Optimal Solutions for Hidden Web Analytics Traps

It is time to tackle some of the toughest issues in web analytics and earn your black belt, the last step to becoming an analysis ninja.

This chapter touches on some of the obstacles you'll face on your quest to be a data-driven analyst and marketer. The quest is not about tools; it is about the right mental model and approach and about thinking differently and internalizing the cost of decisions—from the mundane to the strategic.

You'll use the tactics discussed in this chapter nearly every day of your data-driven life, and if you use them right, these approaches will ensure you massive success.

10

Chapter Contents

Accuracy or Precision?

A Six-Step Process for Dealing with Data Quality

Building the Action Dashboard

Nonline Marketing Opportunity and Multichannel Measurement

The Promise and Challenge of Behavior Targeting

Online Data Mining and Predictive Analytics: Challenges

Path to Nirvana: Steps Toward Intelligent Analytics Evolution

Earlier in the book I discussed the dramatic transformation of the tools landscape. We have so many free, paid, and hybrid choices for every element of Web Analytics 2.0. But what differentiates successful companies from those that are not is their ability to shed old-world tools and approaches.

Let me share a story with you.

I recently visited the senior management of a global company, a leader in financial services. It has a corporate website and numerous micro sites, and it has outsourced its analytics to a large agency. Very bright people work at this global company, and even in the worst of times it has an ample budget. Yet it is one of the least data-driven companies I know. Why?

First, senior management doesn't *get* the Web. Their online strategy, if you strip away the fancy Flash veneer, replicates their TV strategy. Web is not TV! Second, they pay their agency to simply report data. The data is converted into PowerPoint and presented to executives. No one provides any insights because no one is responsible for finding insights.

The company recently rolled out an expensive behavior-targeting system, which brought no significant lift in outcomes—online or offline. Senior management felt the company was now more data driven simply because the technology had been deployed. Furthermore, the company was investing a ton of resources on measuring rich media and widgets, yet they could not answer the simplest of questions like what the bounce rate of the website was.

Now it might seem like this company is an aberration, or perhaps you are thinking, "Thank God we are not that company." Unfortunately, this story is far too common, and you may find that parts of this story match your own. You need to learn a series of approaches to help you create an optimal mental model so that your company does not end up data rich but insight-poor.

 Note: In Chapter 2, I covered the 10/90 rule on how to optimally spend your budget. Following the 10/90 rule is foundational to this chapter, so be sure to check out Chapter 2.

Accuracy or Precision?

In my first book, *Web Analytics: An Hour a Day*, a key exhortation was this: *data quality sucks, so get over it*. It was an acknowledgment that perfect data does not exist on the Web. But it was also my recommendation for a much needed mental model. We have many different types of data on the Web and significantly more of it than other channels such as TV, radio, or magazines. Though the quality of web data may be limited, we can still make valuable informed decisions.

On the Web, we have two fundamental approaches for collecting data: we can be *accurate*, or we can be *precise*. You need to better understand which approach to take for your web business. Simply put, accuracy is *how close to perfect you can get*, and precision is *the degree to which your efforts yield the same results*.

In an ideal world, you want to be both precise and accurate. The difference between the two ideas is illustrated using a bull's-eye target in Figure 10.1. In the first target, the hits are closer to the bull's-eye and have a higher degree of accuracy. But each hit is quite spread out. In the second target, the hits are close to each other, quite precise, but not accurate.

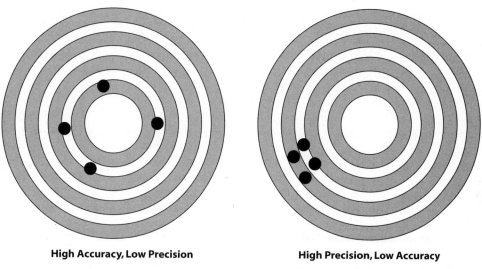

High Accuracy, Low Precision   **High Precision, Low Accuracy**

Image Source: Wikimedia Commons

Figure 10.1 The difference between accuracy and precision

So, which approach should you choose as your strategy for collecting web analytics data? *Precision.* The reason is simple: precision is predictable and therefore reproducible; you can be significantly more confident taking action with insights from precise data. To translate this concept into our target metaphor: if you know where the shot will land every time you fire, you can predict what will happen when you fire the next shot.

Unfortunately, most of us focus obsessively on accuracy. It's good to want accuracy, but it is more important to balance costs and benefits. In the Business 1.0 world, we had fewer data variables and less complexity. We made big decisions, change was slow, mistakes were expensive, and hence the tolerance for risk was low. We needed accuracy.

But that world does not exist online. We factor more variables into our decisions, we need to make decisions faster because of hyper competition, and we can manage risk (see Chapter 7 on failing faster).

With a precision mental model, you know where every shot is likely to land and how far it might be from your goal. Presenting that approach to senior decision makers will translate into driving faster actions and achieving predictable impact for our outcomes. You start by focusing your data strategy in areas where you can be precise.

A Six-Step Process for Dealing with Data Quality

The Web is still a baby. It is going to grow and evolve, in bursts I am sure, but the current methods for collecting data are imperfect. That will change over time, but for now we have to face the facts and figure out how to most effectively optimize our strategy.

We have already agreed to deal with measurement using the precision mental model. Over time you can become more accurate about collecting precise data. Figure 10.2 shows a six-step process I have developed so you can implement a *virtuous data quality cycle* in your company.

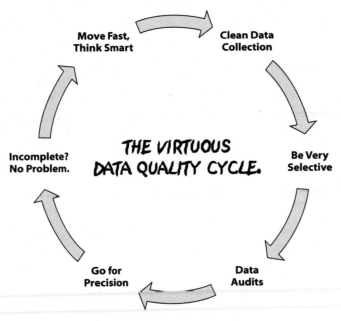

Figure 10.2 The virtuous data quality cycle

Here is more detail on each step of the process:

1. **Collect clean data:** Follow all the best practices to collect your data, and don't do *stupid* stuff. Always use first-party cookies. Ensure all your web pages are tagged. Make sure all the admin settings in your web analytics tool are configured. For a longer list of best practices, check out this post from my blog: http://zqi.me/databp.

2. **Be very selective:** There is no upper limit to the amount of data you can collect on the Web. Collect only as much data as you need now and in the immediate future. Companies tend to implement comprehensive, high-end analytics tools, which can take 18 months! The Web changes every six to nine months. So, by the time you are done implementing, much of what you planned to measure is

irrelevant. Be selective. Plan for a three-month implementation, and start using the data. Implement additional features as you need them. Rinse and repeat.

3. **Audit your data:** Set up a process in your company to periodically audit the data that you collect; you should do this at least once a quarter. The audit will keep your precision high as you collect the most complete data set possible. A number of free and paid solutions, like WASP and ObservePoint, will get your instrumentation up to snuff.

4. **Go for precision:** I have covered all the reasons precision works. Do it. Your analysis will get more accurate as you get more precise!

5. **Don't fret over incomplete data:** Embracing incompleteness is the hardest thing for analysts and marketers to accept. Sometimes this is because of their mental model or because the company is risk averse. Or sometimes it is out of a genuine, but misplaced, desire to give the perfect answer. But waiting for complete data causes paralysis by analysis—an inability to make business recommendations. Be comfortable, I mean be *really insanely comfortable* with incompleteness and learn to make decisions.

6. **Move fast, think smart:** In the context of decision making, the slogan used to be *think smart, move fast.* But on the Web you lose opportunities when you take your time and wait for perfection. The slogan for analysis ninjas is *move fast, think smart.* The Web moves at, well, web speed, and your best investment is in smart people who have a corresponding *speed* built into their DNA. It also means making efficient processes in your company that empower people to move fast. End the multilayered bureaucracy where ownership and execution exist in silos!

You can follow these six simple steps to set up your company to flourish on the Web. Remember, *an educated mistake is better than no action at all.*

What I Am Not Saying

In the context of the six recommendations, it is important to point out what I am *not* saying:

- I am not saying make wrong decisions.
- I am not saying accept bad data.
- I am not saying don't do your damnedest to make sure your data is as clean as it can be.

What I am saying is this: on the Web, your job does not depend on data with 100 percent integrity. Your job depends on helping your company *move fast* and *think smart.* I am also not saying it will be easy.

Building the Action Dashboard

Executives want few things more than a dashboard, and they hate few things more than a dashboard. This paradox exists primarily because dashboards tend to become catchalls fullfull of pies, graphs, and tiny text.

Analysts have tried everything to make dashboards better. We have hired expensive consultants. We have purchased expensive software. We have replaced numbers with fancy visualizations (thermometers, anyone?). We have even tried to stuff as many tabs and metrics as we can into an Excel spreadsheet. But still the dashboards we send are put on autodelete.

Why? Well, often our dashboards stink at helping executives make any decisions. Here are the reasons:

- Dashboards leave the interpretation to the executive. This is a fatal flaw because most dashboards are highly aggregated views of a KPI; they miss the nuance and analysis that only the analysis ninja can give, yet it's rarely shared.

- Most executives want insights and actionable recommendations, but they don't trust their analysis ninjas. Instead, they ask for numbers on paper, so we dutifully cram as many as possible on A4 paper in 6-point font and send it along with a magnifying glass.

- The folks who create dashboards live in a silo. They rarely go out and collect enough tribal knowledge to fully grasp the organizational actions behind the trends and patterns observed in the data being reported.

- Often dashboard creators are "outsiders" such as consultants, and they don't have deep practitioner experience for understanding the entrenched issues within the company, such as the previous three issues. Therefore, they make common mistakes that lead to unactionable dashboards and a loss of credibility.

Creating Awesome Dashboards

If we want executives to use our dashboards and take action, then we must give them information and not data. I attack this problem with psychology: *how can I create a dashboard that will motivate analysts while giving executives the information they need to make the right decisions?*

Recommendation #1 Move to a critical few philosophy for executive reporting (see Chapter 5 for more detail on critical few). Report only the three or four KPIs that define success for the whole business. Kill all the ancillary metrics that are *nice to know*. In the worst case, if you can't kill such metrics, then let the subordinates in the organization worry about them. Eliminate those ancillary metrics from the dashboards.

Recommendation #2 Create an *action dashboard*. It involves a radical redesign of a dashboard and an intense focus away from *reporting the numbers* to *reporting insights, impact, and actions.* The only purpose of an action dashboard is to drive the highest possible executives to quickly understand performance and take action.

Figure 10.3 shows a sample of an action dashboard. Each quadrant of the action dashboard represents a solution to an important human problem. Let's walk through it in detail.

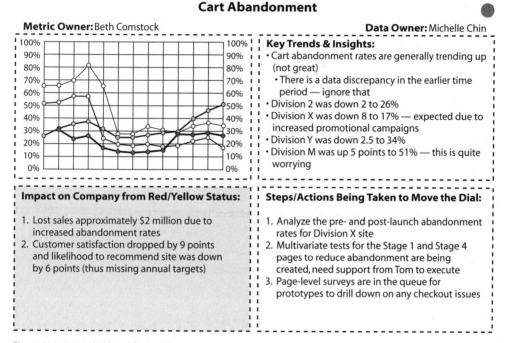

Cart Abandonment

Metric Owner: Beth Comstock   **Data Owner:** Michelle Chin

Key Trends & Insights:
- Cart abandonment rates are generally trending up (not great)
  - There is a data discrepancy in the earlier time period — ignore that
- Division 2 was down 2 to 26%
- Division X was down 8 to 17% — expected due to increased promotional campaigns
- Division Y was down 2.5 to 34%
- Division M was up 5 points to 51% — this is quite worrying

Impact on Company from Red/Yellow Status:

1. Lost sales approximately $2 million due to increased abandonment rates
2. Customer satisfaction dropped by 9 points and likelihood to recommend site was down by 6 points (thus missing annual targets)

Steps/Actions Being Taken to Move the Dial:

1. Analyze the pre- and post-launch abandonment rates for Division X site
2. Multivariate tests for the Stage 1 and Stage 4 pages to reduce abandonment are being created, need support from Tom to execute
3. Page-level surveys are in the queue for prototypes to drill down on any checkout issues

Figure 10.3 Action dashboard for one KPI

At the top of the dashboard, the critical few metric is clearly identified: Cart Abandonment. To add a measure of clean accountability, the dashboard includes the names of the two people responsible for the metric from a business perspective and from an analysis perspective.

The dot on the top right clearly indicates the health of the metric. In this case it's red (although, it appears as gray in a black-and-white book!), unambiguous representation that something is wrong. It can be two other colors: yellow for *don't fire anyone yet but get ready* and green for *send someone a big hug and a box of chocolates.*

The first quadrant, the top-left graphic, shows the trend for the metric, and it is segmented (in this case, the Cart Abandonment metric is illustrated for four key customer segments). This quadrant satiates executive suspicion about whether you know what you are doing. It will be glossed over, and that's OK.

In the second quadrant, Key Trends & Insights, you add value by interpreting trends and supplying context. It also warns which data might be bad. The executives will initially focus on this quadrant. In due time, they will gain confidence in you, the analyst, and then they may skip this section and move on to the good stuff.

Notice we have addressed two important problems: analysts simply puking data out (no more!) and the struggle to earn confidence in your work by showing more than a KPI.

The third quadrant, Actions/Steps Being Taken to Move the Dial, forces the shy web analyst to get out and talk to marketers, website owners, and VPs—whomever it takes to get all the tribal knowledge. The goal is to identify the root cause for the trends in the metric and recommend solid action. You will rarely be able to do this by yourself; you need human contact with others, conversations, and collaborations to identify solutions. It is a fantastic opportunity to become smart about your business.

The Actions/Steps quadrant is key to driving action. You no longer leave metrics to interpretation or postpone action because the next step is unclear. You recommend the next step or the next action. This quadrant will earn you much love from your executives. They will focus on this information, and meetings will transform from everyone arguing about data to executives assigning action items.

The fourth quadrant, Impact on Company from Red/Yellow Status, provides insight for executives who are still unclear about why they need to take action. I think it is also the key element missing from most dashboards—the kick in the rear end. The information in the Impact on Company quadrant answers the question, *As a result of this trend, what was the impact on the company and its customers?* It also forces marketers and analysts to do hard work to estimate the impact and put it on paper.

The Impact on Company quadrant is the killer quadrant—if nothing else drives action, this information will. It illustrates with great clarity exactly how much money was lost, how many customers were upset, or how much opportunity was wasted. Now when executives ignore you, they do so at their own peril and with their butt on the line. Trust me; they will take the action you recommend.

With an improved dashboard, you fix the human problems that hinder good analysis, you address the flaws in the system today, and you become much smarter about your whole business, thanks to the third and fourth quadrants. Win-win-win.

The Consolidated Dashboard

Over time you'll gain a lot more trust from your executives, and all the crappy dashboards can die and be replaced with one that looks like Figure 10.4.

Each quadrant contains the essential pieces from the single "metric action" dashboard: recommendations and expected outcomes. With this you are asking your executives to simply layer their own judgment on the recommendations and assign the recommendations to the relevant people.

Acme Inc. Action Dashboard

VP Who Gets Fired: Victor Cho   **Director for Insights:** Tom Luu

"Critical Few" Metric 2:	**"Critical Few" Metric 2:**
• Recommended action 1 • Recommended action 2 • Expected outcome 1 • Expected outcome 2	• Recommended action 1 • Recommended action 2 • Expected outcome 1 • Expected outcome 2
"Critical Few" Metric 3:	**"Critical Few" Metric 4:**
• Recommended action 1 • Recommended action 2 • Expected outcome 1 • Expected outcome 2	• Recommended action 1 • Recommended action 2 • Expected outcome 1 • Expected outcome 2

Figure 10.4 A consolidated action dashboard

You'll note that there are no numbers on this dashboard. Although many of you reading this book might think this is a bit extreme, I want to assure you that all the work required with the data has happened. The numbers are simply *hidden*—we are trying to drive action, right?

You'll have to earn the trust and respect of your executives to get to Figure 10.4. It will take some time. But you want to get to the point of a consolidated dashboard. You want to create a dashboard that is truly built to drive action.

Five Rules for High-Impact Dashboards

In addition to creating dashboards for your executives and HiPPOs, you'll end up creating dashboards for other folks, such as senior marketers, division heads, and the acquisition team. In those cases, you might not invest the time required for an action dashboard; rather, you'll create a more traditional dashboard of KPIs and graphs.

Many of the solutions I discussed in the prior sections still apply to traditional dashboards. After all, you are still dealing with the same psychological issues. But a unique set of rules applies to traditional dashboards. These rules ensure that your recipients are empowered to understand business performance.

Benchmark and Segment

The first rule of great dashboards is that no metric exists without context because insights should jump out rather than questions. Never report a metric all by itself. Period.

You have many ways to show context. You can use benchmarks (internal or external), goals, or even prior performance. But without context, a metric cannot provide any value on the dashboard, even if it is the most important metric for your business.

The goal in a dashboard is to communicate not just the performance of one metric but also to improve actionability. Segmentation is a key tactic for illuminating the causes of a great performance or a bad one. Figure 10.5 shows one element of a dashboard that effectively incorporates benchmarks and segmentation.

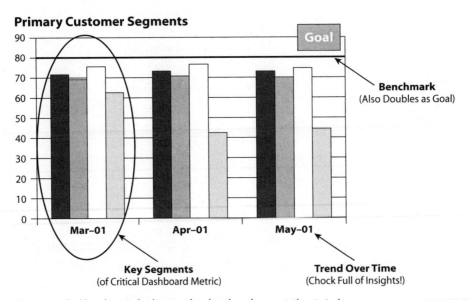

Figure 10.5 Dashboard metric that leverages benchmarks and segmentation strategies

You'll notice that the goal for the metric (80) is clearly indicated at the top of the graph. This clarification alone is worth its weight in gold because it means someone bothered to figure out what the business was shooting for.

The data is not shown just as a snapshot but rather as a three-month trend, which gives nice context to the current performance. Additionally, the graph shows the performance of four individual customer segments, which helps you understand quickly which segment is bringing the party down (the fourth segment).

If the graph showed only overall performance, then this dashboard element would only raise questions or, worse, hide key insights. That's exactly what you are trying to avoid.

Isolate Your Critical Few Metrics

My profound dislike of spamming people with data is probably shining like a noonday sun throughout the book. As analysts, we often think our job is to impress others with how much data we can provide, but we really end up wasting everyone's time.

Often dashboards are 28-tab Excel files or 34-slide PowerPoint decks. In either format, you track too many metrics and rarely segment and highlight performance, which makes it impossible for others to distill a cogent meaning from what happened and take action.

As an analyst, you need to spend lots of time determining the critical few metrics that drive your business. That is, *"What do we care about if the entire house is on fire?"* Do you know the critical few metrics for your business bottom line? Your answer to that question will make or break your dashboard's ability to empower decision making.

As a general rule, your dashboard should contain fewer than 10 metrics (6 is optimal). Remember that you need a goal for each of these metrics, you will segment them, and you will represent the goals and segments on your dashboard.

If you have more than 6 to 10 metrics for your dashboard, then you have not identified your critical few. You need to revisit all your metrics and stress test their importance.

Don't Stop at Metrics—Include Insights

You encountered the principle of insights in the earlier lessons about creating the action dashboard. No dashboard should exist without a cogent set of insights summarizing performance and recommend action.

Most dashboards are a collection of numbers, dials, and graphs; they leave it up to the reader to infer what all that data means. Sadly, such insight-free dashboards are missing the benefit of all the analysis that you put into creating them. Even if you segmented and trended the metrics, you have only summary-level data for critical metrics in the dashboard.

Including a section for insights allows the intelligence from the analyst to bubble up to the highest level. The section should state insights such as the causes for hits and misses and underlying shifts in businesses. Also, include recommended actions, such as what to do next, how to reverse a decline, or a new opportunity on the horizon.

The Power of a Single Page

It might not be the most obvious rule, but if your dashboard does not fit on one page, you have a report, not a dashboard. Additional layers of this rule are as follows:

- Page size = A4

- Print margin = Minimum of 0.75 inch (all sides)

- Font size = Minimum of 10 points for metrics, minimum of 12 points for goals/benchmarks

Limiting yourself to one page leaves little room for doubt or argument. The single-page rule is important because it encourages you to apply rigorous thought as you select your golden dashboard metric. The single-page rule acts as a natural barrier to cramming in too much information, and therefore it makes data presentation easier, it makes the dashboard more understandable and more likely to promote action, and it makes the dashboard portable. Don't underestimate the power of carrying a piece of paper that holds 100 percent of your business performance.

It might seem like an easy enough rule to follow, but condensing your dashboard to one page is a full day's task. Pull out any dashboard you have handy, and try to apply this rule. You'll see instantly how hard the task is. But refining your dashboard is absolutely critical to communicating effectively and driving action.

Churn and Stay Relevant

Contrary to popular belief, dashboards are not carved in stone and hence are not permanent affairs. Everything evolves. Businesses change, people come and go, high-level priorities evolve, and we become smarter. Why should our dashboards and metrics stay the same?

Dashboards, like humans, should constantly evolve. This evolution, however, can be incredibly hard to put into practice because organizations prefer stability and senior management likes predictability.

In reality, to keep pace with real change in the business environment, you can keep 30 to 50 percent of the metrics on your dashboard for a year or more. But you should plan on some level of churn all the time—metrics should be eliminated, almost deliberately, as soon as you discover they are no longer relevant.

Planning for the evolution and churn is mandatory. The only way to ensure that your dashboards don't become stale and end up as worthless, time-consuming pieces of paper is to evolve.

Follow these simple rules about dashboards, and you provide valuable information to your decision makers. The metrics you carefully select and the insights you supply will drive action rather than raise more questions.

Nonline Marketing Opportunity and Multichannel Measurement

Thus far in this chapter, I have covered data collection and quality. I have touched on strategies to create the best possible dashboard to drive action. In this section, I'll touch on one of the most underappreciated and difficult things to measure in web analytics: multichannel marketing.

Shifting to the Nonline Marketing Model

Even today, when the Internet has thrived and changed our lives, most marketing activity is executed in silos. The offline team influences people through TV, magazines, radio, retail, and billboards, and a much smaller, online team handles banners, search, affiliate programs, and email. That marketing execution model implies that our customers behave as illustrated by Figure 10.6, that customers go through four stages—research, selection, qualification, and purchase—either in our offline channels or in our online channel but not in both. That is, of course, absolutely wrong.

Offline Behavior

| Articles in media, conversations with friends |
| Visiting branches and gathering sales literature |
| Talking to staff, or asking questions by phone |
| Buy in-branch or order over the phone and complete by post/in branch |

Product Research and Evaluation
Supplier and Product Selection
Pre-purchase Qualification
Product Purchase

Online Behavior

| Searching websites for reviews and discussion |
| Search by company and product on price comparison/review sites |
| Comparing price, delivery, and support across several possible sites |
| Payment or commit to purchase online and complete by post/in branch |

Figure 10.6 Offline and online behavior silos

We no longer live in a world that differentiates offline marketing from online marketing; we live in a world of *nonline* marketing (a phrase coined by David Hughes, www.nonlinemarketing.com).

There is very little friction for customers between the online and offline worlds; hence, they fluidly move between them as they live their daily lives, as shown in Figure 10.7.

As a customer, I might do all my research online for my digital camera and then visit the store to hold it in my hands and ask questions of the sales associate, and then I might go back online to buy it. You, on the other hand, might see a banner ad online that prompts you to research online, scouring forums to check reviews and ratings, and once you've made your decision, you search for the best price (still online) and finally visit the physical store to make the purchase.

As we consider our marketing tactics and how we influence people, we need to recognize that customers don't make decisions in online and offline silos. If we want to win hearts and minds, we must reconfigure our mental model and, more importantly, our organizations to truly execute nonline marketing campaigns. That translates into showing up at all points of relevance for our current and future customers. Companies that don't grasp this approach will surely fade away.

Figure 10.7 Nonline customer behavior scenarios

Nonline marketing goes against the grain of everything we have been taught so far; it messes with our comfort level. But in a Web Analytics 2.0 world, you must strive to understand the impact of nonline marketing campaigns.

Multichannel Analytics

Consider this scenario from a company that *gets it*. This company runs a paid search campaign for swimwear on www.bing.com. Searchers go to the website to check out all the wonderful tankinis. After customers make their selection, they can promptly decamp for the store and make a purchase there. How does this enlightened company know the online advertising campaign drove the offline conversion?

Or consider the scenario of someone watching television and surfing at the same time. They see the cool new Nike ad and promptly go to the Nike website to make a purchase. How does Nike assign value to the television campaign since they are simultaneously running online campaigns for the same product?

This field of measurement is called *multichannel analytics*. And one single element is the bane of our existence for measuring the impact of our nonline marketing efforts: it is the *primary key*. That is, we seem to have no way of joining the online data to the offline data.

Let's look at a few pictures for a multichannel retailer to understand the challenge. A group of customers looking for various MP3 players visits the retailer's website from search engines. Figure 10.8 shows some of the data that might be captured by a web analytics tool.

	Geek ID	Keyword	U Size
	12345	mp3	XL
	12346	iPod80	L
	12347	Zune	XS
	12348	portable	S

Figure 10.8 Online customer Visits data

The web analytics tool sets persistent cookies, in this case called *geek IDs*, and those cookies are connected to each site visitor. It also captures the paid search keyword that brought the visitor to the site, and just for fun it captures the underwear size of the visitors (though don't ask me how!).

At the physical retail stores that sell electronics, people can walk in and buy MP3 players, amongst other things. Figure 10.9 shows some of the data you might collect in a retail store database: the name of the customer from the credit card, a unique persistent customer ID, the product purchased, and the state where the purchase was made.

Name	Geek ID	Product	Store
Alistair	12345	iPod	CA
Gradiva	12346	Zune	CA
Barham	12349	Walkman	NY
Lily	12348	Sansa	FL

Figure 10.9 Offline customer sales data

Note that these two tables, in Figure 10.8 and Figure 10.9, have a common element, a primary key. In this case it is geek ID. This wonderful gift means that you can join the two tables together with a simple database query and get a table that looks like Figure 10.10.

Name	Keyword	Product	Store	Geek ID
Alistair	mp3	iPod	CA	12345
Gradiva	iPod80	Zune	CA	12346
Lily	portable	Sansa	FL	12348

Figure 10.10 Multichannel merged data set

How glorious! Now you can easily understand which online visitors visited your stores and bought MP3 players. And you can measure the impact of nonline marketing efforts because in the merged data of Figure 10.10 you know exactly how much online efforts contributed to offline sales. You can optimize online campaigns. You can even predict (after collecting enough data) whether underwear size has a causal impact on which digital music player people purchase.

All this action was made possible by a simple thing—the geek ID, or the *primary key*. The problem? *Cue sound of a balloon deflating...*usually no such thing as the geek ID exists in the real world.

The data collected for almost all websites today is unique to online; it is not personally identifiable information (PII), and it is anonymous. When people visit our stores, call our phone centers, and make purchases, they give us their credit card and their names, but they do not, as in Figure 10.9, give us their unique persistent cookie ID.

There are small exceptions, like banks, where your offline data can be tied to your online behavior using the primary key of a bank account ID. But with no cookie ID, you get no primary key and, thus, no soup for you!

Although the current path to hard quantification between online and offline is littered with obstacles, it does not mean you can't track anything at all. You just need to get a little creative and make a leap of faith.

If you can create a small portfolio of initiatives, then you can understand the impact of your nonline marketing campaigns. Pick a few different correlating data points, and you will be surprised at how far you can get in this game! In Chapter 11, we'll learn a dozen multichannel analytics approaches you can use today, from the simple to the sublime.

Note: If your web analytics vendor or consultant says: "Yes, we can track everything online and offline and underwear sizes, and you won't have to lift a finger!" In your sweetest voice ask them, "What is the primary key you use to join the two online and offline data?"

Prepare for them to waffle and hem and haw and backtrack.

The Promise and Challenge of Behavior Targeting

Behavior targeting (BT) is a broad term that covers techniques for targeting ads online and for optimizing content. In the first case, the goal is to improve the effectiveness of the ads and thus improve ROI. In the second case, the goal is to present visitors with relevant content and thus improve ROI. In both cases, you use data collected from the individual's browsing behavior to better target ads or content.

In this section, I will focus on the second case, improving the website experience for visitors by targeting more relevant content to them.

The Promise of Behavior Targeting

Let's use an example to understand the promise of behavior targeting on websites. Say I want to get a handle on my personal finances. I know that Quicken is a software program that does that. So, I type **Quicken** into the search box at google.com. The first search result takes me to www.intuit.com, the company that owns Quicken. The entire page I see at www.intuit.com shows me images and text about QuickBooks, another product Intuit sells.

In addition to images of QuickBooks, I see calls to action on that page: Set Up Your Business, Attract Customers, and Get Paid. No Quicken. No link. No personal finance.

If I persist, I can eventually find a link to Quicken on the website. But I shouldn't have to try so hard, especially when Intuit's website and analytics programs know that I entered the site using the search keyword *Quicken*. That piece of information should be used to display information about Quicken on the home page, thus avoiding a frustrating customer experience.

That is the wonderful promise of behavior targeting. By integrating an intelligent tool or engine into your website-serving platform, you can use data from your customers to optimize their customer experience. This could be as simple as switching the main images on the home page based on the search query, banner ad, or social media link the visitor came on. It could be as complex as learning what pages the customer saw, what products were added to a cart, or what country the customer is located in, and then using that information to show relevant products, promotions, and content.

We spend a significant time and money optimizing our campaigns and the *preclick* marketing experience, or everything that happens away from our websites. Technology now makes it easier to significantly improve the *postclick* marketing experience to ensure the visitor has a relevant experience on the website, which should immediately translate into higher engagement and improved conversion rates.

On-site behavior-targeting platforms include solutions from companies like Omniture, Audience Science, Kefta, and Netmining. Free solutions are even available, such as BTBuckets.

Overcoming Fundamental Analytics Challenges

The data you use for your on-site behavior-targeting efforts will largely be data you already collect with your web analytics tools. When you analyze data from your web analytics tools you face three important challenges: scale, data interpretation, and diversity. They all plot actively against your ability to take fast action. Here's how:

Scale Thousands of visitors may be on your website at any given time. And thousands more are coming. This creates a unique problem of huge numbers that directly impacts the analysis you and your system must do.

Data Interpretation These visitors and pages going back and forth generate tremendous amounts of data, at a level that is difficult for a human, or even our analytics tools, to parse it, interpret it, and identify insights fast enough. Due to our own limitations, that of our organization structures, and our decision-making layers, we struggle to take action even every few days. This is why we can rarely extract even marginal value from getting real-time data.

Diversity Most website owners are pretty bad at understanding all the reasons why people come to their websites (see Chapter 6 for how to overcome this challenge). People may use your website for purposes that you did not intend, and that complicates data analysis and identifying action.

When you do behavior targeting with the right tool, you can overcome the scale, data interpretation, and diversity problems by *automatically* understanding your visitors as they interact with your web presence and showing them the most relevant content. Figure 10.11 shows a schematic of a typical on-site behavior-targeting system.

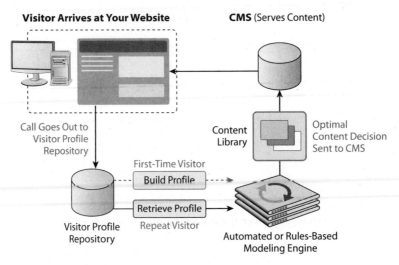

Figure 10.11 How automated behavior targeting works

The top half of Figure 10.11 shows what's happening on your website today. The bottom half is what happens when you use behavior-targeting tools.

You can base your content targeting on business rules that you input into the *modeling engine*. In some solutions, humans are optional (!). These solutions use complex *machine-language algorithms*—they learn from the behavior of similar visitors and then automatically optimize the customer experience.

Let's consider a few examples. In a rules-based platform, a marketer could create a rule that if someone visits three times and they had added a product to the cart in a prior visit, then on this third visit show them a coupon for a 15 percent discount. On the other hand, in an algorithmic platform, after a short learning period, the system might notice a pattern: people who buy product x also tend to buy product y, but only if they come from Utah. So for future Visitors from Utah who add product x to the cart, the system might automatically suggest product y or a bundle of product x and product y.

Behavior targeting helps overcome the fundamental problem of human beings optimizing website experiences. As in the case of Intuit and the challenges outlined earlier, it is clear that human-driven systems have limitations. To get a chunk of intelligence for your website, humans can now be replaced with algorithms.

The tools can't do everything, but used correctly, they can free you to focus on big, strategic business problems (the really important stuff), while leaving the tactical visitor-level decisions relating to content, promotions, and products to the machine. The best BT solutions are still quite expensive, but it is only a matter of time before they become more accessible to every website owner.

Two Prerequisites for Behavior Targeting

Although the promise of behavior targeting is tempting and results are often positive for clients, I find that people seem to treat BT as a panacea. It is important to remember that the principle of *garbage in, garbage out* applies here, more than it does in any other situation. That is because what makes a behavior-targeting platform tick, and produce results, is a mix of its native intelligence and your ability to feed it the right content.

You feed your BT system crap, and it will quickly and efficiently target crap to your customers. And it will target crap faster than you ever could yourself because the system is very efficient.

If you are a medium to large company, you should investigate how BT platforms will help you improve the on-site customer experience. But before you implement an expensive solution, make sure that you cover the following prerequisites, no matter which vendor you choose.

Invest in Solid Customer Listening Posts

Consider what you want to accomplish with behavior targeting: you want the right content to get to the right person at the right time. Now take a step back and answer this question: beyond your web analytics tool, how do you hear from your customers and understand who they are, what they need, and what problems they have?

I suspect that most of us don't have active *listening posts*. These include surveys, usability studies, remote testing, market research, or listening to call center conversations. We discussed these approaches in Chapter 6.

When you leverage these listening posts, you get a solid picture of your customers. When you understand your customers, you can develop the content your BT platform needs to intelligently target the right person at the right time.

No amount of technological coolness from your BT platform can make up for lack of good content. In the end, you still have to get off your quantitative high horse and get out and talk to customers. Monitor your listening posts for at least three months before you implement your BT platform.

Do A/B or Multivariate Testing First

The amazing value of testing and experimentation was covered in Chapter 7. Before you jump into BT, it is a great idea to implement multivariate testing, and run the program for a while.

With multivariate testing, you are not doing behavior targeting, but you are trying to come up with content, offers, products, and layouts to see what works. That process can teach you valuable lessons. You will learn how hard it is to come up with good content that improves the customer experience. You will learn how painful it is for your organization to come up with creative and content: the marketing runaround, the displeasure from sales in approving promotions, the road blocks from legal about what you can say and put out there, the displeasure from your designers about anything simple, and the runaround from your IT teams.

Then there are the incredible lessons about the process. Testing of any sort is not ad hoc. For testing to work, you must create a structured and repeatable process with defined steps and roles, responsibilities, and organizational clarity. As you struggle with MVT, you will discover your company's ability to overcome the aforementioned challenges, and if you are committed, you will be stronger. You will recognize what is broken in your company (people, content, processes), and you must fix it before you can extract a shred of value from your BT platform. This will be a priceless experience.

Conduct your testing for three to six months before you implement your BT platform. The initial three months can run in parallel with the first prerequisite, establishing solid customer listening posts.

After you fix the issues you discover through testing, you can move from making a few changes on your site to creating a relevant customer experience to implementing an automated system that targets behavior on a massive scale.

You can't expect to get a massive payoff from your behavior targeting efforts by simply shifting from a web analytics tool to a complex targeting solution. You need to evolve first and ensure you have a process for understanding your customer needs. You must ensure that your organization has a solid process for feeding good stuff into your targeting platform.

Online Data Mining and Predictive Analytics: Challenges

Predictive analytics is a much bandied-about term that has come to mean everything but the kitchen sink. So, I need to clarify things a bit.

I just covered one type of *predictive analytics*: the attempt to target content or offers to customers using automated intelligence or human-created business rules. Another kind of predictive analytics is used by search engines to improve results based on the searcher's location or previous queries. Both of these strategies have worked well, the latter more than the former. The latter strategy works because of the fewer variables and the depth of data available to search engines.

There is one more kind of predictive analytics, which is perhaps the hardest. This is the attempt to collect years of website data, transfer it into a data warehouse, and mine it to find monetizable trends and patterns.

Wikipedia defines it as thus:

Predictive analytics encompasses a variety of techniques from statistics and data mining that analyze current and historical data to make predictions about future events.

This type of analytics has been used extensively, and successfully, in the offline world across a spectrum of industries, from retail to financial services. Examples include predicting which customers are likely to make delinquent payments, which patients may develop certain conditions, or which employees are at a higher risk of quitting.

Online we may be able to use predictive analytics to mine years of data to predict when a particular customer may buy next, to predict the behavior of paid search visitors over the next 12 months, or to predict which prospect we can best target via a specific online channel. In this segment I'll cover that last type of predictive analytics.

First the punch line: online predictive analytics that apply traditional data mining principles have promised the moon, yet companies have struggled to show any return on the investment. My experience has led me to conclude that a few powerful yet subtle elements work against you when you seek to exploit trends and patterns in your web data. Before you decide to pour resources into online predictive analytics, you need to recognize and address the challenges, outlined in the following sections.

Type of Data

Web data is almost completely anonymous, usually incomplete, and highly unstructured. These issues can severely compromise your ability to deliver insights from traditional data mining and predictive analytics approaches.

It is a challenge to identify complex data trends and patterns for people, products, outcomes, and behavior over significant periods of time when your data set comprises anonymous cookies and sensitive technologies like JavaScript tags. Also, online data is often incomplete and less structured than offline data, which makes it much harder to tie behavior to outcomes.

Yes, if you capture login IDs and you can connect those IDs to actual details from your offline system for every person who visits your site, the anonymity problem

x

eases. But with the average conversion rate in the United States hovering around 1.72 percent, only a tiny fraction of your data set will then be *in the money*.

Number of Variables

Data mining in the offline world is easier because in the offline world we lead a siloed existence. If we have a store, it may compete with another store a few miles away, but life is still simple. You know who your competitors are. A finite number of variables could impact your business, and these variables are easy to identify.

This is absolutely not the case on the Web. On the Web, everyone competes with everyone else; there are no barriers to entry—the customer is a click away from flirting with your competitors and other influence channels online.

How do you identify all the possible variables that went into delivering an outcome on your website (variables that are key to your ability to extract some value from your predictive analytics efforts)?

By now, you accept that you live in a nonline world. This means people don't just interact online with you and your competing influence channels. Rather, they flow between online and offline touch points, introducing even more variables, known and unknown, that you must accommodate in an effective model.

For example, your online data suggests that customers typically make three visits before they purchase. But do you know about their two visits to a store between those three online visits? Anonymity or identity reuse poses challenges as well. Are Tony and all visits attributed to Tony really Tony? Or do his wife and daughter all use Amazon on the same login?

People may behave in crazy ways offline; they have multiple touch points and don't use perfect names and addresses. These problems are exponentially worse online. By the time you control for the variables you can count and account for, you are left with a small glass of water when you started with an oceanful. Your ability to predict anything scalable for actionable insights is deeply limited.

Multiple Primary Purposes

In Chapter 6, I covered the importance of understanding *primary purpose*: people don't visit our websites for one reason; they visit for a variety reasons. I stress primary purpose because most website owners think their site exists to let people do just one thing, when most people visit the site to do many different *jobs*.

You can quickly see how these different jobs become a challenge for data mining and predicting outcomes because:

- You don't know all the primary purposes.
- It is difficult to assign your massive collection of clicks and visits into each primary purpose bucket and then make any predictions.

Your first challenge, incomplete and anonymous data, compounds the problem, as does the next challenge I will discuss.

Multiple Visit Behaviors

You can predict what people want when they walk into your supermarket because the behavior involves a routine. There is actual and emotional cost for multiple visits: it is a nuisance to visit a store and then return six more times. But on the Web this kind of effort is trivial; hence, hardly any website converts visitors on the first visit.

Therefore, as you get ready to analyze your multi-terabyte database, you must answer these questions: *How can you isolate visit behavior in your clicks? With how much confidence?*

On paper, isolating behavior may sound easy, but in practice it is incredibly hard to accommodate for multiple visit behavior, even if you have nixed the problem of collecting data accurately for each person and every visit. Data collection on the Web is simply not there yet.

Missing Primary Keys and Data Sets

You could improve your predictions by merging your data with other sets of customer data beyond web analytics, such as store information or phone channels. If you knew customer touch points and merged the data, then you could understand current behavior and predict future behavior and outcomes.

This nirvana scenario is crushed by a few rather rotten realities. We are all familiar with untagged campaigns and pages. We also know that URL parameters sometimes fail to help us collect data. The problem is that most companies don't apply the required forethought to creating the right *primary keys* to allow data from different channels to be merged. We discussed this concept earlier in the segment on multichannel analytics.

And with names, addresses, and phone numbers collected and stored differently, mining identity data becomes a data reconciliation nightmare and a major challenge for analyzing outcomes.

To yield positive ROI from your data mining and predictive analytics, your company put a lot of forethought into the process of data collection and storage across channels and in the deep bowels of your web, ERP, and CRM systems. When you begin mining and predicting, focus first on these specific challenges before you move on to tools and people.

Pace of Change on the Web

Sure, the big names on the Web, like Google, Amazon, and the *New York Times*, will always be there. For these players, it seems like the Web never changes. For the rest of us, though, the game is not the same. The Web constantly changes, from the way companies compete to the way customers buy.

Doing mining and predictive analytics on past behavior requires a certain degree of *stability* about your future. But if the *environment* changes too much, or even enough, then your predictions from past behavior have only slight chances of success. This is one of the biggest challenges to analysts who apply traditional mining and predictive algorithms to web data.

The Wikipedia article on predictive analytics ends with this statement:

> *Predictive analytics adds great value to business decision-making capabilities by allowing it to formulate smart policies on the basis of predictions of future outcomes. A broad range of tools and techniques are available for this type of analysis and their selection is determined by the analytical maturity of the firm as well as the specific requirements of the problem being solved.*

I'll leave that thought with you and stress that you consider the following:

- The maturity of your firm.
- The requirements of the problem you are solving.
- The six items mentioned earlier in the chapter.
- Whether you have fixed all the *low-hanging fruit*. In the next section, I will outline the steps for this process.

Even with such massive amounts of data on the Web, we fall short in our quest to do data mining, a process that is well established offline. Our problems may just be a challenge for the now. In the future, customer acceptance, better data collection mechanisms, and sanity in complex customer variables will ensure that we can finally deliver on the analytics promise that lives in the data.

Path to Nirvana: Steps Toward Intelligent Analytics Evolution

It is abominable how long it takes to implement a web analytics tool. Some solutions take up to 18 months. Yet in just a few months, the Web can change in myriad ways; therefore, your initial goals and assumptions may not apply by the time your tool is implemented.

So, why does it take months to implement a web analytics tool? Well, we want completeness and perfection, but we need to accept that web analytics implementation is never done and that collecting a complete data set is impossible. You will always want more.

For those two reasons, I recommend a strategy of starting fast off the blocks, making decisions on your web analytics data at the end of the first month, and then evolving over time to make more complex decisions while capturing ever more valuable and complex data from your website. Figure 10.12 shows my recommendation for a structured path to achieving the nirvana stage for web analytics in your company.

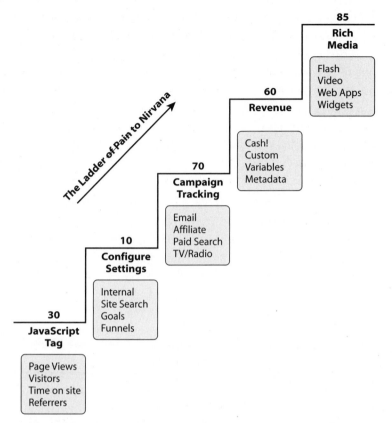

Figure 10.12 Optimal path to successful web analytics evolution

There are five simple steps to analytics nirvana. Each step makes incremental progress, each allows you to get more data and make better decisions, each has associated pain, and each step attempts to balance cost and benefit. Let's cover the logic and benefits of each step to understand the full picture.

You will recognize that many of the concepts I am recommending in the evolutionary process have been discussed before in this book. In this chapter, I'm simply putting them in a specific order to ensure that your execution results in a specific evolution for your company. My goal is simple: insightful actionability from the first week, starting with a small wave and building up to a tsunami!

Step 1: Tag, Baby, Tag!

The first step is to take the simplest version of the JavaScript tag from your web analytics vendor and implement it on your site. Forget everything else. Forget massive world domination (the ultimate perfect tag that on day one will collect ever bit of data you'll ever need!). Find the automatically included footer file on your website, and copy/paste the few lines of the standard JavaScript into that file and—bam!—when you hit Save, 99 percent of your site is tagged.

One percent of your site, such as pop-ups or fragments, may not have the footer. You need to identify those elements individually and tag them. Though tagging these elements is important, at this point it is not critical because these pop-ups and fragments will account only for a minor percentage of content consumption. Put them on the path to implementation, but you don't need to keep fussing until these elements are all done.

You have done nothing particularly complex so far, and the tagging process probably took you just a few days, yet you now possess all the foundational web metrics: Page Views, Unique Visitors, Time on Site, Referrers, Keywords, Loyalty, and Top Pages Viewed.

Just imagine all the decisions you can make right away! You have enough data to know whether your site stinks, you can see what approaches are going well, and you can take an initial peek into customer intent. At this point, you can even identify particular pages that stink by looking at Bounce Rates for top landing pages. And let's not forget, you can already start using key techniques like segmentation (see Chapter 4).

On a scale of 1 to 100, this just involves 30 points of pain. Low pain, high gain.

Step 2: Configuring Web Analytics Tool Settings

With your tags done, you can move on to the easiest step in the whole five-step nirvana process: logging into your web analytics tool and updating the sweet admin. settings.

The good news is you don't necessarily need your IT team for this task. If you have a little technical knowledge, you can update the settings yourself and unlock a raft of new data.

Configuring Reporting

With a few clicks in a web analytics tool, you can configure reporting for your website's internal site search engine:

1. Log into your tool, and click Settings.
2. Click Configure Internal Site Search, and specify the query parameter.
3. Click Save, and you are done. There's no need to touch the JavaScript tag on your site.

In a few hours, you'll have glorious data from your internal site search, and you can understand what visitors on your site are looking for!

Configuring Goals

Being an overachiever, you have surely identified the goals, or micro and macro conversions, for your website (see Chapter 5) before you procured your tool. Another great and relatively painless task is configuring goals in your analytics tool:

1. Log into Settings, and click Add Goals.

2. Enter the Goal Name, choose the Type of Goal, and enter a Goal Value (see Chapter 5 for computing economic value).

3. Enter the funnel steps (if relevant, for example for a checkout process), and then hit Save. Do a happy dance, because you'll have data in a few hours.

With the easy act of updating some settings, you have just accomplished perhaps the hardest task in web analytics: moving your organization to think in terms of Outcomes delivered by your website. Depending on your tool, you may easily configure a host of settings that give you a ton more data for making more sophisticated decisions.

On a scale of 1 to 100 this just involves 10 points of pain. Low, low pain; high gain.

Step 3: Campaign/Acquisition Tracking

It's time to step up your game and focus on your campaign and acquisition efforts. Although vendors often don't make this step clear, simply implementing the web analytics tool does not mean that you can now track your email, affiliate, search, television, or other types of campaigns. Every campaign must be tagged with unique parameters that allow your analytics tool to identify it. (Each tool has its own method or structure for adding such parameters; your vendor can instruct you on how to do this.)

Here's an example. I would like to track all social media efforts for my startup Market Motive (www.marketmotive.com). Simply sharing links to Market Motive on Twitter or Facebook won't help me. I have to encode links with a tracking parameter, like this one:

```
http://www.marketmotive.com/?utm_source=blogs&utm_medium=occamsrazor&utm_
campaign=startupprom
```

Everything after the question mark is a campaign parameter that tells my web analytics tool the type of campaign, the location of the link, and the type of promotion offered in the advertisement.

Campaign tracking is tough because, depending on the size of your company, you'll have to dedicate a few hours to a few people to ensure that every email, search, or affiliate campaign is tagged. You might even have to create a simple database to track the metadata used for these campaigns. You'll have to create a new process for marketers to ensure they request that campaigns are tagged correctly for optimal trackability.

The only exception is Google AdWords and Google Analytics. In that case, all the paid search campaign tracking is done for you with a simple click.

Notice that when you tag campaigns, you are not doing anything in your web analytics tool. Often people blame the tool if their campaigns are not tracked correctly, but poor campaign tracking is not about the tool. Campaign tagging is all about you: your company, your process, and your people.

Tagging your campaigns will take time. But the task is absolutely required because it tracks areas where you are spending money; you want to handle those areas wisely.

On a scale of 1 to 100 this just involves 70 points of pain. It is obvious, but for reasons I've already mentioned, do your campaign tracking as step 3.

Step 4: Revenue and Uber-intelligence

If you are an ecommerce or lead-generating website, then the standard JavaScript tag won't track deep data about orders on your website. You'll have to implement a custom JavaScript tag on your order confirmation/thank you page.

To create a custom tag, you must first spend time with your IT team to understand how your ecommerce platform works and what types of data it will share. You must also work with your HiPPOs and the marketing team to determine what types of deep ecommerce tracking they want. You'll then incorporate both of these pieces of information and work with your web analytics vendor to create a custom JavaScript tag that you implement in your website checkout process.

Creating a custom tag involves work with many different people inside and outside your company. You'll do rigorous QA during this process. For some sites, you may have to review data with your legal team to ensure you comply with the terms and conditions of your site about what data you can collect and where it is stored.

By customizing your JavaScript tag to collect intelligent metadata, you can significantly enhance the types of advanced analysis you do with your web analytics tool. For example, a newspaper publisher can use the custom variables feature of the analytics tool to identify which section of the site visitors saw during their visit. Or a bank can pass anonymous data about visits by existing customers and visits by prospects. Or that the visitor completed a survey during the visit. Or that they participated, unknowingly of course, in an A/B or MVT test.

All this *uber-intelligence* data helps you unleash the power of segmentation because you use data that a web analytics tool does not collect natively. Custom tags empower you to collect *primary keys*, in the form of surveys and tests that allow you to merge analytics data with externally stored data.

To pull all this off, you must collaborate with people driving the strategy for your website, with your most senior decision makers, with your IT team, and finally with your analytics vendor. Getting uber-intelligence data requires lots of customization and lots of effort.

Most companies may never need this level of sophistication, and you certainly do not have to customize on day one. In fact, you may not even think about customization in the first six months of doing web analytics.

On a scale of 1 to 100, this involves 60 points of pain. High pain, high gain.

Step 5: Rich-Media Tracking (Flash, Widgets, Video)

By now you have made a ton of progress in collecting and analyzing data, and that progress has resulted in a truly data-driven organization. You have also optimized much of your website and all of your campaigns, which are driven by sophisticated outcomes analysis.

Finally, we reach the most sophisticated tracking. Increasingly, we live in the world of *fluid web*—a world of RSS, widgets, Flex, video, and Flash. All these applications move beyond static pages and content constrained to your website.

A fluid web is fantastic for creating truly engaging customer experiences. Unfortunately, these applications mean using new and evolving ways to collect the data you need to make decisions. Chapter 9 covered these data collection methods in detail.

To track these applications, you'll touch nearly every corner of your extensive existence: every system, many people, and almost all processes you may have in place thus far.

You have also put a lot of forethought into this step, before you touch the code. With JavaScript tagging, you did not have to think at all. You just took the tag, put it in place, and got a ton of structured data. When you track rich media, you collect data using a very open data collection mechanism, such as event tracking. That means you must know the questions you want answered, and then you must translate your answers into requirements for your developers. Your developers must then code the requirements directly into your rich-media experience—up front—to ensure data gets collected.

On a scale of 1 to 100, this involves 85 points of pain! See why I recommend keeping it as the last step?

If you can successfully implement rich-media tracking, then you will approach true web analytics nirvana.

By following the recommended five-step process of intelligent analytics evolution, you'll avoid a massive 18-month implementation process. You'll avoid hoping that you'll get all the data you need one magical day. Rather than trying to eat the whole analytics tree, you eat your low-hanging fruit first, your JavaScript tags, and simple settings. You then make progress in incremental steps, and you start using data much faster. Over time you'll evolve the sophistication of your organization.

On the Web, revolutions almost always fail. Evolution works.

Guiding Principles for Becoming an Analysis Ninja

This exciting chapter looks at the choicest practical techniques for nearly every facet of your job as an analyst.

The goal is simple: to use proven approaches to help avoid the calamity of drowning in data or getting stuck in paralysis by analysis.

Sourced from real-world experiences, these approaches make the process of identifying insights faster, usually with simple off-the-shelf methodologies. Additionally each addresses a tough marketing challenge on the web.

To be an analysis ninja, you need this chapter. Period.

11

The main tasks of every analytics tool are collecting, storing, processing, and regurgitating data back to you. In this scenario, tables, graphs, and Excel exports abound. Features such as advanced segmentation make the job of a knowledgeable analysis ninja easier, but at the end of the day, our analytics tools lack even basic intelligence.

That is one important reason why I harp on the value of people. The right person with the right mental model and an appetite for hard work can get anything and everything done. This chapter is chockful of techniques for that person to tame gobs of data. There is no definitive list of all available techniques, but those covered in this chapter will help you understand what to look for.

Before we get going, I have to stress one thing. These techniques aren't here because they are cool and sexy. They are here because they help solve a fundamental data/analytics problem or they help solve a fundamental marketing problem on the Web.

Context Is Queen

Often numbers don't *speak* as loudly as they should because you are missing one simple ingredient: context. Context is a piece of data or information that makes you say "I get it now" or "That's interesting. I wonder if...." Context is the quantitative or qualitative information around our key metrics that adds a pinch of color to the data.

The following are six techniques you can use to give context to your performance, starting with one you have already mastered. In later sections of this chapter, I will discuss how to dig deeper into some of these techniques to gain more insight from specific reports.

Comparing Key Metrics Performance for Different Time Periods

Comparing key metrics is the cheapest trick in the book, and it breaks my heart how few people leverage this approach. Figure 11.1 shows how we typically present data to our senior executives; it's a dashboard with key metrics but no insights.

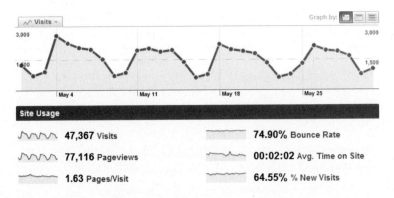

Figure 11.1 Dashboard with key web metrics

The dashboard is cute, but the data tells you nothing. But when you choose a comparable time period, such as the past month or the same month last year, you give context to the data and provide insight. With two clicks of the mouse, we get the picture in Figure 11.2.

Figure 11.2 Comparing performance for two time periods for key web metrics

Even a cursory analysis of Figure 11.2 will yield sweet insights. Although Traffic is down 15 percent for the current time period, Bounce Rate dropped, and Time on Site went up. That means we got more qualified traffic.

A dashboard like the one in Figure 11.2 will also raise the right questions. Early in the month we seem to get a spike in visits, and the spike in May was much lower than April. Why?

By looking at deltas, indicated in parentheses in Figure 11.2, you take attention away from distractions like the raw number, which is all you see in Figure 11.1. This is a worthy accomplishment all by itself!

Providing Context Through Segmenting

It is a crime to report any KPI or metric all by itself in a graph, table, or dashboard. Why? You give no context. But when you segment data, you immediately provide valuable context.

We typically present data as it appears on the left of Figure 11.3. This data is cold and yields nary an insight. I see 116,503 visits and 64 seconds. But, so what?

On the right I added a touch of context by comparing relevant segments of that same data. Now you know some interesting facts about your 116,503 Visitors: approximately half came from search engines, and only a tiny fraction, 5,288, did what you wanted—that is, looked at product pages. More humbling, only a miniscule fraction of Visitors converted.

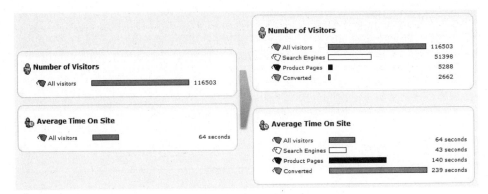

Figure 11.3 Segmented data for key performance indicators

From the second set of data for Average Time on Site, you get a sense for the varied distributions in time that each segment spends on your site. Although 64 seconds might feel like a hurtfully low number for your engaging site, you can see that some people do spend more time on the site—those who make it to product pages. You also know how long it takes for someone to convert, 239 seconds.

You don't have all the answers you need, but you have important questions. Those questions will help focus your initial analysis effort. You'll ask why search engine Visitors spent 43 seconds on average on your site. You'll ask where those Visitors enter: from what keywords and from PPC or organic? What can you fix? Is 239 seconds the right amount of time to conversion?

Spend five minutes supplying context for your analysis, and it will be well worth the effort for the insights you gain.

Comparing Key Metrics and Segments Against Site Average

Yes, averages can lie! And I will briefly discuss that problem soon. But averages can also be your friend, especially for providing the initial context you sorely need to make your mass of web analytics clickstream data actionable.

Say you are curious about your organic search traffic. Click a few times in your web analytics tool, and Figure 11.4 is the view that will greet you. The spark lines give you some sense of the trends, but in the grand scheme you have no clue whether what you are seeing is good or bad.

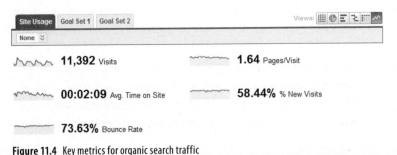

Figure 11.4 Key metrics for organic search traffic

In some tools like Google Analytics, you actually see a view of your data in context, as in Figure 11.5.

Figure 11.5 Key metrics for organic search traffic, with context

Now this is meaningful data! Even a nonanalyst can quickly answer these two questions to gain critical insight:

- How important is this source?

- How well is it performing?

To answer the question about source, you can see that 24.05 percent of the traffic comes from organic search. That is not clear when you see only the number 11,392. With context for your data, you get fast insight: you know that you want to focus on organic search because that number should be closer to 45 percent.

For the second question about how the source performs, you can compare the metrics to the Site Average, which appears under each metric in Figure 11.5. In this case, Average Time on Site for organic search traffic is 5.57 percent higher than the site average. Very good! A quick look at other metrics tells you that performance for this source is good; your only problem is that you need to get more of this traffic. Invest in smart SEO!

Another wonderful idea is to compare key metrics to site averages when you look at segmented aggregate performance, as in Figure 11.5, and you can also do this comparison when you dive deep into data. Figure 11.6 shows an example of using Excel for the same analysis but for understanding which landing pages on the site are performing subpar.

Columns 1 and 2 are from the web analytics tool; column 3 is from the site dashboard; and column 4 is the manually computed delta for individual pages, that is, column 2 minus column 3 (you can do the same calculations for keywords, referrers, campaigns, and so on). And finally, column 5 shows the manually computed, indexed performance.

	1	2	3	4	5	6
URL	Entrances	Bounce Rate	Site Average	Delta	Indexed Performance	In English
/	458,670	13%	35%	-22%	-63%	Yes!
/if/idealist/en/SiteIndex/AssetViewer/vie\	121,192	61%	35%	26%	75%	Ouch!!
/en/job/	120,789	57%	35%	22%	61%	Ouch!!
/en/org/	41,054	66%	35%	31%	88%	Ouch!!
/if/as/Job	29,082	36%	35%	1%	4%	Ouch!!
/?_kk=volunteer&_kt=0b5e299c-e2e5-4(	12,063	56%	35%	21%	60%	Ouch!!
/if/idealist/es/Home/default	10,403	34%	35%	-1%	-3%	Yes!
/if/idealist/en/SiteIndex/AssetViewer/vie\	10,275	37%	35%	1%	4%	Ouch!!
/if/idealist/en/SiteIndex/AssetViewer/vie\	9,855	66%	35%	31%	87%	Ouch!!
/if/as/Find	9,759	21%	35%	-14%	-39%	Yes!

Figure 11.6 Comparing individual page Bounce Rate performance to the site average's Bounce Rate

Note that a negative number is good here, because a lower-than-site-average Bounce Rate is great. If you want to avoid explaining this nuance to your senior decision makers, simply give them the indexed performance using column 6 (or replace column 5 with 6!).

Comparing key metrics and site average is simple yet astonishingly effective because you move beyond the number and metric definitions. You focus on actions for good and bad outcomes.

Joining PALM (People Against Lonely Metrics)

You need someone. I need someone. Everyone needs someone. And so do our metrics.

When we report an important metric by itself, I call this a *lonely* metric. You should pair your important metric with a partner. You'll understand the performance of one and get actionable context from the other.

You might have a table in your dashboard that shows the top 10 referring websites as ranked by Visits. But Visits by itself is not insightful. Add a *best friend* metric next to Visits, such as Percentage of New Visitors, and you hone in on sites that do a swell job of bringing you new visitors (a key goal). They may or may not be the top sites by Visits, and now you know. You can use that information to take better action.

Figure 11.7 shows the best friend technique applied to judge the overall performance of traffic from referring sites.

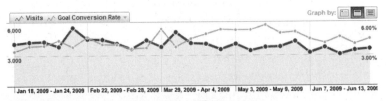

Referring sites sent 102,195 visits via 3,702 sources

Figure 11.7 Applying PALM: using conversions to give context to Visits

If you simply looked at the thicker line, Visits, you might start to freak out that the number of visits from websites that link to you is falling! But with the context of the *best friend* line, the thinner line, you'll notice that Conversion Rates have actually jumped during that time period. Rather than getting fired for not doing your job, you deserve a bonus for pruning sites that were not performing optimally and focusing on those that sent quality traffic. Congratulations!

Tip: As much as possible, try to pick an Outcome metric as the best friend metric—choose something that helps measure the success of your site.

Leveraging Industry Benchmarks and Competitive Data

Industry benchmarks and competitive data are outstanding methods for giving context to your performance. If your cart Abandonment Rate metric is 82 percent or your Time on Site metric is 42 minutes, you need to know whether those numbers are great or whether you need to rally the troops for emergency fixes. Use external context by leveraging industry benchmarks and competitive data.

You can now find industry benchmarks for various web metrics in your web analytics tool. Take a look at Google Analytics, in Figure 11.8, where benchmarking is illustrated in the middle graphs. You can see you are performing better than other sites in your industry, with more Traffic (+29.69 percent) and lower Bounce Rates (−10.21 percent).

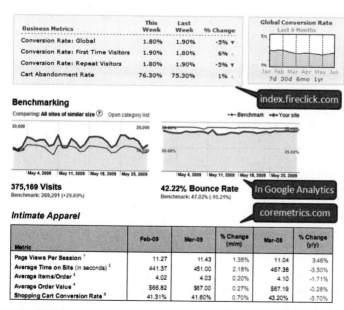

Figure 11.8 Industry benchmarks from Google Analytics, Fireclick, and Coremetrics

The top part of the figure shows the benchmarks available at index.fireclick.com. You can get benchmarks for seven metrics for six different industry verticals. The bottom of the figure shows the performance month over month and for the same month last year for Intimate Apparel websites, from Coremetrics. All of these benchmarks help you better understand your performance, and they are all available for free.

Consider another case. Say I work at Dell, and I realize that traffic to my site has decreased, according to my Omniture data. But I am not worried because of the recession—spending on all things tech is down. I can go get another smoothie.

If I were not lazy, I would spend five minutes getting context for my performance by indexing it against my main competitors. Figure 11.9 shows my performance, dell.com, against my main competitor, hp.com. I have also heard the name Acer resurrected, so let me see how Acer is doing.

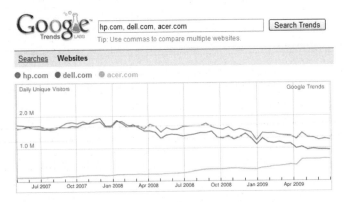

Figure 11.9 Indexing performance by leveraging competitive data

The bottom line is that I should not be so smug. My website kept up with hp.com in the fight for Visitors, but since the middle of 2008, I consistently lost Visitors with each passing month. And that forgotten Acer company has been eating our lunches: Acer's performance rose! If this trend continues, Acer may match Dell's performance in a few months.

It would be impossible to surmise these critical insights just from my website's Omniture data.

Tapping into *Tribal Knowledge*

If there is a killer approach to getting context for your web analytics data, it is through tribal knowledge. This is information about initiatives, marketing programs, website updates, changes, management reorganization, server outages, PPC, direct marketing, and so on—things that impact your website.

Analysts often have no idea what people in other parts of the company are doing on the website or what new acquisition strategies are being tried. So, analysts look at numbers, metrics, and trends, and like tarot card readers, they guess what the numbers mean!

A website has a lot of moving parts, and a lot of people are involved in the holy exercise of creating something of value for customers. The best way to get context for your numbers is to seek out all the players and stay plugged into company processes. You want to know when your marketers send out an email blast, when IT runs a multivariate test, when support has to deal with a broken shopping cart, or when the design team adopts a new media mix model.

Step away from your desk and talk to people, take marketers out for dinner, and create information loops that are closed and include you. Often all it takes to put a trend in context is to know everything that your company is doing. Go get plugged in!

Comparing KPI Trends Over Time

The first recommendation in the previous section compared the performance of two different time periods. Comparing trends over time is an excellent path to finding quick insights and focus areas. Now we'll dive deeper and identify how you can avoid common traps when you apply the technique.

Figure 11.10 shows a typical graph that compares month-to-month or year-over-year performance.

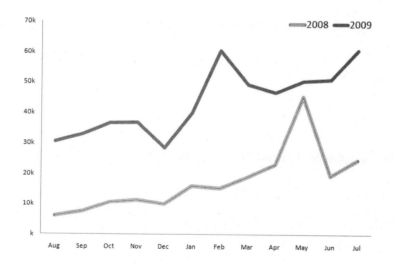

Figure 11.10 Comparing two years of performance

After we exhaust our initial *a-ha* moments, we face the challenge of how to make a more accurate comparison between time frames. There are two important factors to consider:

- Ever-evolving strategies introduce new variables into a KPI's trend (such as product launches or new marketing campaigns).

- The massive change of the Web itself can make data irrelevant (if the population for whom your product is relevant grew by 500 percent in the last year, is last year's data still worth comparison?).

Both these challenges result in a graph, like Figure 11.10, that an analysis ninja should never present to peers or management. You need to dig deeper with your questions about trends and performance.

Your product sales might peak each Thanksgiving (in the United States). But if you earned $15 million in revenue this Thanksgiving and $10 million last Thanksgiving, is that number good? More important, is it good enough?

To answer these questions, you need to collect *tribal knowledge*, seek people who execute your marketing campaigns and your website changes, and ask them about decisions that might have contributed to the trends in the data.

Questions you'll ask will include the following: What is different about this year and last (or this month and last)? Have you doubled the team? Do you have free shipping this year? How much did you spend on AdWords or affiliates in each year? Did you kick off any optimization efforts? How much downtime did the site have over the past 18 months? And other such questions.

Presenting Tribal Knowledge

Your goal when you present data is to provoke an understanding about performance that translates into action. Therefore, you need to annotate your data with the wisdom that explains the trends, as in Figure 11.11.

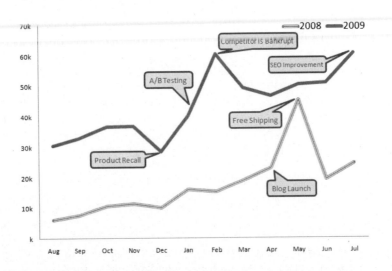

Figure 11.11 Tribal knowledge and analysis incorporated into trend comparison

When you present this graph, the direction of meetings will change from speculation to realization. The graph will shift to the background as the discussion is dominated by insights and action.

Analysis ninjas tend to think our job is to simply report the numbers. Hence, we sit in our organizational silo and rarely interface with other parts of the organization. But if you don't step out and meet with key folks, you'll fail to transform your organization.

Segmenting to the Rescue!

In aggregate, trends can hide insights and hence dirty the data. If you want to compare clean trends, then your best option is to compare related segments within your data. For example, rather than looking at data in aggregate, you could just look at organic search traffic trends or only the performance of email campaigns.

The benefit of comparing segmented trends is that instead of figuring out which of 1,800 variables is causing an impact, you can identify and then investigate just a few relevant variables. This will dramatically speed up your understanding of cause and effect. For example, Figure 11.12 shows the trend comparisons for the same time period as Figure 11.11, but only for affiliate marketing efforts.

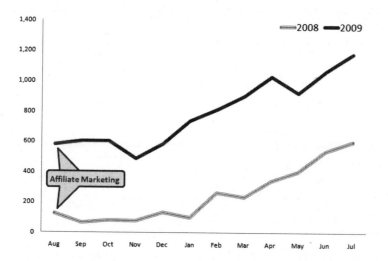

Figure 11.12 Comparing two years of performance for affiliate marketing

The segmented data is very focused. You can now dig much deeper into the trends and understand year-over-year performance. You can identify the efforts your company undertook and their impact on Revenue, Time on Site, and so forth.

The trends also raise questions, not just about affiliate marketing efforts but also for the entire business. Why doesn't the February peak in Figure 11.11 appear in Figure 11.12? In April, affiliate performance surged even as the site as a whole declined. Why? You want your segments to raise exactly these kinds of questions.

Traffic trends can be difficult to compare because so many variables can influence the outcome, even after you segment data and add tribal knowledge. But one of my absolute favorite trends to analyze is Direct Traffic, as shown in Figure 11.13. Direct Traffic is less influenced by other factors, and hence it serves as a great barometer for the overall health of the site. The trend for Direct Traffic alone can tell you where you do *not* have to spend money to get people to your website.

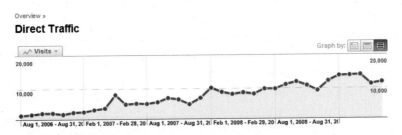

Figure 11.13 Focus on the long-term trend for the "clean" Direct Traffic

By looking at Direct Traffic, you can determine whether you are improving at getting free traffic. You can see whether people remember your site and just show up. You can see whether you have enough engaging content to convince people to return again and again each month. And you can see whether you are acquiring new customers or retaining the ones you converted in the past.

To me that is a clean segment or trend. For your websites, there will be others. Dig, poke, identify.

Beyond the Top 10: What's Changed

When you crack open any web analytics tool, the entire interface will be full of reports that show you top 10 this and top 10 that, from keywords to B2B downloads. The underappreciated problem with the top 10, however, is that it rarely changes for most websites. The only exception may be content-only news websites.

Figure 11.14 shows two months of a Top Search Keywords report. The top keywords look pretty much the same for both months. Yes, subtle shifts occur, but it is the same set of keywords, and most of the words drove the same amount of traffic.

What would you do with this data? You could focus on the minor changes, such as understanding why the keyword *survey questions* dropped from 640 visits to 548 visits, but that would get you minor gains.

But if you add together the traffic from all keywords (the top 10 and all others), notice that in the first month search keywords drove 23,635 visits and in the second month that number was 18,660. That's a drop of almost five thousand! If you were focused on the top 10, then you were focused on the wrong data—on data that accounted for a drop of 145 visits. That's hardly consequential.

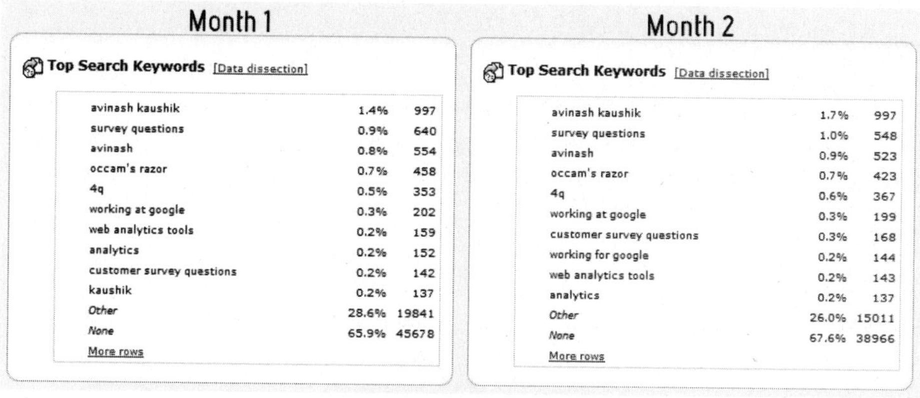

Month 1

Top Search Keywords [Data dissection]

avinash kaushik	1.4%	997
survey questions	0.9%	640
avinash	0.8%	554
occam's razor	0.7%	458
4q	0.5%	353
working at google	0.3%	202
web analytics tools	0.2%	159
analytics	0.2%	152
customer survey questions	0.2%	142
kaushik	0.2%	137
Other	28.6%	19841
None	65.9%	45678
More rows		

Month 2

Top Search Keywords [Data dissection]

avinash kaushik	1.7%	997
survey questions	1.0%	548
avinash	0.9%	523
occam's razor	0.7%	423
4q	0.6%	367
working at google	0.3%	199
customer survey questions	0.3%	168
working for google	0.2%	144
web analytics tools	0.2%	143
analytics	0.2%	137
Other	26.0%	15011
None	67.6%	38966
More rows		

Figure 11.14 Top Search Keywords report for two consecutive months

Most websites are stable businesses with seasonal ebbs and flows. Slight shifts may occur on the surface, but the bigger shifts happen below the surface. These changes can be hard to find.

One challenge is that you can't actually view 19,673 rows of data, which is how 23,635 search keywords visits would appear. Also, because the top 10 reports don't shift much, our marketers and HiPPOs put these reports and dashboards on autodelete. Their rationale is this: *if the data does not shift much, why should I look at it?* It's a fair question.

For this reason I am a huge fan of focusing on the What's Changed report. ClickTracks was the first tool to offer this report, and it is easy to use. You choose any two time periods and ClickTracks will churn through all your website data, apply intelligent mathematical algorithms, and present a report that shows the most significant changes along all your data dimensions. Figure 11.15 shows the What's Changed report for the two months shown in Figure 11.14.

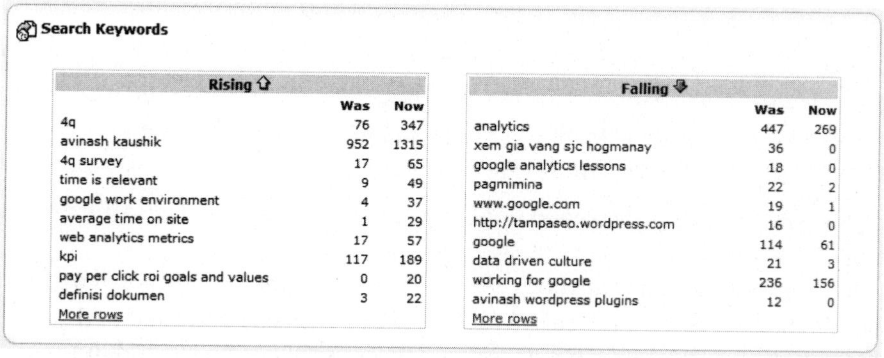

Search Keywords

Rising ⇧	Was	Now
4q	76	347
avinash kaushik	952	1315
4q survey	17	65
time is relevant	9	49
google work environment	4	37
average time on site	1	29
web analytics metrics	17	57
kpi	117	189
pay per click roi goals and values	0	20
definisi dokumen	3	22
More rows		

Falling ⇩	Was	Now
analytics	447	269
xem gia vang sjc hogmanay	36	0
google analytics lessons	18	0
pagmimina	22	2
www.google.com	19	1
http://tampaseo.wordpress.com	16	0
google	114	61
data driven culture	21	3
working for google	236	156
avinash wordpress plugins	12	0
More rows		

Figure 11.15 What's Changed Search Keywords report—ClickTracks

With this report, you instantly know which keywords need your attention because they send a lot more traffic in the current time period, and on the right you can review keywords that are dropping like a block of cement.

Rather than sorting through 19,673 rows of data, you can focus on just the rows of data that are significant. In Figure 11.15, some of my top brand terms are in the Rising category, which validates all my hard work with search engine optimization (SEO). On the other hand, the Falling category contains some keywords that had performed well for quite some time; now I need to figure out why they are dropping and fix the leaks.

You can use the "What's Changed" report to find content or products that are becoming more or less popular, and you can figure out what problems are rising fastest on your tech support website or what social media campaigns are truly fueling the growth of your Facebook-clone website.

Replacing the standard top 10 reports or dashboard items with a "what's changed" table will ensure that your marketers and HiPPOs never again delete your emails or sleep during your presentations, because your data will constantly change. And it will be more actionable.

Other analytics tools are incorporating features so you can create a What's Changed report. In XiTi, you can see Most Significant Rises and Most Significant Falls reports. These use straight percentages to show the data. Although the percentages are not the same as the algorithmic intelligence of ClickTracks, you get better information than from a top 10 report.

In Google Analytics, you can use a Firefox plug-in called Enhanced Google Analytics, created by Juice Analytics (available at http://zqi.me/juicega). In the keywords report, you click the "Who sent me unusual traffic?" button to get two additional reports: keywords with 50 percent higher traffic over the past seven days and keywords with 50 percent lower traffic over the past seven days. In the Referring Sites report, you click the same button to get three additional reports: referring sites with 50 percent higher traffic over the past three days, referring sites with 50 percent lower traffic over the past three days, and new referring sites appearing in the past three days. You can see an example report in Figure 11.16.

The first two reports use a slight variation of the straight percentage method. The third report, at the bottom of Figure 11.16, is one of my favorites because it shows me valuable data that I otherwise could not find. Knowing which sites are new at sending me traffic is fantastic. I can investigate why they suddenly started sending traffic. If they are relevant to my business, perhaps I want to strike an affiliate deal with them or even investigate advertising possibilities.

Referring sites sent 15,694 visits via 1,400 sources

Referring Sites With 50% Higher Traffic Over the Last 3 Days:

	Source	Visits	Pages/Visit	Avg. Time on Site	% New Visits	Bounce Rate
1.	websiteoptimizer.blogspot.com	128	1.68	00:02:38	76.56%	67.19%
2.	blog.iperceptions.com	80	1.26	00:00:53	67.50%	86.25%
3.	markezine.jp	63	1.30	00:00:44	85.71%	87.30%
4.	wel					
5.	ima					

Referring Sites With 50% Lower Traffic Over the Last 3 Days:

	Source	Visits	Pages/Visit	Avg. Time on Site	% New Visits	Bounce Rate
1.	stumbleupon.com	483	1.17	00:00:10	99.59%	83.64%
2.	adsense.blogspot.com	252	1.98	00:02:25	84.52%	54.76%
3.	netv					
4.	wel					
5.	chin					

New Referring Sites Appearing in Last 3 Days:

	Source	Visits	Pages/Visit	Avg. Time on Site	% New Visits	Bounce Rate
1.	smashingmagazine.com	15	1.13	00:00:22	80.00%	86.67%
2.	kartoo.com	9	1.00	00:00:00	0.00%	100.00%
3.	marketingexperiments.com	9	1.78	00:02:27	77.78%	55.56%
4.	atlantaanalytics.com	6	2.33	00:02:59	66.67%	33.33%

Figure 11.16 What's Changed Referring Sites report—Google Analytics

True Value: Measuring Latent Conversions and Visitor Behavior

We all have an unhealthy obsession with *acquiring stuff* on the Web. You can see it as we measure our campaigns: we see how many visits we generated and then how many converted. You can also see the same obsession at non-ecommerce websites where the measure of success is just getting people to open accounts.

Why obsess about the *quickie* Visitor who is opening an account or placing the first order? Why not measure success, true and long-term success, based *on latent visitor behavior*, or behavior after that first purchase or membership sign-up?

When we measure success only when we run a campaign or only for the first action by a visitor, we get only a partial understanding of the impact to our site. Great analysis ninjas should also focus on visitor behavior after that first touch point or conversion.

Latent Visitor Behavior

Let me explain latent visitor behavior through a non-ecommerce example. Let's assume that Facebook is on a quest for world domination. To achieve that goal, it runs a multi-million-dollar worldwide campaign. The analysis team measures success as the number of new accounts opened; the implication being, more memberships = a bigger number = higher company valuation = more venture capital money!

From this campaign, it gets another 500,000 memberships. Was Facebook successful? I say no. Other than PR value, memberships are the least important measure of success. That's because member *behavior* after they join is what adds value to the site.

If Facebook had 250 million members and 249 million never logged in after opening an account, that member number is worthless. But if 200 million log in every day, add more friends, and update their status, then that behavior is valuable.

So, here's a radical idea: why not wait 30 days after the campaign has concluded and measure the behavior of visitors? Metrics like Visitor Loyalty and Visitor Recency measure precisely that (more on these metrics in Chapter 5). Figure 11.17 illustrates the kind of analysis you'll do. You analyze the gap (days) between visits by the Visitors acquired through the campaign 30 days after the campaign expires (or after the Visitor signs up).

Figure 11.17 Post-campaign segmented Visitor Recency analysis

Now you are all set to compare your marketing spending using a higher-order measure of success. Let's take two campaigns and look at their results:

Campaign 1 100,000 sign-ups. Top-bracket Recency: 10 percent (that is, a month after the campaign, 10,000 of these Visitors visited in the last 23 hours on the 31st day.)

Campaign 2 50,000 sign-ups. Top-bracket Recency: 50 percent (that is, a month after the campaign, 25,000 of these Visitors visited in the last 23 hours on the 31st day.)

Which campaign is more valuable? If you used the quickie measurement method and measured only sign-ups, then it would be campaign 1. But with the recommended post-campaign method, where you measure Visitor behavior with Recency, it's Campaign 2. Using *latent visitor behavior*, you focus on details that matter to your business, which is a recipe for long-term success.

You can truly step up the game by combining Recency with Loyalty. You'll know exactly how many times visitors from campaigns 1 and 2 visited your website, which is another excellent measure of post-campaign success.

Let's look at another example. Lots of campaigns in the real world are simply *branding* campaigns using display ads. Measuring success for these ads comprises of either nothing or just the number of Visits to the site. But even if you just want your campaigns to evoke good feelings from visitors, you have something more to measure. Perhaps they visited your site and did not bounce; so, you measure Bounce Rate.

But this chapter is about going even further. If your branding campaign was magnificent, then those visitors will return to your site many times. So, they'll have a high Visitor Loyalty score.

You run two branding display campaigns, campaign 1 on the *New York Times* website and campaign 2 on the Fox News website. Figure 11.18 shows the results of the *latent visitor behavior* as measured by the Visitor Loyalty metric.

Visitor Loyalty — Glorious Campaign # 1

Most people visited: 1 times

Number of Visits	
1 times	47.92%
2 times	13.47%
3 times	7.71%
4 times	4.83%
5 times	3.61%
6 times	2.65%

Visitor Loyalty — Glorious Campaign # 2

Most people visited: 1 times

Number of Visits	
1 times	78.76%
2 times	7.48%
3 times	3.21%
4 times	1.77%
5 times	1.31%
6 times	0.88%

Figure 11.18 Post-campaign analysis using Visitor Loyalty

You can easily see that the *New York Times* branding campaign drove more valuable visitors because only 47 percent visited the website once and never again, while 78 percent of visitors who came from ads on Fox News never returned. You now know where to spend your precious campaign dollars for maximum impact.

Latent Conversions

If you have an ecommerce website, measuring *latent conversions* is even easier. You measure initial success based on conversion rates, but then you wait 90 days (or a relevant time period) and analyze which campaigns drove more repeat purchases. You would value those campaigns higher even if initial conversions were slightly lower.

Despite its benefits, the latent conversion technique is rarely seen in practice. The main reasons are as follows:

- We are too focused on quick success in corporate America.

- Our decision makers are usually impatient; they want data in real time even if it means measuring the wrong thing.

- Doing this type of delayed analysis is harder in many web analytics tools.

In closing, any reporting squirrel can report instant conversions. Only a true analysis ninja will apply the latent conversions and visitor behavior analysis to help the business make thoughtful and cost-saving decisions.

Four Inactionable KPI Measurement Techniques

It is always hard to question principles that the general populace holds to be holy. Yet analytics is hugely underleveraged today because we cram our dashboards and reports with metrics that actively work against us!

These measurement techniques are averages, percentages, ratios, and compound metrics. Each metric is common to our reports, yet their *normal usage* often hides insights rather than helping us identify actions. That word *normal* is very important. Each of these techniques is not bad per se, but the way we use them is suboptimal.

In this section, I'll cover each technique, explain why they don't work, and identify specific solutions. By the end of this section, you'll exponentially improve your ability to find actionable insights from your web analytics data.

Averages

You can't take two web analytics steps without falling into an average—Average Time on Site, Average Conversion Rate, average this, and average that. The attraction of averages is our desire to just get one *representative* number for overall performance.

Yet no visitor to your site is an *average visitor*, and no behavior is *average behavior* when you look at data in aggregate. When we study aggregated data and compute averages, we are saying that average people and average behavior exist. If there is no average visitor or average behavior, how can we expect to find insights?

Consider this: Average Time on Site is 54 seconds. What does that number tell you? Nothing. Averages have an astonishing capacity to give you *average* data. They have a great capacity to lie, and they hinder decision making. But, you can apply different techniques when you work with averages to make the data actionable.

Segmenting Average Data

Segmentation is an effective strategy for teasing out insights from averages. You identify your most important segments for your business and report those along with the overall averages, as in Figure 11.19.

Figure 11.19 Leveraging segmentation when using averages

You no longer rely on an amorphous 54 seconds. You know that nonsearch traffic spends 70 seconds on the site, the hyped social media visitors spend the least amount of time on site, and search engines are not that far behind.

Breaking down the 54-second average gives context to your decision makers; with segmented data about averages, they can ask relevant questions and determine where to place their business focus.

Using Distributions

If overall averages stink, then distributions rock. Distributions are a wonderful way to dissect what makes up the average and look at the numbers in a much more manageable way, as in Figure 11.20.

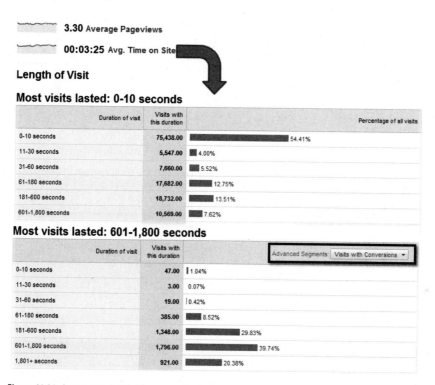

Figure 11.20 Leveraging distributions as an alternative to averages

How cool is this? You know that 54.41 percent of visitors stayed less than 10 seconds (goodness!), and you also see how many visitors actually got into the game and stayed longer than 60 seconds. You can segment those visitors and identify the sources where they came from, the content they consumed, and promotions that appealed to them.

Why stop there? Why not understand the distribution of how long it takes to perform key tasks on your site. The report at the bottom of Figure 11.20 shows the visit distribution for those visitors who convert. It takes more than 10 minutes for a majority of people to convert on your site! In fact, it takes more than half an hour for 20 percent of the traffic.

A previously useless number, Average Time on Site of 3 minutes and 25 seconds, gives you actionable insights when you apply distribution.

Percentages

Nothing is more ubiquitous in our world of web analytics than percentages. But percentages rarely answer the "So what?" or "Now what?" questions on their own because percentages gloss over relevant detail while overselling or underselling the opportunity. As always, you need context when you analyze percentages.

Here's an example:

Conversion Rate from Microsoft AdCenter campaigns: 15 percent

Conversion Rate from Yahoo! Search campaigns: 3 percent

Which campaigns should you invest in? The answer might seem obvious: Microsoft. Now what if your data actually looks like this?

Microsoft: Conversion Rate: 15 percent. Visits: 201.

Yahoo!: Conversion Rate: 3 percent. Visits: 37,925.

Which represents a better opportunity? Yahoo! There is simply not enough inventory with Microsoft. That conversion rate could well be 30 percent, and you'll still focus on the Yahoo! opportunity (while mopping up everything you can get from Microsoft of course).

Here's another example. Figure 11.21 shows three attempts at understanding what actions to take using a standard web analytics report.

When you see the first (top) report, the natural tendency is to say, "Let me find the worst bouncing keywords and fix 'em." So, you click the label for that column, and now it is sorted from high to low. The Bounce Rates are all 100 percent. However, there is one minor problem: each keyword has just one Visit. These are not keywords you want to focus on because you get very low business impact from your actions.

So, you click the column title again to sort from low to high, expecting to find keywords with low Bounce Rates. That report is at the bottom of Figure 11.21. See the problem? Each keyword again has just one Visit.

You really want to identify statistically significant data, where Bounce Rates are meaningfully up or meaningfully down so that you can take action confidently. That is the problem with percentages; they hide insights because we don't include key relevant information or use additional techniques when we report them.

The techniques you'll apply for reporting percentages will be similar to those we used for averages.

Keyword	Visits ↓	Pages/Visit	Avg. Time on Site	% New Visits	Bounce Rate
1. trabajo	59,941	2.32	00:02:00	90.08%	62.29%
2. trabajos	5,928	2.14	00:01:51	90.91%	64.64%
3. idealistas	2,167	5.90	00:06:02	40.66%	30.04%

Keyword	Visits	Pages/Visit	Avg. Time on Site	% New Visits	Bounce Rate ↓
1. "agustin cazaban"	1	1.00	00:00:00	100.00%	100.00%
2. "alejandra parada"	1	1.00	00:00:00	0.00%	100.00%
3. "amanda rudd" ut	1	1.00	00:00:00	100.00%	100.00%
4. "ana m. gonzalez aparicio"	1	1.00	00:00:00	100.00%	100.00%

Keyword	Visits	Pages/Visit	Avg. Time on Site	% New Visits	Bounce Rate ↑
1. " ong de argentina"	1	3.00	00:01:50	100.00%	0.00%
2. "actua ya"	1	2.00	00:13:48	100.00%	0.00%
3. "agora" mendoza	1	3.00	00:00:26	100.00%	0.00%
4. "albergue infantil" bogota	1	4.00	00:00:31	100.00%	0.00%
5. "asociacion de invidentes"	1	2.00	00:00:11	100.00%	0.00%
6. "asociación de invidentes"	1	4.00	00:01:02	100.00%	0.00%
7. "bienestar comun"	1	3.00	00:02:45	100.00%	0.00%
8. "capacity building" jobs	1	4.00	00:00:41	0.00%	0.00%
9. "caro molina" el salvador	1	3.00	00:00:27	0.00%	0.00%
10. "casa cuna" "santa fe"	1	6.00	00:01:22	100.00%	0.00%

Figure 11.21 The challenge of sorting with percentages

Show Relevant Raw Numbers

You already saw me use this technique earlier in the example for Yahoo! and Microsoft. I showed you the raw numbers of visits in relation to Conversion Rate, and those raw numbers helped you decide which search engine to spend money on.

Whether you show the percentage of visits, the percentage of conversions, or the percentage of bounce, including the most relevant raw number will help focus the discussion with your senior management.

Segment the Data

By now you should know you can rely on segmentation to tease out insights. We'll segment again with percentages.

Consider the example in Figure 11.22. In the graph on the left, the percentage trend for Conversion Rate shows that your company is going down the tubes, though it seems to have stabilized recently.

On the right is a segmented view of that same trend. Although the overall Conversion Rate looks terrible, the Conversion Rate metric for Direct Traffic (the top line) has held up quite well at 9.15 percent. In fact, it increased while everything else decreased. The second valuable segment, New Visitors, proves less useful, with a Conversion Rate very close to the overall rate. But now you know where to concentrate your energy.

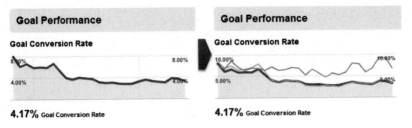

Figure 11.22 Applying segmentation strategy to the percentages technique

User Statistical Significance

The sorting example of Bounce Rate in Figure 11.21 highlighted the difficulty of using percentages to discern what is attention worthy and what is noise.

A/B and multivariate tools identify when treatments have reached a level of significance where we can make decisions. For example, a simple computation might show that version A has x participants of which y percent converted and version B has m participants of which n percent converted. You can contrast this data and identify when the activity has reached a level of statistical significance so that you can use the data to make decisions.

This technique is not available in our web analytics tools today, but you can extract the data manually into Excel and compute statistical significance. Once you have perfected the formulas, many tools allow automated updates of your spreadsheets; hence, it will require negligible effort going forward.

I am hopeful that soon we will have a sorting option called Sort by Statistical Significance to identify only the actionable dimensions of data.

Ratios

A ratio represents the relative magnitude of two quantities. Like percentages, we turn to ratios in our desire to get a *representative* number.

One common ratio is Page Views per Visit, but ratios are everywhere. You can get the ratio of new to returning visitors or the number of replies submitted on a forum compared to articles read.

The challenge with ratios is that the fundamentals can change magnificently. If you report only automated ratios, then you would be none the wiser about such changes. For example, $12 \div 10 = 1.2$ as does $1,200 \div 1,000$. Yet, individually these numbers represent dramatic changes.

You have two approaches to more effectively report ratios, both of which demand that you understand the context of your ratio.

Use Custom Reports to Put the Ratio in Context

Often your standard web analytics reports show only the ratio for a metric. You must leverage the custom reporting feature (learn more in Chapter 3) to add the underlying metrics.

Your analytics report shows the following trend for your critical metric ratio:

August: 4.9

September: 5.0

October: 4.9

November: 5.1

The trend looks steady, so you may not worry about it. But Figure 11.23 shows you should worry, a lot!

	# 1	#2	Ratio
Aug	6,196	30,467	4.9
Sep	8,649	42,905	5.0
Oct	7,500	36,689	4.9
Nov	13,203	66,861	5.1

Figure 11.23 Illustrating the underlying fundamentals of ratios

From August to November the two metrics used to compute the ratios have changed dramatically. Yet the ratio has essentially stayed flat. By creating a custom report and showing the raw numbers, you ensure that the right triggers exist to take action.

Resist Setting "Golden" Rules

We often have our own *golden rules* for ratios. We establish set goals or numbers without any context, such as "We want a ratio of 3.2 for customers to prospects" or "The average page views per visit should be 1.78."

These rules are ineffective because they are too easy to game, for all the reasons I have discussed. When you set goals, they should be motivated by an underlying value, usually an outcome or preferred visitor behavior.

For example, rather than creating a golden rule for Ratio of Visits to Signups, stress Loyalty (the number of times people use the website after the first sign-up). You can measure campaign success by measuring Visits to Signups but hand out a bonus for campaigns that deliver visitors with a high Loyalty number.

Compound or Calculated Metrics

A compound metric is a metric whose subcomponents are other metrics. They were used in the past for esoteric activities the government did not want us to understand, but today consultants and other *industry leaders* are increasingly recommending compound metrics.

The problem is that compound metrics actively work against explaining the basic phenomenon they attempt to measure, and hence, they deliver inactionable insights. Let's look at some examples.

A survey vendor reports a Likelihood to Visit Again metric, which is a number on a scale of 1 to 100. The vendor computes the metric by blending answers from five questions extracted from a 35-question survey. That's a compound metric.

This is another example:

Website Awesomeness = $(RT*G) + (T/Q) + [(z^x)-(a/k)*100)]$

The idea is to take a different metrics from different tools and add, subtract, or multiply them all together to produce a number at the end that tells you how awesome your site is.

Compound metrics may look good on paper, but they present some corrosive problems:

- When you spit out a number, say 9 or 58 or 946, no one except you knows what it means, which causes an anti-actionability bias.

- Even if you, and everyone else, fully understand the intricacies that go into computing the metric, you know nothing by looking at the aggregate number. Say you are computing the Engagement Index metric. Each month the number stays at 58. Is that good or bad? On the other hand, would you know what to do if the number went from 58 to 9 or from 58 to 946? How long would it take to figure that out?

The environments where compound metrics thrive are ones where data is truly difficult to measure. We react to this difficulty by adding and multiplying lots of things. Sometimes compound metrics are excuses for not having the tough conversations that determine relevant goals and what's actually important to measure.

You have several techniques to keep compound metrics under control, from eliminating them altogether to evaluating them frequently to ensure continued business relevancy.

Don't Use Compound/Calculated Metrics

Try everything else before you take the road of compound metrics in your reports or dashboards. Apply the two stress tests in the previous bulleted list to the proposed metric from your consultant or analyst, and see whether the proposal can pass muster. Usually it won't, so move on.

In cases where the compound metric does pass muster, that is, everyone involved understands the data and the numbers make sense, certainly audition the metric for a few months and see whether it provides actionable insights.

Degrade to Critical Few Components

Say you wanted a metric for Website Awesomeness; you might take different metrics from different tools and add, subtract, and multiply them all together to produce a number that tells you how awesome your site is:

Website Awesomeness = (RT*G) + (T/Q) + [(z^x)-(a/k)*100)]

But grinding all those metrics and indices (RT, G, T, Q, and so on) into a mush is the problem; the metrics themselves are not the problem.

You need to go to your HiPPOs and management to learn about the business and its fundamental goals. After you've done this and you decompose individual components of your business, you'll realize that everlasting business success is determined by your critical few metrics, which might be just R, T, and G. Report just those metrics. And don't marry them together into a compound calculated metric. Report the metrics as individuals, easier to report and easier still to understand.

Revisit and Revalidate

If you must use compound metrics, please revisit them from time to time to see whether they still add value. Also check that they add value in all applicable scenarios in your formula.

Many compound metrics give weight to the individual metrics they use. For example, you may give more weight to people who come from search who stay for three pages than to people who come from affiliates and see nine pages. If you use weights, then you must ensure the weights are relevant. You must also revalidate the weights over time to ensure you are not compensating for seasonality or other business nuances.

Every two months, verify that the compound metric has helped you identify actions to improve business performance. Every quarter revalidate the assumptions that you use to create the metric.

There are two schools of thought about analytics. One is that math is easy and accessible with calculators and computers, so go add, subtract, multiply, and divide. This is the mental model of the reporting squirrel, who values data above all else.

The other perspective is that your entire existence is geared toward driving action. You must think, stress test, and be smart about the math you do. Computers and calculators are cheap, but they do not provide the insight required to drive action. This is the mental model of the analysis ninja, who values insights above all else.

Search: Achieving the Optimal Long-Tail Strategy

Search is an essential acquisition channel for most online businesses, and it is also the source of a good amount of our analysis.

My core mission in the next three sections is to explain how marketing has fundamentally changed on the Web and how we must adapt our methodologies to find actionable insights. I hope you'll learn not just the measurement tips but how to adapt to the ever-changing world of marketing and advertising.

Here is an astonishing fact that is hidden right in front of us: your reports with the top 10 rows of data represent a tiny fraction of the available information. Hence, any action you take based on that data will have little impact on your business. Nowhere is this phenomenon more visible than in your search keywords reports. A few keywords, the *head*, will typically drive thousands of visits, while thousands of keywords, the *tail*, will drive a few visits each, as shown in Figure 11.24.

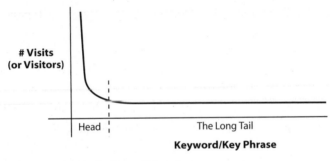

Figure 11.24 The head and long tail of search

Here's a concrete example, data from my blog *Occam's Razor* (www.kaushik.net/avinash):

86,861: Number of total Visits in the month

40,662: Number of Visits from search

26,137: Number of distinct keywords and key phrases

Forty thousand visits resulted from 26,000 key phrases! That is quite astonishing because unlike, say, Amazon.com, I don't sell thousands of items. I write a blog on a single topic, web analytics. Your business website may have thousands of web pages, but thus far my blog has only 200 posts. Yet people looking for content on that single topic searched for it in 26,000 ways!

Let's dive a bit deeper:

13: Number of search key phrases that brought 100 or more visits (the head)

26,124: Number of search key phrases that brought a small number of visits each (the tail)

Here's an alternative way to think about it:

- 13 *head* keywords brought 5,128 Visits to the site. Each keyword contributes a lot.

- 26,124 *tail* keywords brought 35,534 Visits to the site! Each keyword contributes a little, but in total they contribute a huge amount.

This amazing phenomenon, unfortunately, is poorly understood both by leaders who direct web strategy and by analysts who must understand and monetize the long tail.

The "top 10" report for my website will show big numbers; it will have those 13 important keywords. But if I focus only on those 13 words, then I focus only on a total of 5,000 visits. I ignore the big lever I could apply with the keywords that brought 35,000 visits.

That big lever represents the value of the long tail. It is immensely monetizable. If you understand the lever, then you can help your organization create a sustainable competitive advantage. Let's go over a few different ways you can help.

Compute Your Head and Tail

Go into the search report for your web analytics tool, and run a report for keywords and Visits for the last six months. Dump the data into Excel, and create a simple graph that shows keywords on the *x*-axis and Visits on the *y*-axis, as shown in Figure 11.25.

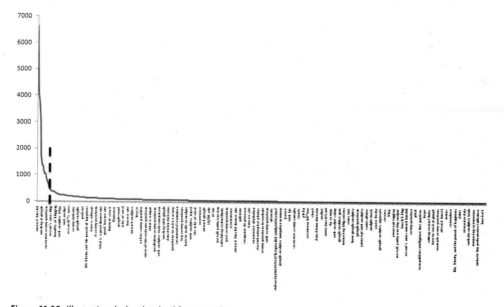

Figure 11.25 Illustrating the head and tail for your website

Whatever your business, your graph will look similar to the one in Figure 11.25 as long as you have done a decent job with search engine optimization. The dotted line shows where the head for my data is. For most businesses online, that will typically consist of 5 to 15 keywords.

Insights You Can Find

With this data, you can vividly illustrate for your decision makers what actually happens with search behavior on your website. The first time you present the report, you will shock them, which is a good thing. Few can imagine that their search world consists of thousands, or tens of thousands, of keywords.

- You can illustrate areas with greatest exposure for your company. For example, your head keywords are most vulnerable to a competitor who can bid high to get their paid search ads to show up higher than yours—thus taking a lot of your traffic.
- The number of words used by searchers will increase as you move from the left (head) to the right (deep tail). This is because people all tend to search differently; for example, what I type to find snack foods might be different from what you type. Hence, key phrases rather than keywords will appear with only a few visits.

Actions to Take

Your head and tail data present a bunch of opportunities. You'll need to analyze the data more deeply and explore the prospects the data reveals.

- Undertake a critical analysis of your head and tail key phrases. Are 10 key phrases enough? Is your head only five keywords? What are the surprises in your long tail? Are all your main key phrases stuffed there?
- Work with your decision makers to document exactly what your search strategy should be.
- Partner with your search agency (or internal search team) to evaluate whether you are giving the right *love and attention* to your head and tail and what changes you need to make with your current strategy.
- If your company has many websites, then the head and tail analysis illustrated in Figure 11.26 is valuable. For example, site 1 needs to revisit its strategy for organic search, because it is too top heavy. Site 3, however, has a very thin head, which could mean that the keyword strategy is missing a sense of focus (remember, you can control the head a lot more than the tail).

% Visits	Site 1	Site 2	Site 3	Site 4	Site 5	Site 6
Head	82%	68%	16%	32%	62%	80%
Tail	18%	32%	84%	68%	38%	20%

Figure 11.26 Benchmarking the head and tail for a portfolio of websites

Understanding Your Brand and Category Terms

A *brand key phrase* or keyword is a phrase or word connected to your *company existence*. Brand key phrases are your company name and names of your products and services. *Category key phrases* are not directly connected with your company; they are generic words and phrases connected to your industry.

Brand and category key phrases for my blog and for my field may include the following:

- Brand key phrases: *occams razor, avinash kaushik, avinash, occams razor blog, 90/10 rule, 90 10 rule, kaushik*
- Category key phrases: *competitive intelligence, path analysis, how to measure success, survey questions, analytics, data driven decision making*

Some brand terms are obvious, such as the name of the blog and my name. Others are not so obvious; for example, 90/10 is a brand term because I authored the 10/90 rule for magnificent web analytics success. Category terms, on the other hand, are specific to my industry but not specific to me or my blog.

Another example is that although Tide, Dawn, Bounty, Duracell, and Oral-B are brand terms for P&G, *clean clothes, sparkling dishes, kitchen supplies, portable power,* and *whiter teeth* are all category terms.

Why Should You Care?

The distribution of brand and category key phrases in Figure 11.27 is a typical distribution that you'll see in your head and tail analysis. As you would expect, the head is dominated by your brand terms. When people type your brand term into Bing or Yahoo!, the search engine will list your website first, and most of those clicks will come to you.

Therefore, the visits on your brand terms tend to be from people who already know you and people who are a lot later in their purchase life cycle. For example, this is someone who types in ThinkPad X301. That's a specific brand term and will be used by someone who knows what they want.

The tail, on the other hand, will be full of your category terms, also known as *generic* or *early-bird* terms. For these terms, you'll be one of many options listed on Bing or Yahoo!, and hence you'll get only a fraction of the clicks.

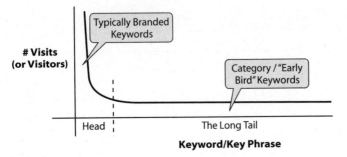

Figure 11.27 Clustering of brand and category key phrases

The people who tend to use category terms are early in the consideration life cycle. I call these people *impression virgins* because they have not yet decided what they want and are open to suggestions. Someone who types in the phrase *lightest long battery life laptop* may not see Lenovo in the number-one slot for that search because the phrase applies to many computers. But if Lenovo does show up, that person may visit their site, be impressed, and convert into a customer.

That's the power of understanding both the type of keyword and the type of customers who exist in the head and the tail.

The Optimal Search Marketing Strategy

Because most companies don't truly understand how search works, most companies execute a poor search strategy. When a marketer gets a pot of money for search engine marketing (SEM), they immediately collect the keywords and key phrases that are most closely associated with the company and bid on them. As a result, marketers expend their SEM budgets trying to show up first in a sponsored listing for their own brand terms.

The SEM Fix

Rather than wasting money on terms that are already linked with your company, you need to go back to Excel and examine your search key phrase analysis. You need to study your head and tail graphs.

First split out the percentage of Visits in your head key phrases that result from SEM (PPC) vs. organic (SEO). Now do the same for your tail key phrases. Next, identify the amount of budget you spend on head and tail key phrases. The result will look like Figure 11.28.

Insights You Can Find

Most of your SEM money is spent on head key phrases, which are just the top 10 or 15 keywords. Almost all of these phrases are brand key phrases, which typically do not bring new prospects to your site.

Aggregrated SEO - SEM (PPC) Analysis		Distribution of SEM Budget
Head key phrases	62%	
Contribution from SEM	44%	90%
Contribution from SEO	56%	
Tail key phrases	38%	
Contribution from SEM	21%	10%
Contribution from SEO	79%	

Figure 11.28 Search budget distribution analysis for the head and the tail

Although you spend such a small part of your budget on your long-tail keywords (your category key phrases), you actually get a huge bang for the buck.

Actions to Take

You need to optimize your SEO and SEM strategies. If you have an effective SEO strategy, then you should rank high when people search for brand key phrases. Check that you are not paying huge bids through your SEM programs to compensate for an ineffective SEO strategy. Fix the root cause; don't put on a Band-Aid.

Figure 11.28 shows that your SEM spending targets people who know you. This approach does not help you grow your business and find prospects. Based on the long-tail phenomenon, your holistic search strategy should look like Figure 11.29.

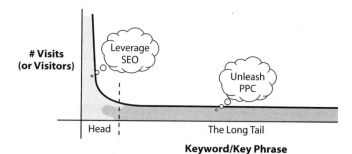

Figure 11.29 Optimal holistic search strategy

Focus your SEO efforts on your top brand terms. If you structure your site optimally, then search engines will index it correctly, and people will find you through search engines. SEO does not have the instant bang for the buck you get with PPC, but it pays off handsomely in the long term.

Focus your PPC efforts on monetizing the long tail. It is difficult to rank high in search results for category terms that apply to many companies and websites. Your main hope is to leverage sponsored results that capture the *impression virgins*.

Fortunately, these long-tail category terms have a lot less competition because they focus on unique niches. Less competition directly translates into lower cost, which allows you to easily spread out your budget over a lot of terms.

In Figure 11.29, the Unleash PPC directive leaks into part of the head area. This is deliberate. There will always be brand terms that are so new to you that you don't have good organic ranking (because your SEO efforts have not kicked in yet). Your only option in these cases is to use PPC. Another example is that you launched a topical television campaign that will last just a few weeks and then go away. Surely that will drive search traffic, but it is too short a time to use SEO to direct that traffic to your site. In this case, you'll also end up using SEO. Or in other cases, you have a huge competitor for the brand terms, and in that scenario you might use both SEO and PPC to compete (of course, only after having run a controlled experiment to validate that that is a good strategy; see the specific case study in Chapter 7).

Executing the Optimal Long-Tail Strategy

I'd like to offer one final bit of guidance. A few years back when I wanted to execute my long-tail strategy, I had some difficulty identifying all the key phrases that I should use in my PPC campaigns. Sure, I had a whole bunch from my web analytics tool. But given the nature of the long tail, there were more phrases that people typed into the search engines that never ended in a visit to my site (all those people went to my competition!).

This problem was recently solved by Google's Search-based Keyword Tool (SbKT; http://zqi.me/s-bkt). The two sources of data that the SbKT uses are the Google searches happening around the world and the results of the Google robot (*googlebot*) that runs around the web crawling and indexing all the websites. When you type in the URL of your website into the SbKT, Google will identify the long-tail keywords that are *relevant* for your website by matching up keywords that users type with the content on your web pages.

Figure 11.30 shows the SbKT report for an electronic retailer's website (the name has been anonymized to avinashelectronics.com for privacy reasons).

From millions of keywords typed by users, SbKT identified 169,235 keywords relevant for this business (but not in their paid search campaigns). A listing of the keywords appears on the left side of the table along with the number of searches in the last 30 days, the competition for each keyword, and the suggested bid (amount you would pay) for a top-three listing in the PPC results.

The next two pieces of data are critical. Ad/Search Share shows two numbers. The first is the current percent of impression share for paid search results. That would be 0 percent for the keyword *african safari* and 2 percent for the keyword *canon lens*. The second number shows the percent of impression share for organic search results: 22 percent for *african safari*. This is useful data because now you know exactly how much share you have of the search results (fix low numbers!) and which strategy, PPC or SEO, needs tweaking.

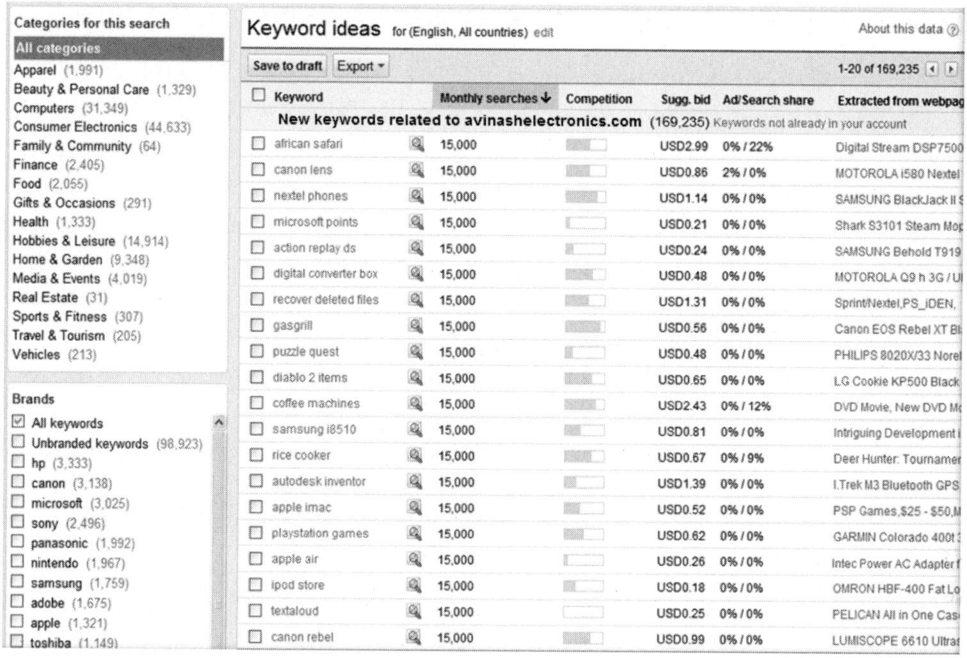

Figure 11.30 Google's Search-based Keyword Tool's report

Finally, the last column on the right shows the most relevant web page on the site for that keyword! This is fantastic because irrelevant landing pages are the bane of a marketer's existence (and the reason for high bounce rates). Now using SbKT you have identified the specific webpage on your site that might be relevant to each keyword.

So, now you know what keywords to consider, which ones to target using PPC or SEO, how much they would cost if you used PPC, and which page on your site to use as a landing page!

You can also do additional analysis in SbKT, such as identify keywords below a certain cost or keywords in specific categories or keywords for specific brands. For a more detailed tutorial on how to use SbKT, please visit http://zqi.me/sbktak.

Understanding how your head and long tail stack up can be a powerful source of insights. If you adapt your SEO and SEM strategy to effectively leverage your strengths (your brand), you can use limited marketing funds to attract new customers to your franchise at an optimal price point.

Remember that analytics is about more than numbers. It may not be in your job description to understand the nuances of the Web, how marketing channels work, or how customers use them. But if you spend time understanding what happens behind the numbers, you can find great insights in your data. Now, go apply this investigative understanding to all the marketing channels you use on the Web.

Search: Measuring the Value of Upper Funnel Keywords

We think we live in a culture of instant gratification. Now! Now!! Now!!!

The reality with customers, though, is more like this: "Let me think about it and ask my wife and check four other places and do all my research over the next few days and then you can have my order."

Yet many of our measurement strategies reflect this Now! culture. Therefore, in Chapter 3, I covered how using Visitors in the denominator was a better measure for Conversion Rate than using Visits. And in Chapter 5, I covered the importance of measuring Days and Visits to Purchase to identify how long it takes someone to purchase. Both of those measures move away from a *one-night stand* mentality to the correct *courtship* model.

In the previous section, I discussed how long-tail keywords introduce *impression virgins* to your website and value proposition. If you apply the multiple visit (not the Now!) behavior to those visitors, you understand the pervasiveness of the phenomenon depicted in Figure 11.31.

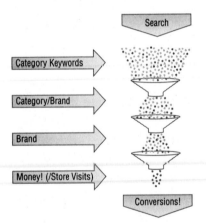

Figure 11.31 The search conversion funnel

Some long-tail keywords will bring Visitors who will convert on your site during the first visit. But the keywords will more likely bring the *impression virgins* to your website when you target the right category keywords. They might visit your site a second time under a brand or category keyword search. Then they'll come back a third time using your brand term. Finally, they'll convert on your website.

These keywords introduce people to your business, but they are not the ones who convert; that happens later in the life cycle, under a different keyword. That means if you run your standard Omniture Site Catalyst keyword conversion reports, you'll see that all *upper funnel* keywords have a Conversion Rate of zero. And since you used PPC to get the Visitors, those keywords actually cost you real money, and the report will show negative ROI. Yet, if these keywords had not brought people to your website in the first place, you might not have gotten the conversion at all!

Here's an example. I wanted to add some American football games to my Android phone. I searched for *mobile football games* on Google. I saw a paid search result for EA Sports (www.eamobile.com). I visited the site and then went off to do more research. A few days later I typed *mobile madden 09* into Google, because it was the game I liked from my first visit. I went to the EA site and purchased the game.

Let's make two small assumptions: PPC cost is approximate, and Mobile Madden costs $13. Here's the Site Catalyst report:

Mobile Football Games: PPC Cost: $2. Visit: 1. Conversion: 0. ROI: -$2.

Mobile Madden 09: PPC Cost: $3. Visit: 1. Conversion: 1. ROI: +10.

Clearly, I would never have visited the EA site if it had not shown up for the upper funnel keyword, yet you would have axed it from your campaign due to "negative" ROI. So, how do you measure the value of these long-tail keywords that are much higher in the funnel (lovingly called the *upper funnel keywords*)?

Here's my simple but extremely effective recommendation:

1. Understand each stage of the customer purchase life cycle. In my simple example, I had two simple stages: curiosity and purchase.

2. Map your keyword portfolio to each of those life cycle stages (curiosity, awareness, interest, consideration, and purchase).

3. Rather than pushing "Every keyword has to convert!" identify specific measures of success for the cluster of keywords in each of the life cycle stages.

Use these guiding principles:

• Early-stage upper funnel keywords are significantly cheaper (curiosity and awareness); hold them to a lower standard.

• Later-stage life-cycle keywords (consideration and purchases) can be expensive. Hold them to a much higher standard.

At the end of this process, your measurement framework will look similar to the one represented in Figure 11.32.

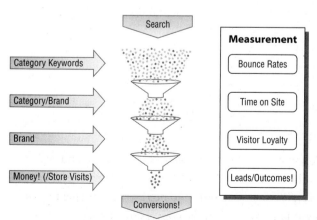

Figure 11.32 Matching unique measures of success with the customer life-cycle stage/keyword cluster

Let's walk through the framework in a bit of detail. Use Bounce Rate to measure those keywords in your portfolio that target early customer consideration steps, such as curiosity and awareness. These keywords cost less; hence, getting that traffic to come and stay on your site is a sufficiently worthy goal. If you do a decent job on the landing page, visitors will find some information, and they will be attracted to your brand or value proposition. Hurray!

For the next set of keyword clusters (interest, consideration), there is a lot more competition. These keywords can be more expensive, and hence you should set a higher measurement bar: demand that these keywords drive traffic that spends a lot of time on your site. These visitors must explore more deeply, read the specification or product details, and so forth.

For your high-cost brand keywords, you ratchet up your expectations. These keywords must attract Visitors that will show a high degree of Visitor Loyalty; that is, they will come for multiple visits and get close to converting (consideration, purchase).

Finally, for your most expensive brand/head keywords, you value success by measuring only conversions, leads, or multichannel offline impact.

Here are the three benefits of this approach:

- You have put together a flexible framework that helps you better value your paid search keyword portfolio.

- You still demand that every keyword you bid on delivers its pound of flesh (value).

- You also map keywords and actions back to the customer consideration life cycle, achieving better targeting and landing page experience on your site.

You may pick different metrics, your customer life cycle might be longer or shorter, or your keyword portfolio might be fatter or leaner than mine. But you'll still build out your framework with the principles I've outlined. The upper funnel analytical framework shows that often you must innovate because one size does not fit all.

Search: Advanced Pay-per-Click Analyses

In Chapter 4, I covered the paid search reports that every analyst, marketer, and VP must use to measure the success of the company's PPC campaigns. In this section, I want to kick things up a notch.

For many companies, measuring click-through rates (CTRs), cost per click (CPC), and conversion rates supplies enough data about their website. But if you run a sizeable paid search program, then you want to step beyond the limitations of your web analytics tools.

You can do more advanced analysis either by pulling data out through your search engine and web analytics tool APIs or by using *third-generation*, dedicated paid search tools from Marin, Kenshoo, and ClickEquations. If you work with a dedicated agency to execute your search strategy, then you can also request (or demand!) that they use the tools at their end for these types of advanced analyses.

The following analyses were done with the ClickEquations Analyst tool, which is part of the ClickEquations PPC platform.

Disclosure: Currently I am part of the ClickEquations advisory board.

Identifying Keyword *Arbitrage* Opportunities

Most web analytics tools dutifully report on search engine data and provide a keyword report. By now you know that you can drill down from the search engine report to look at keywords for that search engine.

The traffic ranking of your site by search engines is fairly well settled. It does not change much month over month. What is important, and usually not clearly visible, is the performance of one keyword across all search engines! This happens because every search engine uses a different algorithm to power its paid or organic search, and thus different keywords perform differently across search engines.

Figure 11.33 shows the clicks coming from different search engines for paid search keywords. The report is sorted to identify high-performing keywords in Yahoo!

Keyword Clicks By Engine

Total Clicks Keywords	Google	MSN	Yahoo	Grand Total
kitten cant breathe			428	428
all doghouse pet food	24	0	343	367
dog food doghouse Balance			256	256
doghouse pet store	395	42	196	633
holistic dog		27	185	212
allergy symptoms cat			171	171
dog supplement	57	1	159	217
doghouse pet	251	22	155	428
doghouse flea treatment	47	7	149	203
dogs grain-free food			140	140
doghouse dog food	197	41	140	378
evo dog food	9	55	132	196
political animals			123	123
premium cat food	14	1	123	138
why does my dog eat poop			110	110
dog food halo			107	107
dry cat food	6	1	102	109
dog food merrick			99	99
pet toy		0	98	98

Figure 11.33 Keyword Clicks by Engine report—ClickEquations

You can quickly identify a whole raft of keywords that perform well on Yahoo! but do nothing in Google. Why? Are you not buying these delightful keywords on Google? Are your bids too low or the ad copy ineffective? You already know they are right for you and they work on Yahoo!, so what can you do to get better performance on Google?

The best strategy is to focus on the same methodology—identify high-performing keywords—but apply it to conversions, as in Figure 11.34. With conversions, you see where immediate opportunities exist (the frowny faces!) and where you are doing OK.

Conversions By Engine Report

Total Conversions	Engine			
Keywords	Google	MSN	Yahoo	Grand Total
doghouse pet store	86	12	41	139
doghouse pet	44	0	0	44
doghouse pet store	27	1		28
doghouse pet	23	2	24	49
doghousepet.com	22	1	12	35
doghouse pet store coupon code	17			17
cat herbal	17			17
all doghouse pet	15			15
doghouse-pet food	13			13
pet doghouse medication	13			13
www.doghousepet.com	13	2		15
doghouse pets	12	0		12
doghouse pet products	12	0	1	13
doghousepet	12	0	1	13
dog incontinence	12	0		12
doghouse pet remedies	12		0	12
doghouse flea	11	0		11

Figure 11.34 Conversions by Engine report

Our second highest-performing keyword is bringing home the bacon on Google, but we are getting eggs with that keyword on AdCenter and Yahoo! The poor performance with the latter search engine highlights a possible sales or revenue opportunity and gives you marching orders to investigate.

Focusing on "What's Changed"

Our search campaigns have thousands of keywords, partly to ensure we are fully monetizing the long tail. It is impossible to review the performance of our keyword portfolios by looking at normal reports—a report with 90,000 keywords would take too long to review.

A better strategy is to focus on *what's changed* by applying simple mathematical algorithms that reveal the 100 or so rows of data where significant shifts have occurred. These rows of data need your attention.

The focus of your What's Changed reports is to show campaigns, ad groups, and keywords that are gaining more impressions, getting more clicks, or producing more revenue (or not) compared to a prior relevant time period. For maximum impact, I encourage you to move beyond the basic Visits or Conversion metrics and focus on metrics that truly matter to your businesses. Figure 11.35 shows the What's Changed report for two such key metrics, Revenue and Gross Profit. The chart shows the list of keywords and key phrases with significant increases or decreases in performance—it's short enough for you to identify problems or opportunities and take action.

What's Changed in Google Campaigns?
Increases and Decreases over the Prior Period

2009-04-21-2009-05-20	Revenue Increased By			2009-04-21 - 2009-05-20	Gross Profit Increased By	
Campaign				**Campaign**		
GS Health-Brands	$	2,729.26	50.80%	GS Health-Brands	$ 2,943.94	135.89%
GS Health-Nat-Remedies	$	2,640.47	888.77%	GS doghouse-Organic Food	$ 2,551.16	529.23%
GS doghouse-Organic Food	$	2,416.78	-	GS Health-Suppliments	$ 2,170.12	357.42%
GS Health-Suppliments	$	2,370.24	3289.72%	GS Health-Nat-Remedies	$ 2,130.43	1442.71%
GS Product Pet Categories	$	1,694.87	3729.91%	GS Food Branded	$ 1,684.33	90.27%
GS Food Branded	$	1,582.33	40.06%	GS Product Pet Categories	$ 1,397.99	267.82%
GCO NE_Optimized	$	1,175.66	386.24%	GS Food Branded Cat	$ 1,076.35	538.17%
GS Food Branded Cat	$	1,132.44	151.60%	NE_Pennsylvania	$ 1,050.14	1315.27%
NE_Pennsylvania	$	1,043.66	979.30%	GS doghouse-Organic Treat	$ 1,034.30	363.87%
GS doghouse-Organic Treat	$	997.88	-	GCO NE_Optimized	$ 1,027.51	1273.09%

Figure 11.35 "What's Changed" report for keywords with significant performance shifts

Scene 1: Good lord, I have to look at thousands of rows, and we stink!

Scene 2: Good lord! I just have to look at a few keywords each day and take actions, and we so rock!

Do you agree that Figure 11.35 is scene 2?

The biggest problem with paid search analytics is that you don't have starting points. The What's Changed report gives you starting points, so you can then go investigate hot leads. Perhaps your competitors have sprung into action. Maybe your quality score has taken a dive. Who knows, the boys in the warehouse may have run out of stock.

Analyzing Visual Impression Share and Lost Revenue

A person types a query into a search engine, and results that match the query appear on the search results page. At the top of the page, and to the right, the paid search ads show up. However, only ads that match a complex set of algorithms actually show up. Variables that go into that decision include the bids, quality score, past click history, location of the person typing the query, and match types used.

Given all these variables, you need to understand your *impression share*, that is, how often your ad shows up on the search results page compared to how often the keyword was queried by a user on the search engine. This concept is sometimes also referred to as *share of voice* or *share of the search shelf*.

Figure 11.36 shows the ClickEquations Analyst report that illustrates the share of voice for the top 20 queries by revenue (translation: our biggest money makers).

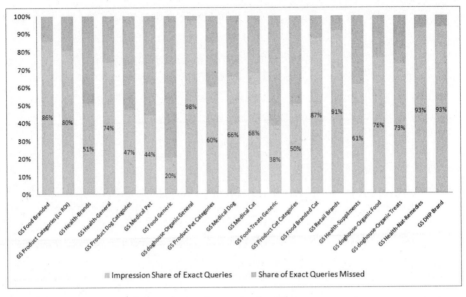

Google Impression Share Exact

"Share of Voice" for queries exactly matching your keywords (Top 20 by Revenue)

Figure 11.36 Google Impression Share Exact report for exact match queries

For GS Food Branded, we have an impression share of 86 percent. So, 86 percent of the time when someone searches exactly for those keywords, our ad shows up. This is good because the more our ad shows up for something relevant to us, the higher the chance that our ad will get clicked, and then the site takes over the conversion job. For GS Health-Brands, on the other hand, our impression share is just 51 percent. Not so great.

The impression share report helps us identify where specific opportunities exist for us to ensure that our ads appear with our best keywords. On the small chance you need HiPPO support to make these improvements, show them the impact of lost impression share. Figure 11.37 shows the lost clicks and lost revenue as a result of lost impression share.

The bars show the potential revenue stream lost, and the line shows the missed clicks. The formula that generates this information takes the average revenue per click from the impressions you get from your campaigns (the real conversion data from your site) and extrapolates to show how much revenue the lost impressions represent.

The previous example is a real customer, and the lost impressions alone (without doing anything else) represent a revenue growth opportunity of 30 percent. Remember, the data is based on actual clicks from ads where you do show up (impressions) and your actual conversions.

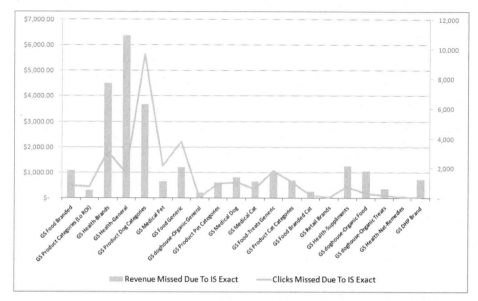

Figure 11.37 Missed clicks and revenue from missed impression share

Winning those missing impressions would require either a budget increase or more significant improvement in bids or quality score. But knowing that potential exists offers a clearer view of specific expansion opportunities than you can usually see with paid searches.

Embracing the ROI Distribution Report

Surely you know the 80/20 rule? Eighty percent of ROI comes from 20 percent of your campaigns. Figure 11.38 shows one of the coolest PPC reports you can use to see that rule in action. The ROI Distribution report shows how many campaigns, ad groups, and keywords fall into three performance bands: Great (exceeds expectations), Good (meets expectations), and Poor (stinks!). Each performance band is based on your ROI goal and on the minimum acceptable ROI.

In the tables you see the raw numbers, the cost vs. revenue breakdowns, and the comparative percentage distributions, which are key to understanding where the 80/20 distributions show up. For example, 8 percent of the Ad Groups are responsible for 54 percent of the revenue, with an astonishing ROI of 9,390 percent! Of course, 86 percent of your ad groups fall in the Poor category, giving you a negative 81 percent ROI. This distribution report is a ruthless way to determine which elements are hurting you and which are helping.

Campaigns

ROI Level	# Campaigns	%	Avg ROI	Spend	Percent	Revenue	Percent
Great (or better)	7	21%	1647%	$ 547	3%	$17,339	34%
Good (in between)	1	3%	169%	$ 1,630	9%	$10,293	20%
Poor (or worse)	26	76%	-54%	$16,267	88%	$23,580	46%
	34						

Campaign Spend-to-Revenue Comparison

Ad Groups

ROI Level	# Campaigns	%	Avg ROI	Spend	Percent	Revenue	Percent
Great (or better)	37	8%	9390%	$ 935	5%	$27,998	54%
Good (in between)	26	6%	163%	$ 862	5%	$ 4,711	9%
Poor (or worse)	389	86%	-81%	$16,177	90%	$18,761	36%
	452						

Spend to Revenue Comparison By Level

Keywords

ROI Level	# Campaigns	%	Avg ROI	Spend	Percent	Revenue	Percent
Great (or better)	174	8%	6826%	$ 896	5%	$32,651	66%
Good (in between)	38	2%	177%	$ 962	5%	$ 5,864	12%
Poor (or worse)	1,921	90%	-94%	$15,981	90%	$11,313	23%
	2,133						

Spend to Revenue Comparison By Level

Figure 11.38 ROI Distribution report for campaigns, ad groups, and keywords

By looking at distribution, you can take a very close and critical look at how many of your keywords are profitable and how many suck wind. You can thus reevaluate your keyword selections, match type settings, bid choices, ad copy, and campaign organization.

Zeroing In on the User Search Query and Match Types

Although the entire business of paid search revolves around keywords, we do not pay enough attention to the role match types play in search queries that trigger paid search ads. We sadly base too many decisions on keyword bids.

In our campaigns, we use *broad*, *phrase*, and *exact* match types to ensure we show up for relevant user searches. Hence, most of our campaigns include keywords that use all or some of these match types. A simple report can help you analyze the impact of different match types on performance. For example, Figure 11.39 shows one such report with three important pieces of data. Column 1 lists queries typed into the search engine, column 2 lists the keyword in your paid search campaign, and column 3 shows the match type.

Search Query	Keyword	Match Type
wysong uretic cat	wysong uretic	Phrase
wysong pet food	wysong pet food	Phrase
wysong geriatrix	wysong geriatrix	Exact
wysong dong food	wysong food pet	Broad
wysong growth age	wysong food pet	Broad
where can i buy wysong pet food in my town	wysong food pet	Broad
wysong food	wysong food	Phrase
discount wysong dog food	wysong dog food	Phrase
wysong dog food	wysong dog food	Phrase
wysong dog food distributors	wysong dog food	Phrase

Figure 11.39 User search query, keyword, and match type report

Right away, you should analyze the performance of individual match types with the user search query to find the clump of specific keywords you bid on. This analysis should spark the following ideas:

- Match type promotions (keywords and search queries you currently buy in phrase or broad match but should be in exact match)
- Search queries that match your broad match keywords but should be phrase match keywords
- A list of negative keywords that you should add to efficiently stop buying unqualified traffic

This search query report may be the ultimate keyword research tool you can get your hands on. And it is free! Use it!

Now that you understand user queries and match types, let's again kick things up a notch! You need to understand the performance of various match types across your entire account. You likely expect exact match keywords that are precise and that carefully chosen targets will perform better than phrase match and certainly broad match. But do they? Figure 11.40 shows the type of comprehensive PPC match type analysis you can perform to answer such fundamental questions.

The report gives you a macro view of your campaign efforts. It shows the results of all your hard work in finding and promoting keywords to exact matches, and it shows whether you increased the percentage of revenue you get through broad matches.

When you understand the macro view, you can dive deeper into analyzing key metrics such as Revenue Per Keyword by Match Type. There you find that the revenue is much higher for exact, a bit lower for broad, and even lower for phrase. The results are a function of how each match type works and the relevance to the user query. If you don't see clear results, dive deeper.

I have stressed Outcomes a lot in this section, so I'd be remiss if I did not share one of my favorite reports, a summary of Cost, Revenue, Gross Profit, and Net Profit by each match type (see Figure 11.41). Your HiPPOs will love this report.

Match Type Analysis (Google)

Match Types by Keywords and Revenue in Google

Match Type	Count	Percent	Cost	%	Revenue	%	Conv	%	Assists	%	Rev/KW
Broad	3803	45.73%	$ 28,798.67	64.19%	$ 55,523.37	41.43%	1104	46.76%	696	50%	$ 14.60
Exact	2731	32.84%	$ 9,091.41	20.26%	$ 62,172.38	46.39%	960	40.66%	529	38%	$ 22.77
Phrase	1783	21.44%	$ 6,974.26	15.55%	$ 16,323.53	12.18%	297	12.58%	166	12%	$ 9.16
Total Keywords: 8317			$ 44,864.34		$ 134,019.29		2361		1391		

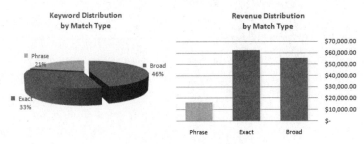

Figure 11.40 Match type keyword, revenue, and conversion analysis

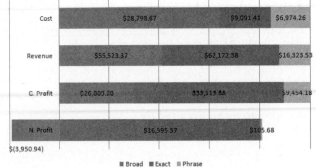

Figure 11.41 Bottom-line outcomes report by match type

For this specific client, every dollar spent on broad match yields a much lower return compared to phrase or exact match types. The client needs to work immediately on negative keyword expansions to further optimize their spending.

When you focus on Cost, along with three key outcomes (Revenue, Gross Profit, and Net Profit), you can see a multidimensional picture of your performance quickly.

 Note: By default, your web analytics tool, as well as many search analytics tools, won't be able to compute your profit because they don't have cost of goods sold (COGS) information. Specialist tools, like ClickEquations, can do it because it exports COGS data from your company financial systems. That enables search campaign optimization based on what matters the most to you: net profit.

Advanced Principles for Becoming an Analysis Ninja

The toughest challenges in online measurement are the touchiest. Gaining a Conversion is complex: a Visitor may visit your website multiple times and be exposed to multiple online marketing campaigns. And because we live in a "nonline" marketing world, the influences on a Visitor are not limited to online channels. We see television ads and billboards. Therefore, our Outcomes are no longer limited to online Conversions; we might do our window shopping online, but we convert offline.

This chapter deals with the most demanding measurement topics. We'll look at different approaches to one of the hottest challenges of the moment—multitouch campaign attribution analysis. Then we'll examine the measurement options for multichannel analytics. In this chapter, ninjas earn their sabers.

12

Chapter Contents
Multitouch Campaign Attribution Analysis
Multichannel Analytics: Measurement Tips for a Nonline World

Multitouch Campaign Attribution Analysis

No other topic, except perhaps mobile analytics, currently gets as much press as *campaign attribution*. And no other topic generates as much passion and mudslinging. Welcome to the world of assigning credit (or, more correctly, blame!).

In this section, you'll develop an appreciation for the problem, identify whether it impacts you (this is one step everyone forgets to cover), dissect available solutions, and finally peer into the future by considering two promising solutions for attribution that are currently still in the labs.

What Is All This Multitouch?

Throughout this book I have stressed that it usually takes a few visits for someone to convert on your website. During the visits leading up to the conversion, the customer was likely exposed to many advertisements from your company, such as a banner ad or affiliate promotion. Or the customer may have been contacted via marketing promotions, such as an email campaign. In the industry, each exposure is considered a *touch* by the company. If a customer is touched multiple times before converting, you get a *multitouch conversion*.

Let's look at a few specific examples. Figure 12.1 shows five scenarios of advertising and marketing exposures occurring prior to the conversions. The legend at the bottom of Figure 12.1 tells you the campaign the customer was exposed to in each scenario. In this case, our campaigns are Yahoo! banner ads, MSN home page promotion, Google organic search (yes, organic should be treated as a campaign), affiliate promotion, and email campaign.

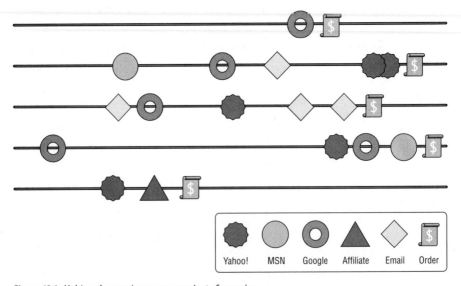

Figure 12.1 Multitouch campaign exposures prior to Conversion

In the first scenario, life is simple: someone visits Google, does a search, clicks an organic listing, and converts on the site. Who gets *credit* for the conversion? Google organic search does.

In the second scenario, life is not that simple. The customer saw (but did not click) a promotion on the MSN home page; however, a few days later the customer did an organic search on Google and visited our website, the next day received an email campaign from us, and then days later saw two banner ads for our product on the same day while reading news on Yahoo!, clicked the second one, and placed an order.

Who gets credit for this conversion? The Yahoo! banner ad? The email campaign? The first promotion on the MSN home page that might very well have introduced the customer to our brand? It is not clear who should get credit.

Multiple campaigns raise other issues as well. In the third scenario, the customer ignored our first email promotion, later did an organic search, saw but did not click a Yahoo! banner, was still not convinced of our value proposition, and hung back. We sent an email with a promotional price and got no result. Finally, a personalized email campaign based on past history appealed to the customer and led to a conversion event. Should any of the other campaigns get any credit? Clearly they failed to do their job. Yes? No? You can make many different cases depending on your perspective.

How about the fourth scenario? Should the first Google organic campaign get any credit since it happened a week prior to the conversion?

These are incredibly hard questions to answer because attribution often comes down to a qualitative judgment. Each person's answer might be different. The reason marketers, advertisers, publishers, and HiPPOs will fight to the death on this issue is quite simple: each wants a piece of the action, and each wants credit for the conversion (if not all, then some of it) so they can stay in business (or get promoted).

What is clear is that for some Conversions, your customers are being exposed to multiple campaigns. What is not clear is what to do about it, and that's what we'll spend the rest of this section on.

Do You Have an Attribution Problem?

In the heat and passion exuded by gurus, bloggers, and, OK, authors on this multitouch issue, one small detail gets overlooked. It's this question: *"Do you, website owner, actually face an attribution problem? If yes, what's the size of the problem?"*

For intellectuals, multitouch attribution presents a chance for an appealing brain exercise. But as a website owner, your fiduciary duty is to establish whether you actually have a problem and not get caught up in the hype. Amazingly, that is quite easy to do.

Log into your Webtrends or other analytics tool, and click Ecommerce Reports. Click the standard Visits to Purchase report, as shown in Figure 12.2. A quick glance at this report will tell you whether you should run like your head is on fire or just be a cool cucumber and chill.

Visits to Purchase

Most purchases occured after: 1 visits

Visits to Purchase	Transactions	Percentage of all purchases
1 visits	384.00	76.95%
2 visits	50.00	10.02%
3 visits	28.00	5.61%
4 visits	8.00	1.60%
5 visits	3.00	0.60%
6 visits	1.00	0.20%
7 visits	5.00	1.00%
8 visits	4.00	0.80%
9-14 visits	3.00	0.60%
15-25 visits	9.00	1.80%
26-50 visits	4.00	0.80%

Figure 12.2 Visits to Purchase report

In Figure 12.2, 86.97 percent of Conversions happened in two visits or less. In this case, you may not have a multitouch attribution problem. Or your problem may be minor, and solving it should be a lower priority (first fix the Bounce Rate of your home page or the Abandonment Rate of your shopping cart).

If you want to be perfectly sure, go ahead and click the standard Days to Purchase report. It will tell you how many Conversions happen on the same day and whether they happen across multiple days and hence multiple visits. If you see 80 percent of Conversions happening on the same day, you might not have an attribution problem. But if only 5 percent of Conversions happen during the first two visits and a majority of Conversions happen after 15 visits, you may need to spend some of your precious resources on multitouch campaign attribution analysis.

Don't jump into action quite yet.

After you recognize the attribution problem, you want to leverage the power of segmentation to identify where to focus your initial effort. Figure 12.3 illustrates the desirable outcome for a portfolio of campaigns.

Export | Email | Add to Dashboard | Beta Advanced Segments: Paid Traffic

Overview »

Visits to Purchase

Most purchases occured after: 1 visits

Visits to Purchase	Transactions	Percentage of all purchases
1 visits	399.00	77.03%
2 visits	54.00	10.42%
3 visits	28.00	5.41%
4 visits	8.00	1.54%
5 visits	3.00	0.58%
6 visits	1.00	0.19%
7 visits	5.00	0.97%
8 visits	4.00	0.77%
9-14 visits	3.00	0.58%
15-25 visits	9.00	1.74%
26-50 visits	4.00	0.77%

Export | Email | Add to Dashboard | Beta Advanced Segments: Yahoo! Display Campaigns

Overview »

Visits to Purchase

Most purchases occured after: 15 visits

Visits to Purchase	Transactions	Percentage of all purchases
1 visits	1.00	0.65%
2 visits	2.00	1.30%
3 visits	4.00	2.60%
4 visits	4.00	2.60%
7 visits	2.00	1.30%
8 visits	1.00	0.65%
9-14 visits	1.00	0.65%
15-25 visits	120.00	77.92%
26-50 visits	19.00	12.34%

Figure 12.3 Visits to Purchase segmentation exercise for campaigns

I have identified that Visits to Purchase for paid search traffic is not an issue (87.45 percent convert in two visits or less). But for my Yahoo! display campaigns a large percentage of Visits to Purchase happen after 15 days! Therefore, for the initial focus area, I'll segment all Visitors from Yahoo! and get them prepped for deeper attribution analysis.

You can also go through the Days to Purchase exercise to cross-check your findings. Here is your bottom-line magnificent accomplishment:

- You saved time and resources by going through an exercise to identify whether you have a problem.

- You saved time and resources by finding the optimal starting point for your multichannel attribution exercise.

Congratulations.

Attribution Models

Once you have quantified that you do have a problem that demands that you go through the multitouch attribution analysis then the next step is to understand what model you could use to attribute credit (assist) to each touch point (campaign).

No multitouch attribution model is universally accepted at the moment. One commonly used model exists, along with other emerging models, one of which may become the standard down the road.

In a multitouch scenario, it is impossible to know the influence or impact each touch has on the customer. Without that information, you are going to use your understanding of your business, or even your best guess, for how to attribute credit.

Let's assume a scenario where a customer purchased a $75 product. The challenge is how to assign credit for that revenue to the various campaigns. Figure 12.4 shows five potential attribution models. Let's look at each one briefly.

			1	2	3	4	5
Touch	Ad Channel	Action	Credit (Last)	Credit (First)	Credit (Even)	Credit (Split)	Credit (Custom)
1	Email Promotion	Open	$0	$75	$10.7	$6.3	$15.0
2	Yahoo! Banner	View	$0	$0	$10.7	$6.3	$3.8
3	MSN Home Page	Click	$0	$0	$10.7	$6.3	$9.0
4	Google PPC	Click	$0	$0	$10.7	$6.3	$13.5
5	Affiliate	Click	$0	$0	$10.7	$6.3	$5.3
6	Bing Organic	Click	$0	$0	$10.7	$6.3	$15.0
7	Yahoo! PPC	Click + Convert	$75	$0	$10.7	$37.5	$13.5
			$75.00	$75.00	$75.00	$75.00	$75.00

Figure 12.4 Multitouch campaign attribution models

Last-Click Credit

Because it is impossible to guess what influence each campaign played in the decision to purchase, the founding fathers of analytics decided that the last campaign should get credit. Today this is the standard attribution model in most web analytics and campaign analytics tools.

In Figure 12.4, the Yahoo! PPC campaign gets credit for driving $75 worth of revenue to the company. All other campaigns get zero credit. A reasonable person could argue that perhaps the Bing, Affiliate, Google PPC, MSN, and email campaign deserve some credit as well.

My POV: A case can be made that *some* credit should be given to campaigns that touched the customers in a reasonable period immediately prior to the conversion. Although last-click credit is the standard today, it is not optimal for identifying how best to spend our budget in different marketing channels.

First-Click Credit

A minority amongst analytics tools use the first-click method for campaign attribution. The rationale is this: "*If it were not for the very first campaign touch the customer might never have known we existed, she might never have considered our product.*" Well, OK then. In this case, the email promotion gets the credit for driving $75 of revenue, and all other campaigns get zero. You might then dismiss the value of all other campaigns and focus resources on email promotions.

You can configure most web analytics tools, like Google Analytics, to give credit by default to the first campaign (a *campaign* would include organic and referrals, both typically free sources and not just paid marketing).

My POV: I think first-click credit skates on really thin ice. If the first campaign was so magnificent, why did it take six more campaigns to get the customer to convert?

Even-Click Credit

Some web analytics tools, such as Coremetrics, and some search analytics tools, such as ClickEquations, now provide a standard report that uses the even-click method for attribution.

The rationale for even-click credit is this: "*We have no idea how to assign credit, and since we live in a democracy and are peace-loving human beings, let's just give everyone equal credit.*" In this case, each of the seven campaigns gets credit for driving $10.71 of revenue. Thus, you might keep investing equally in all campaigns in the chain.

My POV: This approach is suboptimal. If the six campaigns prior to the one that converted were so fantastic, why did it take so long to convert? Or, why give the second one, the Yahoo! banner, any credit? The customer did not even click it! This approach is a punt to avoid making the hard decision.

In the Olympics, everyone who runs the race does not get a participation medal. Analysis is done. The winner gets gold, the next runner gets silver, and a third person gets bronze. Why should your campaigns be any different?

Split Credit

Though none of the current tools in the market offers this as a standard model, you can see how a small group of enterprising folks came up with it.

The rational for split credit is this: "*We give 50 percent of the total credit to the last campaign, and we'll split the other 50 percent equally amongst all other touch points.*" I call this the *some are more equal than others* model!

In this case, the last campaign, Yahoo! PPC, gets $37.5 worth of revenue credit. Each of the other campaigns gets $6.3 worth of credit. The result from this attribution model is that you'll invest more in the last-touch campaign and then invest an even amount between all others.

My POV: This model is perhaps a bit more palatable. Mind you, it is not totally yummy, but at least it is not dead on arrival. The person who brings home the bacon deserves a lot of credit (50 percent). But the democracy bit is still in action, so you give equal amounts of revenue credit to a view-through and a click. This is the unpalatable part.

Custom Credit

Because all the previous attribution models miss the mark in different ways, some vendors have created and marketed the custom-credit modeling functionality as a possible path to enlightenment.

The rationale for custom credit is this: "*We have no idea what your business is, what campaigns work for you, how you value view-throughs and clicks, or how you might want to assign credit. So, here's an open model; you figure how many touches it takes and how you want to assign credit to each touch.*" That sentiment holds a lot of truth.

In Figure 12.4 earlier, I decided that I value my campaigns using the following percentages:

Email 20 percent (because they might be a customer, I do a lot of work, and I deserve a lot of credit)

Yahoo! banners with view-through 5 percent (because I don't value view-throughs)

MSN home page promotions 12 percent (because this is a scatter-shot approach)

Google PPC 18 percent (because I can show up only for exact match relevant queries so these are very targeted)

Affiliate campaigns 7 percent (because the affiliates server customers who have already been exposed to other campaigns, so I value them a bit higher than view-throughs)

Bing organic 20 percent (because I love organic traffic, it's free, and I love Microsoft)

Yahoo! PPC 18 percent (for the same reason as Google PPC)

This rationale gives me the revenue credits that you see in the Credit (Custom) column in Figure 12.4. While the logic is complex, it is unclear if it can be transferred to other businesses.

You might take a different route and use a *decay model* of giving the last campaign 30 percent of the credit and five campaigns prior to that one 25 percent, 20 percent, 15 percent, 7 percent, 3 percent of the credit respectively, and any campaign beyond that 0 percent. That would be based on your understanding of your business, customers and conversions.On a recent project, I came up with a truly custom model for a client in the printing services business. The last click got 75 percent of the credit, and I then used a decaying function for the remaining 25 percent, which applied to clicks in the last 14 days. I wanted to give the most weight to the converting campaign and go back only 14 days because that was the consideration life cycle for a typical customer for this business. The end result was a custom credit model that used *split*, *custom*, and *decay* to come up with an optimal solution for this business.

You can see why attribution analysis under the custom-credit model is hard to generalize. Depending on the wisdom, experience, and critical-thinking capabilities of the analyst, you might get great results or an empty bag.

My POV: The success rate with the custom-credit model is medium to low. It's not because of the technical capabilities of your analytics tool; it's because of these three challenges we humans face:

- Understanding the obvious or nuanced elements of what influences people online
- Understanding past performance enough to propose a model that reflects the truth
- Assuming that past performance is an indicator of future success

Often these assumptions are proven false online, and hence the models are hit or miss.

Of course, if your analytics tool lets you apply a custom-credit model, you can compare the even and split credit models to see whether they work better. Or you can experiment with various custom models. Just be careful, will ya?

Core Challenge with Attribution Analysis in the Real World

Path analysis. In a nutshell that's the core challenge in trying to do productive attribution analysis for our campaigns.

Most new analysts want to do website path analysis because they believe one golden series of clicks, *the path*, leads to business success. They want to know whether Visitors to the site are following such a path. If not, then what path are they following? Hidden behind that rationale is a belief that the Web has structure, just like a bookstore or a supermarket.

Path analysis turns out to be a terrible waste of time because the Web is not structured; it is chaotic (you can learn more about path analysis at http://zqi.me/akpath). There isn't one path to success; there are thousands. In addition, website owners define success on our site differently than our customers. This mismatch makes path analysis even more useless for unstructured experiences.

These two challenges bedevil our multitouch attribution analysis efforts as well. The first assumption behind attribution analysis is that you can identify a particular *path* for converting visitors (example: email —> organic search —> display —> conversion). But the sheer chaos of the web experience often makes identifying such a path unfeasible.

If we want to get to a clean path, similar to Figure 12.4 earlier, we might order it along these lines: "*Let's figure out whether we need to do display first, then YouTube, and finally paid search. Once we know that, we'll spend money correctly on marketing.*" However, when we look at all converting Visitors and re-create their campaign path to Conversion, we find very diverse data—1 percent converted after a path of display, search, then email, and 5 percent converted after a path of organic search and then paid search. Tiny fractions of your converting Visitors followed too many different paths. Unfortunately, our reality looks more like Figure 12.1 (and those are just five converting Visitors!).

The second assumption behind attribution analysis is that even if you understand the campaign path to Conversion, you can then take that information and change how you spend your marketing budget.

Here's a very simplistic example. So far, you have spent 70 percent on display advertising, 20 percent on YouTube, and 10 percent on search. You do the attribution analysis, and it turns out 100 percent of your converting Visitors followed this campaign path: display (banner), YouTube, search. You use even-credit attribution analysis, and now that you know what's happening, you triple your marketing budget and decide to spend 33 percent on each. Will you have success?

Even in our simplistic case, that might not happen. Every marketing channel—display, YouTube, search—has a natural threshold of available inventory (impressions). Although you can allocate 33 percent of your spending on YouTube, if no one will watch your video, why allocate that budget? You might as well spend it all on search where there are available impressions.

In doing attribution analysis, we might be answering the wrong question: "*How can I assign credit to each campaign?*" This leads to a path analysis type of effort. The question we should answer is this: "*How can I optimally allocate my budget across available advertising and marketing channels?*"

Promising Alternatives to Attribution Analysis

Many companies and agencies are experimenting with alternative approaches to attribution analysis. No clear winner has yet emerged from these experiments.

Let's look at two examples that hint at options that may one day help us improve our efforts to allocate our marketing and advertising budgets.

Media Mix Modeling

Media mix modeling leverages the marketing mix optimization method from the offline world. Our goal is to determine how much money to spend on each media channel, as illustrated by Figure 12.5.

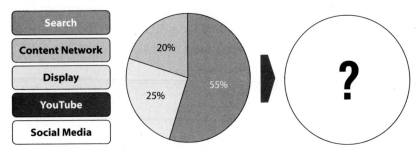

Figure 12.5 Media channels and current budget distribution

On the left are available media channels. The current budget allocates 55 percent to search, 35 percent to display, and 20 percent to the content network. What should the allocations actually be?

If your goal is to determine how much to spend on each media channel, then why not answer that question directly with a randomized media mix experiment rather than attempting conversion attribution analysis?

In the offline world, companies use the following approach to create a media mix model: in a well-directed experiment, a company will choose certain markets (states, cities, or designated market areas) and spend a varied mix of the marketing budget in each channel of their portfolio.

For example, in Ohio, the marketing spend would be as follows:

20 percent TV, 70 percent newspapers, 10 percent radio

In Florida, it would be as follows:

35 percent TV, 35 percent newspapers, 30 percent radio

In California, it would be as follows:

70 percent TV, 15 percent newspapers, 15 percent radio

As soon as they execute these campaigns, they start to collect conversion data, isolated by geographic regions. An analysis of this data helps determine the optimal mix of media to achieve the lowest *cost per acquisition*. The company uses that data to spend the budget optimally.

The answer, however, is not perfect forever. The company must rerun experiments based on seasonality, new product introductions, and other such variables.

You can apply a similar methodology to the Web to solve the problem posed in Figure 12.5. Although a media mix model is a bleeding-edge approach, it holds much promise because online we can run experiments quicker and at a lower cost.

Applied to the online world, the media mix method combines the best of rapid, controlled experiments (more in Chapter 7) and leverages real-world facts to make decisions.

Challenges of Online Media Mix Modeling

No specific tools or accepted methodology yet exists for media mix modeling. If you want to create an optimal media mix model, you must learn from models in the offline world and implement your own program.

Ironically, it is much easier to collect data in the data-poor offline world for media mix models. Online your ad spending likely happens through different agencies and systems, so you must rationalize cookies and centralize large amounts of data. As companies move to integrate datasets, this will become less of an issue. For example, Omniture's Genesis platform allows you to bring in many different sources of data (display, search, social media, and so on) and provides for easier analysis, even though the media mix modeling experiments are run outside the Genesis platform.

Marginal Attribution Analysis

The concept of marginal attribution is quite simple. Rather than trying to attribute Conversions to different media channels, you can answer a more meaningful question by designing an experiment that helps you do *marginal attribution analysis.*

For example, you spend 55 percent of your marketing budget on display and 45 percent on search. This results in $2 million in total revenue from those programs. Some people may have seen only display ads and others just search ads. Some people saw both.

Now it turns out that you have just received an additional $200,000 marketing budget and you need to know how best to allocate that budget between your search and display options.

In doing marginal attribution analysis your approach will be to take a part of that budget, say $10,000, and allocate it to one part of your portfolio, say display advertising campaigns. You'll then measure the outcome (Conversions) for this experiment. Any increase in Conversions will be attributed to that $10,000 increased spend in Display.

Under this methodology it does not matter what the last touch point was; in our simple scenario it would have been search for all the incremental conversions. The focus of our analysis is to understand how much additional revenue we added from changing one variable in our ad spend budget (in our case an additional $10,000 on display). You would do this until you identify the point of diminishing returns for a particular channel.

If you use all media channels—affiliate, email, search, display, and social media—then change only one variable (media spend), identify incremental conversions, and do marginal attribution analysis.

Marginal Attribution Analysis Challenges

With marginal attribution analysis, it is difficult to control all the variables that could impact your experiment, especially online. You would have to construct the experiment to be as clean as possible and identify variables you can and cannot control. You are also changing one thing at a time, which can take time.

Neither media mix modeling nor marginal attribution analysis is easy, but with such tough questions you are forced to think outside the box, to be patient, and to be willing to experiment.

I hope that these advanced methodologies will move us away from tough, sometimes frustrating, attribution analysis work toward scalable, efficient, and predictable methodologies.

Parting Thoughts About Multitouch

This has been a tough section of the book with no easy answers. I wish that were not the case, but we are very early in our evolutionary cycle here. Until these methods have sorted themselves out, here are three parting thoughts:

- A percentage of your Conversions will come from multiple marketing touch points. Before you do anything, figure out what that percentage is and what channel is most impacted.

- If multitouch attribution is a big problem for you, then you should move beyond assigning 100 percent of the credit to the last click, understand all the models and their limitations, and then pick the best possible attribution model and apply it.

- Stay plugged into new and evolving methodologies in this space. If you are a large company with large marketing budgets, then it might be wise to experiment with new methodologies such as media mix modeling or others like it.

Good luck.

Multichannel Analytics: Measurement Tips for a Nonline World

In Chapter 10, I covered the delightful world of nonline marketing. Key insights from that section were to break down the silos between our online and offline efforts and to identify why measuring multichannel impact is such a challenge.

In this section, I am excited to cover the options available for measuring the online impact of our offline campaigns and the offline impact of our online campaigns.

Before we get going, let me stress that there is no magic pill here. But we do have a number of wonderful options to get us close to understanding the impact of our nonline marketing campaigns. Also, some of these options are not for the fainthearted; they are for the brave and true analysis ninjas!

Tracking Online Impact of Offline Campaigns

For every billion dollars spent on online marketing, multiple billions are spent offline on TV, magazines, radio, and billboards. Spending on those channels vastly surpasses spending on the Web. So, it is no particular shock that offline marketing has a big impact online.

Perhaps after seeing your ads on TV, people run to buy your competitors' products (OK, just teasing you; they run to buy your products!). They search for you. The next time they see your flashing banner on a website, they are more likely to click through.

Increasingly, companies are also actively driving customers to multiple channels. At the end of the ad, you'll see a phone number listed as well as a URL for a website. That makes it even more important to track the impact of the URL.

Here are my recommendations, starting with the simplest, for measuring the impact of offline advertising and marketing efforts on your website.

Vanity URLs

Remember, a major problem with nonline measurement is that we don't have a primary key. So, why not *create* one? Using vanity URLs, also called *redirects*, is one of the oldest tricks in the book for creating a primary key.

The idea is very simple. You have an ad in a magazine. Rather than printing the URL of your website, you use a vanity URL that redirects people to your site (or better still, the best page on your site). In the process of redirection, your web analytics tool captures useful data.

Here's an example. I run an ad for QuickBooks, the wonderful accounting software for small businesses. My television ad ends with the URL `www.usequickbooks.com`. That's the vanity URL. When someone types it into the browser, the URL redirects them to this page:

`www.quickbooks.intuit.com/?campaign=tv_nbc_dec_2009`

The customer typed in the easy-to-remember URL, and I get deep tracking from my web analytics tool (see Figure 12.6). I can measure how much revenue TV contributes to the bottom line. I can also see that Conversion Rate from the TV campaign is multiple times higher than for all other Visitors to the site.

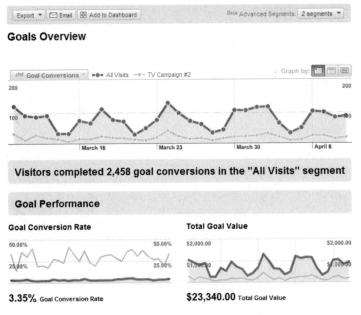

Figure 12.6 Tracking online impact of television campaigns

In addition, you can also measure what pages these Visitors read, their Bounce Rate, how many days it took them to convert, and their Loyalty and Recency metrics.

Vanity URLs can include your main domain and an offer or tracking parameter in them, such as www.sears.com/101 for a billboard on highway 101 in California or www.starbucks.com/20off for a Starbucks ad that gives $20 off a $100 purchase. You can do this for any offline ad. Just remember three small details:

- Make your vanity URLs easy to remember. If you use www.reallyreallyhardandtoughtorememberurl.com, no one will remember it. Ditto for www.e2r.com/astringofrandomnumbersandalphabets.

- Make vanity URLs permanent redirects—always good for SEO.

- Absolutely ensure the redirect is encoded with tracking parameters (version of the ad, name of the magazine, location of the billboard, offer in the radio ad, and so on).

Tip: When you analyze these campaigns, you can filter out any traffic with a referrer. That will ensure that if your vanity URL gets posted online, then those clicks are excluded (because you used a permanent redirect, those clicks will come with the referral information and the ad clicks won't).

Unique Redeemable Coupons and Offer Codes

Coupons and special offer codes are another relatively easy way to track the online impact of offline marketing. In your offline advertising campaigns, you can use unique coupons or tracking codes that will become the primary key for tracking online impact. Figure 12.7 shows two such examples, Dell on the left and 1-800-FLOWERS on the right.

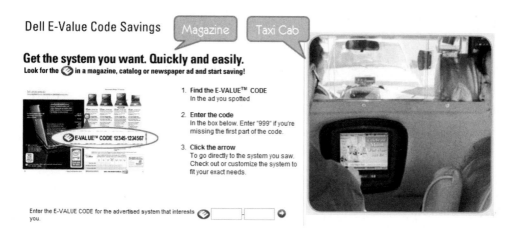

Figure 12.7 Using coupons to track impact

In the case of Dell, the catalog that I get in the mail contains ads for preconfigured systems that are on sale at their website. To help me locate these systems better, each system has an e-value code. I can go to dell.com and type my code to locate the system quickly. That makes me a happy customer. But it also makes Dell happy because now it can track my click on the website back to a physical catalog. Because Dell can use unique codes by country, geography, catalog issue number, or even the person (me!), it can do deep tracking of the online impact of its catalogs.

In the case of 1-800-FLOWERS, I was watching a TV built into a New York taxicab. At the end of the ad for Mother's Day flowers, this call to action appeared on the TV screen: "Use the code TAXI on our website to save $10." Bam! Primary key! During the checkout process for my Martha Stewart Vibrant Blossom Bouquet, I used the code TAXI. The web analytics tool captures that data, and the analyst at 1-800-FLOWERS can easily establish the impact of that taxicab TV campaign.

Of course, the persistent website cookie means you can also track future purchases by the same person or other Visitor behavior, allowing you to learn more about your customers in a way that you can't via other channels.

Oh, and in both cases, for Dell and 1-800-FLOWERS, I could have picked up the phone and placed my orders (using the same tracking/coupon codes). That means both organizations can easily track the channel preferences of their customers (and even segment by location to learn, for example, that people in Michigan order through the phone and those in Texas prefer the Web).

Online Surveys and Market Research

In Chapter 6, I discussed the many benefits of using online surveys. One additional benefit is to identify the primary reasons people visited your website. As an example, you can use the completely free on-exit 4Q survey (http://zqi.me/ipsi4q) to track offline drivers of traffic. You simply add the question in Figure 12.8 in your survey.

☑ How did you arrive at the website today?

○ Typed the URL into a browser
○ Bookmark /favorites
○ Used a search engine
○ Clicked on a online banner ad
○ Saw the URL on a billboard
○ From a magazine ad
○ From a social networking website
○ A friend sent me a link
○ Other

Figure 12.8 Visitor source question in 4Q

Analysis of this data will complement data you already collect from your web analytics tools. It will also fill some major gaps in your analytics tools, such as answering why you have so much Direct Traffic (could be your offline campaigns!).

Online surveys like 4Q also measure customer satisfaction and task completion rates. So, you can take the visitors driven by your offline channels from Figure 12.8 and segment their results to understand whether they could complete the task they came to your site for. You offered a phone and a free charger in your magazine ad: could those visitors find the phone with the free charger and complete the purchase? Now you know.

Correlating Traffic Patterns and Offline Ad Schedules

Because we are talking about tracking the impact of offline activity, we are handed a great lever to measure the online impact. You know when ads run and where. Why not use that information to set up a baseline for your site and then measure the impact when campaigns are live?

Let's look at a good example. A company decides to promote a new product using radio ads across the United States. Even if I tell you nothing else, you'll understand exactly what Figure 12.9 is showing.

On the left is data from before the campaign was executed, and on the right is data, Visits, for the duration of the campaign. With this data, an analyst can easily measure the impact in several areas:

- Raw impact in terms of Visits (or metrics like Conversions)
- Specific radio markets where the ads proportionally drove more traffic online
- With access to the media plan, whether the audience for particular types of radio stations (for example, news, rock, or country) was more likely to connect with the ad and visit the website

Before: Baseline Data   After: Radio Campaign Results

Dec. 8–29 : 27 Cities   Jan. 19–Feb. 9 : 100 Cities

Figure 12.9 Online impact of radio campaign across different regions

Figure 12.9 is visual, is direct, and powerfully illustrates impact. Although it is not the deepest analysis you can do, images like these work very well when you present data to your HiPPOs.

As an analyst, you don't have to stop there. If you followed my earlier advice to use vanity URLs in your radio ads, you can do some very cool tracking. Figure 12.9 shows the aggregate view of the impact. But you can do more. You can take data for your radio campaigns and correlate that offline campaign reach with various traffic streams on your website to find actionable insights. Figure 12.10 shows precisely such analysis.

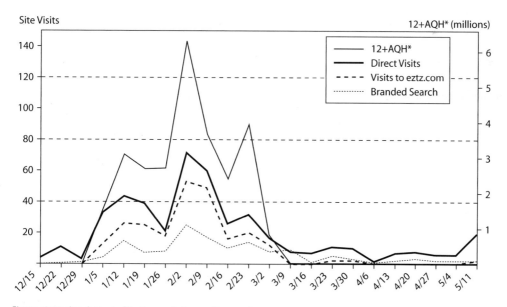

Figure 12.10 Correlating traffic streams during a radio campaign

The first line is the campaign data (reach in millions from the radio campaign). The third line is the first thing you should look at; it represents Visits that were a direct result of people typing in your vanity URL (in this case eztz.com).

Nice. You get a clear correlation between the ad airing on radio and the traffic spiking on the site, and the ebb and flow also match nicely. You can also compute the point of diminishing margins. The campaign line has three peaks, but although the third peak was higher than the first, the amount of traffic driven was much lower. You may have maxed out audience reach by then.

These two lines, the campaign reach via radio and visits via vanity URL, may not quite capture the holistic impact. For that, you should add the other main traffic streams to the graph to see whether you can detect impact.

In Figure 12.10, you'll notice that both Direct Visits and Branded Search show a near-perfect correlation to the radio campaign. That's an indicator of how many people used the vanity URL to visit the site. In this case, lots of people visited the website directly or came via search engines on the keywords containing the product advertised on radio!

The radio ad deserves credit for the tight correlation between the traffic streams with the campaign line. Now you understand the impact your radio campaign has produced, and you can see how it actually drove search traffic.

Remember, though, that correlations don't imply causality. In this case, the campaign was run in a way that minimized other influences, which you may not always be able to do, and care was taken to do clean analysis. For example, you might have noticed the search trend was only for brand searches for the new product being advertised on radio, not for all search traffic.

When you do correlations—an effective analysis strategy—be careful not to jump to causal conclusions. Instead, stress test the insights the data gives you.

Leveraging the Power of Controlled Experiments

I discussed controlled experiments in Chapter 7, you can also deploy them in the service of your multichannel analytics efforts. Let's learn their benefit using a practical example.

A national company wanted to raise awareness of its products through offline campaigns and specifically drive traffic online. The marketing team proposed using print ads (local newspapers) and doing a celebrity event across major U.S. states.

Rather than run the campaign in an ad hoc manner, the company conducted a controlled experiment. The campaign rolled out in three phases: it launched the first print ad, then it launched the second print ad, and finally it held the celebrity event.

To collect data optimally, the team also collected data during 30-day periods before and after the experiment. The goal was to compute lift during the campaign as well as compute any permanent lift after the campaign concluded. Figure 12.11 shows the data for the campaign.

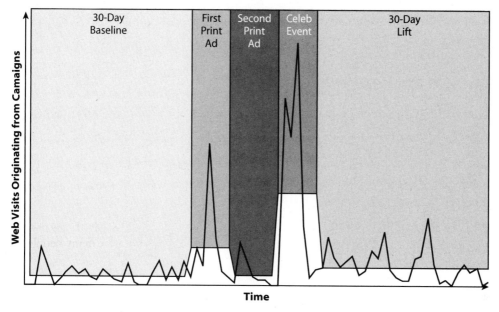

Figure 12.11 Offline marketing controlled experiment

The first print advertisement had a big impact on the website traffic; it caused a huge spike in traffic and then sustained over a few days before things settled down again. The second advertisement had only a marginal impact, so the company reached diminishing margins of return very quickly through print media.

The team observed two interesting phenomena with the celebrity event. A huge initial spike occurred as news of the event went out. That the event spiked traffic was not surprising, but the amount by which it did was a surprise.

The post-campaign measurement showed a sustained lift of more than double the traffic to the site, which was a positive result in terms of retaining new customers introduced to the brand. Additionally, since the team executed the experiment across multiple states, they could understand aggregate behavior in Figure 12.11, break it down by geography, and identify return on investment from each campaign. Although Figure 12.11 shows only the web visits, the team could also measure website outcomes and compute cost per acquisition (CPA) to bring an additional layer of accountability to the offline campaign.

Using controlled experiments is a simple methodology if the test is structured with a great deal of planning up front. Many teams must coordinate so that the campaign can be executed as planned and analysts can collect the required data.

With controlled experiments, you cannot always control all the factors in the test. Do the best you can, and in the post-campaign analysis go back and look again at traffic patterns and ad schedules, as in Figure 12.10.

These five methods—vanity URLs, unique coupons and codes, online surveys, traffic patterns and ad schedules, and controlled experiments—can help you quantify how your offline marketing activities add value to your online channel.

Tracking the Offline Impact of Online Campaigns

Now we move to the other side of the multichannel journey: measuring the offline impact of our online activities. You may have 2 percent Conversions on your ecommerce website, but what happens to the other 98 percent of Visitors? They may have gone to your store to buy. They may have called your phone center to conclude their purchase.

If you have a wonderful website for luxury cars, your customers cannot order your product online. But you want to know how your website contributes to potential customers purchasing your ultra-expensive car. Or if you organize a protest against chopping down giant redwood trees, you may post flyers, canvas door to door, and galvanize supporters through online social sites. You probably want to know the specific impact of your online efforts on your successful protest.

These questions and more come up every day in conversations and usually don't get answered. Measuring the offline impact of your website is critical for one reason only: understanding the complete value your website adds to your business.

As an example, you need to know that a banner ad campaign on the *New York Times* website is delivering an average order value of $90 *and* that the same people are subsequently buying $200 worth of products through your offline channel. That changes how you think of your campaigns, right? Or, say your technical support website reduces $50 of cost every time it answers someone's question online so they don't have to call you.

The path to hard quantification of online-to-offline impact is littered with small obstacles for now, but you still have areas you can track. The current obstacles simply mean that you need a little creativity and thoughtfulness.

If you are willing to create a small portfolio of initiatives, then you can get a decent understanding of the hidden offline impact of your web presence. Pick a few correlating data points, and see how far you can get in this game!

The following are my recommendations, starting with the simplest, for measuring the impact of your website on your offline channels.

Measuring Offline Calls to Action

Multichannel businesses are *littered* with offline calls-to-action, such as the Wal-Mart website providing store locators so people can find the nearest store. You could track the usage of this offline call to action as a proxy for the site's offline impact.

A customer may visit Walmart.com to find a digital SLR camera, zeroing in on the Nikon D700. While the site may convince the customer that this is the best camera, she may not want to buy it online. She can click the Store Finder link in the top navigation, type in a U.S. ZIP code, and end up on a page like this:

```
http://www.walmart.com/storeLocator/ca_storefinder_results.
do?serviceName=ALL&sfatt=ALL&rx_title=&rx_dest=/index.gsp&sfsearch_
zip=94043&%23.x=0&%23.y=0&%23=Find
```

The analyst at Walmart.com can use the previous URL to track how many people use the website and then visit the store. Two wonderful pieces of information sit in that URL. The number of Visits that contained that page, ca_storefinder_results.do, can be measured over time. And a savvy analyst can go one step deeper and measure not just the search results page but also the product page viewed or that an item was added to the cart, which are both strong signals of customer intent of purchase.

Analysis ninjas know that you can't stop at just measuring Visits. You have to quantify the goal value (more in Chapter 5). Figure 12.12 shows the steps required to set up the goal and the subsequent report.

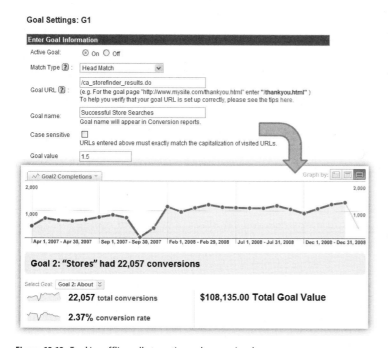

Figure 12.12 Tracking offline calls-to-action and economic value

Creating a goal is simple; you can simply use the page name. The next step is critical, identifying a Goal Value, which in this case is $1.5. You'll have to work with your finance department, you can merge your online and offline data (more on this a bit later), or you can run experiments to identify this value.

The report at the bottom of Figure 12.12 shows the trend over time of the site's impact on your store. Furthermore, it also shows the economic value generated by the site (the previous data is not for Wal-Mart; if it were, then it would have at least three more zeros behind it!).

> **Note:** There is another delightful piece of data in the previous URL, sfsearch_zip. This parameter contains the ZIP code that was searched. You can configure your web analytics tool to capture this data, and then you can report the geographic locations where online customers are more likely to visit your stores. A report like this lets you optimize your online and offline marketing efforts.

You also have a much stronger proxy for an offline store visit, the directions page! On the Walmart.com site, I can pick the nearest store to my ZIP code and then print driving directions. When I type my starting address into the browser, I get a page with this URL:

```
http://www.walmart.com/storeLocator/ca_storefinder_directions.do?sfsearch_
street_1=1600+Amphitheatre+Parkway&sfsearch_city=Mountain+View&sfsearch_
state=CA&sfsearch_zip=94043&x=41&y=12&edit_object_id=2280&continue=&sfatt=
```

An analyst can now track Visits where this stronger proxy for customer intent exists by tracking the page ca_storefinder_directions.do.

To get maximum insights, I would do all of the previous and track Visits that used the store locator after viewing a product page or adding something to cart. I would track the geographic locations and merge that data with store locations. Finally, I'll need to set a store value, such as $6 for each directions page, and present that data to my management team.

The previous examples are just two possibilities of offline calls to action on a website. Other examples include requests for product catalogs or making appointments to test-drive cars at dealerships.

Tracking Phone Calls and Live Chat

During my visit to the Marks & Spencer website, I decide to buy the Captain Hideaway Bed with Mattress. But rather than making a purchase on the site, I placed a phone order. Under current circumstances, my purchase is invisible to the web analytics tool, even though the website convinced me to make the purchase.

But you could track all these phone calls: you can track the nice calls that result in orders and the nasty calls that result in technical support questions because the site is not helping your customers.

You have two approaches available for tracking how your website drives phone traffic. First, you can use a unique phone number on your website and track calls and conversions using your existing system. You won't have to do any additional work, except getting the unique phone number. However, if your company's bureaucracy stands in the way, several web-based options, such as TeleCapture, can give you a unique phone number, program it to ring to your company's existing number, and provide rich reporting on the number of calls, unique callers, and missed calls. Bureaucracy nuked!

Increasingly, you can also bring call data into your web analytics tool. Solutions from companies such as Mongoose Metrics (U.S.) and Fresh Egg (U.K.) let you add unique phone numbers to your website. Any activity from those phone numbers gets sent over to your web analytics tool, where you can study both your online impact and offline calls in one place.

These solutions give you more sophistication because you can track offline calls driven by your search, banner, affiliate, or other types of individual campaigns. You just add a JavaScript tag to the landing page (or entire site) for the campaign where you would normally show the phone number. When a Visitor comes to the site, they see a unique phone number tied to the specific campaign (say, for the keyword *avinash rocks*). Now you can track down to a keyword or campaign level how many Conversions happened online and how many calls were generated offline.

The phone system in many companies allows marketers to track conversions by individual phone numbers, and an analyst can use this data to track conversions. If you don't have such a system, then you can use solutions from companies like ClickPath to take the data all the way down to Conversions.

Finally, if you provide phone call and live chat functionality, such as on your ecommerce or technical support websites, then numerous solutions, such as LivePerson, will integrate your phone and chat data with your web analytics solution. You update your analytics JavaScript tag, you configure LivePerson with your analytics account ID, and you are on your way.

Using Unique Coupon Codes and Offers

We used the coupon and code strategy effectively in the earlier section on tracking the online impact of offline campaigns. You can leverage the same idea in reverse.

I can visit www.target.com today and print custom coupons for products I want to buy. When I redeem the coupons in my neighborhood Target store, their analysts can use the company's existing data warehouse to report the percentage of store customers who were driven from their website.

Here is a specific example that was executed by my friends René Dechamps Otamendi and Aurélie Pols. Their client, Panos (www.panos.be), wanted to use the website to drive people to their restaurants. René and Aurélie's team created a campaign with a game for site visitors to play; at the end of the game, the visitors got a single-use coupon for Panos. Figure 12.13 shows the data they collected from this campaign and the key metrics with salient insights.

Panos can measure the end-to-end value of its campaign. The campaign ran for 18 days. During this time, almost 59,000 people visited the site and played 109,000 games, and that resulted in 42,000 coupons. Of those coupons, 59 percent were redeemed in restaurants; that's a huge redemption rate. The cool thing is Panos can measure cost per acquisition, which was less than 2 euros. Cooler still is that since these were single-use coupons, they could capture and report on fraud! You have to be proud of humanity: of the 42,000 coupons, only 189 were fraud attempts!

Some figures: (campaign duration=18 days!)

\# of visits to the website : 58.627

\# of page views: 1.057.769 (18 pages per visit)

\# of page views the busiest day: 155.071

\# of games played: 109.024

\# of games/sent eCoupons: 2,6

\# referal visits: 16.024

\# eCoupons sent: 41.701

\# eCoupons printed: 35.319

\# eCoupons exchanged in POS: 20.659 (58,9%)

\# eCoupons fraud atempts: 189 (less than 2 per POS)

Near 60% of eCoupons exchange rate

Cost per profiled email address: less than 2 euros!

Figure 12.13 Panos online-to-offline campaign analysis

Marrying and Mining Online and Offline Data

Companies such as Safeway or Macy's use the principles for tracking coupons and codes to tie offline behavior to online activity. For example, a supermarket that issues club cards could analyze the online and offline behavior of their customers since customers can use the club card in either place during the ordering process.

In another example, Marks & Spencer could spend a lot on online campaigns and measure the Average Order Size for each of those campaigns. But now with the credit card, name, and address information in the company ERP systems, it can also track additional purchases in stores in the subsequent 30 days. Recently I worked on such an analysis, where for every dollar spent online from paid search campaigns, customers spent six dollars in the offline store in the following 30 days. As an analyst, you can help your senior management value the effectiveness of your online marketing by emphasizing the one-to-six ratio.

The cost of this sophisticated analysis is simply your ability to capture the right primary keys and your willingness to step outside your world of web analytics tools. The rewards are magnificent if you do.

Using Surveys to Predict Offline Impact

In Chapter 6, I covered the glories of collecting qualitative data to hear directly from your customers. One methodology I covered in some detail was on-exit surveys. You can extend that methodology to measure offline impact.

Companies such as iPerceptions, CRM Metrix, and Usability Sciences all allow you to do online surveys where you ask Visitors to rate their experience and answer some follow-up questions. You can use this data to compute metrics such as Likelihood to Purchase, as shown in Figure 12.14. You can see that as a direct result of visiting the website, 54 percent of people are more likely to make a retail purchase—you can see the value your website added to the process.

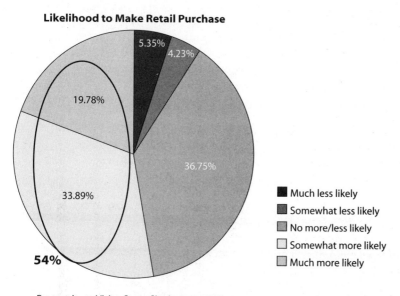

Likelihood to Make Retail Purchase

- Much less likely
- Somewhat less likely
- No more/less likely
- Somewhat more likely
- Much more likely

Propensity to Visit a Store: Site Impact +54%

Figure 12.14 Likelihood to make a retail purchase

If you trend this percentage over time, you can measure the effectiveness of your website in catering to your offline purchasing customers. It is a great complement to your online conversion data.

This is not the only piece of data your survey will collect. By isolating the Visitors who buy offline, you can then analyze why they visited the site, what features worked for them, and what did not work for them. You can then optimize your website to the needs of all Visitors.

Another common strategy of multichannel retailers is to use point-of-sale surveys. For example, if you make a purchase at Target or eat a meal at Pizza Uno, you'll notice an invitation on your receipt to fill out an online survey (in exchange for a sweepstakes entry or a coupon for a future visit). This survey asks you to rate your experience in the physical store, and it also asks questions about your visits to their website and how it influenced the store visit. Bam! You have data that identifies the value of your website for your offline existence.

Conducting Controlled Experiments

Controlled experiments are another effective strategy you can use; I covered such experiments earlier in discussing the online impact of offline campaigns and extensively in Chapter 7. Let me share some ideas that could inspire you to create your own controlled experiments to measure offline impact of online campaigns.

If you want to see whether your website drives traffic to your stores, you can conduct an email campaign to customers in a few different cities or states, drive them to your site to learn more, and see whether you get a lift in area store visits.

Another approach is to run geographically targeted PPC campaigns to deliver a certain message or call to action on google.com. Measure the impact on your site from those campaigns, and correlate it with the data (signal) you pick up in your call center by comparing performance for those regions with that of other regions.

Finally, here's one of my all-time favorite experiments. For one week, a top retailer did not send newspaper inserts in Arizona, New York, and Indiana. Instead, it ran banner ad campaigns on related sites and drove people to their website to look at relevant and unique offline sales in their local ZIP codes. The retailer removed an offline marketing medium to measure whether online-only marketing was as effective in driving people to stores *and* for buying items that would have appeared in the weekly paper circular. By creating an experiment with test states and control states (all others!), the retailer collected data that proved the value of switching to online-only marketing in two of those states.

The core idea is to try a targeted approach so that you can correlate the data to your offline data sources and detect a signal (impact). By isolating your approach to different states that are far from each other, you isolate *pollutants* to your data (things beyond your control that might give you suboptimal results).

As with all controlled experiments, this methodology takes time and effort. But nothing else will be more impactful for your business and prepare your marketing for the future.

Leveraging Primary Research

In addition to controlled experiments, the second technique that I have learned from our well-established offline brothers and sisters is good old-fashioned market research to isolate the impact of your online presence on your offline channels: field surveys, focus groups, interviews, and more.

Let me give you an example. Twice a year a tech company collects the names and information of all the folks who purchased something, online or offline. The company then sends that information to their market research agency folks who, using a portfolio of methodologies, polls those customers to discern all the drivers that caused the purchase.

The data was a gold mine of information related to product attributes, television ads, the website, impressions from visits to a store, percent of people who touched multiple channels before they purchased the product, and so on.

I remember when I got a decision maker to pay some attention to the website in that company. I had one slide in the analysis presentation that showed two pieces of data: 24 percent of purchasers listed the company website as the most trusted source of product information, and 40 percent of purchasers used the website during the purchase-consideration process. That data got me money for analysts, and that data gave the poor, starved web team two resources to improve the website—all from one slide. But that's the power of data.

Conducting a market research survey can be a great way to understand the influence of each online and offline channel. Doing periodic custom studies that focus on either a specific geography, a customer type, or a product can also yield valuable insights relating to the website's value to the offline channel.

Before we close this chapter, I'll be remiss if I did not mention once again that none of the previous methodologies will be a panacea. Think of multichannel measurement as a portfolio approach; you will have a few techniques to collect multiple data points. If you are a small or medium business, use the first three techniques in each section. If you are a large business, you'll include those, but the latter techniques will offer you the highest impact.

Have fun.

The Web Analytics Career

Of all the careers you could embark upon, perhaps none is quite as future proof *as a career in web analytics. Most channels are data-starved, but the Web is not. In fact, at the core of any success on the Web is data. And guess who's at the center of all that data? An analysis ninja!*

I believe the Web will evolve, that everything about online marketing and customer experience will evolve, and that we cannot predict what will be possible. To power all that evolution we will need smart people who can make sense of all the complex data.

This chapter shares my advice on what it takes to develop a career in analytics, the choices available, and how to identify optimal people for this dynamic field.

13

You'll be surprised at the diversity of careers available in the field of Web Analytics 2.0. No longer is analytics run by an IT person sitting on top of log files!

There are generalist roles in web analytics—usually in small or medium companies—but increasingly you'll see specialist roles as well. Analyst roles are very specialized in search, display, on-site merchandizing, and social media because of the deep subject-matter expertise required. Web Analytics 2.0 areas such as experimentation and qualitative analysis tend to require analysts with specialist skills. Then there are specialized roles related to tool implementation and technical optimization. As businesses grow, or internalize the data advantage, more management roles have appeared.

In all of these positions, data plays a primary role. A quick glance at job boards shows that data plays an increasingly important secondary role in traditional non-analyst roles, such as marketers, site owners, and campaign optimization specialists. That is a good sign from a career growth perspective in that you can get really deep into data analytics and still expand your career prospects if you have business skills.

Lots of people will rule the web world, but if you love data, then you'll sit at the head of the table.

Planning a Web Analytics Career: Options, Salary Prospects, and Growth

In this section, I'll share the many nuances of a web analytics career and outline a simple and easy-to-understand framework to help you make the right career choice. Each choice implies a level of salary you can command, a company division where you might work, and the amount of job growth you can expect.

Although much of this section applies to anyone working at a company of any size, some of the job growth perspectives might not apply if you work in a small company. In small companies, you have only so much headroom in any specialist role, including analytics, and people tend to have hybrid roles (translation: do many jobs for small pay!). If that's you, then you'll still benefit from understanding the landscape, and you'll learn how to recognize points where you must shift your career or move to another company.

 Note: Although this section emphasizes web analytics, the framework and guidance provided will apply to jobs and careers in other analytics careers as well, for example, in business intelligence or financial analysis.

From my own career in web analytics, I have come to realize that most prospective analysts don't recognize the two critical choices they must make; these are choices that will have a dramatic impact on success. You must choose one from each of these options:

- *Choice 1:* Technical or business
- *Choice 2:* Individual contributor or team leader

You have four possible outcomes, and your choice will propel your career in very different directions, slopes, and lengths. You need to do some introspection before you choose. To help you, I have developed the Avinash Kaushik Web Analytics Career Introspection Guide:

Give each of these questions deep thought, and write down your answers:

- *Do you like being an individual contributor?* You like to be master of your domain and controller of your destiny. You like setting agendas, while others deal with the actual work. You are truly at peace with your introvert self. Be honest with yourself.

- *Do you like managing people?* You rejoice at the prospect of helping mold careers. The prospect of collecting self-reviews, getting 360-degree feedback, and writing a performance review for each employee each quarter does not make you want to jump off a building. You see a matrixed bureaucratic organization, and like former President Bush, you say, "Bring it on!"

- *Do you love "code" and think there's nothing better than parsing scripts to make magic happen?* Your true *analyst* skills are sourced from your mastery of how to solve every technical problem with every tool known to humanity. You can implement anything, and if you don't already know it, then you can figure it out by glancing at a 500-page technical document. You can decode and reconstruct a debugging tool like WASP in two days. You can hack the Google Analytics tag to capture people's height and eye color.

- *Do you love being in strategy meetings?* Your true *analyst* skills come from all the time you have spent with marketers and business leaders dissecting company initiatives and goals. You possess some mastery at translating "measure something" from a VP into three critical few metrics that bedazzle her. You understand the long tail and how to recognize insights that revolutionize your search campaigns.

Answering these four questions honestly and critically is much harder than you think. Self-awareness is the process of figuring out where you shine, and truly knowing and accepting where you suck. It takes time to get going, and it is more of a lifetime journey. Self-awareness comes with great benefits. For example, over time I have learned to maximize the roles and situations where my strengths will boost success.

Your answers to the four questions will ensure that you don't end up in a job that you'll hate or where you very quickly rise to your level of incompetence. Remember, there is no wrong answer here. There are jobs available in companies, at vendors, and with consultants for each choice you might make.

With that introspection done, let's look at each career choice. For each, I'll cover the broad implications, career prospects, salary prospects, and long-term job title growth (promotion prospects).

Technical Individual Contributor

Many people wrongly believe that to make lots of money you must be in management. The reality is that you can also be well compensated as a senior individual contributor. Roles in this category include senior project manager, senior architect, and implementation god.

Technical individual contributors report to a director or VP. You get to set policy, rules, and regulation, and you only have the barest of dotted-line responsibility for project implementation. You might be the master liaison between the business team and your vendor to make sure that all the technical tag and tool hacking happens.

In this role in the vendor world—such as at Webtrends or IBM—you go to various clients and show off cool detailed stuff. You answer technical questions from wise guys employed by the client. You may be the army of one tapped to do rapid prototyping to prove the vendor is better than Google Analytics or Omniture. Or you may be the point of contact for the first 60 days when your company is trying to impress a new client with fast help. Make no mistake—this work can be fun. You get to travel and meet new companies and people.

It is quite likely that you'll sit in the IT (CTO/CIO) function.

Career Prospects

Career prospects are pretty sound at large to extra large companies, which can afford a dedicated position. The vendor world, of Omniture, Webtrends, Nedstat, and the like, probably has more jobs of this type. It would be harder to find these roles in medium to large companies.

Salary Prospects

Salary for a technical individual contributor starts at $40,000 and may reach $100,000 or beyond at vendors. It is hard to find people who are *really* good at this role. If you are one of them, then you are in demand.

Long-Term Job Title Growth (Promotions)

Job growth for an individual contributor is a bit dicey. If you stick to web analytics, your title might tap out at one of the titles mentioned (say, senior of this-and-that or an architect). That does not mean there isn't a long future and plenty of hay to be made.

If you want more job growth, then you'll have to gradually move to the world of business analytics rather than web analytics and into business intelligence roles in IT. Both of these areas provide individual contributor title growth, and easier switches to other leadership roles should you show promise.

Business Individual Contributor

If you are an analyst today, then you are likely in an individual contributor role on the business side.

If you are a web analyst in IT, the best career move you could make for yourself is to a marketing or business function. A strong analyst role in IT is tough to achieve because there is so much emphasis on being a good little reporting squirrel.

Roles for you on the business side in this category include senior analyst, internal evangelist, single point of contact (SPOC) for chief marketing officer (CMO), and central business liaison.

In the client world, a business individual contributor can report to anyone from a director to the CMO. Your job is heavily business focused—understanding various businesses and their strategies and providing über-analysis, providing cross-functional analysis, creating management dashboards, or administering the rollout of Yahoo! Web Analytics across 90 business sites.

In some rare cases, you can become the internal analytics champion; I had the privilege of doing this for a while. You'll have to be good at your analytics *game*, but perhaps more important, you must be a strong businessperson—an MBA or *strategic* type. You work with VPs, CMOs, and senior leaders, and you identify measurement strategies for their impossible-to-answer questions. As the champion, you pull your organization up by the bootstraps, and the effort is quite gratifying.

A business individual contributor in a vendor world may be a product manager for the analytics product or for certain features. You might also be a professional services rep (sorry, "strategic solutions consultant"). You may also be responsible for the analysis of the vendor's own website and marketing campaigns.

Career Prospects

Except for small companies, you have lots of room to grow in this role. However, you must be a very strong businessperson. You must understand the ecosystem, business strategy, and Web Analytics 2.0 measurement strategies. You should be a smooth talker (you know, an *effective communicator*). A deep understanding of statistics and advanced math is helpful though not mandatory. JavaScript-hacking skills are optional.

If your strength really is in a technical area, see the previous role or the next one because you won't find success as easily in a business role.

Salary Prospects

Salary prospects in this business position range from $70,000 to $120,000 with client companies, though not so much with vendors. From my humble experience, less than 10 percent of people in our field truly have the skills for a business role to rise beyond the analyst or senior analyst title. If you are one of those 10 percent, then congratulations.

Long-Term Job Title Growth

As an individual contributor on the business side, you are afforded a lot more flexibility. You could be promoted to internal consultant on business analytics projects (beyond web analytics). If you excel in an individual capacity, you can even switch to a leadership role, such as team management, or you may tackle other complex ventures for a company, such as creating a *data strategy* or becoming the chief privacy officer.

On the vendor side as well you'll have many opportunities to be promoted and grow, though they might not be as numerous as in a company role (simply because vendors don't really need that much analytical horsepower). You could switch to a *professional consultant* role, in which case you'll work with other companies on behalf of your vendor employer.

Technical Team Leader

Roles in the category of technical team leader might include manager of analytics implementation, senior manager of website analytics, or group manager of web operations reporting. In the early genesis of web analytics, this role was a lot more prominent in companies. The shift to JavaScript-based ASP solutions caused a shift of web analytics to the business side. It also eliminated the need for a large IT staff to support web analytics (since the technical heavy lifting happens outside the company).

For example, seven years ago I first took over web analytics at my company. A four-person IT team supported the process of running Webtrends on the company's server log files and churned out 200 reports. The shift to an ASP-based solution meant only one job remained for a senior technical individual contributor. The other jobs evolved or were replaced with people who did analysis.

With the shift to ASP-based solutions, most companies will not have a large enough technical team dedicated to web analytics to require a senior technical team leader role. If the role exists, then the technical team leader will usually report to a director. In some companies, you can carve out a nice technical team lead career in a web analytics team in marketing.

A vendor probably has more technical team lead opportunities. Here you can manage the technical aspects of the analytics product or manage the technical army of consultants who work with clients.

This role requires an ability to leave behind your lone-ranger mentality and the deep-rooted habit of doing all the technical stuff yourself. It is harder for technically oriented people to blossom into people managers, but that's what you sign up for as a technical team leader. You must be comfortable with losing some of your awesome hacker skills as your leadership and delegation skills mature.

Career Prospects

If your company uses an ASP-based solution (for example, Google Analytics, XiTi, Unica), then the aforementioned limitations will impact how far your career as a technical team leader can go. In all except very large companies, such a role may not even be an option.

Some companies have in-house, hosted analytics solutions that may require a robust technical team. The opportunities are few, but you can have a role as web analytics technical team leader that will last a while.

As a team leader, you will live or die on your ability to inspire and motivate people, not on your ability to write code or keep up systems. If you are a technical team leader, then your people skills more than anything else will limit how much you can grow.

Salary Prospects

Salary prospects for a technical team leader range from $50,000 to $100,000.

Long-Term Job Title Growth

Promotions for a technical team leader will be limited if your company uses an ASP-based model. And remember, ASP is not just for web analytics; it now applies to testing, behavior targeting, surveys, and more, further reducing the need for companies to keep large technical teams in-house.

For in-house implementations or data warehouse extensions, you can expect nice growth. You may run into natural ceilings if you stick with web analytics, but you can break through those by moving to technical leadership roles in CRM, supply chain, or ERP.

Good technical team leaders are hard to find; if you have awesome technical skills today and you are willing to grow your people management skills, you will be adored. If you are a technical team leader, stay with analytics roles as long as you can grow and then switch to another arena.

Business Team Leader

When people think of making more money in web analytics, they think of working as a business team leader. While wanting this job is fine, you should go through the Avinash Kaushik Web Analytics Career Introspection Guide first to ensure that what you want is what you are good at.

Roles in this category include senior manager of web analytics, director of web research and analytics, and team lead for Coremetrics reporting. If you work in a pure online business, then you might even see the occasional VP of business analytics.

This role in a company setting increasingly reports to a senior director, a VP, or, in companies that get it, the CMO. Ideal candidates are supreme analysis ninjas with streaks of good leadership skills. They are motivators, inspire confidence, are inherently unselfish, and can charm the pants off senior management.

I cannot overstate this enough: ideally you have grown from a reporting squirrel to an analysis ninja, but your hardcore technical skills are vastly overrated in a business team leader role, where you must inspire and lead.

A business team leader, in a pure web analytics fashion, is less necessary in a vendor setting. Vendors need to sell. However, you might be hired to analyze nedstat.com or unica.com for internal use. Or you might find work as a business lead for the $300/hour professional services division.

Career Prospects

You have lots of room to grow as a business team leader because web analytics has become a more serious sector for many companies. Numerous companies recognize that a tool that costs half a million dollars is worth squat, as are hundreds of reports floating around the company. These companies are urgently rethinking their tool strategy and looking to put solid leaders in charge of analytics. The long-term prospects look very positive.

Your limitation as a business team leader is whether you can truly execute on Web Analytics 2.0 and move beyond clickstream.

Salary Prospects

Salary prospects for a business team leader can range from $90,000 to more than $170,000. Strong leaders with analytical minds are the rarest of the rare in corporate America. If you are good, then you have no limits.

Long-Term Job Title Growth

Your ability to get promoted depends a bit on your company size. In medium to large companies, you might tap out at director or senior director. If you are in a large or multinational company, you may reach VP.

In either case, if you are good at your job, you can shift to a role as a business function leader or consider other corporate roles. It is reasonable to say that if you have strong business skills and superior competency with data, then there is no real limit to how high you can go.

Figure 13.1 summarizes the four roles and shows a handy matrix that you can use as part of your decision-making process.

	Individual Contributor	Team Leader
Business	Career: * * * * Salary: $35k–$120k+ Title: * * *	Career: * * * * * Salary: $90k–$170k+ Title: * * * * *
Technical	Career: * * * Salary: $40k–$100k+ Title: * *	Career: * * Salary: $50k–$100k+ Title: * *

Figure 13.1 Analytics career paths and growth possibilities

Please consider the salary data in the matrix as a general guide. The numbers will be very different depending on your company, the business, and its location. Use those factors, and other data, to compare the information in each box.

Cultivating Skills for a Successful Career in Web Analysis

Anyone who wants to cultivate web data analysis skills will benefit from the information in this section. From marketers who want to understand their ROI better to a usability expert who wants to use quantitative data to help create better qualitative analyses—you will acquire practical information.

I am often asked what skills are required to be good at analyzing web data. This is a tough question to answer because there are many paths to nirvana. But in this section I'll offer specific ways in which you can develop skills that will help you, regardless of the actual path you take.

In this book I have already covered the important *intangibles* of analytics, such as being comfortable with incomplete data, truly embracing multiplicity, accepting that a perfect answer never exists, and realizing change is the only constant on the Web. These intangibles are the real key to your success. Without the right mental model, nothing else matters.

That said, here are some *tangibles* that you can focus on to develop superior analytical skills.

Do It: Use the Data

You can't be a great analyst if you don't put this book down, get in the mud, and wrestle the data pig. Sure, you'll get dirty, but there is absolutely no other way to learn.

Much of what you learn in school or university education is theory. Your courses are taught by well-intentioned people, but the real world is ever evolving, complicated, and messy.

Even if you already have a Master's or a PhD in web analytics, your real journey as an awesome analyst only starts when you get out in the real world.

I often recommend that future analysts find a nonprofit, perhaps one whose services are near and dear to your heart, and volunteer to help implement a website analytics solution and analyze that data. Nonprofits are very difficult to analyze; you have no Order Now buttons, and you often get little guidance with Goals and Outcomes. You'll be working in the deep end of analytics, yet with every hour you spend on that data, you'll learn a ton about yourself and about web analytics. Any work that you produce will help them do their part to change the world, and it will give you tangible, real-world experience.

Get Experience with Multiple Tools

You have not worked with web analytics until you have fairly deep experience with three or four different tools. The reason is simple. Each tool in our world comes with a unique set of frustrations, from the way code is implemented to the way the tool won't segment unless you have predefined "evars" and "sprops" and user-defined variables up front.

If you use multiple tools, then you will learn more than what buttons to press to get what reports; you'll learn how messy the world of web data really is. Let me hasten to add that when I say multiple tools, I don't just mean limiting your experience to multiple clickstream tools like Google Analytics, Omniture, or Unica's Affinium NetInsight. I really mean multiple tools that cover the complete spectrum of Web Analytics 2.0.

Get deep experience using Compete, Webmaster Tools, iPerceptions's 4Q, FeedBurner, PercentMobile, Google Website Optimizer, or TwitterFriends. You'll stretch your brain and learn how these tools can liberate you from the limitations of website clickstream data. You will find better answers to your questions.

Play in the Real World

Far too often we allow our jobs to limit our education and experience: *"All I know is ecommerce because that is all my company does."* Or, *"All I know is lead gen because that's my world."*

These excuses are extremely corrosive and sadly indicate how we allow our environment to limit our full potential and stunt our professional growth.

Your company will rarely give you the time to truly learn and grow. But the world around you is always changing and growing. If you don't keep pace, you go stale. So, you need to step out and take charge of your own education.

Here is a small portfolio of ideas you can use to ensure that you have the best education possible about data-driven decision making—regardless of the level of support you get from your organization.

Web Analytics Education

My own education about web analytics was transformed after I started my blog. The total cost was $65 ($5 to buy a domain and $5 a month to host it with an ISP). A few simple posts per month got me a few thousand page views per month. That was more than enough for a learning platform—a place where I could implement web analytics tools and play with real-world data.

In the last few years I have implemented at least 25 analytics tools on my blog. I have learned about implementation, customizing data capture, data analysis, and tracking challenges.

Experimenting with different tools on your own blog means your company can't limit your ability to learn. You are in charge of your own destiny; you control whether you stay fresh or go stale.

If starting a blog is too much, then grab your dad's business site or ask a non-profit to let you analyze their site. Beg your "social media god" brother-in-law for access to his blog or media presence so you can do analysis.

Beyond a Web Analytics Education

It is eternally frustrating to me that *web analysts* limit their education to Omniture, Webtrends, or Google Analytics. Why not get really smart about search engine optimization analytics?

Your company has a SEO team who won't let you in? No worries. Claim your blog in Webmaster Tools from Google and Microsoft. Log into the tools, check out all the wonderful reports, and educate yourself about the data that is missing from Site Catalyst yet absolutely key to understanding SEO performance.

Want to get smart about competitive intelligence? Don't wait for your boss to give you access. Log into Compete, Google Insights for Search, and Google's AdPlanner, and learn about psychographic and demographic audience segmentation for free!

All of my A/B and multivariate testing education came from using Google Website Optimizer on the website of a nonprofit that I work closely with. They got more donations, and I got a valuable education. Win-win.

Online Advertising Education

A few years back the company I worked for did no display advertising and did not use AdSense. So, I implemented display ads in my RSS feeds and implemented AdSense on my blog. I got an education worth its weight in gold by working in the real world.

You can read blogs about online marketing or attend presentations at popular conferences on those topics. But the pain of actually implementing ads and working with AdSense teaches you tangible lessons. You learn the challenge of merging the data sets and trying to reconcile first-party and third-party cookies.

You do not learn theory. You get real-world practice. And you can do it all on your own; you don't need permission from anyone.

Social Media Analytics Education

Last year I read about a new tool to measure Twitter. I visited the tool and punched in some names, and I quickly concluded that the tool was fatally flawed. So, I started a Twitter account to learn about this fledgling social medium and its potential impact on influence and marketing.

After three months of committed participation, I finally understood what made the medium unique, how to define success, how to measure it, and, most important, how to ignore the crap metrics floating around it.

My dedicated time and effort produced two powerful Outcomes:

- I learned a lot about online measurement in all its forms.
- I stay on the cutting edge of the web evolution.

In the same vein, my Flickr, YouTube, FriendFeed accounts exist as conversation channels and because I want to learn, from experience, how best to measure them.

The Bottom Line on Online Marketing and Analytics Education

Don't let your web analytics vendor or your employer limit your education or your potential. Don't let their business tactics and restrictions make you yet another analyst who can't survive a real-world interview. Stay current and relevant by controlling your own experience and education.

You will add value to your current employer by being smarter than you are supposed to be, and if you and I ever sit for an interview, we can have a fun conversation!

What are you going to do today? What is one new task you can add to your education in the next three months?

Become a Data Capture Detective

Web analytics is a mystery, not a puzzle. Puzzles have a factual answer waiting to be found. Mysteries rarely do; furthermore, mysteries require judgment and assessment of uncertainties surrounded by too much information. Therefore, an analyst should be a *detective*—someone comfortable looking through lots of data and focusing on areas rich in the type of information that will yield insights. An analyst should be someone who can take seemingly disparate pieces of information and form a hypothesis about possible connections.

The best analysts have a deep technical side, in the sense that they possess an understanding of JavaScript tags, URLs, parameters, redirects, and web pages. They are better able to answer this question: *"How does the data get collected, and then how it is interpreted by the analytics tool?"*

To see practical examples of how important it is to know how data is collected and interpreted, go through Chapter 8. You'll notice that a competitive intelligence tool can be gold or garbage, not because of the reports it provides but because of how data is collected. This knowledge applies to your testing tools, to your qualitative tools, to your ad server, and to everything else you'll do.

Before you use the data, ask how it's collected. Then ask again three more times until you get the right answer.

Rock Math: Learn Basic Statistics

We have all come to analytics from different backgrounds, often with unconventional experiences. This is a good thing. But often we are all missing one key arrow from our quiver: basic knowledge of statistics.

I highly recommend getting a solid grounding in basic statistics. Great analysts know how to leverage the awesome power of statistics, such as leveraging statistical significance (http://zqi.me/akstat) and statistical control limits (http://zqi.me/akctrl). Also, traditional clickstream analysis is becoming less insightful because the complexity of the Web and customer behavior increases every day. For this reason, I recommend a focus on customer experience and on experimentation and testing. To truly exploit these approaches for your business, you need to be good at statistics.

Survey analysis tools frequently use complex multivariate regression models to identify actionable insights. These models bring hard-core quantitative power to the qualitative realm of survey responses. You need to understand how these models work.

Likewise, if you do multivariate or A/B testing, then you need to know the basics of statistics as you analyze the data and make decisions based on when the result set has reached the desired confidence levels.

You don't need a PhD in statistics, but being familiar with statistics will greatly enhance your career in web analytics. The wonderful thing about statistics is that the training will teach you how to think analytically and look at every problem differently.

Ask Good Questions

Remember, as an analyst, you have access to a large number of tools and a ton of data. You will not perish because of a lack of either, but you will perish if you cannot ask the right questions.

Here are some examples to get your juices flowing:

- When your boss asks for a report, politely ask what question she wants answered. Then identify the right data to answer that question. Always ask "Why?"

- For every metric that you report, ask the question "So what?" three times. Each question will typically provide an answer that raises another question. Ask "So what?" again. If at the end of the third question you don't get a recommendation for action, you are using the wrong metric.

- We covered this earlier, but always ask "How was this data collected?"

- Never accept, or show, a top 10 report or a static dashboard. Always ask, and show, "What's changed?" When you go on that quest, you'll realize the difficulty of the task and the incredible power of the answers.

- When faced with a HiPPO's opinion, ask "So, your hypothesis is *xyz*, right? Can I create a test based on that?"

- Your best friend is this question: "And how is that important?"

Good analysis provides good answers. Be curious.

Work Closely with Business Teams

Analytics originally grew up in the IT team. Therefore, in many companies, the analytics team runs on a service model: *"Give us a request, we will fulfill it in three weeks, and you'll have your report."* You can see how that approach is counterproductive.

The service model is suboptimal because it shows a lack of understanding for business strategy and for *tribal knowledge.* You can fix both issues by working closely with the business team. You can attend their staff meetings. You can set up recurring meetings with your key stakeholders. You can join business-planning sessions. You can ask for access to intranet web pages and databases where current marketing programs are stored. You can make 10 percent of your time available to answer ad hoc business questions.

When you gather these details, you'll know the top three priorities of your business. This can help you focus and project a clear line of sight between the work you do and what's important to the company.

By participating in planning meetings and knowing the marketing calendar, you'll know everything going on in your company that applies to your web analytics data. No longer will you run and report your wonderful insight of a spike in search data only to be told, *"Yes, we know; we just spent $1 million on a paid search campaign on Bing."* If you already know about the campaign, then you can do segmented analysis and report performance specific to the campaign.

By working closely with the business team and outside your analytics/data silo, you gain key knowledge for effective analysis. And you endear yourself to people who matter (which is very important at salary review time).

Learn Effective Data Visualization and Presentation

You might think that well-crafted Excel reports and custom segments that yield insights will drive action by your employer. Sorry. Your ability to sell and convince others drives action. I cannot tell you how often great work is neglected because the analyst did not visualize or present it effectively.

The most effective reports and presentations are simple, direct, and visualize data that asks the right questions and supplies answers. Invest time in training yourself about data visualization techniques. If you need inspiration, visit the *New York Times* Visualization Lab (http://zqi.me/nytvlab).

Figure 13.2 is one of my favorite examples of data visualization, Death & Taxes by Jess Bachman. Just think how hard it is to make sense of the U.S. federal budget. Yet Jess has done a magnificent job of pulling it all together in a poster, with a pinch of creativity and lots of patience.

Even at this tiny size you can see that the government spends half its budget on the Department of Defense (all of the left side and the big circles on the bottom right!). Everything else (Health and Human Services, NASA, Education, and Energy) are the small bubbles in the middle and top right.

Figure 13.2 Annual U.S. federal budget visualized

Consider the powerful insights you get when you can explain in one quick shot something as fuzzy as the federal budget, which is $1.421 trillion for 2010:

Military/national security: 63%

Nonmilitary/national security: 37%

Oh, and that big giant circle you see in the background? That's the national debt. It is so huge it barely fits on the poster (a message in itself). You can see more at `http://zqi.me/jessba`.

We can't all be Jess. But we can be better than the tables and graphs we create today from analytics tools and Microsoft Excel. Improve your presentation skills, and your effort will pay off huge dividends. Sure, you have to present to only eight people sitting around a conference room table or maybe just to your CMO in his office. But you need to be able to communicate, energize, and evangelize all in one shot.

Take classes in effective presentation skills. Watch YouTube videos of every great speaker in history, and take notes. Learn how to be great at PowerPoint.

Stay Current: Attend Free Webinars

Are you tired of hearing me tell you how much the Web and web data change every day? They really do. A truly effective way to stay current with the latest and greatest, and get tips on new types of analyses, is to attend a webinar.

Nearly all vendors offer free webinars. Omniture in particular has done a great job of sharing useful information. You'll find Omniture's webinars at `http://zqi.me/omnedu`. Most industry organizations such as SEMPO (`http://zqi.me/sempo1`) and the WAA provide regular webinars to their members, often for free. Use these webinars first, and make it a goal to attend two a month.

Organizations like Marketing Profs (`http://zqi.me/mktprofs`) and my startup, Market Motive (`http://zqi.me/mmotive`), also provide online webinars and trainings. The quality is very high, but you must pay or be a member to attend.

Stay Current: Read Blogs

If you don't have an RSS feed reader, then it is possible that all your information is old. Most of the current knowledge about anything in the world, from cooking to analytics, is now contained in blogs. I spend at least 10 hours per week reading blogs to ensure that I am up to speed with the latest evolutions online.

There is infinite information out there, and you need to be discerning and choose the highest-quality stuff. You must pick the right blog to read and ignore ineffectual blogs. I know. It's tough.

To get you started, here is a list of quality blogs that are relevant to our ecosystem:

Junk Charts (`http://zqi.me/junkcharts`) Kaiser's blog is one of my favorites. He takes apart some of the most commonly used data charting and visualization techniques and provides his take on better alternatives.

Kaizen Analytics (`http://zqi.me/mnotte`) Michael Notté currently works at Toyota Europe, and he shares wonderful insights from his experience in the weeds as a practitioner.

Dónde está Avinash cuando se le necesita? (`http://zqi.me/gmvera`) Gemma Muñoz Vera's Spanish blog on analytics is so good that I read it using Google Translate even though I know that some of the translation is not optimal! Gemma works at a bank and is another rare practitioner.

Web Analytics in China (`http://zqi.me/wachina`) Sidney Song's Chinese blog covers all elements of the web analytics space in China and contains numerous real-world insights.

Web Analytics Inside (`http://zqi.me/taden`) Timo Aden's German blog covers the broad world of web analytics as well as includes tips and insights on effectively using Google Analytics.

Trending Upward (`http://zqi.me/shelbyt`) Shelby Thayer currently works at a university, and her blog contains her daily experience, frustrations, and deep insights of how to use analytics for a higher-education website.

Non-Line Blogging (`http://zqi.me/dhughes`) David Hughes is a digital marketing consultant and is a source of some of my best learnings in the space of multichannel, email, and other marketing techniques.

Seth Godin's blog (`http://zqi.me/sethgo`) Seth has one of the top-ranked blogs in the world. He is thought provoking, pithy, and full of brilliant insights. If I could read only one blog in the world, it would be Seth's.

Analytics Talk (`http://zqi.me/cutroni`) Justin Cutroni is the author of the book *Google Analytics Short Cuts*, and his blog covers all things advanced Google Analytics.

Marketing Productivity blog (http://zqi.me/jimnovo) From his site: "Jim Novo is an interactive customer retention, defection, and loyalty expert with nearly 25 years of experience generating exceptional returns on customer marketing program investments." Need I say more?

Visual Revenue (http://zqi.me/dennism) Dennis Mortensen is the director of Data Insights at Yahoo!; his blog covers all things Yahoo! Web Analytics.

ClickEquations blog (http://zqi.me/cqblog) Craig Danuloff shares his insights and takes search engines to task on this blog. If you want to be up to speed on all things search, or just listen to some of Craig's conspiracy theories, then this is the place to be.

FutureNow's Marketing Optimization blog (http://zqi.me/grokdot) My friend Bryan Eisenberg's team writes this blog. It covers everything from analytics to ecommerce to testing to really anything that is connected to improving websites.

Google Analytics blog (http://zqi.me/gablog) The official Google Analytics blog is updated frequently with tips, videos, helpful how-to posts, and lots more.

Omniture blog (http://zqi.me/omblog) Omniture has one of the best vendor blogs. It covers a very diverse ecosystem, from analytics to search to testing to ecommerce optimization. You should read it even if you don't have Omniture.

These 15 blogs give you insights into a wide spectrum of knowledge. You'll find my blog at www.kaushik.net/avinash.

I want to close this section with one last bonus skill that I think is hugely underrated: common sense. We live in a complex, data-rich world. There really is no limit to how complicated we can make our metrics and analytical approaches. Keep your "common sense applicator" handy, and don't forget to apply the Occam's Razor.

An Optimal Day in the Life of an Analysis Ninja

Career planning. Check. Cultivating skills. Check. Ongoing education. Check.

In this section, I'll cover the last piece of the *how can I have a successful career in web analysis* puzzle.

Perhaps the most important thing you can do with your career is ensure that you take your finite time and focus on activities that will add value to your company.

First some context: I suspect that you are not, nor do you aspire to be, a report writer, and I suspect you have not just started in analytics. The distribution of effort I recommend here is for analysts who have been doing reporting for about a year and now want to kick their career up a notch. There's nothing wrong with being a report writer; we all start there. We just don't want to stay there forever.

Figure 13.3 shows how an analysis ninja should spend the workweek in order to maximize opportunities for massive success.

Figure 13.3 Distribution of activities for an analysis ninja

Let's look at each element in detail:

20% reporting Although I wish you could escape reporting completely, sadly you can't. You must still do reporting, but your reporting efforts should evolve to focus on custom reports in support of your company's strategic objectives.

On the bright side, reporting is a great way to keep in touch with reality.

20% analyzing acquisition strategies You want to know what your company is doing to attract traffic to your website. Are they using search, affiliate marketing, banners, or email marketing? What else?

Your company spends considerable money on these efforts, and anything you can do to change, adapt, or improve them through data will permanently endear you to your peers and management. Your effort analyzing acquisition strategies yields dual benefits. Your insights reduce cost, and they help improve ROI. Your company makes money on both sides.

20% on-site customer experience Use a mix of clickstream and qualitative methodologies to analyze the customer experience on your website.

If you are not reading open-text voice of customer responses from surveys, sitting in on a usability study, or executing a remote usability study (now as cheap as $10 per participant!), then you are not focused on customer experience. For more actionable ideas, see Chapter 6.

There is no better way to victory than making your customers happy.

20% staying plugged into the context Most analysts suffer because of a lack of context. The company puts you away in a corner with an analytics tool and expects you to produce earth-shattering insights. That never works, which is why I stress "context is queen" in Chapter 11.

As an analyst, you need to use 20 percent of your time staying plugged into what else is going on in the marketing organization, on the website in terms of operational changes, and with senior management (anyone higher than your boss) to know their strategic pain points and imagine how web data can solve them.

Web analysis is not a silo, and every analyst needs to be plugged into the *tribal knowledge* so that they can look at the right data and provide relevant insights.

10% explore new strategic options You always want to move the ball forward in your company. Therefore, you should spend a chunk of time experimenting with new and different ways to move your programs forward.

Think testing, competitive intelligence analysis, multichannel integration, and usability. If you work alone, say in a small company, implementing these options can be difficult (especially with 10 percent of your time). But think of small ways to show that web analytics creates better customer experiences and a strategic advantage through data.

10% bathroom breaks, email, oh, and lunch! I am generous, aren't I?

I realize that each company is unique and each analyst is unique. But I hope that this picture provides a semblance of universal guidance for anyone who has the word *analyst* in their title.

Do a quick back-of-the-envelope summary of how you spend your day or week and then compare it to this picture. What do you find? Now go fix it.

Hiring the Best: Advice for Analytics Managers and Directors

Remember the 10/90 rule from Chapter 2? It outlined all the reasons that investing in people has a far bigger impact on your company than investing in tools. So, you have signed on to correct the 90/10 ratio in your company. You post a job. Lots of resumes arrive. Now you need to ensure that you pick the right person for the analytics generalist or analytics specialist job.

I am not going to cover the typical skills that you might find listed in an analytics job description. That's because although some of those skills might be helpful—such as experience with tools, spreadsheets, or JavaScript—the lack of those skills does not mean that the candidate will be unsuccessful. After two weeks of training, any human can click the right buttons in a tool.

True success will not come from clicking the right buttons; rather, it will come from bringing the right approach to the table: an analytical mind and a *web aptitude*.

Key Attributes of Great Analytics Professionals

The complex organism of the Web demands a stunning amount of flexibility from people who must analyze it. Web analysis requires an atypical ability to let go of past experiences and learned behaviors quickly so as to invent new, appropriate solutions.

The following traits count in the making of a great analyst:

The person actually *gets* the Web. In their blood the candidate is a web being who marvels at the beauty of the Web; they use it, they love it, they *get* it (critical if they are ever to *walk in the shoes of* your website visitors and make sense of all the clicks!).

The candidate has mental flexibility. The prospective analyst is an inherently flexible being who is open to new tools, metrics, mental models, and more. In fact, they have experience proving that, at every new job, they ditched the old junk and moved an employer to the latest optimal mind-set—not technology but mind-set. (It is critical for someone to recognize the evolution of the Web and understand the newest measurement opportunities.)

Entrenched mind-sets will not win the battles of web analytics.

Change will not kill them. This attitude is different from mental flexibility. Human beings love the known; most fear change, and a few can't see opportunity because they can't or won't change. Yet for the foreseeable future, the only constant in the web measurement space is change—as you build out a team, you want people who are ready for change.

They are curious. An ideal candidate constantly tries new approaches; you can see evidence of curiosity in their experiments with the latest and greatest in social media, or even in media channels that look like they will fail. Failing is OK. Not trying is not OK.

Prefer curiosity over intelligence, if you must choose.

They possess critical thinking skills. From Wikipedia, "Critical thinking consists of mental processes of discernment, analyzing, and evaluating. It includes all possible processes of reflecting upon a tangible or intangible item in order to form a solid judgment that reconciles scientific evidence with common sense."

You want an analysis ninja, right? Not a report writer? You can find critical thinking in a guy flipping burgers at McDonald's or doing advanced statistical analysis. Look for it.

In a nutshell, I can teach anyone to click buttons in Omniture or Webtrends. I can teach anyone the definition of Bounce Rate in Nedstat or XiTi. It takes a few weeks, but I can teach you how to create labels in ClickTracks or segment data in Google Analytics. But, I cannot teach someone any of the previous five traits.

Experienced or Novice: Making the Right Choice

After rounds of interviews, many of us must choose between a seasoned analyst with a lot of experience in the field or a freshly minted college grad. Which candidate will bring the maximum bang for the buck? Hidden in that question is the assumption that the experienced candidate will be expensive and the college grad will work for peanuts. The answer of course is, *it depends*!

In my decision-making process, I evaluate based on one specific criteria: *Does the company have a strong web analytics program or a person who can provide mentoring and thought leadership?*

If the answer is yes, then you can hire the smart graduate and teach him the new mind-set of Web Analytics 2.0. If the answer is no, then you are better off paying more and getting someone with the latest thinking and experience. This person can get a grip on your current analytics strategies and point your company in the right direction. When she has established credibility through success, perhaps she can hire the young folks.

If you don't have someone who can provide guidance and a strategic execution plan, then any college grad will wither. It is important to choose the right person at the right time.

The Single Greatest Test in an Interview: Critical Thinking

In the attributes section, I listed the importance of critical thinking skills. Unlike other attributes, critical thinking can be hard to test. Or perhaps I should say people tend to test for it in the wrong way. For example, many companies are famous for giving out puzzles and riddles during interviews and asking for solutions. That is a cute technique. I have rarely see success at those puzzles as any predictor of future success.

To help spark your creativity, let me share my favorite test for critical thinking: give the candidate a real business problem that needs critical, analytical thinking, and ask them to solve it. It could be a numbers (web analytics) problem. It could be a competitive problem. It could be a page-level problem. But the problem should be real for your company or a company you know.

The scenario is a little unfair because you will know more about the problem than the candidate. But you are not looking for the perfect answer. You are interested in the following:

- The solution the candidate comes up with
- How the candidate thinks

The latter is perhaps even more important than the former. You want to see creativity and a surprise in some facet of the solution. If the candidate is a solid critical thinker, he should come up with an interesting solution, an approach you might not have considered, if for no other reason than you are too close to the problem.

Because you are in analytics, you want part of the solution to involve numbers (how to look at data to solve the problem, qualitative or quantitative—it does not have to involve hardcore numbers).

When the candidate provides the solution, you want to push back a bit, regardless of the answer. Throw a curve ball, try to say something totally silly, or point out a flaw. You want to see whether you can influence the candidate to change his answer. You want to see if he can defend his original answer (most people fail here), give a rationale, or ask clarifying questions. You want to see how fast he can think and what happens if he is backed into a corner.

If the candidate is a critical thinker, she'll think uniquely and, for lack of a better word, survive. In fact, she will love the challenge and reply with specifics and not ambiguous FUD. It is amazing how quickly you can cut through to see a candidate's content-free big words, lack of thinking capability, or lack of experience.

Even if the candidate knows that you will be testing him, it is nearly impossible for him to "prepare" for it. For the most part, a candidate's answer to a reality-based problem will reveal his true nature in the position.

Go try it and let me know how it goes (feedback@webanalytics20.com).

Tip: There is one more reason for pushing back politely. You are also looking for a certain personality type. Most interviews are stacked against a candidate. By pushing them a bit, very respectfully and in a very dignified, nonchallenging way, you try to assess their personality type.

Can't be a push over. Can't have a "report writer mind-set." Can't be "pushed" too easily to change opinions. Can stand up and defend. Can't make stuff up. Can't get flustered. Can say "I have no idea" at the right moment. Can give a complete answer, even if it's wrong.

HiPPOs, Ninjas, and the Masses: Creating a Data-Driven Culture

14

I'll close the book by covering the most difficult topic of all: culture.

In a channel with so much data, organizations barely scratch the surface of transforming themselves into data-driven entities.

You can accelerate your company's transformation. You can make changes in your everyday life—in how you approach data, present analyses, enthuse your peers, communicate, and, yes, even how you embarrass people.

This chapter covers strategies and practical approaches to overcome the penultimate barrier that stands before you.

Chapter Contents

Changing how people think and how companies behave is difficult because it is not about being rational, presenting data, or hoping one day management will magically see your way. In my experience, changing how people think is about digging below the surface, understanding the root cause behind *faith-based initiatives*, and, most of all, understanding human psychology.

People sometimes don't use data because they are afraid of how it will reflect on them. Or they may have always worked a certain way and they don't want to change. Usually people want 100 percent certainty that data is accurate. More often than not, they just don't understand all the ways in which the world of marketing and influencing people has changed around them.

You should be aware of all these obstacles and other such *hidden* matters at your company. You need to identify and understand them, and then you must create a strategy to address them, even though that may not seem to be your job. It is. You can never *win* until you understand why your company makes largely *faith-based* decisions rather than *data-based* decisions.

In this chapter, you'll see unique solutions to addressing the issues I have identified below the surface—issues that address the root cause. You'll see some themes repeated in some of the sections; you should focus on those the most.

It is my fondest hope that you'll be the evangelist, the champion, the *ninja* who will transform your company. Know that I am rooting for you!

Transforming Company Culture: How to Excite People About Analytics

If you can't get people excited, rabidly excited, about data and analytics, then really you have no place to go! In talking to marketers, sales folks, website owners, and management, you'll learn that they fear web analytics like climbing Mount Everest or that they believe it's useless, messy, and full of "dirty data."

Or often *web analytics* translates in people's minds as *counting hits*. People would rather pull off a fingernail than learn how to leverage their website data. This is all so sad because web analytics is like Angelina Jolie: it's sexy, it kicks butt, and it is a goodwill ambassador!

So, how do we get to a point where others in the organization are excited as well?

- Accept that web analytics might have less impact than it should. Once you accept that, then you can move on and do something about it.

- You can make incremental progress every hour and every day. Realize that it is hard to win an Olympic medal in swimming, but that should not scare anyone from learning to swim. There is a shallow end of the pool where you can get started and get better over time. In web analytics, it is suboptimal to go into a 15-month implementation and expect a massive payoff on day one.

- Get everyone in your organization more excited about using data by making it more appealing than pulling off fingernails. Attempt to convert them into raving data lunatics—people who will do anything to get their hands on data before making their next decision!

Follow the first two tips, and I will help you with last one.

Do Something Surprising: Don't Puke Data

You are undeniably smart. When you interact with a new team or get your first web analytics tool installed, your first tendency is to impress the marketers and decision makers with the quantity of data you have. You proceed to puke out data.

Reports go out. The adventurous amongst you might even export into Excel and send 16-tab spreadsheets along with the directions to heaven. Try to resist that.

Your decision makers expect you to overdose on data, and they are wary of data pukes. So, surprise them. Give them a gift—the gift of an answer. Have a conversation with someone who wants to talk to you, and listen. Ask these questions:

"Please tell me a little bit about your job…"

"What aspects of your life or job touch our website?"

"What's one question you wish you could get answered about our website, or what's one thing you could learn from our website Visitors?"

Now go back and answer one solitary question. Don't send a report. Call your decision maker, and tell him the answer. He'll be hooked after you do this once or twice.

Remember, you can't convince people by puking data out. You can't expect that *they'll figure it out*. Repeating things 16 times or moping about how *they don't get it* does not work. Smile, go have a conversation, and come back with an answer.

Start with Outcomes and Impact, Not Visits

Open any web analytics tool, and you see Visits and Visitors, Time on Site, Repeat Visits, and Pages staring back at you. And so you rush all those metrics out the door. You try to explain cookies and exits to your decision makers. You might as well be talking Sanskrit.

When you start your analysis, start by showing how wonderful web analytics is at measuring Outcomes, the reason for your website's existence. (Pick up tips and ideas from Chapter 5.)

Show your decision makers how much money your website is making, how many leads you got, and macro and micro Conversions. Show them how the site drives traffic to your retail stores. Decision makers understand these concepts. And they'll be hooked.

Then they'll ask:

"Where do these people come from?"

"Why is that only $14 million? What about all the great persuasive content we have?"

"Only 15 people out of 20 million checked out our store locator. Why do you think that is?" (Because the link is invisible!)

"Our 'pathetic' website generates more leads than all our salespeople combined?"

All the right questions!

In any job you'll be asked to provide *traditional web metrics*. But when you start with traditional metrics, your peers and HiPPOs cannot appreciate the power of web analytics or why it is important to listen to you. Avoid that false start.

Remember this: it's the outcomes, stupid.

Create Heroes and Role Models

It is really hard to convert an entire organization, whether you have 20 people or 20,000 people.

You need to find a willing partner in your company, a leader who will listen to you. I mean really listen. It does not matter whether they spend a lot of money or run the magnificent corporate site or a divisional micro site. But it must be someone who will allow you to tag the site correctly and consider your insights from data for implementation on the site. Then you must put your heart and soul and all your skills as an analysis ninja into finding actionable insights. Live and breathe their business. Make the decision maker an absolute hero through data-driven decision making.

Heroes rarely want to stay in their cubicle farm or corner office. They want to fly around and talk about their heroism. They want to brag. Let them tell your data story. Let them excite their peers. Let them show how they did it.

Other decision makers will get jealous and want to become heroes (or get a bigger bonus). They will ask the original hero how she got so smart. And all roads will point to you.

If You Want Excitement, Make It Fun!

So, perhaps not everyone thinks analytics is Angelina Jolie. But have you tried to make analytics sexy and fun? You have so many opportunities to make web analytics fun.

When you're trying to transform your corporate culture, do the second item in the list first; that is, try making analytics fun. It is always exciting to make money, improve conversions, and measure multichannel impact. Then try the rest of the items in the list.

Hold Contests

The first time I ran a multivariate test, I wanted everyone to be excited, so I held a contest. I charged $1 for entry and challenged the entrants to guess the percentage improvement in Conversion Rate.

Everyone wanted a piece of that contest. My testing team had 25 dollars before the test started! Guesses were all over the place: 5 percent and 20 percent and 9 percent. As soon as the test went live, everyone logged into the testing tool to check out the results, which gave me an opportunity to explain statistical significance! There were questions about why *B* was not winning or *D* or whatever they were rooting for.

It was a hoot. My peers learned about testing, and they learned that to have a huge impact on conversions, you need to create versions that are very different. They were surprised when the conversion in the test improved by only 0.75 percent.

The winner had guessed .65 percent and had been teased beforehand because it was such a low number. I was the winner. Of course, I put my winnings, $25, toward buying cookies for the office.

Here are some ideas for more contests:

- Hold a quarterly contest to see who can figure out the most useless metric on your dashboard.
- Give a prize to the marketer who figures out the most creative use of VOC or the department that logs the most actions taken.

People love to play, and they love to win. Tap into that psychology, and let your imagination soar.

Hold Internal Conferences

You don't need to go outside your company to learn and share. You can hold a half-day internal conference in your own company every quarter, where marketers come and show off their key knowledge to everyone else.

Find the biggest conference room you can (or book a conference room at a nearby hotel), mike up your internal company folks, have them do presentations, and let them teach. It is exciting—and an honor—for people to stand up, present, and teach. Oh, and don't forget to invite their bosses.

If you want to go all out, print shirts, or hand out a plaque to the presenters, something they can proudly display on their desk. Notice you also just made someone a hero.

Hold Office Hours

We often live in our caves. Requests come in via a ticketing system, they are prioritized, and Excel reports go out.

Each week you should set aside half a day where anyone can come and ask you and your team any question they want. Although this might not seem like much fun, you'll become more accessible, and people will know that when they want to learn, you are there.

Or schedule an hour where you invite marketers and decision makers to shout out questions, and you show them live, with Yahoo! Web Analytics or Webmaster Tools, how you can answer their questions on the spot.

Web analytics is exciting. It can be an amazing high when you figure out a new way to analyze the data or answer a real business problem. Go share some of your passion; it can be contagious.

Deliver Reports and Analyses That Drive Action

Earlier I covered a specific issue related to reporting: don't puke out data. But you have many more ways to make your decision makers cry with happiness at your reports or presentations.

In this section, I'll show you specific ideas to help you identify what makes for magnificent analysis. I will help you present your thoughts on data so you offer the best insights and drive the greatest action.

After you complete any set of analysis and before you present the data, apply the filters outlined in the following sections will ensure you send out gold.

The "What's Your Point?" Filter

When I read any *analysis*, the following questions and comments go through my mind:

- "What's your point?" Give me value, not data.
- Based on your point, "What do you want me to do?"
- If relevant, and usually only if asked, give me the data (and please don't make me think or have to compute 19 percent of 8,296 Visits!)

Remember, your report recipients want the answer to the first question the most. The answer drives action.

If there are any rivers of data in your reports, consider redoing your *analysis*. For example, if you lead with your key finding at the top of the report, it should be in the form of the biggest change or a simple text summary statement. Consider replacing your normal "Here are all the metrics we were asked to track" with "Here is the impact analysis on revenue and customer satisfaction in the last month."

Your senior decision makers want to make decisions. Look at your presentation, Excel spreadsheet, automated dashboard, and ask yourself the question, *"What's my point?"*

Bonus point: If you did a good job with the graph, you should not have to repeat in English underneath the graph what it is showing.

The Hard Tie to Business Outcomes

If you have learned anything in this book (or the earlier section!), then it is that you should be as obsessed with Outcomes as I am. Your data should easily link to revenue, leads, increased customer satisfaction, donations, ads clicked, task completion rate, and so on.

Your analysis must focus on clearly established business outcomes. If your boss or client has not set the Outcomes, then you must.

Present Multiple Perspectives: True Web Analytics 2.0

My first instinct when I receive analysis is to see whether the analyst used more than one data source.

Google Analytics and Omniture are great tools. You need them to answer the *what*. But you also need the *why?* and the *what else?* to get robust answers that have deeper customer and competitive insights. If you do not answer the latter questions with your analysis or if your data has no context from other sources, then you have not done enough work.

For example, if you show the traffic trends from search to your site, you should also include a line on the graph that shows your main competitor's traffic. Or when you show the Conversion Rate for your site, you should also show the Conversion Rate for your industry vertical. Either of those inclusions makes your report massively better.

You don't have to despair about the limits of company tools. You can get more data by using free services like Compete, Google Insights for Search, Trends for Website, or the Fireclick Index.

The Unböring Filter

The furniture store IKEA used this slogan as a part of its advertising campaigns: unböring.

Web analytics is not perceived as particularly exciting. Our huge piles of data do not help matters either. Yet we always do the same thing: we send out tables and graphs. Why not do something fun in your report, as in Figure 14.1? You could easily show the data in a table, but would it have the same impact?

Pest Control Category: Query Volume

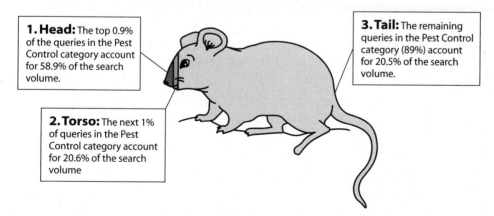

1. Head: The top 0.9% of the queries in the Pest Control category account for 58.9% of the search volume.

2. Torso: The next 1% of queries in the Pest Control category account for 20.6% of the search volume

3. Tail: The remaining queries in the Pest Control category (89%) account for 20.5% of the search volume.

"Head" terms are high volume but can be quite competitive.
"Tail" terms are lower volume but tend to be less competitive and to convert better.

Figure 14.1 Head, torso, tail analysis for pest control category

My friend Rachel Meyers created the brilliant slide in Figure 14.1. The client was a pest control company, and the data came from web search queries. Rachel used Photoshop to create the visual and even went so far as to measure the rat in pixels to ensure that the head, torso, and tail represented data to scale! The result was an unböring presentation of data that communicated the value proposition to the client effectively and engaged them in ways a table never could.

Write an essay. Make a quick video with a customer. Use a motion chart (http://zqi.me/mcharts). Be unböring.

Connecting Insights with Actual Data

In many presentations of analysis, the connection between the data and the insights derived from that data can be hard to see. We have all developed our own best practices and preferences, and hence we sometimes jump to making recommendations based on those practices and preferences rather than grounding our presentations in data.

Often I read advice like this: "Redesign the navigation." My first thought is why? Based on what? Or, "Internal search should be everywhere." Why? Surely, it is a best practice, but why for this site?

Tie your recommendations to the data on hand. Include your feelings in an appendix if you feel strongly. But make sure that every recommendation you make is supported by the data in the analysis.

The Expectations of Scale Filter

An audience imposes a differing set of expectations on different people. Willem is my boss, and you work for me. When Willem presents analysis, his audience expects it to be strategic, calculated, and chockfull of insights. Expectations might be lower for me, because I am just a cog in the wheel. I might get by with just nominal insights. Since you work for me, you'll exceed expectations if you simply answer audience questions with data they can interpret. I call these different levels *expectations of scale*.

The bigger you are, the more an audience expects from you: more insights, more rigor, more everything. Look at your rank. Does your analysis reflect the depth that your rank implies? It better.

Having Something Unique to Say

When you get in front of senior management or your biggest HiPPOs, do something that makes you stand out. Don't rely on text formatting or 3D pie charts—that approach has been done to death. Have something unique to say.

For example, everyone will report that a metric was 53 percent for keyword z and 56 percent for keyword q. But you can stand out by computing the statistical significance. Rather than just reporting the two numbers, you can show how much confidence your decision maker can have in those numbers.

Or in a real-world example, an analyst began her review by stating that she was leaving out a time period that could distort the data. Her decision showed an understanding of the data and the business.

You can try measuring the offline impact of online activity: it is a tough task, but it will make you stand out (see tips in Chapter 11).

Business life can be a contact sport; if you want to win, then you must have a unique value proposition (UVP). Never let analysis leave your computer without making sure that you have included unique information that will stand out.

Apply these recommendations to your reports and analyses, and you ensure that your work drives action. You don't have to apply all of them to every report. You'll probably apply the first few, and as business requirements get more complex, you will apply other approaches that work best.

Changing Metric Definitions to Change Cultures: Brand Evangelists Index

Web analysts rarely think deeply about the story we tell with our data. Yet we must consider the implications of data in a grander context, connect with business goals, and sometimes be bold enough to try to change company culture.

This is a story about a specific metric, Brand Evangelists Index, and my attempt to change a culture and set a higher bar for everyone in the company. It is my hope that you can apply the parable of the story to every metric you report.

Let's look at how changing the definition of a metric can impact a company's culture.

The Case and the Analysis

The data in question was survey data about a daylong conference for current and prospective customers. We had asked attendees to rate each presenter on a five-point scale, in answer to the question, "How satisfied were you with the presentation and content?"

You could get this kind of data from a free website survey, like 4Q from iPerceptions: "Based on today's visit, how would you rate your site experience overall?" Or you can use free page-level surveys from Get Satisfaction or Kampyle, using this question: "Please share your ratings for this page." In all of those cases, you can analyze how the content or website performed.

On the surface, performance does not seem to be a difficult problem to analyze. Figure 14.2 shows two common paths analysts take in reporting this data.

Sessions	Not At All Satisfied	Not Satisfied	Satisfied	Very Satisfied	Extremely Satisfied	1 Avg	2 Sat
Jonny Buckland	0	0	6	12	0	6.0	100%
Will Champion	0	1	2	14	1	5.7	94%
Chris Martin	0	0	0	3	15	6.0	100%
Guy Berryman	0	2	14	2	0	5.3	89%
Brian Eno	0	1	4	11	2	5.7	94%
Apple	0	0	7	8	3	6.0	100%

Figure 14.2 Computing scores for presenter performance

The most common choice seems to be this: just average it! The actual formula is to average the last three columns. When your boss eyeballs this report based on a simple average, she says, "Looks like everyone performed well today. Let's uncork the champagne."

But a more experienced analyst would look at the more traditional *satisfaction computation*. In that formula, you add the three ratings and divide that number by the total number of responses. For example, Jonny's performance is calculated: (6+12+0)/18.

The average, 6.0, is a number hanging in the air naked, without context, and hence it is hard to truly *get*. The percentage, 100 percent, on the other hand, has some context (100 is max!), and so an executive can *get it*.

Using the percentage, everyone does not get champagne. Jonny, Chris, and Apple get it because they did spectacularly well. Will and Brian get a hug, and Guy gets a handshake.

The Problem

You have two problems with your data here, one minor and one major. You saw the minor problem with Guy's case: percentages have a nasty habit of making some things look better than they are. Human beings seem to think anything over 75 percent is great. So, maybe we should not use percentages.

The major problem, however, is that this kind of analysis:

- Rewards meeting expectations
- Does not penalize mediocrity

Both problems are signs of business as usual—a *let's get our paycheck* attitude. Why is it acceptable to simply *meet expectations*? But that's what including the Satisfied rating in the metrics calculation does. Accepting a rating of Satisfied essentially translates to this: "As long as we don't stink, let's accept that as success."

And no one should be let off the hook for earning a Dissatisfied rating. That's what happened here because the scores from the Not At All Satisfied and Not Satisfied columns are not included in your metric's calculation.

Every business should try to be great. Every interaction should aim to create delight. We should measure and reward people based on those high standards because we can create *brand evangelists* through outstanding customer interactions.

Our customers love us because we work hard and because we set such a high bar for ourselves. That will translate into customers going out and telling others about us. They become our brand evangelists.

But that's not what our current metric is measuring or valuing.

The Solution

Although influencing the company culture was not a part of my job description, I changed the formula to try to do just that. To measure the correct values, I made two major changes and one minor change to the calculation:

- Partly inspired by the Net Promoter concept, I discarded the Satisfied rating.

- I added a penalty for any negative ratings (even the slightly negative).

- I indexed the results for optimal communication.

I called the new metric Brand Evangelists Index (BEI), and I used the following formula:

{ [(Very Satisfied + Extremely Satisfied) − (Not Satisfied + Not At All Satisfied)] ÷ Number of Responses } × 100

The Results

With the new formula, the differences between each person are remarkable. The scores now provide a radically different understanding of the quality and impact of each speaker. Figure 14.3 shows the ratings of each presenter with the BEI calculation.

Sessions	Not At All Satisfied	Not Satisfied	Satisfied	Very Satisfied	Extremely Satisfied	1 Avg	2 Sat	3 BEI
Jonny Buckland	0	0	6	12	0	6.0	100%	67
Will Champion	0	1	2	14	1	5.7	94%	78
Chris Martin	0	0	0	3	15	6.0	100%	100
Guy Berryman	0	2	14	2	0	5.3	89%	0
Brian Eno	0	1	4	11	2	5.7	94%	67
Apple	0	0	7	8	3	6.0	100%	61

Figure 14.3 Calculating a tougher BEI metric

Compare Jonny's current scores with his previous scores, for example. His scores were pretty solid before, but now they are less stellar. Will, who initially scored worse than Jonny, is now 11 points higher than Jonny. That's because the BEI rewards Will's ability to delight customers (he had a lot more people in the Very Satisfied column and one in the Extremely Satisfied column).

Compare the unique case of Guy Berryman. In other computations Guy was dead last, but there were just a few points difference between him and Will and Brian. But the BEI shows that Guy was not just a little bad, he was awful! He received a few bad ratings and failed miserably at creating customer delight. He failed at creating brand evangelists. His scores now reflect this.

Note that Apple did all right, but she could use some mentoring and evolution.

The Outcome

Initially a few people were upset by the BEI. Some stones were thrown. But I presented the concept of the Brand Evangelists Index to the VP and the CMO. They adored it because the Brand Evangelists Index did the following:

- Demanded higher return on investment
- Set a higher bar for performance
- Was truly customer-centric

The BEI became the standard for scoring performance, and over the course of the next six months, it helped the company hone in on, and reward, the truly high performers. Those who did not perform well could get additional training and improve their performance, or the lowest performers could find more optimal jobs in the company.

An Alternative Calculation: Weighted Mean

There are many different paths to a destination. In that spirit, I wanted to share another methodology to accomplish our goal of setting high standards through metrics. This methodology was shared by Carmen Gerea on my blog post about BEI.

Carmen suggested a methodology called *weighted means*. It would involve giving each rating a different weight and then computing the mean as the score:

Not Satisfied At All = -2

Not Satisfied = -1

Satisfied = 0

Very Satisfied = 1

Extremely Satisfied = 2

This system achieves the goal of setting high standards by *penalizing* the negative scores, ignores the scores that *meet expectations* (Satisfied), and rates positive scores higher. Note that in this case, unlike in BEI, Extremely Satisfied is valued even more than Very Satisfied.

Figure 14.4 shows all four methods, with Weighted Means in the fourth column. Chris is still clearly a superstar, by a wide margin. Jonny and Will also come out as they did before. We don't see as much difference now between Brian and Apple. In Brian's case, he has more Very Satisfied scores, but Apple trumps him with a few more Extremely Satisfied scores.

	1	2	3	4
Sessions	Avg	Sat	BEI	WMn
Jonny Buckland	6.0	100%	67	67%
Will Champion	5.7	94%	78	83%
Chris Martin	6.0	100%	100	183%
Guy Berryman	5.3	89%	0	0%
Brian Eno	5.7	94%	67	78%
Apple	6.0	100%	61	78%

Figure 14.4 Four methods for computing performance

In my career I have developed a bias toward *indexed scores* because I have found that when people know the upper and lower limits, they can more quickly internalize the data. BEI does this by using a scale of 0 to 100.

All in all, the Weighted Mean methodology also helps accomplish our purpose. You can use the methodology that best suits your unique situation.

The Punch Line

The approach you take in defining metrics can have a big impact on how your company thinks and how it measures success. Here are three lessons I hope you'll take from the story of BEI, as you go about creating *key performance indicators*.

When you create your own *key performance indicators*, check to see whether they help accomplish these three tasks:

- They demand higher return on investment.
- They set a higher bar for performance and motivate employees.
- They are truly customer-centric; that is, their computation favors your customer rather than just your company.

If you assess the metrics you report based on the previous goals, you will have a disproportionately positive impact on your company.

Slay the Data Quality Dragon: Shift from Questioning to Using Data

In Chapter 10, I discussed the six-step cycle of virtuous data quality. The cycle helps us become more accurate about collecting precise data. But data on the Web will never be quite as perfect as, say, reporting your taxes to the IRS or reporting your company's financial numbers under the Sarbanes-Oxley Act. But web data can still be magnificently useful.

Often you will run into organizations with HiPPOs and cultures where even an iota of doubt can cause them to clamp down tighter than an armadillo and do nothing. People in these organizations want certainty; they don't want to jeopardize their jobs, and many organizations punish failures, even minor ones, quite severely.

In such companies, web strategy becomes faith-based rather than data-driven. The website stinks, and the organization fails to capitalize on the value of the Web.

Perhaps you work in such an organization. Then, this section is for you. It contains practical strategies to deal with the cultural problems highlighted previously. It shares nuances you can exploit, tactics you need to renounce, tactics you might consider doing more, and bosses you need to ditch.

But before we go on, we need to outline three prerequisites.

- You understand that data collection is imperfect on the Web, and that is OK.

- You have internalized and started executing the six-step mental model on data quality from Chapter 10.

- Your gallant efforts to make progress with your data are stymied by the benevolent overlords (or as we often lovingly refer to them, the HiPPOs).

Got that? OK, let's dive in and look at 10 specific strategies you can use to move your company from data paralysis to data-based confidence.

Pick a Different Boss

The first option I want you to consider after you've given it all you've got is to pick a different boss. There is an entire generation of leaders that don't get it. Many of them, sadly, will never get it. I don't blame them. They have seen the world one way, and they can't change now. We simply have to wait that generation out—wait for them to get promoted or take on other life challenges.

When I have found myself in situations where the HiPPO's mental model has no chance of movement, I try to switch bosses. Life is too short. There is too much money to be made. There are too many customers to be satisfied.

If you can, move on. Find someone who is open to accepting the new data-quality mental model and who will work with actionable recommendations (even if they agree to try just one or two things first). When you have that small opening, work *really* hard to make your new boss a hero. The impact will be huge for you, for the boss, and for the company.

If you work at a small company, switching bosses is not an option; you have one boss, and that's that. You can follow the recommendations below.

Meanwhile, remember to polish up your resume in case you need to find a better place of employment. I am not saying you should quit as soon as you see resistance. I am saying that you should consciously recognize untenable situations and know when it's time take your skills to a better situation.

Educate Your Organization About the "Perfect" Source

More than once I have opened the mind of executives by detailing the irrational faith they put in other sources of imperfect data.

Take TV as an example. Nielsen uses a dataset of 18,000 to 30,000 people to measure the viewing habits of 200 million plus Americans. In a world of fragmented consumption, no sophisticated math can account for all the inherent anomalies, and you are left with high-grade, nonrepresentative "data." Consequently, network CEOs have been forced to put canceled shows back on the air despite the data of "low" Nielsen ratings because of massive fan rebellions or huge DVD sales.

Just imagine what happens to the capacity of a data set of 18,000 to 30,000 when you measure the nonmajor networks or the really long tail. Current TV anyone? Yet Nielsen ratings and GRPs are accepted as *the truth*. Even with 30 percent inaccuracy through the third-party Omniture 2o7.net cookie, your web analytics data is better than that.

Or, here's another one: web panel–based data sources are considered definitive sources of good data though they have only few hundred thousand participants (not to mention the sampling bias).

Start a revolution:

- Solve the major problem. Educate yourself about imperfect data. This is often the key flaw.

- Present a dispassionate and nonpersonal education of each data source and its value.

- Highlight how web data is less imperfect and how it provides more information, which is missing in other sources.

Ask for actionable insights to be implemented from web data. I'll cover more tips on how to educate your boss in the "Five Rules for Creating a Data-Driven Boss section."

> **Note:** I am not saying Nielsen, or ComScore or other panel-based sources, are not trying hard enough or not doing their best to apply optimal mathematical algorithms. The problem is with the core data they collect and how much they collect. No amount of pretty math can accommodate for the new world order of content consumption on TV. For more, please see Chapter 8.

Distract HiPPOs with Actionable Insights

Dazzle your HiPPOs with your intelligence! Distract them the way you distract a baby by jingling some keys.

When you present data, you need to change the focus from silly, unactionable aggregated numbers like Visits or Average Page Views per Visitor and instead highlight key sources of traffic. Using the insight of traffic sources, you can then run controlled experiments to measure offline impact. You can focus on improving conversions for your campaigns. And you can identify the top five reasons Visitors to your site fail to complete their tasks.

Your senior management does not know what to do with total Visitors or Unique Visitors. If you can distract them by giving them interesting insights, they'll focus on value. Use the specific examples provided in Chapter 5 as your starting point.

Dirty Little Secret 1: Head Data Can Be Actionable in the First Week/Month

Throughout this book I stress the *need for speed*. So, it is criminal to wait 18 months to implement an analytics tool. You get *big enough* information—the head data—in the first week. You don't need complete data because it won't change your decision or insight.

Figure 14.5 is a simple picture you should stick next to your monitor as a constant reminder. It outlines how you can make your biggest decisions based on only 90 percent accurate data, because getting that last 10 percent won't change anything.

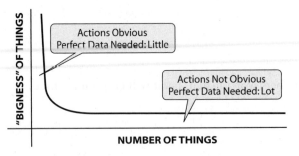

Figure 14.5 Balancing the need for perfect data vs. actionability

On the left is the *head*, where you can make big decisions quickly even with imperfect data. On the right is your *tail* where you need more precision because of small numbers and small decisions. It's ironic, right?

You job during your first week with a tool is to analyze the head data—the places with big numbers and events. Say your imperfect data shows that 60 percent of your traffic comes from Google and from the keywords *Avinash rocks* and *Michelle is awesome*, while *HiPPOs stink* accounts for 40 percent of that traffic. You can start taking SEO/PPC action right away because marginal data-quality improvements in those big numbers won't really change your approach.

Or say you discover that www.nytimes.com sends huge traffic to the game pages of your website. You can start moving on that now.

Tell your boss to start moving quickly on these areas because the numbers are large enough; they indicate the need to monetize opportunity x or fix problem y.

Dirty Little Secret 2: Data Precision Improves Lower in the Funnel

Visitors on your site pass through a funnel until you reach that small number of Visitors who convert on your site. Here is the typical way the funnel flows:

All site visitors→

Visitors who see category pages →

Visitors who see product pages→

Visitors who add to cart→

Visitors who start checkout→

Visitors who abandon→

Visitors who complete their task.

From that final number of Visitors, you can measure revenue, leads, average order size, and so on. As you go deeper into the *funnel*, you deal with fewer and fewer Visitors, as well as fewer sources, keywords, pages, and vagaries of nature. If you tagged your site completely, used first-party cookies, and so on, then not much can mess up data at the end of the funnel. The data set is smaller; it's impacted by fewer vagaries of nature.

So, when you start your web analytics journey, start at the bottom of the funnel, not the top. You won't find yourself mired in quicksand. And it is easier to reconcile data at the bottom of the funnel.

With data from the bottom of the funnel, you can compare your orders in Yahoo! Web Analytics with your ERP system. You can compare your leads in Google Analytics with Salesforce. The numbers won't match, but it will be a million times easier to discover why.

You start at the bottom of the funnel, and you start with measuring Outcomes. Guess what? All HiPPOs love Outcomes!

By the time you get to the top of the funnel, the following will happen:

- You'll actually be smarter.

- Your management will be significantly more evolved in their thinking.

Hurray!

The Solution Is Not to Implement Another Tool!

Bigamy, on the surface, sounds really attractive. It is not. Monogamy rules!

You believe data collected by Webtrends is poor, so you implement Omniture. Or you think Omniture is not working right, so you implement Google Analytics as well. Rather than solving your problem, you've just compounded it.

It is hard enough to follow the six-step virtuous cycle (Chapter 10) with one tool. It takes a lot of effort to understand just one tool, get it right, and make decisions. Two tools means reconciling a lot more data, it means understanding the nuances of more tools, it means chasing two vendors, it means more confusion, and it means minor hell. More than anything else, it means using up a ton of time and taking your eyes off the prize.

Remember, there is nothing particularly magnificent about how Omniture collects data. Google Analytics does not have patent-pending exclusive CIA techniques in its tags. Webtrends has no secret sauce.

Just use tags. Have 'em on all the pages. Use first-party cookies. After you do this, any tool is pretty close in data collection. You can try different analytics tools at the start, but pick one and stick with it unless you find massive limitations.

Recognize Diminishing Marginal Returns

You should work to improve data quality, but realize that after a certain point your efforts are wasted. I have come to adore the classic principle of diminishing marginal returns. Figure 14.6 illustrates the concept: the star denotes the point of diminishing returns.

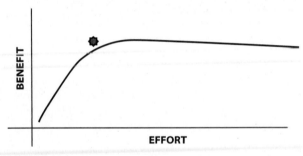

Figure 14.6 The point of diminishing marginal returns

If you put in four weeks of effort and fix big gaps, you need to ask yourself whether you get any more ROI from trying to improve quality by another 3 percent. The fact that you'll feel good does not count.

Data quality seems to be such a holy crusade that it is hard to consciously walk away. But the wise know when to walk away. Remember, your job is not to collect perfect data. Your job is to increase revenue, reduce costs, and improve customer satisfaction and loyalty.

The principle of diminishing marginal returns is lovely because it tells you to work *really* hard and then to stop at a certain point. Be rigorous about realizing when you have reached that point. Then move on!

Small Site, Bigger Problems

You are a part-time analyst or a professional consultant. You are hired to do Omniture analysis at a company, and you find that even a 3–5 percent error is a big deal because of small overall numbers for the site. You then spend hours and days trying to make data collection more accurate. This is a terrible use of time and resources.

If you work for a small company and you get a small number of Visitors on your site, then you must recognize that your big problem is not data quality; your big problem is not enough Visitors. Stop with the data quality. Be productive for your business.

Focus on doing SEO to get more free traffic. Mine your existing customer data to find new ideas for products or customer sources. Though you are an analyst, spend three weeks doing marketing.

My point is that the best use of your time is not chasing a 5 percent error; it's getting an additional 150 people to your site. If you are a small site, focus on the actionable *head* data.

Illogical Customer Behavior and Inaccurate Benchmarks

Many challenges with data accuracy stem from the clash of logical tools with illogical customer behavior. Web analytics tools expect and work on the basis of a set of logical rules. But to a great extent, the Web, and our own behavior, is illogical.

Most of us behave illogically only a small percent of the time (quickly bouncing between sites, changing our minds, missing obvious buttons, or missing relevant results). I have never seen a case where, with enough work and experimentation, I could not explain even the most illogical behavior. Yet in pretty much all of those cases in the end all that effort put into finding the explanation was not worth the ROI. Worse still, that effort distracted from getting the real work done.

Another quest that distracts well-meaning analysis ninjas is this: why aren't there benchmarks for how *bad* web data is? In asking for such benchmarks, you are asking for what Donald Rumsfeld famously called the *unknown unknowns*.

The Web is such a complex beast that getting ranges for inaccuracy is just not possible right now. The huge differences between how sites are built, experiences are created, technologies play, and the needs of each tool for each site adds to the complexity.

You know a lot of the knowns in web analytics. Take action on that data, and also try to identify the known unknowns (do audits using tools like Maxamine, ObservePoint, or WASP), and try to fix them.

Benchmarks, in this case, can become crutches or excuses.

Fail Faster on the Web

The greatest gift the Web gives you is the ability to fail faster and at low cost. This translates into an awesome ability to take higher risks. You can also move fast with less than 100 percent confidence, and if you are 1,000 percent wrong, you can control the damage. This privilege does not exist in the offline world.

If you have only 80 percent confidence in your data, you can send a small email blast and test the waters to see what will happen. You can send three different offers to different geographies to validate a hypothesis. You can try five versions of the home page and see which works because you are not designing a catalog or newspaper ad that must be printed on a deadline.

If you had 100 percent confidence in your data, you would commit to spending $500,000 on affiliate marketing. But if your confidence is a little lower, you can commit to a four-week pilot program with a budget of $50,000. You take on lower risk, still have the possibility of high reward, and have a near 100 percent chance of making a more confident decision for the remaining $450,000.

Don't wait. Just go.

Five Rules for Creating a Data-Driven Boss

Your first job anywhere might be to actively work on creating a boss or bosses who are at their core data-driven. To help you give your *bestest* shot at creating a truly data-driven boss, I want to share effective strategies I have learned from my own experiences and failures.

Get Over Yourself

Your critical first step is to get over yourself. Ouch! You were hired because you bring unique skills. You are likely smarter than everyone else when it comes to data. Hence, you want to do amazing things and create a multidimensional statistical regression formula with 15 variables that could predict the temperature of your website every second. But your boss stubbornly wants a report that shows referring URLs and trends in visits. You are disappointed at how little value you are adding. Get over yourself.

You have to figure out how to talk to your boss and his peers at their—possibly less-data-smart—level. Remember, it takes time for any organization to evolve, and lots of analysts and marketers let their egos get in the way. Learn how to communicate with your boss or her boss. Give them what they want so that they will get on the evolutionary cycle.

Also remember that your boss is more aware of organizational context: business focus, strategies, and goals. That information is critical to your success; you need that context and intelligence to solve the right web analytics mysteries.

Solve for evolution; don't be discouraged, leave your feelings aside, and communicate (really) to understand your boss's perspective. Then figure out how you can solve for your boss and not you. For now.

Embrace Incompleteness

Many of us come to the world of web analysis with experience in traditional analytics, where things can be counted to the last drop. On top of that, we are classically trained to not take risks and to only make decisions based on data we can swear on to be accurate.

At several points in this book (including this very chapter), I have covered the problems with the mental model of complete data. It is impossible to collect data perfectly. Data is ugly, dirty, and incomplete.

Yet, despite this, all analysts, especially the smart ones, can't resist. Avoid that trap. You and your boss must embrace incompleteness; it will set you free.

Always Give 10 Percent Extra

Organizations run on reports and so do your bosses. They ask questions, and you give spreadsheets. Then they ask for more, and you automate the production of the spreadsheet. Initially, you were providing data, and then you started providing data without even looking at it! How is anyone going to find actionable insights?

Your boss is 15 steps removed from data; you are closest to it. Yet you let yourself become a reporting squirrel. As the person closest to the data, it is your job to analyze and provide insights. Look at the data, understand what you see, and make recommendations.

Make a conscious choice about the job you want: reporting squirrel or analysis ninja?

Note: Bosses: When you pay consultants to do "data work," also make this conscious choice—are you paying the consultant to be a squirrel or an analysis ninja? Don't hire a squirrel and expect them to do a ninja's job.

When your boss asks for a report, give her 10 percent extra. You must visit the website, click around, experience it, and then return to the data and connect the dots. Only you can do this because you are the smartest person in the room.

Now give your boss the 10 percent extra: your insights that she did not ask for. Make a recommendation. Tell her what is working and what is broken.

You create a data-driven boss by giving her actions she can drive from data, not by giving her spreadsheets or reports or only what she wants. At the end of each week, ask yourself, did you give your required 10 percent extra?

Got ninja?

Become a Marketer

I find that great analysts are not simply data people. They are customer people. Yes, analysts are all critical thinkers, with curiosity and common sense, but great analysts are also marketers.

Different parts of the organization care about different issues, but marketing cares about the business from a very unique perspective. If you want to change your boss and your company, then you'll have to become a marketer—someone with an understanding of marketing principles, someone who can be a customer advocate, and someone who can evangelize the purpose of data in creating customer centric-decisions.

Think like a marketer, and execute with that mind-set. Your job is to *market* your data in unique and innovative ways that solve for the customer.

Take a course in marketing at the local university, read up on it (start at Seth Godin's blog), and partner with the marketers in your company and absorb. Your boss will love you, and your career will soar.

Business in the Service of Data. Not!

Lots of companies are data rich and tools *richer*. In fact, in many companies, extensive data efforts to mine logs and then mix and merge them leave them with…nothing.

OK, not nothing. They have just invested years of time, people, and money on a ton of technology. They have all that. What they don't have is a list of even five decisions that were made based on the data—they have no insights.

In the obsession with capturing, shaking, and baking data, the core reason for the data is forgotten. When the rare person asks, "What has all this complexity delivered for the company?" The answer is, "We have lots of reports."

The stress on data and reports is a classic sign of an ecosystem where the business exists to produce data to employ people. Data should exist to serve the needs of the business. Embrace that mind-set if you want to change your management's mind-set about how decisions should be made. Do an inventory, and ask around: how many decisions have been made based on data that can be traced directly to have added value to the bottom-line revenue numbers?

When you undertake data projects, apply this approach: go small, deliver in a month, and then measure whether the work had an impact on the bottom line. If yes, continue to invest more. If not, then dump the project, and do something new.

Traditional IT projects tend to be multiyear undertakings that delivered in the traditional worlds. That does not work on the Web. On the Web, things happen too fast, they get complex too fast, and every data project you undertake starts to decay almost immediately. Embrace speed and flexibility and 80 percent good enough.

You do not make data-driven decisions by spending 95 percent of your time collecting, storing, and processing data rather than analyzing what you have. You want a data-driven boss? Spend 80 percent of your time analyzing data and producing insights.

Adopt the Web Analytics 2.0 Mind-Set

Following the Web Analytics 2.0 mind-set in your execution model will mean that you can represent more than clicks to your bosses, and you can represent the customer voice with qualitative data. It will mean you can fight the HiPPO-driven opinions with data beyond clicks. It will mean you can get context from data that is outside your website and in your competitive ecosystem.

Creating a data-driven boss is not difficult; you just need to follow most of the previous rules. So, may your days be brighter and your bosses more data-driven!

Need Budget? Strategies for Embarrassing Your Organization

You know exactly what is necessary in order for your company to achieve Web Analytics 2.0 greatness. You attend a conference and hear all the speakers share deep insights. At the end of one of my speaking engagements, you come up and say, "Thanks, Avinash; that was really great. You've opened our eyes. But..."

I know what's coming next:

"Our senior management won't let us do that."

Or, "We have been banging out heads on this one for six years."

Or some such variation.

Bottom line: *It is not my fault; it is their fault.*

Sometimes our problems as analysts are not our own fault. You may be too low on the totem pole, or management may be close-minded. So, what do you do to move the ball forward? Certainly not buckle in and put in another five years on the job doing mediocre reports and adding no value.

You need to *embarrass your management!*

Yes, that does sound like career suicide. But stick with me. I have observed that often analysts try to bring about change by arguing with management. Or we are insulted that they won't accept our recommendations.

Your own credibility and expertise cannot always drive change. You need to take *you* out of the equation. Depersonalize things. That's because the HiPPO at the table has his own priorities, experiences, context, and opinions. His experience gets priority over your experience, context, and opinion. And while most HiPPOs won't yield to your Chinese data torture, they will yield to customers and competitors.

When I say embarrass your senior management, that's what I mean. Use your customers and competitors to help you move the ball forward—to buy a new tool, hire another analyst, kill hideous home pages, spend money on SEM and SEO, and so on.

Senior managers are biased toward themselves, but they bow to customer data and competitive opportunities. The rest of this section contains six strategies for bringing the voice of the customer and perspective from competitors to the table and for winning big.

Implement an Experimentation and Testing Program

Experimenting and testing is the biggest no brainer, and it kills most stupid ideas. It is the best way to take yourself out of the game.

Saying no to an executive idea can be tricky. But it is easy to say: *"Excellent idea. Why don't we split traffic and send 50 percent of the home page traffic to your idea and get customer feedback?"*

Testing is great because you can get the most important person's opinion: the customer's. After being proven wrong a few times by customer preferences, even the biggest HiPPO will back off and give you all the support you need to make appropriate changes. You have no excuse to avoid testing. See Chapter 7 for easy ways to start.

Capture Voice of Customer

The Voice of Customer metric is another excellent way to remove your opinion from the table and use the customer to get management to change. You can do something simple, such as using the free 4Q survey from iPerceptions and asking your website visitors *the three greatest survey questions ever* (see Chapter 6).

In one shot you'll help your decision makers understand why people come to your website. And, you'll get Task Completion Rate, so you can tell management precisely which tasks Visitors are unable to complete and where you need to focus improvement.

It is not your opinion. It is not their opinion. It is the customer's opinion, which depersonalizes the whole situation and focuses management on being customer centric.

Here is a quick example. A support website received a task completion and customer satisfaction score of 21 out of 100. Essentially that score was saying the site existed to create *net detractors* (people who would hate their experiences and spread the word!), not the intended *net promoters* (people who would be delighted with the experience and spread the word!). The company would have been better served by shutting down the site. Yes, some customers would be upset that the company did not have a support site. But at least they would not be actively turning people off after experiencing the site.

As soon as senior management received the survey responses, they were so embarrassed they immediately appointed a director and gave him a small staff to create a best-in-class support website.

See what I mean by embarrassing management? That site had existed as is for five years. Then a small effort by some *rogue* analysts changed it all.

Deploy the Benchmarks

If you want more resources for your website, then it's time to benchmark your performance against your competition. Benchmarks can come in handy as a way to set context around your own performance, whether for vogue metrics like Conversion Rates or for metrics that should be in vogue like Abandonment Rates.

Remember, comparing benchmarks for one point in time is usually suboptimal. But when you trend over time, you can reduce some of the vagaries of time, seasonality, and other formulas. So, understand how the benchmark is computed, make sure you have access to the best possible data, and then go compare trends.

With benchmarks, you are solving for the same problem as with Voice of Customer: you provide an external opinion that your manager can digest more easily.

Chapter 8 contains a number of sources you can use to get benchmarks, including sites such as the Fireclick Index, tools such as Google Analytics, or associations such as shop.org.

Competitive Intelligence: Your New Best Friend

In Chapter 8, I also covered the wonderful insights you can gain from competitive intelligence analysis—insights that are powered by having access to your data and to data about your competitors.

Here is an example. Our company *owned* a category keyword (let's call it *accounting software*), we thought we defined market. There were only two companies competing in this category, us and our evil nemesis. Our web analytics tool reported that we got lots of traffic for our keyword; it made up a good chunk of our overall traffic, and it was growing at a nice clip over time.

The first time I logged into a competitive intelligence (CI) tool and looked at our *share of search* for the keyword *accounting software*, I was dumbfounded. We had 6 percent share of all the searches, and we had never heard of the top five sites that were getting traffic for *our* keyword. Someone was eating our lunch, and we had no idea!

I did some analysis of that data and presented it to senior management: they needed to take search seriously because we were leaving so much money on the table. With my CI data and my recommendation, I got all the money I had been begging for to do SEO.

That's what I mean when I say use competitive intelligence data to *embarrass* your management team. I had stressed the importance of SEO for months, but it took a quick bit of data from a CI tool to get management to move.

Hijack a Friendly Website

One of my early strategies when I kept getting resistance from senior management was to hijack a friendly website. I could not convert management with words, so I tried to show them that I deserved to be heard.

I went around the company meeting various website owners and judged their need for data and their willingness to cooperate and take action. Then I picked a small site where the owner wanted to drive change and, more importantly, was open to our help. I tagged the site correctly, integrated their humble campaigns, shared actionable insights with the owners, did a few A/B tests, and so on.

In three months, the site's performance improved dramatically. We made the website owner a hero in the company.

The website owner then went around presenting this improved site to executives, other business unit leaders, and even the CEO. When people asked him how he did it, he told the story of working with our team. Then everyone wanted to work with us.

Make someone else the center of attention when you need resources. Not you. Find a willing partner, inside your direct responsibility or outside. Find a big or small site where you can make progress. Then show 'em what you can do.

If All Else Fails...Call Me!

Sometimes you need someone from the outside to hold up a mirror, bring credibility and gravitas, help create a road map, and charge large sums of money so your CEO will take you seriously.

Find a respected industry thought leader and get them to do a presentation or a small strategic consulting gig that involves understanding, shredding, and then recommending the optimal web strategy (notice I did not say *web analytics*) for your company. Hearing advice from an outsider often gets senior management really listening, and that drives change.

When you look for such an external person, use the following criteria:

- They are battle-hardened from years of being a practitioner.
- They are empathetic; that is, they consider your internal experience, not just their outside experience.
- Their feet are firmly planted in the future, not the past.

If the earlier tips don't embarrass your management into action, then find the right outsider to help. If all of them are busy, you can call me as a last resort.

Strategies to Break Down Barriers to Web Measurement

In this, the penultimate section of the book, I want to share best practices and tips to deal with the biggest barriers to creating a successful web measurement strategy. Many of these tips reiterate advice that we have learned in this chapter and throughout the book.

The 2009 Econsultancy Online Measurement and Strategy Report (http://zqi.me/econcm) identified the following 11 barriers to successful web measurement strategy:

- Lack of budget/resources (45 percent)
- Lack of strategy (31 percent)
- Siloed organization (29 percent)
- Lack of understanding (25 percent)
- Too much data (18 percent)
- Lack of senior management buy-in (18 percent)
- Difficulty reconciling data (17 percent)

- IT blockages (17 percent)
- Lack of trust in analytics (16 percent)
- Finding staff (12 percent)
- Poor technology (9 percent)

That's a lot of barriers. The list also makes for some depressing reading, especially for people such as yourself who have been working so hard for so long to evangelize the value of data.

But worry not. Although the obstacles are certainly huge, they are surmountable. I'll use the framework provided by the Econsultancy report and share my *from-the-frontlines* view of how to overcome these barriers.

First, a Surprising Insight

We live in a culture where every analyst, blogger, and consultant presents their comparisons on web analytics tools. You cannot take a step without falling into a pile of opinions about why one tool is great and another is bad.

Yet the top 10 barriers have absolutely no connection to features and barely have any connection to tools. The tools barrier is the last one listed. This should not be a surprise to anyone who believes in the 10/90 rule. But it is still sobering to realize that most of the barriers to your company's success are unconnected to your technology.

Tools are an important part of the mix, but don't look at them to deliver you or your company to the Promised Land. For that you'll have to tear down the more mundane and more difficult barriers such as management, politics, budgets, and organization structures.

Let's look at best practices for the individual barriers identified in the report.

Lack of Budget/Resources

In some sense, the budget and resource problem never goes away. It bedevils you when you are small and just want to buy a web analytics tool, and it bedevils you when you are a multinational and you want to plunk down a million dollars to buy a behavior-targeting platform.

How do you overcome the budget and resource challenge? *Start for free, and earn your right to ask for budget.*

Any tool you want is now available for free, from web analytics to behavior targeting. Why are you asking for a tool budget? Although you may not want to work with a tool for a year or two and then switch, no one knows how the world will look in 18 months. So, why are you planning for five years?

Implement Yahoo! Web Analytics, Google Website Optimizer, or BT Buckets— and boom!—you have powerful clickstream, outcomes, experimentation, and behavior-targeting platforms at your service. For free!

If and when you run into limits with these tools, you'll have a proven track record of success that will make it easier to ask for a budget for Webtrends, SiteSpect, and Kefta. The only reason you'll get turned down is if you showed no value to the company.

Here are few more tips for getting more budget:

- Don't focus on the value of the resource; instead, quantify the value of the outcome you will deliver. *"I want an analyst for our tech support site because I can reduce calls to our phone center, reduce costs by $1.6 million, and increase satisfaction by 5 points."*
- Enroll your customers and competitors to help you (see the previous section). In this way you show management your needs in the context of business and competition.

Lack of Strategy

The second barrier to success is a lack of strategy. If the barrier to an effective web measurement strategy is that your business has no web strategy, then you should look for another job, because this barrier is a few pay grades higher than a marketer or an analyst.

Strategy is a HiPPO problem. Your HiPPO truly needs to get the Web and create a web strategy. And you can help her. But she needs a rough strategy in place already, or this is a lost cause.

If you are a director or a VP perhaps, you can try to plant the seeds for a strategy—especially if you notice that IT owns measurement/analytics (usually a kiss of death). Get analytics moved to a business function.

Here are some other tips to help create an effective web strategy:

- If you are at a large company with many divisions and no consensus, then try to pick one division/country, and make them a hero. Don't try to get everyone to agree on a set of metrics.
- If you think your boss wants to create a strategy but needs a final push, check out the earlier section "Five Rules for Creating a Data-Driven Boss."

Siloed Organization

Silos can open up if you can show value. Everyone wants a bonus, and they want to get promoted. Oh, and they also want to help the company. So, exploit those facts, and remember that it's going to take some hard work on your part.

Start small, show some value, and then go bigger. That was my strategy. When I started, it was me and one analyst in the "center," and no one would listen to us. But we proved the value of data to one siloed team in the company, and they wanted to move together.

After some painful business gyrations to break down the IT and analytics silo, we were able to spend more time working faster and better with the help of that team. We proved more value and earned credibility.

When time came for the company to step up to the next level and the question was *how?*, our request to merge the quantitative and qualitative analysis team was heard with an open mind. That change allowed us to deliver increased value, which in turn increased management's trust in the team, which in turn begat more resources and support.

Make the best of what you have today. Work hard all day. Strike oil. Go back to work harder the next day. Most people don't want to work this hard. Most people don't have the kind of patience required. In those cases, it is easy to complain and wait for someone else to fix the silos.

Lack of Understanding

Lack of understanding is a generic barrier that might yield statements like this: *"No one understands me, no one appreciates me (except my mom!), no one will help me."*

If your company does not understand the value of data, then someone from your management team needs to attend a vendor webinar (Omniture does a bunch of these for example, as does MarketingProfs). These webinars present one client's experience, which may get your boss to appreciate the value of your data.

If management does not understand what analytics can do, get Google Analytics, slap it on a micro site, and improve organic search to show how you can improve the number of Visitors from search. Notice everything in this sentence is free except your time.

If your boss does not understand what technologies exist in the market, do a quick Bing search, identify the main vendors, and get them to come do a dog-and-pony show for you (online or in person). Sure, there will be some showmanship, but you and your boss will also learn a bunch.

Here are some other tips for creating understanding:

- If you are a low- or mid-level employee, then realize that you can't take direct action. Find a sugar mommy or sugar daddy who will help you.
- I'll repeat this again: you create understanding by *doing* rather than by *talking*.

Too Much Data

Finally, a web analytics problem! I was quite surprised that only 18 percent of survey respondents complained about too much data. It just goes to show how many people still execute Web Analytics 1.0, or clickstream-only strategies. If they were truly using Web Analytics 2.0 strategies, more people would complain about too much data, and it would be a good thing.

OK, it's time for tough love: we practitioners create the problem of too much data. We are simply so eager to impress others about how much data we have and how we are so fantastic that we make reports with 28,205 metrics. Who cares!

Two words: *critical few*. You must not send a single report out, not even a number via email, until you have identified your critical few metrics. That process starts with the question: what the heck are we solving for with our website?

Identify the one Macro Conversion (big goal) for your website and up to three Micro Conversions (other smaller goals). Now focus on just the few metrics that help you measure the success of your chosen Conversions, with the highest priority being the Macro Conversion. Do nothing else until you have mastered these goals and their metrics. Don't irritate your colleagues with lots of reports.

If you can't get management to identify goals, update your resume, and apply for other jobs. While you are waiting, focus really hard on reporting only those metrics that will help increase revenue, reduce costs, and increase satisfaction. You can't go wrong with those three.

Lack of Senior Management Buy-In

A few pages back, I addressed the problem of getting senior management on board with analytics. Read the earlier section "Strategies for Embarrassing Your Organization." Use the strategies outlined there to *embarrass* your management. They are simple and very effective.

At the end of the day, to get management to buy into analytics, you must leverage your customers and competitors. They give context to your own web performance. The context of customer satisfaction and competitor performance *always* drives management to change.

Also, remember that there is a difference between reporting and analysis. Be an analysis ninja, and provide value with your analyses; don't be a reporting squirrel.

Difficulty Reconciling Data

Let's tackle the problem of data reconciliation at two levels. At a macro level, you know by now that it will be impossible to reconcile data, especially because you have now adopted a true Multiplicity strategy (Chapter 1).

With Multiplicity, you use different tools with different data sources and different metrics. So, it is absolutely OK that the data won't reconcile. You get exponentially more value using these data sources than the alternative.

You need to educate management about why the numbers differ. They won't accept it entirely. Start with making small decisions based on multiplicity data, show value, earn trust, and move to bigger things. Use the strategies mentioned earlier in this chapter.

At a micro level, the data reconciliation problem refers to reconciling numbers between Google Analytics and Nedstat, or between HitWise and Compete. If this is your case, then please use the "The Ultimate Data Reconciliation Checklist" section in Chapter 4 to identify where the issues might be and fix them. You'll never get the numbers to match perfectly, but if you get close to 10 percent delta, you are pretty much there. Move on to other problems.

IT Blockages

The IT team is burdened with ensuring that the company's systems and infrastructure are up and running. Often we must go to the IT team to get anything implemented on our website, from a new button that converted better in an A/B test to rearchitecting the site to make it more SEO friendly. IT *blockages* may happen in large companies, and they can manifest as someone telling you to *talk to the hand* or get in line.

My recommendation is that if you can then take direct ownership of large parts of the IT work required, primarily tagging, then follow the strategy I outlined in "Siloed Organizations." But, your company simply may not allow you to touch the site. In this case, you are stuck with IT, to do both web analytics work and online marketing work, and IT is an organization that tends to be ultra-conservative. Use the sparkling power of data to unclog the blockages.

My friends Shane Atchison and Jason Burby are authors of the book *Actionable Web Analytics*. They have long advocated creating models that identify the cost of delays. Figure 14.7 shows one such model.

Monetize potential returns

PURCHASE FUNNEL

Wireless Homepage	120,428
Step 4 Combined*	9,177
Conversion Rate	7.62%
Value of Purchase	$ 50 *(adjust $ value to see impact) First month only*

Future Conversion Rate:	Orders	Incremental Orders	Monthly Incremental Value	Impact to FY06 (July Launch)	Impact to FY06 (Sept Launch)	Impact of Three Month Delay
7.62%	9,177	-	$ -	$ -	$ -	$ -
8.00%	9,634	457	$ 22,862	$ 480,102	$ 137,172	$ (342,930)
8.25%	9,935	758	$ 37,916	$ 796,226	$ 227,493	$ (568,733)
8.50%	10,236	1,059	$ 52,969	$ 1,112,349	$ 317,814	$ (794,535)
8.75%	10,537	1,360	$ 68,022	$ 1,428,473	$ 408,135	$(1,020,338)
9.00%	10,839	1,662	$ 83,076	$ 1,744,596	$ 498,456	$(1,246,140)
9.25%	11,140	1,963	$ 98,130	$ 2,060,720	$ 588,777	$(1,471,943)
9.50%	11,441	2,264	$ 113,183	$ 2,376,843	$ 679,098	$(1,697,745)
9.75%	11,742	2,565	$ 128,237	$ 2,692,967	$ 769,419	$(1,923,548)
10.00%	12,043	2,866	$ 143,290	$ 3,009,090	$ 859,740	$(2,149,350)
10.25%	12,344	3,167	$ 158,344	$ 3,325,214	$ 950,061	$(2,375,153)
10.50%	12,645	3,468	$ 173,397	$ 3,641,337	$ 1,040,382	$(2,600,955)
10.75%	12,946	3,769	$ 188,451	$ 3,957,461	$ 1,130,703	$(2,826,758)

▲▰ ZAAZ

Figure 14.7 Monetizing impact of website improvements

The current Conversion Rate metric and its value are identified at the top left. In the first column are subsequent improvements to Conversion Rate metrics, based on the goodness that Zaaz will bring to the table. The columns indicate incremental orders and value and, sweetness, the impact of launching the changes in a month or in four months. The last column shows the cost of the delay.

Assuming Conversion Rate improves to just 8 percent (from the current 7.62 percent), the impact of a three-month delay in implementing the recommendation would be $342,930! That gives you (and the IT team) an immediate solid number to rally around and discuss the cost of making changes. If it would cost IT $50,000 to hire external contractors and get this done ASAP, then it is worth taking on that cost.

Now the reality is that the improvements are expected to increase the Conversion Rate to 9.25 percent (shown in Figure 14.7 by the row marked by the box). The cost of a three-month delay in implementation will be $1,471,943 in lost revenue!

Do you think you could get IT to get unclogged? You betcha.

Figure 14.8 shows another model from Shane and Jason; this one monetizes the lost opportunity from delays in implementing the recommended changes.

Lead generation monetization

Visit-to-Lead Conversion						
Monthly Site Visits			21,000 (Estimated)			
Monthly Inquiries from Site			500 (Contact, Literature Request, Webinar, Tour and TD Inquiries)			
Current Visit-to-Inquiry Conversion Rate			2.381%			
Value of Inquiry			$ 238.00 (adjust $ value to see impact)			

Future Conversion Rate:	Inquiries	Incremental Inquiries	Monthly Incremental Value	Annual Incremental Value	Lost Opportunity - Delaying Optimizaiton 3 Months	Lost Opportunity - Delaying Optimizaiton 6 Months
2.381%	500	-	$ -	$ -	$ -	$ -
2.50%	525	25	$ 5,950	$ 71,400	($17,850)	($35,700)
2.75%	578	78	$ 18,445	$ 221,340	($55,335)	($110,670)
3.00%	630	130	$ 30,940	$ 371,280	($92,820)	($185,640)
3.25%	683	183	$ 43,435	$ 521,220	($130,305)	($260,610)
3.50%	735	235	$ 55,930	$ 671,160	($167,790)	($335,580)
3.75%	788	288	$ 68,425	$ 821,100	($205,275)	($410,550)
4.00%	840	340	$ 80,920	$ 971,040	($242,760)	($485,520)
4.25%	893	393	$ 93,415	$ 1,120,980	($280,245)	($560,490)
4.50%	945	445	$ 105,910	$ 1,270,920	($317,730)	($635,460)
4.75%	998	498	$ 118,405	$ 1,420,860	($355,215)	($710,430)
5.00%	1,050	550	$ 130,900	$ 1,570,800	($392,700)	($785,400)
5.25%	1,103	603	$ 143,395	$ 1,720,740	($430,185)	($860,370)
5.50%	1,155	655	$ 155,890	$ 1,870,680	($467,670)	($935,340)
5.75%	1,208	708	$ 168,385	$ 2,020,620	($505,155)	($1,010,310)
6.00%	1,260	760	$ 180,880	$ 2,170,560	($542,640)	($1,085,280)
6.25%	1,313	813	$ 193,375	$ 2,320,500	($580,125)	($1,160,250)

◢▟ ZAAZ

Figure 14.8 Lost opportunity because of implementation delays

Invite your IT and business decision makers to a conference room. Serve them soft drinks. Put Figure 14.8 on the screen. Ask them: "*How much money can we afford to lose by not implementing these recommendations?*"

The problem with our standard approaches in dealing with business or IT delays is that we use everything except data to make our case. Change your strategy. Don't pick political battles. Use data.

Lack of Trust in Analytics

If your company does not trust analytics, then my best advice is in the prior section of this book. Go back a few pages, and read the recommendations outlined in the section "Slay the Data Quality Dragon: Shift from Questioning to Using Data."

It takes a small amount of dedicated effort on your part to change the core mental approach to data quality. The change is doable; just use the recommended strategies (and don't forget to pray once a day!).

Finding Staff

Sure, you get it: people are the key to success! But finding staff for your team is certainly not easy. I can completely empathize with this challenge.

I think the root cause of the problem here is that we tend to look too narrowly. We look for people with 10 years of Omniture experience or with experience in Webtrends, Optimost, iPerceptions, and making coffee. These people are very hard to find; you've narrowed the pool of potential candidates way too much. We are a young industry, and that means it is hard to find people with deep experience in one specific tool.

In addition, so much has changed in any analytics tool and on the Web in the last five years that any tricks you knew from five years ago are irrelevant now.

When you look for analysts, consider looking for people in the finance function. Look for people who are doing traditional business intelligence work. Look for fresh college graduates who have the Web in their blood, and then spend a couple weeks teaching them which buttons to click in your analytics tools. And don't close your eyes to other possibilities. A peer of mine just hired someone who was on the HR team doing people analytics, and she is turning out to be the best web analyst ever!

Refer to the end of Chapter 13, where I outline key attributes to look for when hiring analytics professionals, and find answers to such questions as whether you should hire experienced professionals or young college grads.

Poor Technology

Finally, we get to blame tools! Yes!

On a serious note, if you are looking for technology to do traditional web analytics or Web Analytics 2.0, then you are in luck. Lots of powerful technology exists, both free and expensive tools.

The only places I find "poor" (I hate that word; I prefer *early evolution*) technology is on the bleeding edge. If you cannot collect rock-solid data for mobile analytics, social media analytics, or distributed content analytics, then you have my sympathy. As analysts, we have not quite figured out what these media are, and they change with every passing day. It will take us some time to figure out the optimal data collection and associated technologies.

But other than that, don't give, or accept, the excuse "poor technology."

I hope I have given you solid starting points to attack some of the tough organizational, mental model, and people problems connected to web analytics. These approaches may take you a few steps away from your *analyzing data* job. But nothing will actually move action by your company more than overcoming these barriers.

Who Owns Web Analytics?

My first book, *Web Analytics: An Hour a Day*, ended with a perspective on where analytics should sit in an organization. This question is so important that I wanted to end my second book with the same question, albeit with some new guidance.

Web analytics started its life in the IT organization, primarily because at that time *web analytics* meant servers, log files, and complex handwritten code to parse the log files and pump out reports. Recently, data collection has shifted to JavaScript-based solutions and therefore data collection, storage, and processing moved into the *cloud* (hosted by your application service provider rather than in-house). This has eliminated the need to maintain IT teams for web analytics, except perhaps to implement tags and other required code on web pages.

Additionally, the website itself has evolved from being a "toy" or "brochureware" to becoming an increasingly integral part of the business both online and offline.

Because of these trends, web analytics has become a strategic function. Nothing highlights this change more than the fact that we no longer report cute things like browser versions and screen resolution as we did in our IT-centric days.

I strongly believe that web analytics should be owned by the business function, optimally the function that owns the web strategy. Web analysts need to think, imagine, and move at the pace of the business. The measurement of success needs to be closely aligned with the people in your company who define success and set strategies to achieve it.

To Centralize or Not to Centralize

If you are in a medium or large company, you must answer another important question. Should the web analytics team be centralized or decentralized? Centralization is a model where all of the analytics team sits under the auspices of, say, the corporate marketing function and from that perch serves the needs of multiple business teams.

Decentralization is a model where each business team has their own analytics team (and perhaps even their own tools) and that team meets all the local needs of business leaders. There might be some collaboration with other teams in the company, but for the most part execution is siloed.

Centralization allows the team to develop a common set of tools, standards, and processes that can then be applied across the entire company. No one has to reinvent the wheel. The downside of centralization is that after a few years, in larger companies this team itself becomes the bottleneck to making data-driven decisions. As a centralized team, they end up implementing a request process to pump out reports. They are far removed from the front lines and hence miss the context to do valuable analysis for local business units.

In a decentralized model, the analysts are aligned directly with the business units, they are close to the problems and the pain, they have the context they need, and they can really do analysis rather than just pumping out reports. The downsides of decentralization in a large company are that everyone runs their own fiefdoms, multiple tools persist, and everyone ends up learning the same lessons after putting in the same amount of effort, often dealing with the same challenges. In a nutshell, there are no efficiencies of scale.

I have found that a centralized decentralization model works best for most companies with established analytics teams, especially large companies. It provides the best of both worlds. Under the centralized decentralization model, the company has a central team that is more like a center of excellence for web decision making. The team implements a standardized web measurement system across the company in partnership with other units, and it also establishes various contracts, selects technology solutions, creates best practices and, most of all, keeps the company on the cutting edge.

Under this model the central team does not take on all the reporting and analysis tasks for the business and functional units. Each business unit has a web analyst or a senior web analyst. The business unit typically funds this analyst and therefore has some skin in the game. The analyst in turn is very close to the business unit and can understand much better the challenges the team faces and can respond accordingly. Although the analyst works as part of the business unit, the analyst still taps into and uses the centralized standard web analytics platform and hence has to worry about only data analysis and not data capture, processing, and storage. That problem is solved centrally for the analyst. Additionally, the centralized team can share best practices and standard dashboards and knowledge and expertise.

Evolution of the Team

Web analytics typically starts decentralized and then becomes centralized and then ends up decentralized again. In the second stage of the evolution, you must stop the process and deliberately execute a centralized decentralization strategy to ensure you position the company to gain maximum analytical benefit at the lowest possible cost.

- If your company is very early in the web data evolution, your analyst should sit in the division that is most analytically savvy.

- If your company is a bit more evolved, then align the analytics team as closely as possible to the person/team responsible for the web strategy. If that's not possible, align them with the person/team deciding what to change on the website (data will inform that change more readily).

- Aim for a centralized decentralization model.

Good luck, and God speed!

About the
Companion CD

In this appendix:

What you'll find on the CD

System requirements

Using the CD

Troubleshooting

What You'll Find on the CD

The following sections are arranged by category and provide a summary of the goodies you'll find on the CD. If you need help with installing the items provided on the CD, refer to the installation instructions in the "Using the CD" section of this appendix.

Podcasts

The disc contains an hour of audio with two interesting podcasts. *Web Analytics Simplified* is a quick primer that will help you reenergize your analytics efforts and deal with common challenges. *Social Media Analytics* is an exploration of the ways in which you can measure the impact of your social media efforts.

Videos

The four hours of videos included on the CD cover a wide spectrum of useful instruction in topics from actionable web analytics to actionable small-business KPIs to innovative uses and measurement of Twitter efforts. There are also videos on web analytics vendor comparisons and how to achieve analytics nirvana. Finally, don't miss the exclusive video about the future of web analytics and what cool things might be around the corner.

Resources and Presentations

The Resources and Presentations section of the CD extends the content in the book by making additional concepts easy to understand. The PowerPoint presentations synthesize the essence of key concepts (multichannel analytics, Web Analytics 2.0, smart paid search, and more), the web marketing Excel models and dashboards are tools you can adapt quickly to your business, and the user guides for Google Analytics and search engine optimization will have you up and running in no time. Be sure to check out the presentation of five key web analytics frameworks that will help influence your current and future strategy.

Adobe Reader

For Windows and Mac
We've also included a copy of Adobe Reader so you can view PDF files that accompany the book's content. For more information on Adobe Reader or to check for a newer version, visit Adobe's website at www.adobe.com/products/reader/.

System Requirements

Make sure that your computer meets the minimum system requirements shown in the following list. If your computer doesn't match up to most of these requirements, you may have problems using the software and files on the companion CD. For the latest and greatest information, please refer to the ReadMe file located at the root of the CD-ROM.

- A PC running Microsoft Windows 98, Windows 2000, Windows NT4 (with SP4 or later), Windows Me, Windows XP, or Windows Vista

  or

  A Macintosh running Apple OS X or later
- A CD-ROM drive

Using the CD

To install the items from the CD to your hard drive, follow these steps:

1. Insert the CD into your computer's CD-ROM drive. The license agreement appears.

> **Note:** Windows users: The interface won't launch if you have autorun disabled. In that case, select Start > Run (for Windows Vista, select Start > All Programs > Accessories > Run). In the dialog box that appears, type D:\Start. exe. (Replace D with the proper letter if your CD drive uses a different letter. If you don't know the letter, see how your CD drive is listed under My Computer.) Click OK.

> **Note:** Mac users: The CD icon will appear on your desktop; double-click the icon to open the CD, and then double-click the Start icon.

2. Read the license agreement, and then click the Accept button if you want to use the CD.

The CD interface appears. The interface allows you to access the content with just one or two clicks.

Troubleshooting

Wiley has attempted to provide programs that work on most computers with the minimum system requirements. Alas, your computer may differ, and some programs may not work properly for some reason.

The two likeliest problems are that you don't have enough memory (RAM) for the programs you want to use or you have other programs running that are affecting the installation or running of a program. If you get an error message such as "Not enough memory" or "Setup cannot continue," try one or more of the following suggestions and then try using the software again:

Turn off any antivirus software running on your computer Installation programs sometimes mimic virus activity and may make your computer incorrectly believe that it's being infected by a virus.

Close all running programs The more programs you have running, the less memory is available to other programs. Installation programs typically update files and programs, so if you keep other programs running, installation may not work properly.

Add more RAM to your computer This is, admittedly, a drastic and somewhat costly step. However, adding more memory can really help the speed of your computer and allow more programs to run at the same time.

Customer Care

If you have trouble with the book's companion CD-ROM, please call the Wiley Product Technical Support phone number at (800) 762-2974. Outside the United States, call +1 (317) 572-3994. You can also contact Wiley Product Technical Support at http://sybex.custhelp.com. John Wiley & Sons will provide technical support only for installation and other general quality control items. For technical support on the applications themselves, consult the program's vendor or author.

To place additional orders or to request information about other Wiley products, please call (877) 762-2974.

Index

Index

Note to the Reader: Throughout this index **boldfaced** page numbers indicate primary discussions of a topic. *Italicized* page numbers indicate illustrations.